K 2-

THE GEYSERS OF YELLOWSTONE

The Geysers
of Yellowstone
THIRD EDITION

T. Scott Bryan

University Press of Colorado

Third Edition © 1995 by T. Scott Bryan
Second Edition © 1991 by T. Scott Bryan
First Edition © 1979 by T. Scott Bryan

Published by the University Press of Colorado
P.O. Box 849
Niwot, Colorado 80544

All rights reserved.
Printed in the United States of America.

The University Press of Colorado is a cooperative publishing enterprise supported, in part, by Adams State College, Colorado State University, Fort Lewis College, Mesa State College, Metropolitan State College of Denver, University of Colorado, University of Northern Colorado, University of Southern Colorado, and Western State College of Colorado.

The paper used in this publication meets the minimum requirements of the American National Standard for Information Sciences — Permanence of Paper for Printed Library Materials. ANSI Z39.48-1984

ISBN: 0-87081-365-x

Cover Photo: Great Fountain Geyser is the largest in the Lower Basin. Eruptions estimated as tall as 230 feet have been observed.

Contents

Tables, Figure, and Maps

Preface

This is the third edition of *The Geysers of Yellowstone*. The entire text has been rewritten and virtually every description revised on the basis of activity as recent as July 1994. A number of significant new geysers have been added. Every effort has been made to make this the most up-to-date and comprehensive reference ever produced on the geysers of Yellowstone National Park. It is intended to serve those who have been geyser gazers for years as well as those who have never seen a geyser. In the hope of assuring historical and numerical accuracy, the manuscript for this edition was reviewed by many of the people named in the following paragraphs.

The maps are based on highly accurate maps produced by the U.S. Geological Survey (USGS) during the 1960s. The locations of roads, trails, streams, and thermal features are precisely. Users will have to remember that the scale is small, however, so that real distances may be much greater than they seem on the map. The exceptions are the maps of the Gibbon and Lone Star Geyser Basins, for which no detailed USGS maps exist, and the index maps to the Upper and Lower Geyser Basins; these are based on enlargements of standard 15-minute topographic maps.

Whether formally named or not, every geyser was given a serial number in the previous edition of this book. These numbers identify the locations of the features on the maps. In order to avoid renumbering every hot spring, geysers that are new in this edition have been given numbers starting where the second edition left off. For example, the last Upper Basin geyser described in the second edition was #186, and it remains #186 here. New to this edition is Bronze Spring, the first geyser described in the Geyser Hill Group of the Upper Basin; it appears in the text and on the maps as #187.

Special words of note are needed about the names of the geysers as they appear in this book. There has always been a tendency for geyser gazers (myself included) to invent names for unnamed features in an offhand way. There is good reason for discouraging this practice. Often, the feature does have a historic name. Also, different people might use different names for one spring. In fact, the only persons who technically have the right to apply names to thermal features are the Park Superintendent and the Chief of Interpretation, who may follow the suggestions of the Research Geologist.

Nevertheless, numerous informal names have been applied and are now largely accepted because of extensive popular use. Many of these names are included in this book. Any geyser that has received a widely recognized but unofficial name is designated first as an unnamed geyser (UNNG); this is followed by an abbreviation for the hot spring group it is a member of and then a number. The informal name is given parenthetically and within quotes. An example from the Upper Geyser Basin is "194. UNNG-CGG-7 ("Gizmo Geyser")." The meaning here is:

194.: This is the forty-fourth geyser described in the Upper Geyser Basin.
UNNG: The geyser is officially unnamed.
CGG: The geyser is a member of the Geyser Hill Group.
7: This is the ninth unnamed geyser described within the group.
("Gizmo Geyser"): This name has received extensive use in verbal and/or written reports about the geyser's activity; it is widely recognized but has not received official sanction.

This technique was adopted for the second edition of this book. It seems to have been helpful, so this edition continues the numbering scheme. May we never again suffer the long-standing confusion as to "which unnamed geyser is that?"

There are cases in which a geyser's name is given within quotes without a number. Another example from the Upper Geyser Basin is "Uncertain Geyser." As with the earlier example, such features are still officially unnamed, but here the given informal name is so deeply entrenched by use that it is considered to be acceptable although not official.

Lee H. Whittlesey has done an incredible amount of work on Yellowstone's place names. Now employed as Yellowstone's archivist, Lee conducted extensive research in places like the National Archives in Washington, D.C., the U.S. Board on Geographic Names in Reston, Virginia, and numerous regional libraries. The result is a work titled *Wonderland Nomenclature: A History of the Place Names of Yellowstone National Park*, a typescript volume of more than 2,300 pages; an abridged version, *Yellowstone Place Names*, is published by the Montana Historical Society. Lee's work was added to significantly by independent and cooperative research by Rocco Paperiello and Marie Wolf of Billings, Montana, and Mike Keller of Kalispell, Montana. The many historical revisions in this book have been extracted largely from these efforts.

This book is also filled with extensive numerical revisions. Geysers are dynamic. Their eruptive activity is seldom stable for very long, and keeping track of all the changes can be difficult. When I first wrote *The Geysers of Yellowstone* during the mid-1970s, there were very few geyser gazers. Now more than 250 have banded together as The Geyser Observation and Study Association (GOSA), a nonprofit corporation dedicated to studying, understanding, preserving, and simply enjoying geysers. My greatest thanks go to all of the members for their valuable information, stimulating discussions, thoughtful ideas, brainstorm revelations, and fun times.

Dr. Donald E. White of the U.S. Geological Survey is responsible for developing many of the modern theories about how geysers and geothermal systems work. He provided ideas vital to this book and, in fact, his favorable review of the first edition probably assured its publication.

Dr. George D. Marler was *the* ranger-naturalist geyser gazer of Yellowstone for several decades before his death in 1978. Had he not kept extensive and detailed notes about the geysers and their dynamic changes throughout the years, relatively little would be known about long-term changes in geyser action and their meaning for us today. His numerous publications and reports, although sometimes contradictory, are indispensable references now held in either the archives of Yellowstone National Park or the special collections library at Brigham Young University.

Research Geologist Rick Hutchinson and the ranger-naturalist staffs at the Old Faithful Visitor Center and Norris Museum keep the daily logbooks of geyser activity accurate and up-to-date at all times during the visitation seasons; this is especially vital during the winter when geyser gazing is severely limited.

We must remember, too, those who were here during the early surveys of Yellowstone. Researchers such as Hayden, Hague, Peale, Weed, Allen, Day, Fenner, and many others set the stage for us by helping to create, maintain, and understand what Yellowstone is really all about. Saxo Grammaticus, who saw and described Iceland's Geysir, became the first geyser gazer we know of more than 700 years ago — unless that distinction belongs to Homer who, in the *Iliad*, seems to describe a small geyser near the ancient city of Troy as far back as 700 B.C.

Above all, tremendous appreciation goes to my wife, Betty. My writing *The Geysers of Yellowstone* was her idea, and her patience and encouragement kept me at a project that might never have happened otherwise.

Thank you, one and all.

THE GEYSERS OF YELLOWSTONE

Chapter 1

About Geysers

What is a geyser?

The definition in general use was devised by Dr. Donald E. White of the U.S. Geological Survey. It reads: "A geyser is a hot spring characterized by intermittent discharges of water ejected turbulently and accomplished by a vapor phase." It sounds simple, but it really is not. The definition includes several gray areas that can be interpreted in different ways. How hot is hot? How high must the turbulence be? Are there limits as to how long or short the intermittent action must last? Such questions will probably never be answered to the satisfaction of everybody, but there are two similar varieties of hot spring that definitely do not qualify as geysers. *Intermittent springs* undergo periodic overflows but never actually erupt. *Perpetual spouters* (called *pulsating springs* in some parts of the world) may have spectacular eruptions, but their action never stops. In all three of these cases, however, the cause of the action is the same — namely, water boiling into steam at some depth belowground.

What makes a geyser work?

Three things are necessary for a geyser to exist: an abundant supply of water, a potent heat source, and a special underground plumbing system.

The water and heat factors are quite common. There are hot springs in virtually all of the world's volcanic regions.

The plumbing system is the critical aspect. Its shape determines whether a spring will be quiet or will erupt. It must be constructed of minerals strong enough to withstand tremendous pressure, and it must include a permeable volume so as to hold the huge amounts of water that are ejected during an eruption.

Nobody really knows what a plumbing system looks like from top to bottom — it is, after all, belowground and filled with hot water and steam. Considerable research drilling has been done in some of the world's geyser areas, and none has yet found any large, open water storage caverns. This fact led to the conclusion that a geyser's main water reservoir was a complex system of small spaces, cracks, and channels in the porous rocks that surround the plumbing system.

In 1992 and 1993 an experimental probe used at Old Faithful Geyser expanded on this idea and resulted in considerable changes in our understanding of what a plumbing system looks like. Equipped with temperature and pressure sensors and a video camera, the probe was lowered into Old Faithful's vent. At a depth of only 45 feet, past a spot barely 4 inches wide, it found a cavity about the size of a large automobile. The temperature was 244°F (117°C), fully 45°F (25°C) hotter than the normal surface boiling point at that altitude. The researchers reported that the action resembled a seething "liquid tornado" of unbelievable violence. Years ago, in New Zealand, people were able to scramble down into an inactive hot spring. There they found a chamber with smooth walls punctured by numerous small openings. Once upon a time this must have been the scene of wild boiling like that witnessed inside Old Faithful, and its existence supports the notion that Old Faithful's inferno is normal rather than unique.

This is quite unlike the standard model of a plumbing system, which has the water flowing upward rather quietly at depth into a single main tube. Still, this revised model probably applies to all geysers. It makes the water supply network more complex but changes nothing about how geysers actually operate. The character and eruptive performance of every geyser are determined by the geyser's plumbing system, and, as in all of nature, no two are alike.

With this, enough information is available for us to reconstruct a basic plumbing system. An example is shown in Figure 1. It consists mainly of a tube extending into the ground, with many sharp bends and constrictions along its length. Connected to this main pipe are small open spaces and, especially, layers of water-storing sand and gravel of high porosity. Most of this plumbing is fairly close to the surface, and even the largest geysers extend to a depth of only a few hundred feet. Finally, much of the plumbing system is coated with a water-tight and pressure-tight lining of *siliceous sinter,* or *geyserite.* The mineral is also deposited outside the geyser and in and about the quiet hot springs. Of course, the geyserite is not magically created by the water. Its source is quartz (or silica) in the volcanic rocks underlying the geyser basin.

The water that erupts from a geyser arrives there only after a long, arduous journey. Water first falls in Yellowstone as rain and snow, then percolates through the ground to as much as 12,000 feet below the surface and back up again. The round-trip may take at least several hundred and sometimes thousands of years. This can be determined with reasonable accuracy by studying the *tritium* ("heavy heavy hydrogen") content of the geyser water. Tritium is radioactively unstable and decays with age. Young water contains considerable amounts of tritium, whereas old water contains little or none. Tritium is nearly absent in most Yellowstone waters. In fact, it is commonly believed that the water erupting from Old Faithful today fell as precipitation roughly 500 years ago — around the time Columbus was exploring the West Indies.

At depth, the water is heated by contact with the enclosing volcanic rocks. Once heated, it dissolves some of the quartz from the rocks. All of this takes place at very high temperatures — over 400°F (205°C) in many cases; and 460°F (237°C) was reached in one shallow research drill hole. This silica will not be deposited by the water until it has approached the surface and cooled to a considerable extent.

Now an interesting and important phenomenon occurs. Although it was the mineral quartz that was dissolved out of

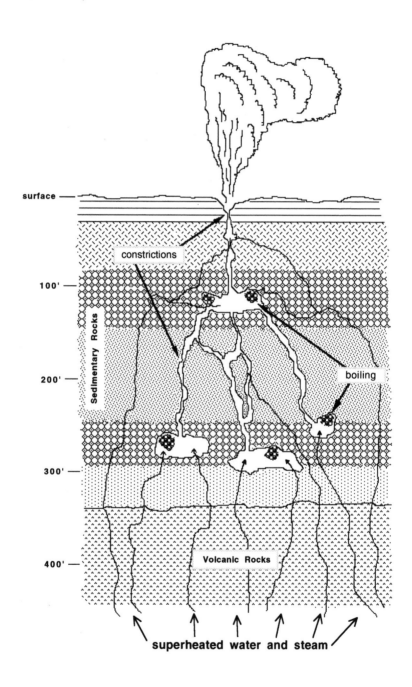

surface

100'

200'

300'

400'

Sedimentary Rocks

constrictions

boiling

Volcanic Rocks

superheated water and steam

the rocks, the deposit of geyserite is a non-gem form of opal. The mechanisms involved in this process are complex, involving temperature, pressure, acidity or alkalinity of the water, and *time*.

How a geyser erupts

The hot water, circulating up from a great depth, flows into the plumbing system of the geyser. Because this water is many degrees above the boiling point, some of it turns to steam instead of forming liquid pools. Meanwhile, additional cooler water is flowing into the geyser from the porous rocks nearer the surface. The two waters mix as the plumbing system fills.

The steam bubbles formed at depth rise and meet the cooler water. At first they condense there, but as they do they gradually heat the water. Eventually, these steam bubbles rising from deep within the plumbing system manage to heat the surface water until it also reaches the boiling point. Now the geyser begins to work like a pressure cooker. The water within the plumbing system is hotter than surface boiling, but it is "stable" because of the pressure exerted by the water lying above it. (Remember that the boiling point of a liquid is dependent upon the pressure. The boiling point of pure water is 212°F [100°C] at sea level. In Yellowstone the elevation is about 7,500 feet [2,250 meters], the pressure is lower, and the boiling point of water is only about 199°F [93°C].)

The filling and heating process continues until the geyser is full or nearly full of water. A very small geyser may take only a few seconds to fill, whereas some of the larger geysers require several days. Once the plumbing system is full, the geyser is nearly ready for an eruption. Often forgotten but extremely important is the heating that must occur along with the filling. Only if there is an adequate store of heat within the rocks lining the plumbing system can an eruption last for more than a few seconds. (If you want to keep a pot of water boiling on your stove, you have to keep the fire turned on. The hot rocks of the plumbing system serve the same purpose.) Again, each geyser is different from every other. Some get hot enough to erupt before they are full and do so without any preliminary indications of an eruption. Others may be completely full long before they are hot enough and so may overflow quietly for hours or even days before an eruption occurs. But eventually, an eruption will take place.

Because the water of the entire plumbing system has been heated to boiling, the rising steam bubbles no longer collapse near the surface. Instead, as more very hot water enters the geyser at depth, more and larger steam bubbles form and rise toward the surface. At first, they are able to make it to the top of the plumbing with no problem. But a time will come when there are so many bubbles that they can no longer simply float upward. Somewhere they encounter some sort of constriction in the plumbing. To get by, they must squirt through the narrow spot, forcing some water ahead of them and up and out of the geyser. This initial loss of water reduces the pressure at depth, lowering the boiling temperature of water that is already hot enough to boil. More water boils, forming more steam. Soon there is a virtual explosion as the steam expands to over 1,500 times its original, liquid volume. The boiling becomes violent, and water is ejected so rapidly that it is thrown into the air. People standing near very large geysers sometimes both hear and feel a thudding, popping sound. Research indicates that this happens because the superheated water is ejected so quickly, and then additionally explodes into steam within the air, that the total speed exceeds the sound barrier — the thuds are caused by small sonic booms within the column of steam and water.

The eruption will continue until either the water is used up or the temperature drops below boiling. Once an eruption has ended, the entire process of filling, heating, and boiling will be repeated, leading to another eruption.

Why are some geysers regular, others irregular?

The inflow of water into a geyser system is usually constant. Thus it would seem that the activity of any geyser should also be continuous. But only a few geysers are classed as regular geysers. In order to be regular, a geyser must either be isolated from other springs or be connected only with springs whose own activity is so steady that it does not affect the geyser. Old Faithful is the most famous example of regularity. Its eruptions can be predicted with about 90% accuracy. Several other geysers, including Riverside, Daisy, Lone Star, and Castle, are even more regular, sometimes operating with almost stopwatch-like precision.

But most geysers are irregular. The time interval between eruptions is erratic. One time it may be just minutes between the plays, the next time several hours. In no way can these geysers be predicted.

The mechanism behind this has been termed *exchange of function,* as first described by G. D. Marler in 1951. This basically means that water and energy can be diverted from a geyser to some other hot spring or hot spring group (another geyser is not necessarily involved). This happens because the plumbing systems of most springs and geysers are intertwined with those of others. The activity of any one of those springs must affect all the others within the group.

Just what makes exchange of function take place is unknown. Many exchanges are very small scale in both extent and time and require a knowing eye to detect them. Others can be of great significance. Indeed, one group of active springs may suddenly stop functioning altogether while a nearby group of insignificant springs becomes animated with an exchange that might last for many years. Perhaps the best example involved Daisy Geyser and nearby Bonita Pool in the Upper Geyser Basin. For years Daisy was one of the largest and most regular geysers in Yellowstone, whereas Bonita overflowed only slightly. Suddenly the energy shifted toward Bonita. Daisy was drained of the energy necessary for eruptions as Bonita overflowed heavily and underwent frequent small eruptions. The result was that

Daisy erupted just three times in over 13 years. During the mid-1970s the energy flow gradually shifted back toward Daisy. Now it erupts as regularly and frequently as before, and Bonita again lies quietly below overflow.

This exchange was triggered by the 1959 earthquake (see Chapter 2), and continuing seismic and tectonic events frequently modified the activity. Most other large-scale exchanges of function have had similar tectonic causes, but others just seem to happen now and then; a few have been almost predictably regular. Just how the exchange process takes place is not completely known. There are a number of potential causes, and any one observed effect could be the result of several independent processes acting together. It is, however, interesting to note that exchange of function is either rare or unknown in most of the world's geyser fields except for Yellowstone.

Why are geysers so rare?

There are few places on earth where the three requirements for the existence of geysers are met. The requisite water supply poses no great problem; in fact, a few geysers are able to exist in desert areas, places normally thought of as dry. But the heat source and plumbing systems are tied to one another and are much more restrictive.

Nature's most potent heat source is igneous activity. The heat is supplied by large bodies of molten or freshly cooling rock at great depth. Given a proper water supply, hot springs are possible in any area of geologically recent volcanism. (In geology, "recent" can be as much as several hundred thousand years ago.)

Most hot spring areas do not contain geysers, however, because there is a catch. Not just any volcanism will do. The plumbing systems must be pressure-tight, and this requires silica-rich rocks to provide the source of the geyserite that lines the plumbing systems.

The answer is *rhyolite*. Rhyolite is a volcanic rock very rich in silica; it is the chemical equivalent of granite. Rhyolite itself is rather uncommon, though, and large recent fields of it are found in few places. Yet virtually all geysers are found in such areas. Most of the exceptions to this rule are still associated with recent volcanic activity, although their rocks — dacite, andesite, and basalt — are somewhat less rich in silica. And as seems to be usual in science, there are a few completely anomalous geyser localities, such as Beowawe, Nevada (see Appendix), where the activity is not associated with recent volcanic action nor even directly with volcanic rocks of any type or age.

Not only is Yellowstone a major rhyolite field, but it is of very recent origin. Although the last major volcanic eruption was 630,000 years ago, minor activity continued up to as recently as 70,000 years ago. Yellowstone could well be the site of further volcanic eruptions. That is another story entirely, but for now the Park is incomparably the largest geyser field in the world.

How many geysers are there in Yellowstone?

This chapter opens with a basic definition of "What is a geyser?" and notes that there are a number of gray areas and transitional kinds of springs. When such features as bubbling intermittent springs, variable perpetual spouters, and random splashers are eliminated from consideration, the number of geysers actually observed to be active in Yellowstone in any given year may approach 500.[1]

That is an amazing number. The second largest of the world's geyser fields, Dolina Geizerov on Russia's Kamchatka Peninsula, contains about 200 geysers. New Zealand cur-

---

1. This count of 500 active geysers is somewhat controversial. In part it depends upon the very definition of *geyser* that opens this chapter. What is a geyser to one observer may be a noneruptive boiling spring to another, and a perpetual spouter that pauses its eruption only briefly and very rarely may be listed either way by different people. Virtually all observers will agree that Yellowstone contains a minimum of 300 frequently observed active geysers during any given year and that at least 600 and perhaps 800 have erupted since the national park was established in 1872.

rently stands third with perhaps 40 active geysers. El Tatio, Chile, ranks fourth with 38, and Iceland holds around 25. All other areas contain fewer, and taken together the entire world outside of Yellowstone has a total of around only 400 geysers. (See Appendix for more about the rest of the world.)

Yellowstone, in other words, probably contains *at least* 55% of all the active geysers on earth. The number of geysers is not stable, however. They are very dynamic features, affected by a wide range of physical factors and processes. The slightest change in the geologic environment may radically alter, improve, or destroy the geysers.

Recent studies of historical literature have shown that much about Yellowstone had been forgotten. Many springs taken to be "new" geysers in recent years have proven to have been active during the 1800s. Nevertheless, the number of active geysers appears to be increasing. Recently, a geochemist with the U.S. Geological Survey, who has conducted studies in Yellowstone since the 1950s, stated that back then you could easily count the number of geysers on Geyser Hill on two hands. This book describes 52 geysers on Geyser Hill, and at least 36 were active during 1993. Allen and Day of the Carnegie Institute counted 33 geysers at the Norris Geyser Basin in 1926; 72 are now known. The same situation exists throughout Yellowstone.

This is not a matter of there simply being more or better observers. The apparent fact is that there really are more active geysers today than perhaps ever before in recorded history (eliminating only a few weeks immediately following the earthquake in 1959). We don't know why this is so, but the "good ol' days" of geyser gazing are right now.

Chapter 2

Some Background on the Yellowstone Geysers

Geysers are beautiful and rare. Wherever they are found, they have attracted attention for the duration of their known history. Outside of Yellowstone some geysers have been watched for hundreds, even thousands of years. Within the Park they have been observed for far longer than recorded history. The Indians certainly saw them and wondered about them.

But just *what* the Indians thought about the geysers is uncertain. Few tales have come down to us, and most were probably embellished by the trappers who passed them on to us. We do know that at least some of the Shoshone Indians called the geyser basins "Water-That-Keeps-On-Coming-Out." But despite popular notions about native religions, the Indians were obviously not afraid of the geysers in any way. Remains of their campsites have been found within most hot spring areas of the Park. In some of these places obsidian chips left over from toolmaking litter the ground, suggesting that these areas were virtual factories for the production of arrow and spear points.

In at least one place in the Park, an unknown native piled logs about the crater of a geyser. Why this was done will always remain a mystery, but it further suggests that Indians did not fear geysers. Perhaps they did hold a special reverence for them, though. One story claims that geyser eruptions were the result of underground battles between spirits, but these wars had no effect on mortals. Whatever the Indians thought, they harbored no great myths about either Yellowstone or its geysers, at least that we know of.

Their stories about the geothermal wonders, however, may have attracted early explorers to the Yellowstone Plateau. The first was probably John Colter. A member of the Lewis and Clark Expedition, he was so intrigued by the trapping and trading potential of the Montana-Wyoming area that he left the main party in 1806. Moving south along the Yellowstone River, he may have visited the huge terraces of Mammoth Hot Springs.

Colter's reports, although factual, were regarded as pure fancy and therefore were ignored. But other mountain men soon moved into the region and emerged with similar stories, always too fanciful and fantastic to be true.

Twenty-eight years later, Warren Ferris gained credit as Yellowstone's first tourist because his visit was specifically motivated by the stories he had heard. His journal contains an exquisite description of the Upper Geyser Basin and details about several large geysers (interestingly, *not* including anything similar to Old Faithful). In the later 1830s, Osborne Russell traveled throughout the Park area. His written descriptions of some of the geysers and hot springs were so accurate that the individual features can be identified from them today. Yet even these learned observations seemed unbelievable to "civilized" people back east. When mountain man Jim Bridger, soon to be known for his tall tales, drifted into the Yellowstone country and confirmed the findings of the others, people listened, but they probably did so only for a laugh.

The stories didn't stop, though. In time the versions of what Yellowstone really was had become tremendous. Clearly, there had to be some honest answers.

Several attempts to lead organized expeditions into the Yellowstone country were made during the 1860s. Because of frequent Indian scares throughout the region or a lack of financing, planned expeditions continually fell through until 1869, when Charles Cook, David Folsom, and William Peterson, all from the mining town of Helena, Montana, decided to go it alone.

They rode up the canyon of the Yellowstone River (missing the Mammoth Hot Springs) to Tower, over Mirror Plateau to the Mud Volcano area, around Yellowstone Lake to West Thumb, and finally northwest into the Lower Geyser Basin. They were thrilled by Great Fountain Geyser and amazed at the Midway Geyser Basin. Here, figuring they had seen enough, they moved down the Firehole River and so missed the fantastic Upper Basin by just four miles.

Cook, Folsom, and Peterson kept records of what they saw, and their report renewed the enthusiasm of three men who had thought of making the trip earlier. Bigger names were involved this time: Henry Washburn, the surveyor general of Montana Territory; Cornelius Hedges, a judge; and Nathaniel Langford, who later became the first superintendent of Yellowstone National Park. Along with an Army contingent, led by Lt. Gustavus C. Doane, for protection, these men and others set out in late summer 1870 on what has become known as the "Discovery Expedition."

It was a long journey, one that saw hardship and tragedy, but eventually the explorers reached the Upper Geyser Basin. One of their first sights was Old Faithful erupting against an afternoon sky. In the next day and a half they saw eruptions of numerous other geysers, large and small. They named several, including Beehive, Giantess, Castle, Grotto, and Old Faithful. After recording their findings, they left the basin.

The Washburn party spent their last night in what is now Yellowstone National Park at Madison Junction. Around a campfire they discussed the marvels they had seen. Almost everyone wanted others to be able to see what they had seen. But how to achieve this?

Popular stories say that it was there, around an evening fire in the middle of a wilderness, that the national park idea was born. Judge Hedges is supposed to have said it first: withdraw the entire area as a park, excluded from settlement and protected for all time by the government. The plan was agreed upon, and all worked to that end upon their return to Montana.

The campfire tale is a modern legend that is undoubtedly not true, but somewhere, somehow the park concept was invented, and some members of the expedition began to work on it. But most Easterners *still* would not believe the reports, despite the integrity of the explorers. In fact, one article reportedly submitted to a magazine was returned with the cryptic rejection: "Sorry, we do not print fiction."

But the leader of the northern part of the Geological and Geographical Survey of the Territories, Dr. Ferdinand V. Hayden, did believe the reports. He organized and led a complete survey of the proposed Park area during 1871. The Hayden survey's report, combined with the excellent photographs of William H. Jackson and paintings by Thomas Moran, convinced the nation, or at least the U.S. Congress. On March 1, 1872, fairly soon, really, after all those "tall tales" of the trappers, President U. S. Grant signed the bill establishing "The Yellowstone Park" into law.

Thanks to the efforts of those early explorers, we are able to visit what is certainly the greatest, most wonderful geothermal area on earth and see it as nature made it. More than 120 years later, Old Faithful still merits its name; Grand, Clepsydra, Kaleidoscope, and the other geysers continue to spout skyward, just as they have for millennia. The preserve we call Yellowstone has barely changed. Or has it?

The geysers of Yellowstone often seem to be extremely permanent features. Time after time, day after day, they go through their eruption cycles with little or no apparent change. Just think: a geyser that erupts every 10 minutes will have had well over 6,000,000 eruptions since the park was established.

But at 11:37 P.M. the night of August 17, 1959, the entire Yellowstone region was jarred by a severe earthquake. With a Richter magnitude of 7.5, it ranks as one of America's major tremors. Just outside the Park twenty-eight people were killed by landslides. There were no fatalities in Yellowstone, but structural and road damage was severe.

One of the greatest and longest-lasting reminders of the quake was its effect on the geysers and hot springs. On the night of the tremors and within the next few days, hundreds of geysers erupted, including many hot springs that had not previously been known as geysers.

The 1959 earthquake caused Sapphire Pool to erupt violently, some bursts reaching over 125 feet high. With declining force, the activity persisted into 1961. Only two minor eruptions have been seen since then. (National Park Service photo by George Marler.)

Exactly what caused these eruptions is difficult to say with certainty. It might have been a twofold event. With some geysers, compression resulting from the quake might have forced a small amount of water out of the plumbing systems, causing subsurface boiling and eruptions. In others, especially those that did not erupt before the earthquake, the underground water circulation patterns may have been altered so that more energy was channeled to these springs. Whatever the reasons for the increased activity, most geysers died down quickly. Many springs returned to their pre-quake state within a year. But some new activity continues to this day, and changes such as these might be permanent — "permanent" in human terms, at least.

Geologic study has shown that the surface opening of every hot spring in Yellowstone, be it quiet pool or geyser, probably formed as a result of steam explosions, which are commonly associated with earthquakes. The shaking of the ground creates cracks in the siliceous sinter, and these rifts

The entire history of Seismic Geyser — its birth, growth into a major geyser as much as 75 feet high, and decline back into quiescence — was the result of the 1959 earthquake. (National Park Service.)

tap the hot water source below and become the sites of new springs. Several are known to have formed as a result of the 1959 earthquake.

One of these, Seismic Geyser, is a major geyser. At first, the crack steamed quietly. With time the force of the steam became greater, until a steam explosion opened a large crater during the winter of 1961–1962. Within the crater was a small geyser. Again, as time passed the activity of the geyser became more powerful; by 1966 Seismic was playing as much as 75 feet high. But that force was too great. A 1971 explosion opened another crater known as Seismic's Satellite. Eruptions from the new vent, small as they were, were enough to prevent any further eruptions by Seismic itself. Now, even the activity of the Satellite has declined, and the members of the Seismic complex only boil gently.

Seismic is but one example of this process. The Yellowstone region is the site of frequent major earthquakes; over the past century there has been one quake about every 25 years. On June 30, 1975, a quake of magnitude 6.1 shook the Park. No resulting changes could be found in the Old Faithful vicinity, but one backcountry area was affected. Changes resulting from the Borah Peak, Idaho, earthquake of October 28, 1983, were more dramatic. Even though that tremor was located more than 150 miles from Yellowstone, its magnitude of 7.3 had impressive effects. Exchange of function dramatically changed the performance of many springs on Geyser Hill, and related to those changes was a major slowdown by Old Faithful. Here and there throughout the Park were other notable changes in eruptive activity, and many of these have persisted. The story of a magnitude 4.9 earthquake on March 26, 1994, is still being written. That shock occurred a few miles northwest of Madison Junction, within Yellowstone, and although it was a relatively small tremor, changes in the hot spring activity at the Lower and Norris Geyser Basins were seen over the next few weeks.

Every year, in the Yellowstone Plateau, up to 2,000 tremors are recorded by seismographs. Mostly far too small to be felt by people, these quakes are normal events. There is little doubt that Yellowstone has been shaken by a great many major shocks over the ages. The resulting thermal changes must be nearly infinite in number. One day in the future even Old Faithful will meet its demise, but something new might replace it at the same time.

Of course, not all change and variation are the result of major earthquakes. Yellowstone can be subtle, too, and perhaps nothing shows this as well as the spectrum of colors seen in the hot springs and their runoff channels. Just as each geyser or pool is different, each geyser basin has its own personality. None of the coloration is ever exactly the same, neither from place to place nor from time to time.

The broad flats and cones of the geyser basins are accented by tones of white and gray. These stark colors are caused by the geyserite that, when underground, is so important to the existence of geysers (see Chapter 1). It normally forms very slowly, sometimes at the rate of only $1/100$ of an inch per year. Most deposits vary from a few inches to a few feet thick. Obviously, such specimens took many, many years to form. Yet they are delicate and beautiful, too. Pause somewhere in the basins to take a close look at the lustrous, pearly beads and compare them with the wafer-thin, artistic laminations of other spots. As you do this remember the tremendous age and rarity of this geyserite. Don't try to take a piece with you. In time it will dry out and crumble into dusty gravel like that you see elsewhere in the basins. Leave the formations untouched for others to see.

Minerals other than siliceous sinter are also present, although they are more rare. Most common are bright yellow sulfur and red-brown iron oxide. These deposits are especially prominent in the Norris Geyser Basin. At various spots throughout Yellowstone the sinter is sometimes stained dark gray or black because of impurities of iron sulfide or manganese oxides; interestingly, smaller amounts of manganese oxide cause a fine pink color. Brilliant red and orange-yellow arsenic compounds appear at Norris and Shoshone. Small popcornlike aggregates of complex sulfate minerals show up as white and light yellow puffs on gravel in barren, acid flats. The minerals are everywhere, always with different combinations and compositions.

The hot pools themselves are often deep blue or green, a coloration that led some early Yellowstone explorers to believe they had found a bonanza. Copper in solution will turn water blue or blue-green, and that is what they thought they had found — a fabulously rich copper mine without having to sink a shovel into the ground. But any deep body of water will look blue. Water absorbs most of the colors of the rainbow, but not the blues and blue-greens. Those colors are reflected back, giving the water its color. If any other material is present in the water or lining of the crater walls, that tint will be added to the blue. Most common is the yellow of either the mineral sulfur or hot water bacteria. This blending of yellow and blue can produce a green of incredible intensity and richness.

The brilliant yellows, oranges, browns, and greens in the wet runoff channels are caused by thermophilic ("temperature-loving") cyanobacteria. (Although commonly referred to as *algae,* cyanobacteria is a photosynthetic bacteria very different from algae, which is a plant. The word *cyanobacteria* is now used in place of the old term *blue-green algae*.) These microscopic organisms have been studied extensively. You can tell the approximate temperature of a stream by the color of its cyanobacteria. If there are no cyanobacteria, the temperature must be greater than 167°F (75°C). If the bacterial mat is bright yellow, the temperature is around 160°F (71°C); brilliant orange, about 145°F (63°C); the dark browns come in at about 130°F (57°C); and pure green shows up at around 120°F (50°C) and below. In relatively narrow, fast-flowing channels, one often sees a v-shaped pattern to the colors. The stream cools more slowly toward the center. There the cyanobacteria that thrive in higher temperatures are able to survive farther from the source of the stream; less tolerant organisms hug the edges of the channel, where the water cools more quickly nearer the source. If stringy, pale yellow or pink strands of bacteria are visible in a very hot runoff, one can be fairly sure the temperature is over 180°F (82°C). In areas with acid runoff, where true algae can survive, this color-versus-temperature scheme fails, and bright green is the biological color. Still other runoffs support a mixture of cyanobacteria and algae, which produces different color schemes altogether. One of these is a nearly fluorescent chartreuse.

The natural Yellowstone and its thermal features are constantly changing. Now, too, there is another cause of great change, one that causes change that is more extensive and destructive than that of Mother Nature's greatest earthquake. It's called people.

A century ago some people with vision fought to protect and preserve Yellowstone's environment. A fact often forgotten is that the Park exists not because of its forests and wildlife but, rather, because of its geysers and hot springs. They are what make it so unique that it attracted the early explorers and now draws over 3,000,000 visitors each year. It's well that they did so, for we now know that Yellowstone contains fully 55% of all the geysers in the world and is one of only two geyser fields that has any real measure of protection. Yet the remains of an old slat-back chair and other debris were removed from Old Faithful during a 1980s cleanup project. Please, let's not let the Park's founders down.

To leave the boardwalks and trails within the geyser basins is highly destructive to the formations. The slightest bit of trash thrown into a pool can clog it forever. Wandering off the trails is dangerous. Thin crust can look completely solid, but in many places it is only inches thick, brittle, and underlain by a boiling pool. More people have been killed by thermal burns than by the notorious grizzly bears. Leaving the trails is also illegal. Obey the signs in the geyser basins. Help yourself and others to have safe, enjoyable visits to the greatest geyser field of all . . . now and in the future.

Chapter 3

Geysers of Yellowstone National Park

Yellowstone National Park, Wyoming, is the home of Steamboat Geyser, the tallest active geyser in the world. It is the site of Giant Geyser, which may have the greatest total water discharge of any geyser when it has one of its rare eruptions. Smaller is Bead Geyser, which operates with amazing precision. And so on. Pick nearly any category you wish and you will probably find the "best" example among the geysers of Yellowstone. This should not be a surprise. Yellowstone is by far the largest geyser field on earth. Its 600 geysers, most of which are described in the following pages and of which 300 erupt frequently, make up at least 55% of all the geysers on our planet.

Geysers have long fascinated mankind. A possible single geyser (Gayzer Suyu), near the site of ancient Troy in Turkey, is mentioned in Homer's *Iliad*, written around 700 B.C. The first accurate description of a geyser eruption came from an English monk in Iceland in A.D. 1294. Anywhere geysers have been encountered at any time, they have always been noted. Therefore, for all their rarity, geysers are among the more familiar features of our natural world. But except for Yellowstone, one must do a lot of traveling to see other good examples. The next best geyser fields — in order, Kamchatka, New Zealand, Chile, and Iceland — combined contain fewer geysers than does Yellowstone. (For more about these and other world localities, see Appendix.)

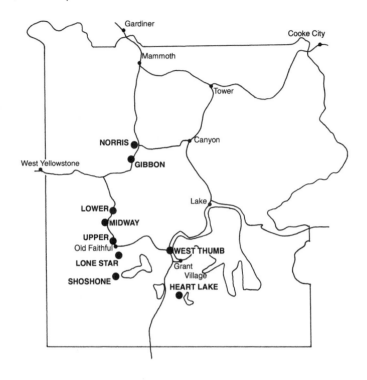

Map A. Geyser Basins of Yellowstone

Within Yellowstone are more than 10,000 hot springs of various types. Overall, fumaroles (steam vents), mud pots, and quietly flowing springs are much more common than geysers. The geysers are found in only a few relatively small areas. These are the "geyser basins" — specifically, Upper, Midway, Lower, Norris, West Thumb, Gibbon, Lone Star, Shoshone, and Heart Lake (see Map A).

These geyser basins are not necessarily true basins but are simply geographical areas in which hot springs, including geysers, are found. The basins are not large. For example, all of the more than 200 geysers of the Upper Basin are located within an area just 2 miles long and $1/_2$ mile wide.

The Upper Geyser Basin is the most important. There

are more geysers here than in any other area of either Yellowstone or the world. This is the home of Old Faithful, Beehive, Grand, Riverside, and most of the other famous geysers. Interspersed among them are hundreds of other beautiful hot springs.

The Lower Geyser Basin covers a much larger area — about 12 square miles — but the geyser groups are more widely scattered. Some of the better known individual geysers here are Great Fountain, Clepsydra, White Dome, and Fountain. This is also the location of the Fountain Paint Pots, which is among Yellowstone's largest assortment of mud pots.

The Norris Geyser Basin is the third largest, in both area and number of geysers. To many, it is the most interesting because it is different from any other basin. Part of the water at Norris is acid, some of it more caustic than battery acid. All of the other geyser basins discharge mostly alkaline water. Norris is the site of Echinus Geyser, one of the more beautiful and regular geysers in the Park, and Steamboat, the tallest in the world when active.

The Midway, West Thumb, and Gibbon Geyser Basins contain fewer geysers than the rest. They are, however, accessible areas, with relatively little walking necessary in order to see the geysers. Each has its own attractions and is well worth the time it takes to see it.

Three other geyser basins lie in the backcountry. The Lone Star Basin is about $2^1/_2$ miles by trail and includes two large and several small geysers. The Shoshone and Heart Lake Geyser Basins lie at greater distances. Few people visit them, so they remain comparatively untouched. Marked trails lead to these basins, but none of their features are identified by signs. Although one is free to wander among the hot springs, the hiker should remember that all thermal areas are dangerous and that extreme caution is necessary.

In the following descriptive chapters, the geysers are detailed according to geyser basin. Each area is further subdivided into groups, within which the geysers are described according to the order in which they lie along the trail. Every set of descriptions is followed by a table summarizing the activity of that group.

Chapter 4

Upper Geyser Basin

The Upper Geyser Basin is the first area to be described. This is always the case, and it is not just because of old habit. The Upper Geyser Basin is the home of Old Faithful and several other major spouters along with dozens of smaller geysers.

The Upper Basin is the greatest concentration of geysers anywhere in the world. More than 200 geysers, better than 20% of the world's total, are found within this area of only about $1^1/_2$ square miles. The hot springs are scattered among several nearly contiguous groups (Map B). Most of them lie within a few hundred feet of the Firehole River or its Iron Creek tributary, and seldom is the basin more than $^1/_2$ mile wide.

The Upper Geyser Basin understandably attracted the greatest attention of the early explorers of Yellowstone. Many of the names given the geysers and pools here were applied during the early 1870s. Although it was recognized that all of Yellowstone was worth preserving, it was probably the Upper Basin above all else that provided the greatest wonders and led to the founding of the world's first national park.

With four exceptions, all of the groups of geysers are threaded by boardwalks and other trails. The areas that are not — the Cascade, "Old Road," Myriad, and Pipeline Groups — can still be visited to some extent by way of trails or roads along their margins. Because of the thermal dangers involved, however, casual wandering through these groups is illegal, and persons doing so are subject to arrest.

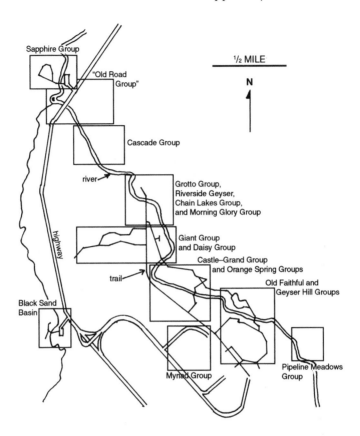

Map B. Index Map to the Upper Geyser Basin

Ranger-naturalist tours occasionally explore them, and, if nothing else, most of their geysers can be viewed from more distant roads and trails.

To properly see the Upper Basin one *must* spend two or three days in order to wait for the large and famous geysers to erupt as well as to experience the smaller features. There are minor details to be observed in the basin, too — the colorations, forest life, thermophilic communities, and so on — many of which are found nowhere else in the world. To spend less time is to cheat oneself.

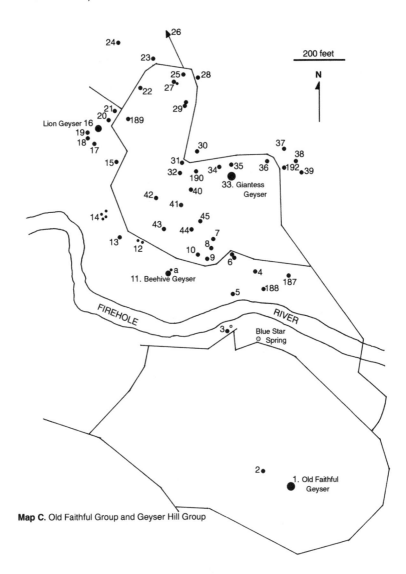

Map C. Old Faithful Group and Geyser Hill Group

Old Faithful Group

Only five springs are described as belonging to the Old Faithful Group (Map C, Table 1). In reality, the group is probably an isolated portion of the Geyser Hill Group, but because of its location on the opposite side of the Firehole River, it seems separate.

Two of the springs are not geysers. Between Old Faithful and Chinese Spring is a very pretty pool. The origin of Blue Star Spring's name is obvious; so is the huge amount of trash that unthinking visitors have thrown into the crater. Right next to Chinese Spring is East Chinaman Spring; it boils, overflows, and generally has a geyserlike appearance, but it has never been known to erupt.

1. OLD FAITHFUL GEYSER is the most famous geyser in the United States, as it should be. However, technically, at least, it is not the best-known geyser in the world. That distinction belongs to the Geysir in Iceland, the namesake of all geysers. There are geysers that are higher, more frequent, more voluminous, and so on, but no geyser anywhere can match Old Faithful for a combination of size, frequency, and regularity of eruptions. It can be viewed from the many benches near the Visitor Center, Inn, and Lodge. A more scenic view is from Geyser Hill, across the Firehole River, from there the greater distance allows Old Faithful to be really seen. It is one of the finest sights in Yellowstone.

Old Faithful was "discovered" by the Washburn Expedition in 1870. As Langford wrote in his journal, "Judge then our astonishment" when, as they entered the Upper Geyser Basin that September 18 afternoon, the first thing they saw was Old Faithful in full eruption. Unbelievably, here was one of the towering columns of water the mountain men had talked about for so long. Although they spent just $1^1/_2$ days in the Upper Basin, the members of the expedition were so impressed by this geyser's frequent activity that they called it Old Faithful. On the basis of their observations, several other geysers could have received the name, but Old Faithful is the only one that has remained true to the name for well over a century.

Many rumors about Old Faithful make the rounds. Many believe it once erupted "every hour, on the hour." Others swear it is far smaller than it once was or that it used to play for many minutes longer. Following the earthquake at Borah

Peak, Idaho, in 1983, dozens of newspaper, radio, and television reports said Old Faithful was dying. None of these stories is true. Old Faithful is a natural feature. It is subject to changes and one day will alter or stop its behavior. But for now it is very much the geyser it has always been.

Over the years more data have been gathered about Old Faithful than any on other geyser. The long-run average interval between eruptions was near an hour until the 1959 earthquake. The actual average of more than 46,000 intervals was 64.91 minutes. Since 1959 there has been a tendency toward longer intervals, and the 1983 earthquake caused the intervals to increase to an average greater than 78 minutes. The average of the 6,723 recorded eruptions in 1990 was 78.17 minutes, the highest value ever registered. In 1993 that average had dropped to around 75 minutes. How tall an eruption might be is subject to much variation, but the average for 211 eruptions during June 1985 was $123^1/_2$ feet, only 3 feet less than a similar calculation done in 1878. And, as always, the eruptions last from $1^1/_2$ to 5 minutes.

Old Faithful is regular enough to allow the rangers — and you — to predict the time of the next eruption with fair precision. There is a direct relationship between Old Faithful's duration and the following interval. A short eruption means that less water and heat have been discharged, that a shorter time span will be required to regain that water and heat, and therefore that the interval between the eruptions will be shorter than average. For example, if an eruption lasts 2 minutes, it will be around 55 minutes until the next one. On the other hand, a long duration (say, near $4^1/_2$ minutes) will lead to a longer interval; the prediction will be for about 88 minutes. The known range among intervals is from 30 to 120 minutes (plus two controversial but probable intervals of only 12 and 18 minutes), and, in fact, Old Faithful usually has either a long or a short interval. Eruptions occurring on the actual average (such as the current 75 minutes) are uncommon.

Much of the belief that Old Faithful is slowing down and that it isn't as powerful as it once was probably results from different viewing times. It is possible that such stories arise when a person visited the geyser years ago and happened to see an especially fine eruption. The height can exceed 180 feet. Any smaller play on another occasion will make the geyser seem to be weaker. A person's memory can also play tricks; a remembrance from years past is often magnified. All of the evidence is in contrast: Old Faithful has not changed to any great degree.

Shortly before Old Faithful begins to play, water splashes periodically from the vent. Sometimes this "preplay" will continue for 10 to 20 minutes before the eruption begins, but usually Old Faithful begins to spout after only a few such surges. One splash will be heavier than the others and will be sustained for a few seconds, and the eruption is on. The water column rockets rapidly to its maximum height, which is known to range from 106 to 184 feet (note that as with any geyser, strong wind can "chop off" the top of the column to a much lower height). After a minute or so, the column begins to shrink and slowly drops. Short duration eruptions stop abruptly, whereas those of longer durations end with a minute or two of low jetting and a weak steam phase.

Each of Old Faithful's eruptions is different from every other, and all are magnificent. Old Faithful Geyser *is* one of the natural wonders of the world.

2. UNNG-OFG-1 ("TEAPOT GEYSER") is located on top of a low geyserite mound about 150 feet northwest of Old Faithful. Although eruptions may last as long as several hours, at only 2 feet high and viewed at quite a distance, they aren't impressive. Few people notice this small geyser, and its interval has never been accurately determined.

3. CHINESE SPRING. In the early days of Yellowstone Park, there were many more concessions than at present. One of these was used by a laundry. One day the proprietors (who may have actually been Japanese) were doing some wash when the spring erupted and scattered clothes across the surrounding landscape. And so the name. Chinese Spring rarely erupts, but when it does the water column surges to 20 feet for about 2 minutes.

Geyser Hill Group

On Geyser Hill, the white, sinter-clad area directly across the Firehole River from the Old Faithful Group, are well over fifty geysers (Map C, Table 1). Some of these are among the largest anywhere; many others are almost inconspicuously small. It is worth mentioning that this concentration of geysers would, by itself and with no other geyser in Yellowstone, be the second largest existing geyser field on earth.

Most, if not all, of the hot springs on Geyser Hill are connected with the other members of the group. Exchange of function is extremely common. There are also two mysteries that have only recently been discovered, neither of which has a clearly identified cause. One is a tendency for several of the geysers to exhibit diurnal behavior — in general, short intervals by day and substantially longer intervals at night. Superimposed upon this is a weekly cycle known informally as the "Geyser Hill Wave," which causes fairly regular weekly increases and decreases in the intervals of many geysers in the group. It takes a great deal of observational experience to become familiar with these changes, but understanding them makes the activity on Geyser Hill anticipatable if not outright predictable.

Geyser Hill is traversed by a loop trail. It connects with other trails leading to Old Faithful, the Grand Geyser area, and Solitary Geyser–Observation Point.

187. BRONZE SPRING is the first pool encountered to the left of the boardwalk as one arrives on Geyser Hill from Old Faithful. It is usually a quiet and rather nondescript pool, but on occasion it undergoes significant eruptions. These are most commonly associated with the weekly cycles that take place within Geyser Hill. Most eruptions are only a few feet high, and some consist of little more than bubbling and surging, but exceptional bursts higher than 15 feet have been seen.

188. SILVER SPRING lies a few feet west of Bronze Spring (187) and also responds to the weekly Geyser Hill Wave

cycles. Over the course of several days, the water rises slowly in the crater. When the crater is full, intermittent boiling eruptions may dome the water as high as 2 or 3 feet. Then, *if* nearby Little Squirt Geyser (4) erupts, the pool level in Silver Spring will rapidly drop out of sight. During this part of the cycle, frequent eruptions can reach up to 8 feet high over the course of several hours.

4. LITTLE SQUIRT GEYSER was named because of the squirting nature of the small eruptions. Its original name was Gnome, and sometime later it was less formally referred to as "Spiral." Unless it is playing, the location goes unnoticed by most, since the vent is only a 3-inch hole in the geyserite. Before the 1959 earthquake, Little Squirt was very irregular. Since then it has been active during most seasons, but it is likely to erupt only at the culmination of the weekly Geyser Hill cycles. Since it can skip opportunities, the intervals fall at about one week or multiples of one week. Most durations are 12 to 18 hours, throughout which the squirting reaches 4 feet high. Exceptional eruptions can last for many days. Months-long dormant periods are also known.

5. CASCADE GEYSER was active during the early days of the Park, and for part of the 1890s it was a showpiece, with eruptions high as 40 feet recurring in intervals as short as 10 minutes. It became dormant in 1898. Except for a brief rejuvenation in late 1914, only brief eruptive periods have occurred since then. In 1948, 1950, and following both the 1959 and 1983 earthquakes, Cascade had eruptions as high as 25 feet. The most recent active phase of importance, during January 1988, lasted less than three days. The intervals then ranged from 14 to 145 minutes and the durations from $1^1/_2$ to $2^1/_2$ minutes; the height was 12 feet. Although there was evidence of activity in 1990, only a single eruption by Cascade has been seen since 1988; in July 1992, there was a brief eruption not more than 3 feet high. Because few observers give Cascade more than an occasional glance, such minor eruptions might actually be quite common.

6. THE ANEMONE GEYSERS. Anemone is a double spring. Two vents about 10 feet apart are the sites of semi-independent geysers. Most of the time the two act separately with little apparent relationship between them, but during some periods an eruption of one will invariably follow that of the other. The geysers sometimes play simultaneously. Both craters are shallow basins lined with pearly beads of sinter; the larger is tinted pinkish-gray and orange, the smaller pale yellow.

"Big" Anemone, nearest the boardwalk and the larger of the two, normally shows the greater activity. During most seasons it erupts every 7 to 10 minutes. Some of the spray reaches over 8 feet high, and angled bursts may reach the boardwalk. Eruptions usually last about 40 seconds. If "Little" Anemone erupts for an extended duration, the interval before "Big" does so again may be as long as 15 or 20 minutes.

"Little" Anemone plays from the vent farther from the boardwalk. Its eruptions are smaller than those of its neighbor, but they generally last considerably longer. Most plays begin near or shortly after the eruptions of "Big" Anemone. On rare occasions near constant activity by "Little" will render "Big" dormant for days at a time.

7. SURGE GEYSER is an old spring or geyser rejuvenated by the 1959 earthquake. Before then the crater was there, but no eruptions had ever been recorded. Following the earthquake, Surge erupted frequently until 1963. Since then it has sometimes been active in concert with Giantess Geyser (33), proving that there is an underground connection between the two. Such eruptions, lasting as long as 1 minute and reaching 8 feet high, were last seen in 1984.

8. SPUME GEYSER (previously listed as UNNG-GHG-1) had occasional eruptions during the early days of Yellowstone, but then none occurred until brief, active episodes following the earthquakes of 1959 and 1983. The ragged crater was considerably enlarged by the 1983 eruptions, which burst powerfully to at least 10 feet high. The action died down rapidly, and the crater now acts as a drain for runoff flowing from the upper part of Geyser Hill. The same crater contains the vent of Spew Spouter.

9. PLUME GEYSER is of fairly recent origin. In 1922 a small steam explosion created its vent. After about five years of activity, it fell dormant in 1926. Only one possible, brief active phase in 1930 interrupted the dormancy until 1940. Since then it was continuously active until 1992. For a long time, Plume did seem to erupt "every hour, on the hour": the average interval was almost exactly 60 minutes. However, as time went on it gradually became more irregular until, just after the 1959 earthquake, it seldom erupted. By 1962, though, it was again a highly regular geyser, and the new average interval was only 27 minutes. This was the case until 1972.

Plume is a good example of how geysers may change themselves. In late December 1972 another steam explosion added an extension to the vent. Much of the eruption now issues through this new opening. Plume is still fairly regular, but the eruptions are massive bursts to 20 or 25 feet rather than the slender 40-foot jet of old.

Plume's modern activity is complex. A model of precision until the late 1980s, its behavior was modified only infrequently by such outside forces as eruptions by Giantess Geyser (33). By 1988 it was realized that Plume was undergoing slight but regular interval variations. This pattern has grown stronger every year. During 1992 and 1993 Plume behaved in a strongly diurnal fashion. Daytime intervals could be as short as 25 minutes; at night, it slowed to intervals as long as 70 minutes and occasionally fell completely "asleep" for several hours in the morning and early afternoon. The cause of this phenomenon is not completely known, but it may have to do with the temperature of runoff water flowing into Plume's plumbing by way of Spume Geyser (8) — cold water quenches potential eruptions. For a few weeks in March and April 1993, and again during winter and spring in early 1994, Plume was completely dormant. When it reactivated, it played on an erratic pattern, with little of the diurnal effect being apparent. Plume is also a participant in the Geyser Hill Wave, which alternately increases and decreases the average intervals on a weekly basis, no matter what other activity pattern might be underway. Plume, once a model of constancy, has become one of the most complex and intriguing of geysers.

10. UNNG-GHG-2 is a ragged hole a few feet to the left of Plume Geyser (9). During most seasons eruptions are frequent, reaching 1 to 2 feet high, but dormant periods are known. The twin vents of another small geyser lie a few feet beyond GHG-2.

11. BEEHIVE GEYSER is the second or third tallest regularly active geyser in Yellowstone. During most of recorded history it was an infrequent performer, with eruptions many days apart. Starting in the early 1970s and continuing through 1993, it had unprecedented activity. Beehive eruptions became nearly a daily sight. Average intervals were mostly between 16 and 20 hours within a range of 9 to 28 hours, and only for very short times did it revert to the historical mode of infrequent eruptions.

The eruptions issue through a cone 4 feet high that is shaped like an old-fashioned straw beehive. The vent within the cone is very narrow and acts like a nozzle so that a slender column of water is shot under great pressure to as high as 200 feet. To observe an eruption of Beehive from the boardwalk near its cone is a unique experience. The awesome display combined with the pounding roar of steam escaping at great speeds is unforgettable. Viewed at a distance the impression is very different. Then the slenderness and height of the jet become apparent, with needlelike rockets of water towering above the surroundings. The entire eruption, including a concluding steam phase, lasts about 8 minutes.

It is difficult to tell when Beehive might erupt. Water spraying out of the cone tells little, although it often attracts a considerable crowd. Such splashing happens throughout most of the quiet interval, and only in the last few minutes

Beehive Geyser, in Geyser Hill, is among the largest cone-type geysers in the world. The steady jetting reaches between 150 and 200 feet high. Unfortunately, Beehive sometimes goes days or even weeks between eruptions.

before an eruption do the splashes become notably large and frequent. One of these eventually triggers the full display. Accurate knowledge of the weekly Geyser Hill cycle allows reasonably accurate eruption times to be predicted, but these will never be more precise than plus or minus a few hours. Of greater use is Beehive's Indicator (11a), whose performances are almost invariably indicators of a pending eruption.

11a. BEEHIVE'S INDICATOR plays out of a small vent a few feet to the front-left of Beehive's cone. Historically, when Beehive had days-long intervals, the Indicator was rarely active, but since the early 1970s it has been true to its name. Almost without exception, every eruption of Beehive is preceeded by an eruption of Beehive's Indicator. The steady water jet of the Indicator reaches 6 to 10 feet high, usually starting 10 to 25 minutes before Beehive erupts (the known range in lead time is from less than 1 to about 45 minutes). Since it is readily visible from a distance and has such a long duration, the Indicator provides ample opportunity for people to get close to Beehive, if not actually onto Geyser Hill for the promised show.

Unfortunately, the use of Beehive's Indicator is not 100% reliable. It sometimes erupts for long durations (up to an hour) without resulting in play by Beehive. These "false Indicators" are uncommon, but in August 1992 they completely took over the activity from Beehive. Totally unlike anything ever seen before, the Indicator erupted every 3 to 5 hours for durations of about 50 minutes. Beehive was dormant from August 7 until the Indicator stopped its unusual performances on September 1. A similar episode took place during July–September 1994. Still less common are "midcycle Indicators," which play a meaningless, weak, and brief jet of water about halfway through Beehive's interval.

There is another indicator vent for Beehive. Interestingly, even though this "Beehive's Second Indicator" lies between the Beehive's Indicator's vent and Beehive's cone, it is rarely active. When it is, the play is more of a small splashing. The Second Indicator bears a less certain relationship

to Beehive, and durations as long as 6 hours, without resultant eruptions by Beehive, are known.

12. SCISSORS SPRINGS. These two small springs used to flow
steadily. The rivulets from each converged a short distance
from the pools then split again, so that the entire formation
resembled a pair of shears. By 1950 one spring had stopped
flowing; the other stopped soon thereafter. In 1973 they suddenly sprang to life again, not only overflowing but acting as
small geysers a few feet high. The activity has waxed and
waned several times since then, and now only the right-hand
spring intermittently overflows.

13. DEPRESSION GEYSER was affected dramatically by both
the 1959 and 1983 earthquakes, which caused considerable
increases in its activity. Before the 1959 tremors, Depression
was so inactive that it hadn't even been given a name, even
though there had been some action in 1947–1948. Now the
pale blue-green pool plays fairly regularly. The intervals have
been increasing slowly through the years and are now
between 5 and 9 hours long. The play, 6 to 10 feet high, lasts
about 3 minutes from a full pool then continues in a weaker
fashion from a lower water level for another 2 to 3 minutes.

14. UNNG-GHG-3. In the flat area a short distance to the right
(northwest) of Depression Geyser (13) are a number of
spouters and geysers. Most are very small, although one has
been known to hit 8 feet high. The number of these springs
acting as truly periodic geysers varies from five to nine.
Records indicate that they were active only during 1947,
1959, and 1962 until beginning the modern, nearly continuous action in 1972.

Across the boardwalk from these geysers' vicinity are several ragged explosion craters. Although all probably formed
in prehistoric times, several had eruptions as a result of both
the 1959 and 1983 earthquakes. Although they reached as
high as 10 feet, none were regular or frequent enough to be
given a name except for a pencilled "Blowout" next to one
on a single map.

15. "POT OF GOLD SPRING" (previously given as GHG-4) is immediately next to the boardwalk midway between Arrowhead Spring and Heart Spring. It was named during the post-1959 earthquake studies and was a cool, quiet pool lined with orange-yellow cyanobacteria until 1980. It has had several eruptions since that time, some of which were simultaneous with eruptions by Giantess Geyser (33). A series of eruptions on July 28, 1988, reached up to 4 feet high. About 12 feet to the right of Pot of Gold is another crater, which was only a tiny hole in the geyserite until some small but explosive eruptions in 1985 enlarged the crater and littered the boardwalk with chunks of geyserite.

THE LION GEYSER COMPLEX (numbers 16-21 plus 189). Situated on a high sinter mound rising steeply from the Firehole River at the far northern end of Geyser Hill are four geyserite cones. These constitute the Lion family. Related to them are three other springs, below and to the northeast of the mound. All seven are geysers, and together they make up the Lion Geyser Complex, one of the most active sets of geysers in Yellowstone.

16. LION GEYSER issues from the largest cone on the mound, the one farthest north and nearest to the boardwalk. Lion is also the largest geyser in the pride. Lion is perhaps the classic example of a cyclic geyser, in which there are distinct series of eruptions. The initial eruption in a series has a duration of around 6 minutes, during which water is jetted to between 50 and 70 feet high. One exceptional eruption was measured at 98 feet in 1988. The subsequent eruptions of a series recur at intervals of 1 to $1^1/_2$ hours (rarely, 3 hours); with durations of 2 to 4 minutes, they are considerably weaker than the initial eruption and rarely reach more than 30 feet high. Most series consist of two to four eruptions, although a few have only the initial eruption and others see as many as nine eruptions.

The number of eruptions within a series roughly controls how long a "cycle interval" (series start to next series start) will pass until the next eruptions take place — the more eruptions within a series, the longer the time between series. If there are only one or two eruptions, the cycle interval is usually only around 6 to 8 hours long; longer series produce cycle intervals as great as 19 hours. (Lion has always been a cyclic geyser, but the cycle intervals and durations have shown wide variations; at one time the cycle durations were as long as 36 hours, but then the intervals between active phases were as great as 9 days.)

During the quiet between series, Lion occasionally splashes as if about to erupt, and these splashes sometimes seem ready to trigger an eruption hours before the initial one actually takes place. Perhaps it was this action that resulted in Lion's original name, Niobe. Niobe is from Greek mythology; bewailing the loss of her children, she was turned to stone and remained forever wet with tears. The modern name came about because of the loud roars of steam that gush from the vent just before all of Lion's eruptions other than the initial ones.

17. LITTLE CUB GEYSER is the only other member of the Lion Complex to be frequently active year after year. It is the small cone on the far left (south) of the mound, farthest from Lion. Little Cub normally erupts every 45 to 90 minutes, possibly varying in accord with the weekly Geyser Hill Wave. It is somewhat larger than it looks from the boardwalk, and it sends some spurts up to 10 feet high throughout the 10-minute duration. Just off the right-hand side of Little Cub's cone is the "Cubby Hole," which plays a few inches high in conjunction with Little Cub.

18-19. LIONESS GEYSER AND BIG CUB GEYSER are the two center cones, on the left and right, respectively. These two geysers seldom erupt, but when they do they often play in concert with one another. Lioness can reach 30 feet and Big Cub about 40 feet high.

The Lion Complex clearly shows exchange of function, both between other complexes of geysers and among its own members. When Lion Geyser is having active cycles, Lioness and Big Cub are dormant. Since Lion has been far and away the dominant geyser during all of recorded history, eruptions by the other two have been rare. The last active phases of Lioness and Big Cub took place during 1947, when there were twelve eruptions; in 1951, with a single play; and in 1952, when there were seven eruptions by Lioness and eight by Big Cub. The Borah Peak earthquake of 1983 produced a dormancy in the entire Lion Complex. When activity resumed in 1985, it seemed as though both Lioness and Big Cub were about to enter a new active period. The only eventual result, however, was a single solo eruption of Big Cub on August 6, 1987. Both geysers boil and sputter vigorously at times and seem to be on hair-triggers. Someday they are bound to be seen again.

20. GOGGLES SPRING is the irregular crater a few feet north of Lion's mound. It was named during the 1910s for uncertain reasons but just when automobile traffic and driving goggles became common in Yellowstone. The shallow, round, orange pool next to Goggles' crater used to contain a small vent of its own, but it has long been choked with trash and debris. Goggles Spring was probably active in some fashion during the 1920s and evidently played in concert with one eruption of Giantess in 1952, then did not erupt again until 1985. Following the rejuvenation of the entire Lion Complex from its 1983–1984 dormancy, there was an increase in activity by all the members of the complex. Goggles shared in this by having several eruptions in concert with those of nearby North Goggles Geyser (21) and Lion. The eruptions were brief and not more than 6 feet high, but the bursts were jetted with enough force and at such a low angle out of an empty crater that they reached the boardwalk 20 feet away. No jetting eruptions have occurred since 1985, but boiling up to 2 feet high in company with nearby North Goggles was seen in 1993.

21. NORTH GOGGLES GEYSER was evidently the site of frequent action before recorded times, as it has large runoff channels leading away from its small cone. Historically, though, it was rarely if ever seen prior to the 1959 earthquake. Since then, it was active in most seasons through

1985 and again in 1993 and 1994. North Goggles has both minor and major eruptions. During most years the minors are the only variety seen. These are very brief and seldom more than 10 feet high. Studies indicate that they are most likely to take place during the quiet cycle interval of Lion Geyser. Major eruptions, which were the dominant form of activity only during 1985, are spectacular. Almost always occurring in concert with Lion, they reached as high as 50 feet. The steady water jet pulsated throughout the eruption but only began to decline near the end of the 4-minute duration. Major eruptions were followed by a short but briefly powerful steam phase. In 1994 a few eruptions of a possible new "intermediate" type were seen. Occurring during active cycles by Lion, as was the case with the majors of 1985, these generally lasted about 1 minute, reached perhaps 20 feet high, and concluded without a significant steam phase.

189. UNNG-GHG-10 is a small pool located about 30 feet across the boardwalk from North Goggles Geyser. Although seldom noticed, it is generally active as an intermittent spring, repeating quiet overflows every 7 to 9 minutes. Sometimes, usually shortly before the time of Lion's initial eruption, GHG-10 has eruptions on the same frequency. Most bursts are a foot high or less, but some jetting up to 10 feet has been observed.

22. EAR SPRING is a prominent, small pool right next to the boardwalk. Its water is usually superheated (the water temperature is above the local 199°F [93°C] boiling point) so that there is a constant sizzling and bubbling about the rim of the crater. True eruptions are extremely rare. One reported as 15 feet high took place during 1957; the 1959 earthquake produced a few eruptions perhaps 2 feet high, and additional plays of that size were observed in both 1986 and 1992. Also, in association with eruptions by Giantess Geyser (33), Ear Spring sometimes undergoes heavy surging without actually splashing. In the opposite fashion, Ear Spring is infrequently found cooler than boiling and slightly below overflow.

23. PENDANT SPRING is usually a quiet pool. It was once known as "Algous Pool" when it was cool enough to house a thick growth of cyanobacteria. More often, as now, it has been too hot for cyanobacteria to grow, and it has had geyser eruptions during at least three episodes. During both the 1870s and 1960s, the eruptions had durations of several hours and heights of 1 to 2 feet. Briefly following the 1983 earthquake, the plays were just seconds to minutes long, but some bursts reached up to 6 feet. Pendant Spring has been dormant since 1987.

24. UNNG-GHG-5 lies among some old craters near the woods beyond Pendant Spring (23). Active as a perpetual spouter of very small size prior to the 1983 Borah Peak earthquake, it had frequent eruptions up to 5 feet high during 1984. GHG-5 then gradually declined, and it is again a perpetual spouter.

25. BEACH SPRING played as a 10-foot geyser during 1939, on a smaller scale during 1947, and during a few brief spans since. Mostly, it acts as a cyclically boiling intermittent spring. Much of the time the water lies low within the crater. Every few minutes it fills and covers at least some of the beachlike terrace around the pool. Only then does it undergo vigorous superheated boiling and rare bursting. The duration is a few seconds.

27. BEACH GEYSER AND UNNG-GHG-7. These two small geysers lie a few feet beyond Beach Spring. The larger, right-hand (northern) geyser may be the historical Beach Geyser (UNNG-GHG-6 in previous editions). These two geysers are closely related to one another, largely filling, erupting, and draining in concert. Beach Geyser had frequent eruptions as high as 15 feet during 1939, the same year in which nearby Beach Spring (25) was also active as a notable geyser. Now it plays up to 4 feet high, whereas the smaller GHG-7 seldom exceeds 2 feet.

Across the boardwalk from Beach Spring and GHG-6 and 7, a trail leads through the forest and up the hill to

Solitary Geyser (26). Along the way is a lush forest meadow with some of the finest wildflowers you can find anywhere — most prominent in midsummer are columbine, monkshood, Indian paintbrush, chives, and sticky geranium. This trail continues from Solitary Geyser across the mountainside to Observation Point and then back to the starting point of the Geyser Hill loop trail.

26. SOLITARY GEYSER was, contrary to most accounts, active as a small geyser during the early years of Yellowstone, but it was dramatically and artificially altered in 1915. In that year permission was given to use the water of the seldom visited spring for a swimming pool. Solitary Spring immediately became Solitary Geyser. A deepened runoff channel had lowered the water level enough to allow boiling to take place at depth — and, consequently, eruptions began. The play was frequent and powerful, reaching 25 feet high. The Old Faithful Geyser Bath was closed in the late 1940s and the runoff channel was repaired, but eruptions continue despite the renewed high water level. Although most modern eruptions recur every 4 to 8 minutes and last about 1 minute, with bursts less than 6 feet high, much as was described in 1887, a few hitting 15 to 20 feet can still be seen with a little luck or patience. This is a good illustration of how delicate these hot spring systems are — after more than 40 years, the system still has not stabilized.

28. AURUM GEYSER was so named because of the golden color of the iron oxide stains inside the little cone. Eruptions were rare prior to the 1983 earthquake, with Aurum constantly boiling and bursting within its vent at almost all times. Since then it has been fairly regular, with most intervals between 3 and 5 hours. For reasons unknown, Aurum sometimes tries to regress to its pre-1983 behavior, resulting in intervals as long as 20 hours. However, occasional intervals of less than 1 hour have been seen, too. The play is angled toward the boardwalk, reaching up to 20 feet high and sometimes inundating the walk at the peak of the 1-minute eruption.

29. DOUBLET POOL is one of the most beautiful blue pools in the Upper Geyser Basin. It is slightly intermittent in its water level and overflow. Most of the rare eruptions have been nothing more than boiling at the times of high water, but on two occasions associated with eruptions by Giantess Geyser (33) and once following the 1959 earthquake, Doublet Pool had true bursting eruptions reaching perhaps 2 feet high.

Near the runoff west of Doublet Pool is a small geyserite cone. Usually active as a perpetual spouter, it was given the very informal name "Singlet Geyser" on the basis of frequent geyser activity in 1993 and 1994. It is less than 1 foot high.

30. PUMP GEYSER was a seemingly unchanging perpetual spouter 2 to 3 feet high for many years until the 1983 earthquake. It is now a true geyser, albeit with both intervals and durations only a few seconds long. The water is sprayed under considerable steam pressure so that it fans up and out of the long vent as far and as high as 6 feet. The geyser was named in allusion to a small perpetual spouter nearby that is called The Pump.

31. SPONGE GEYSER got its name because the geyserite decorations on the outside of its cone resemble a sponge. Also, according to some, the entire eruption could be soaked up by a sponge. The cone is remarkably large given the tiny size of the eruptions, and Sponge was possibly once a more significant geyser or boiling spring. When active, water stands near the top of the cone, and eruptions 6 to 9 inches high recur every minute or so. More commonly in recent years, Sponge has been dormant, the water lying far out of sight deep within the cone.

32. PLATE GEYSER was named because of platelike sheets of geyserite about the crater. It was named when the 1959 earthquake triggered the first known eruptions. It was then inactive until the late 1960s, and it remained at best an infrequent performer from then until the 1983 earthquake. Most eruptions, when any took place, were in association with Giantess Geyser (33). Such eruptions lasted only

a few seconds. There has been much more action since 1983, and Plate has been a regular geyser during several seasons. Intervals range between 1 and $2^{1}/_{2}$ hours. With durations of up to 3 minutes, the highest bursting water jets can reach 15 feet.

190. UNNG-GHG-11 ("ABRUPT GEYSER") made a dramatic appearance in May 1992. It plays from an old crater along a fracture; Plate Geyser (32) and Slot Geyser (191) occupy other craters on this same rift. The eruptions are spectacular but uncommon. The play begins with an abrupt gushing of water out of the vent, which instantly builds into a sharply angled water jet as high as 20 feet. After the initial surge, the play slowly declines in force until it ends with a few final weak, steamy bursts. The durations have ranged between 8 and 40 minutes; the intervals have varied from a few hours to days. There is a clear relationship between Abrupt and nearby Plate Geyser (32), with Abrupt playing only when Plate is having intervals that are shorter than average. Also, all observed eruptions by Abrupt have started during or within a few minutes after play by Plate. However, although Plate has had similar performances in the past, the evidence indicates that the 1992–1994 activity is Abrupt's first ever. It may well meet its demise as abruptly as it appeared.

191. SLOT GEYSER evidently lies within another crater on the fracture that also incorporates Plate (32) and "Abrupt" (190) — but exactly which vent it is is controversial. It may be identical to the "second new thing" that was active near Abrupt in 1992, but not all observers agree. In any case, its activity has been rare, with eruptions not more than 1 to 2 feet high. (Because of its uncertain location, Slot Geyser is not shown on Map C.)

33. GIANTESS GEYSER is one of the largest and most powerful geysers anywhere in the world. You must be very lucky in order to see it erupt, though. During most of recorded history it has averaged only two or three active episodes per year. Recently, it has had some better seasons, and the all-time

Giantess Geyser averages only two or three eruptions per year, but its water jets may approach 200 feet high shortly before it enters a steam phase that is sometimes audible more than a mile away.

record for activity was set in 1983, when it had forty-one eruptive episodes (all before the Borah Peak earthquake on October 28). Given the infrequency, it is amazing that the Washburn Expedition saw Giantess during its $1^{1}/_{2}$ day visit in 1870. The explorers described it as "the grandest wonder" of their trip.

During the long quiet phase, the large pool boils periodically around the edge of the crater. An active episode begins during one of these "hot periods." In general, there is no indication as to when eruptions will begin, except that a recent study has determined that the hot periods become slightly stronger and more frequent during the last few hours of the quiet phase. In addition, since Giantess is a member of the Geyser Hill Group, its activity is affected by the mysterious weekly cycles of the Geyser Hill Wave. Look especially for voluminous "north-face boils," which spill large volumes of water onto the surrounding platform. The action truly begins when surging starts to pour a tremendous flood of water over all parts of the platform. After several minutes this sometimes ceases briefly, and the water level drops several inches within the crater. But then the eruption begins in earnest, with jets of water being rocketed to as much as 200 feet in height.

The entire eruption may last from 1 to 43 hours; the 1959 earthquake caused one eruption of more than 100 hours. Each of these phases consists of a number of separate bursts of activity and can be classified into types. The water phase type will jet water for 5 minutes at intervals of 25 to 50 minutes, over a total of about 24 hours. In the steam phase type, the water gives way to powerfully roaring steam, usually during the second or third water eruption. At first this roaring can easily be heard more than a mile away, but then it steadily declines and ends after about 12 hours. First observed in 1959, and the most common eruption type since then, is the mixed phase. This begins like the steam phase but reverts to water phase after 3 to 8 hours; the mixed phase eruption lasts as long as 43 hours. Finally, first observed in 1981 is the short or aborted phase, which ends after a brief and very weak duration. Following any of these varieties, the crater will take a few hours to 3 days to refill. Then there is only occasional boiling until the next active phase begins days to months later.

A geyser as great as Giantess would be expected to have an effect on other springs in the area, and indeed it does. Vault Spring (35), Infant Geyser (36), Teakettle Spring (34), Dome Geyser (39), Plate Geyser (32), Doublet Pool (29), Ear Spring (22), Pot of Gold Spring (15), Beehive Geyser (11), Plume Geyser (9), and Surge Geyser (7) are all definitely and rather directly connected to Giantess. This is known because of the reactions of these springs to the eruptions of Giantess. In fact, they are all part of one subsurface system, and it is these numerous connections that make Giantess an infrequent and irregular performer.

34. TEAKETTLE SPRING is not a geyser; perhaps it never was. It is mentioned here because it does have a large geyserlike cone. The water level is deep within the crater, where it can be heard boiling and splashing. The pool was full until 1947. In that year nearby Vault Spring (35) began erupting after a long dormancy. The water in Teakettle immediately began ebbing.

35. VAULT SPRING was known as a geyser in the early days of the Park, when it occasionally erupted several hours *before* nearby Giantess Geyser (33) began an active period. Rare eruptions in concert with Giantess were seen in the 1920s and 1930s, but no consistent action was known until 1947. In that one year it had remarkable activity, with intervals of 40 to 50 hours, durations of 12 to 24 hours, and heights of 15 feet. More recently it has exhibited two modes of behavior. Most commonly, it begins to play a few hours after Giantess starts and is usually done erupting before Giantess has quit. On infrequent occasions, it has independent active episodes. In both of these modern cases, the intervals are commonly around 1 hour, with eruptions 6 to 20 feet high over durations of 4 or 5 minutes.

36. INFANT GEYSER is a spring that seems to have somehow become partially disconnected from the rest of the Geyser

Hill Group. Prior to the 1959 earthquake, the water level stood well below overflow, and small eruptions took place only in concert with Giantess (33). After the tremors, Infant began having eruptions on its own several times a day. Gradually the water level rose, and when the crater began to overflow in 1964, the eruptions ceased. During all of this time the water was clear and alkaline like the other Geyser Hill springs. Infant has since dropped to the water level of old, but it is now murky and acidic. It still shows the connection with Giantess, however, having small eruptions during some active phases of Giantess.

37. MOTTLED POOL lies uphill across the boardwalk from Infant Geyser (36). Nothing of it can be seen from the boardwalk (and, of course, you must stay on the boardwalk). There isn't much to see, anyway. Deep within the crater eruptions rise from a small pool. Frequent but brief, most of the splashes are only 1 to 2 feet high. Mottled Pool probably had some eruptions during the 1800s, but it was described as "extinct" in 1927. The modern activity might date to the 1959 earthquake, and it has continued without change since the early 1970s.

192. PEANUT POOL was a forgotten name and an ignored crater until 1991, when it began to have eruptions. The play was never more than 1 foot high, and Peanut Pool had reverted to an empty hole by the end of 1992.

38. BUTTERFLY SPRING, named for the shape of the crater, has had episodes of true geyser eruptions as high as 6 feet, but it now acts as a 1-foot perpetual spouter with one of the wings filled with gravel.

39. DOME GEYSER was generally an erratic and infrequent performer, with long dormancies, until 1972. The play, however, was as high as 30 feet. Its modern activity is on a much reduced scale. Active episodes take place at intervals of several days to a few weeks. A series of eruptions, consisting mainly of vigorous boiling but little splashing, then takes

place for a day or more. There is probably a direct relationship between Dome and Giantess Geyser (33). Most active episodes of Giantess have begun during exceptionally long intervals by Dome. In turn, an eruption by Dome seems to eliminate any real probability of a near future Giantess eruption.

OTHER GEYSERS OF THE GEYSER HILL GROUP. Six other geysers of this group are worthy of mention. Because of their mostly small sizes and their locations well away from the boardwalk, they are not easily viewed.

40. MODEL GEYSER is a small spouter of frequent activity, regular at times and very irregular at others. Best viewed from the boardwalk near Sponge Geyser (31), it plays from a fairly obvious yellowish-brown crater in the central portion of Geyser Hill. The eruptions reach about 4 feet high. A smaller unnamed geyser lies a few feet beyond Model, and still another is found just to Model's left.

41. DRAGON GEYSER is a beautiful blue pool, again best seen from the vicinity of Sponge Geyser (31). Dragon is known to have had very few eruptions during Park history. The most recent was during 1992, when play mostly less than 2 feet high with occasional bursts of 5 feet was recorded. Washed areas around the crater following the 1959 earthquake implied that some sort of voluminous eruption took place that night.

42. ROOF GEYSER usually cannot be seen except for its steam cloud. It lies completely below ground level in a deep hole, over which is a "roof" of geyserite. The small pool erupts every few minutes for a few seconds. During 1993, however, it was frequently seen to spray fully 4 feet above the ground.

43. UNNG-GHG-8 is just one among a collection of craters atop the hill above Scissors Springs (12) that erupted following the 1983 earthquake. GHG-8 was the only one of these to have persisted in its activity. Eruptions up to 20 feet high

recurred on an irregular but frequent basis into 1986. None are known from any of these craters since then.

44. UNNG-GHG-9 ("BORAH PEAK GEYSER") was in existence prior to the October 1983 earthquake, but it was much more active for several years following those shocks. It had both minor and major eruptions. All intervals were a few minutes in length. The minor eruptions had durations of only a few seconds, whereas the occasional majors lasted as long as 20 minutes. With either type, the height was 3 to 4 feet. Borah Peak has recently become a much less important geyser. It is often dormant, and its few eruptions are minor splashing only 1 foot high; it is frequent and stronger when Giantess (33) is active. The crater is nearly impossible to see from the boardwalk.

45. BENCH GEYSER was once very active, but the runoff from the frequent eruptions by Giantess Geyser (33) during the early 1980s completely filled it with gravel. Its site is marked by a gentle drift of steam in cool weather.

Table 1. Geysers of the Old Faithful and Geyser Hill Groups

Name	Map No.	Interval	Duration	Height (ft)
Anemone Geyser, "Big"	6	7–10 min	40 sec	6–8
Anemone Geyser, "Little"	6	7–30 min	sec–min	2–4
Aurum Geyser	28	3–20 hrs	1 min	20
Beach Geyser	27	minutes	minutes	4–15
Beach Spring	25	minutes	1–2 min	boil
Beehive Geyser	11	hrs–days	5 min	150–200
Beehive's Indicator	11a	with Beehive	1–45 min	6–10
Bench Geyser	45	extinct?	seconds	6
Big Cub Geyser	19	[1987]	4–8 min	40
Bronze Spring	187	min–hrs *	sec–2 min	2–15
Butterfly Spring	38	steady	steady	1
Cascade Geyser	5	[1988]	1 1/2–2 1/2 min	3–40
Chinese Spring	3	rare	2 min	20
Depression Geyser	13	5–9 hrs	6 min	6–10
Dome Geyser	39	min–hrs *	5–10 min	boil–30
Doublet Pool	29	rare	minutes	2
Dragon Geyser	41	unknown	seconds	2–5

Table 1 continued

Ear Spring	22	rare	1–2 min	boil–2
Giantess Geyser	33	0–41/year	1–43 hrs	100–200
Goggles Spring	20	[1985]	seconds	6
Infant Geyser	36	rare	hours	2
Lion Geyser	16	1–3 hrs	2–6 min	30–98
Lioness Geyser	18	[1952]	5–10 min	30
Little Cub Geyser	17	45–90 min	10 min	10
Little Squirt Geyser	4	days	12–18 hrs	4
Model Geyser	40	minutes	minutes	4
Mottled Pool	37	sec–min	seconds	1–2
North Goggles Geyser	21	min–days *	sec–5 min	6–50
Old Faithful Geyser	1	30–120 min	1 1/2–5 min	90–184
Peanut Pool	192	[1992]	minutes	1
Pendant Spring	23	[1987]	sec–min	1–6
Plate Geyser	32	1–2 1/2 hrs *	3 min	6–15
Plume Geyser	9	min–hrs	1 min	3–25
Pot of Gold Spring	15	[1988]	seconds	4
Pump Geyser	30	seconds	seconds	6
Roof Geyser	42	minutes	seconds	2–6
Scissors Springs	12	minutes *	1–2 min	1–2
Silver Spring	188	seconds *	seconds	2–8
Slot Geyser	191	rare	minutes	1–2
Solitary Geyser	26	4–8 min	1 min	2–20
Sponge Geyser	31	seconds *	seconds	6–9 inches
Spume Geyser	8	[1984]	seconds	8
Surge Geyser	7	[1984]	1 min	8
UNNG-GHG-2	10	sec–min *	minutes	1–2
UNNG-GHG-3	14	sec–min	sec–min	1–8
UNNG-GHG-5	24	steady	steady	1–2
UNNG-GHG-7	27	minutes	sec–min	2
UNNG-GHG-8	43	[1986]	minutes	20
UNNG-GHG-9 ("Borah Peak")	44	minutes	seconds	1–4
UNNG-GHG-10	189	7–9 min *	seconds	inches–10
UNNG-GHG-11 ("Abrupt")	190	hrs–days *	8–40 min	20–25
UNNG-OFG-1 ("Teapot")	2	infrequent	hours	2
Vault Spring	35	1 hr *	4–5 min	6–20

* When active.
[ ] Brackets enclose the year of most recent activity for extremely rare or dormant geysers. See text.

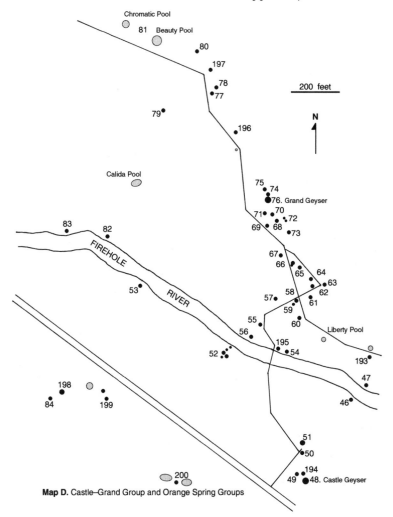

Map D. Castle–Grand Group and Orange Spring Groups

Castle Group and Grand Group

The Castle Group and Grand Group of geysers (Map D, Table 2) are the most extensive in the Upper Basin. They include over forty geysers, most of which are active to some degree all of the time. Four of the geysers are very large, and if there is any area in Yellowstone where one can be assured of seeing a major geyser other than Old Faithful erupt, this is it. In addition to the numerous spouters, the groups also contain several beautiful pools. Despite the nearness of the groups to one another, any physical subsurface connection between them is only hypothetical.

The Castle and Grand Groups can be approached in two ways. A paved trail leads directly from the Visitor Center, past the Inn and lower Hamilton's Store, to Castle Geyser. The other route leaves the Geyser Hill loop near North Goggles Geyser and leads through the Sawmill Complex directly to Grand Geyser.

46. SPRINKLER GEYSER is difficult to see well; the best viewing spot is from the boardwalk across the river, near Liberty Pool. Named in the 1870s, it has probably been active at all times since, but because of its inconvenient location no long-term study of its behavior has ever been performed. Probably a cyclic geyser, it is in eruption more than it is not. Intervals seem to be less than 40 minutes long (usually much less), and the durations range from just 5 to 30 minutes. In 1993 the action was quite regular, with both intervals and durations around 10 minutes, so that Sprinkler was in eruption about 60% of the time. The height is up to 10 feet.

47. SPATTER GEYSER is directly across the Firehole River from Sprinkler Geyser (46). Its only known activity was a result of the 1959 earthquake, when its behavior made it a near twin of Sprinkler. Spatter returned to dormancy in 1962, and its crater is now nearly filled with debris slumped from the slope above.

193. UNNG-CGG-6 is a small pool on the west side of the boardwalk; across the walk where there is a railing is a larger, deeper yellow-green pool sometimes called "Rubber Pool" because of the way its sides seem to bend and wiggle as the pool pulsates. CGG-6 acts mostly as an intermittent spring with short intervals and durations, but when it is overflowing it occasionally splashes a foot or two high. The numerous cool springs in this area are known as the Frog Pools. Several erupted the night of the 1959 earthquake yet now have no apparent inflow of thermal water.

48. CASTLE GEYSER always attracts a lot of interest. It was named in 1870 by N. P. Langford and G. C. Doane, who felt the cone resembled the ruined tower of an old castle. Over 12 feet high, the huge geyserite structure is one of the landmarks of the Upper Basin, spectacular even when the geyser isn't erupting.

Castle must be a very old geyser. The cone itself probably required several thousand years to form; estimates of its age run from 5,000 to 15,000 years. The lower figure is probably more accurate, but to consider that Castle has likely been continuously active during that entire time makes it even more amazing. However, the history of the cone is not the whole story. The cone is built atop a series of flat deposits that in turn rest upon a huge sloping geyserite mound that was formed by an even earlier hot spring over still more thousands of years. Some estimate that hot spring activity similar to what we see today has been underway in Yellowstone for at least 200,000 years. It is possible that among the first of those springs was Castle's immediate predecessor.

When we talk about the personalities of geysers, Castle heads the list. It has been known to undergo at least four different types of eruptions. Most common through the first century of the Park was a steady steaming, punctuated every few minutes by water jets 40 feet high. When that type of action took place, Castle had an extremely powerful eruption every several weeks. Well over 100 feet high, the 10-minute water eruption was followed by a steam phase lasting several hours. More recently have been times when Castle did not give off such frequent splashes of water. Instead, on relatively short intervals it had eruptions lasting only 4 minutes that were not followed by the steam phase. On still other occasions, this same sort of action resulted in durations of just 2 minutes. This kind of play, called a minor eruption, still takes place, but it is seldom a regular part of Castle's modern activity.

Most typical of Castle since the 1959 earthquake has been a fourth kind of eruption. Steam wells quietly out of

The huge sinter cone of Castle Geyser, perhaps the most massive free-standing cone of geyserite anywhere, is topped by eruptions that most commonly reach around 80 feet tall.

the crater until about 3 hours before an eruption. Then occasional splashes rise above the top of the cone. The surges increase in size and frequency until an especially heavy one initiates the eruption. Interestingly, in 1992 and 1993 most eruptions had very little of the preliminary play but, rather, started with almost no warning. For about 20 minutes water is jetted into the air as an almost continuous column. Some jets are only 30 feet high, but many reach 70 or 80 or even 100 feet. As the eruption progresses, water is slowly lost from the system, and the steam phase begins. At first it is very powerful, producing a deep, thunderous roar while darting sharp water jets through the billowing steam cloud. Then over the next hour or so, Castle slowly calms down. The interval between major eruptions is highly regular at 11 to 12 hours. People with experience are often able to predict Castle's eruption within just 10 minutes — remarkable, given the size of the geyser.

Minor eruptions still occur. During the first few minutes of its eruption, Castle has occasional brief pauses. Minors happen when it somehow doesn't restart from such a pause. Common in some seasons and rare in others, the minors have lost the 2- or 4-minute durations of before and now may last from 1 to 7 minutes. Very crudely, the duration of a minor eruption controls the length of the interval until the eventual major — 1 minute of duration equals 1-plus hour of interval. This can be used only as a rough guide, and "minor intervals" as short as a few minutes have been seen. Only once have consecutive minor eruptions been observed.

Castle's changeable nature makes it one of the most interesting geysers in Yellowstone. At any time it could revert to some form of activity from the past, and it undoubtedly has some new tricks to spring on us in the future.

49. TORTOISE SHELL SPRING has a remarkably large geyserite cone of its own, but lying as it does immediately at the base of Castle's cone it seems hardly noticeable. In spite of this proximity, remarkably, there is little, if any, connection between the two. Even the most powerful eruptions of Castle do not visibly affect Tortoise Shell. This spring is one of the hottest in Yellowstone, with superheated water temperatures as great as 207°F (97°C) having been recorded. The result is a constant, violent boiling strong enough to throw considerable water out of the open crater. Rarely, brief eruptive bursts send spray as high as 6 feet, but because the action is constant overall, Tortoise Shell is not considered to be a geyser.

194. UNNG-CGG-7 ("GIZMO GEYSER") was an assortment of quietly overflowing, slightly bubbling vents until 1988, when it began having strong eruptions. The play rises from at least four openings in the geyserite platform at the base of Castle's cone. Ongoing studies indicate that Gizmo's activity follows a cyclic pattern controlled by Castle Geyser (48). For a short time after Castle has played, Gizmo is quiet. It then begins to erupt, with intervals of 3 to 15 minutes and durations of 1 to 5 minutes. The most noticeable part of an eruption comes when one of the vents temporarily produces a loud steam jet that sends spray up to 15 feet high.

50. TILT GEYSER is often dormant because of runoff from Crested Pool (51) flowing into its craters. When active, though, it frequently catches people by surprise. The vents attract little notice even though they are located right next to the boardwalk. Thus, people gathered around Crested Pool (51) and waiting for Castle Geyser (48) to erupt are often startled by the sudden gurgling and gushes of steam near their feet. The original Tilt Geyser is the single vent to the right. It has seldom actually erupted since the development of the twin vents closer to the walkway, but it is still an intriguing part of the geyser. The new vents were formed as a result of a small steam explosion on July 6, 1976. Most of the eruption now comes from these openings. They splash from a few inches to 6 feet high for durations of $1^1/_2$ to 3 minutes. The intervals are usually quite regular at any given time, ranging from 45 to 100 minutes.

Much of the runoff from the new vents flows into the original Tilt, thoroughly drowning it. At the end of the eruption, the water drains down the vent. A narrow vortex of a whirlpool produces a loud sucking sound, and, when the last of the water disappears down the hole, it gives forth with a final loud gurgle. This entire process may take several minutes to complete. Don't leave Tilt too soon. The sounds are great!

51. CRESTED POOL is 42 feet deep and intensely blue. Like Tortoise Shell Spring (49), the water is superheated. Boiling around the lip of the crater is constant but fairly variable. On frequent occasions a sudden surge of hot water will rise to the surface, causing a violent boiling that may dome the water up as much as 8 to 10 feet. This is the sort of action that triggers true bursting eruptions in some other boiling springs, but none is ever known to have happened at Crested Pool.

Crested Pool is not only very beautiful but is also very dangerous. The spring is partly surrounded by a railing because it has taken human life — a young boy who was running through the steam cloud and possibly couldn't see where he was going. Yet you see people climbing the railing and trying to balance on top while taking "that special picture." It could be special, all right. Don't climb the railings.

52. "TERRA COTTA GEYSERS" is the name for what is really a number of separate hot springs, all of which have been known as geysers since 1878. In practice, they have come to be called "Terra Cotta 'A,' 'B,' 'C,' 'D,' and 'E' " — awkward, especially since the original Terra Cotta Spring is a small brick-red spring about 100 feet to the northwest. In fact, two of these geysers have officially approved names: "Terra Cotta 'B' " is Dishpan Spring and "Terra Cotta 'C' and 'D' " together are Washtub Spring. Since the use of "Terra Cotta" for these geysers has become common in recent years, the name is now being applied to the entire cluster.

Unnamed vent "A" is by far the most active. Spouting from several openings, the major part of the play reaches 5 to 10 feet high at a slight angle from the vertical. Intervals are usually around 2 hours, and durations are a few minutes.

Dishpan Spring (vent "B") is considerably less active than "A," but its strongly angled eruptions can reach fully 20 feet high and are strong enough to play into the river. The durations are again a few minutes long. **Washtub Spring's** (vent "C") erupts from a small square pool. The eruptions are uncommon and last only a few seconds while reaching 15 feet high. Vent "D" is the rarest of all, with only a few eruptions being seen each season. Its bursting play can hit 20 feet through most of a duration of 5 minutes. Lastly, unnamed vent "E" is a small geyser, hardly visible from the boardwalk but quite frequent in its action.

53. SPANKER GEYSER has been remarkably constant in its activity. Rising from the left bank of the Firehole River far downstream from the boardwalk bridge (which provides as good a view as any), it is actually a perpetual spouter. Most bursts are less than 6 feet high, so that steam is often all that is visible of Spanker.

54. CHIMNEY CONE, though often marked with a sign reading "Chimney Geyser," is not a geyser and probably never has been. Such a tall and narrow cone is more typical of springs that flow only a slight volume of water very steadily over many years. A small spring at the base of the cone bubbles and splashes a few inches high as a near perpetual spouter; perhaps the sign would more accurately refer to this "Chimney Cone's Spouter" than to the cone itself.

195. UNNG-CGG-8 has infrequent eruptions out of a pair of vents near the boardwalk in front of Chimney Cone (54). The first known vigorous eruptions took place during 1992. More eruptions, often in series with intervals of only a few minutes, occurred during 1993. The maximum height was 4 feet. Just to the right of CGG-8 is another small spring. It, too, punctuates its normal bubbling with infrequent eruptions.

55. SCALLOPED SPRING has never acted as a natural geyser in recorded times. There are ways of making hot springs erupt unnaturally, and Scalloped Spring was a victim of such activity. The induced eruption was evidently quite powerful, with a heavy discharge of water. No details about the play were recorded, for the people who caused it did not report their illegal act. The pool never recovered, and the water level now lies several feet below the ground surface. The Scalloped Spring incident is an example of how fragile these springs are; induced eruptions were not meant to be and often destroy or alter the spring.

56. DELETED TEAKETTLE GEYSER got its name when it was decided that too many springs in Yellowstone had been named "Teakettle." Apparently, the intention was that the name of this particular geyser be name deleted entirely from the records; instead, a "deleted" notation became added as part of the name. The geyser erupts from a small cone right on the brink of the steep Firehole River bank. The cone indicates that Deleted Teakettle was a geyser in the past, but no eruptions were recorded until the 1959 earthquake. For several days thereafter, it underwent frequent, 10-foot-high eruptions. Then the activity declined; by 1964 it only boiled up about 1 foot high. Eruptions of this sort continue. Recurring every few minutes and lasting around 1 minute, some briefly reach 2 to 3 feet high at the start of the play. Those with a sharp eye will notice that the water level in South Scalloped Spring drops slightly when Deleted Teakettle erupts and then recovers to overflow during the quiet interval.

SAWMILL GEYSER COMPLEX (numbers 57 through 66a). The Sawmill Geyser Complex is one of the more active groups of geysers in Yellowstone. Every one of its springs has a history as a geyser. Often you'll find yourself surrounded by activity, with eruptions rising from as many as five or six geysers at once. The entire Sawmill Complex is cyclic in its activity. It is usually Sawmill, Tardy, and Spasmodic Geysers that have the significant eruptions, which is known as the "Sawmill mode" activity. Rarer in most years is the "Penta-Churn mode," in which Sawmill seldom plays and long durations by Tardy and Spasmodic can be ended by otherwise rare play in Penta and Churn Geysers. Whichever mode is in force, when the eruptions end (within a few minutes of one another in most cases) the water of every spring in the group drops from a few inches to several feet below the full level. This often leads visitors to comment about the dead craters that no longer erupt. Wrong; return in an hour or two to see a very different set of hot springs. All of the springs refill simultaneously, and the next eruptive cycle usually begins about the time Sawmill reaches its first overflow.

No place in Yellowstone better expresses exchange of function. What is "normal" at one time may be replaced by an entirely new pattern of activity at another time as the energy shifts back and forth between the members of the complex. Also, the entire complex is known to be connected with the neighboring Grand Complex, and some observers believe it is also related to the springs of the Castle Group across the river.

57. CHURN GEYSER is one of the least active members of the Sawmill Complex. Although it was known as a 10-foot geyser in 1884, it was named because most of its known activity was little more than a surface commotion of the water. After the 1959 earthquake it would sometimes boil up a foot or two and overflow, but no modern eruptions were seen until 1971. It is now known that Churn is likely to be active only when the Sawmill Complex is playing on the uncommon Penta-Churn mode in company with Penta and when Sawmill itself has gone several hours without playing. Then, during an active period that may last as long as 2 hours, Churn often has a series of eruptions. Intervals are a few minutes. The bursting play reaches 15 feet high for a duration that may approach $1^{1}/_{2}$ minutes.

58. SAWMILL GEYSER is the namesake and largest member of the Sawmill Complex. During eruption water spins about in the crater, resembling a large, circular lumber-mill blade. Sawmill is a very interesting fountain-type geyser. The eruptions are a series of separate bursts of water; some are not more than 3 feet high, but others easily exceed 35 feet. Throughout the eruption there is a copious discharge of water.

Studies during the past few years have shown that Sawmill has eruptions of three distinctly different lengths. The most common are durations of 30 to 50 minutes. Others last between 9 and 20 minutes or more than 80 minutes (occasionally longer than 4 hours). Since eruptions do not have durations of other lengths, it seems clear that these three different types involve progressively greater portions of the plumbing system, almost as if Sawmill is three geysers in one. The longer the eruption, the deeper the drainage of the entire complex when it ends. A "deep drain" following an exceptionally long duration happens about once a day and may be associated with otherwise unusual eruptions by some of the smaller members of the complex. Whatever the case, Sawmill is in eruption about 30% of the time overall, and a typical interval is between 1 and 3 hours.

59. "UNCERTAIN GEYSER" was named at a time when its activity seemed to bear little relationship to the surrounding geysers. The small, round vent lies nearly hidden within the deep sinter shoulders of the far (southern) side of Sawmill Geyser's (58) crater. It appears that Uncertain can erupt under only two circumstances. By far the more likely is when the Sawmill Complex undergoes a deep drain; Uncertain almost invariably erupts about $1^1/_2$ hours after the start of the drain. The other, far less common condition is when Penta Geyser (62) appears ready to erupt. Play by Uncertain prevents the eruption in Penta. There are exceptions to any rules, and Uncertain has also been seen playing in concert with Sawmill. The play is a steady jet of mixed spray and steam reaching 10 to 15 feet high. It can last from 2 to 5 minutes and is followed by a long, weak steam phase.

60. TARDY GEYSER looks and acts a lot like the much more impressive Sawmill Geyser (58), and indeed it was once known as "Little Sawmill." The name was originally applied to a geyser near Grand (76) but may have been transferred to this geyser because of a tendency for Tardy to have a series of brief, steamy eruptions near the end of Sawmill's exceptionally long plays. When the Sawmill Complex is operating

on the Sawmill mode, Tardy undergoes eruptions of relatively short durations while Sawmill is playing. Under the Penta-Churn mode, Tardy gets a jump on Sawmill. In company with Spasmodic Geyser (63), eruptions may have durations as long as a few hours. Sawmill is almost completely dormant during these episodes. Tardy's jets reach about 10 feet high. Tardy also sometimes erupts during the deep drains of the Sawmill Complex, and these noisy bursts of steamy spray can reach up to 20 feet.

61. UNNG-CGG-1 ("TWILIGHT SPRING") lies to the right of the boardwalk as one walks from Sawmill Geyser (58) toward Penta Geyser (62). Water is constantly rocking about in the crater, occasionally splashing over the edge. When the water level drops during a deep drain of the Sawmill Complex, CGG-1 sometimes erupts. The splashes reach up to 2 or 3 feet above the ground and, therefore, up to 4 or 5 feet above the pool level.

62. PENTA GEYSER, once called the "Handsaw," is a very enjoyable geyser. Its eruption, jetting up to 25 feet high from the main vent and splashing 1 to 4 feet high from four other openings, rises from a small cone only about 7 feet from the boardwalk. Penta is also a complex and irregular geyser. During most years, the Sawmill Complex operates almost exclusively on the Sawmill mode, and eruptions by Penta are rare at best. Many seasons have passed with only two or three eruptions being recorded. During other years, such as 1992 and 1993, the Penta-Churn mode is more common. Then Penta can be seen on a daily basis, and intervals as short as 6 hours are known. As the long eruptions of nearby Tardy (60) and Spasmodic (63) Geysers progress, the water level in Penta slowly rises. If it reaches near or to overflow, an eruption by Penta is possible, although by no means certain. Many such cycles sometimes pass before Penta finally responds. The play ordinarily lasts either 35 to 50 minutes *or* longer than 2 hours.

During 1984 and occasionally since, a second type of eruption has been seen in Penta, one that might explain the relatively large geyserite cone in a geyser that is normally very inactive. This can best be described as a steam phase eruption. Often seen near the start of or during a deep drain by the Sawmill Complex, these brief eruptions spray mixed steam and water a few feet high and do little more than moisten the cone.

63. SPASMODIC GEYSER plays from at least twenty separate vents. When erupting, the activity is constant or nearly so from the numerous small openings near the boardwalk. Every few seconds to minutes there will be a momentary increase in intensity, and then all of the vents spout strongly. Meanwhile, there is bursting and boiling in the two deep, blue pools. A last vent is located on the far side of the craters, somewhat between the two pools. When Spasmodic as a whole is erupting, this geyser plays every 1 to 2 minutes up to 10 feet high, the action lasting a few seconds. Spasmodic is active during both modes of Sawmill Complex activity.

64. OVAL SPRING had no recorded episode of geyser eruptions prior to the 1959 earthquake; it was never more than a quiet, greenish pool. The 1959 tremors induced an eruption, and for the next several weeks Oval boiled heavily. By 1960 it had resumed its prequake state, and only a few further eruptions were seen until the 1980s.

The modern activity is of several different sorts. Most eruptions take place when Oval Spring's water level has dropped during a deep drain of the Sawmill Complex, and they show that Oval is really three geysers in one. Rising from in front of the large cavelike opening exposed at depth, bursting eruptions sometimes occur in series with intervals of a few minutes, durations of seconds, and heights from 1 to 20 feet. Other eruptions can take place in a second vent to the northeast (right-front) of the cave; these are seldom more than 1 to 2 feet high. The most powerful sort of activity is very rare, observed only a time or two each during 1983, 1985, 1989, and 1990. These eruptions blasted white, muddy water at an angle out of the cave itself, jetting 12 feet high and well across the boardwalk. Finally, on a few occasions in the 1970s and 1980s, this same vent played when the pool was completely full.

65. OLD TARDY GEYSER was identified as the original "Tardy" in the previous edition of this book. That is incorrect, but the name *was* applied to this geyser for a time, and when it was corrected several years ago, the "Old" was prefaced to the name. Old Tardy is fairly irregular in its performances. A member of the Sawmill Complex, it follows the same cyclic rises and falls in water level and eruptions as the rest of the group. Intervals range from a few minutes to many hours. Corresponding durations are from seconds to hours, but in almost all cases the height is 10 to 15 feet.

Few would be surprised to visit the Sawmill Complex someday to find a large new crater in the vicinity of Old Tardy Geyser. Between it and Oval Spring (64) is a narrow opening within one of Old Tardy's runoff channels. A geyser whose eruptions seldom rise high enough from a subterranean pool to reach ground level, this "UNNG-OTO" [Old Tardy–Oval] developed from a steamy patch of ground during 1987, as did an all but invisible fracture on the west side of Old Tardy.

66a. "CRYSTAL SPRING'S GEYSER" (also known as "Slurp Geyser") plays from a round hole in the runoff channel at the edge of Crystal Spring (66). It is inserted here, before Crystal Spring, because despite the one foot of surface distance between the two, they are decidedly separate from one another at depth. Crystal Spring's Geyser is a member of the Sawmill Complex. Its activity is very erratic and generally infrequent, most likely to take place during a deep drain of the Sawmill Complex. The play is a long duration chugging within the vent, the spray reaching no more than 1 foot high and producing limited runoff.

THE GRAND GEYSER COMPLEX (numbers 66 through 76) includes at least ten springs, all geysers, as members of one closely knit complex. In addition, the complex is known to be connected with other hot spring clusters. Grand is clearly related to the Economic Geysers more than 400 feet to the north, the Sawmill Complex to the south, and probably to the miscellany of springs in the meadow to the northwest. Grand Geyser itself has been unpredictable through most of its history; the fact that it can now be predicted with considerable accuracy is a wonder.

66. CRYSTAL SPRING is the shallow, nearly colorless pool at the top of the formation north of Old Tardy Geyser (65). Its rare geyser activity proves it is a member of the Grand Geyser Complex. On most occasions, water rocks about within the crater, and every few minutes it rises to cause a brief overflow. Crystal is thus an intermittent spring, although it failed to perform very well during 1992 and 1993. A few major eruptions have also been recorded. There were some in 1931 and 1932 when it was called "Gusher Geyser," and it was active again in 1973, 1977, and 1983. In each case bursts fully 20 feet high were seen. A series of smaller, 2-foot eruptions occurred in late 1987.

Just north of Crystal Spring, near the spot at which the two branches of the trail merge, is Belgian Pool. Generally relatively cool (about 180°F [81°C] in the hotter part), this spring received its name because of the death of a Belgian tourist who fell into the water in 1929. There are records from the 1930s of a Belgian Geyser. It is possible that it and Belgian Pool are the same.

67. BULGER SPRING might be an independent spring, a member of neither the Sawmill nor Grand Geyser Complexes. The term *Bulger* was commonly applied to small geysers and spouters by Yellowstone's early geological explorers, and this fact alone implies that Bulger Spring was a frequent performer during the 1870s. It apparently remained so through the 1890s but then was nearly dormant until the 1959 earthquake. Now it is again a frequent performer, exhibiting both minor and major eruptions. As with most geysers, minor activity is the more common. These eruptions have durations of only a few seconds and last barely long enough to produce runoff away from the cone. Major eruptions can

have durations as long as 10 minutes and substantial runoff. Each kind of eruption sends bulging bursts of water about 6 feet high.

68. EAST TRIPLET GEYSER is at present the least important existing member of the Grand Complex. Prior to 1947 it erupted fairly often. Since then, however, most seasons have seen no activity, and the crater is only a shallow, muddy hole. Minor eruptions up to 5 feet high are rare. In the general area of East Triplet are the miscellaneous vents known collectively as "the Sputniks" (72). These springs and spouters show a close relationship to West Triplet (69) and Rift (73) Geysers. Their overall action has increased in recent years and could portend renewed activity in East Triplet, which has joined their activity with vigorous bubbling.

69. WEST TRIPLET GEYSER lies in a symmetrical funnel-shaped vent near the boardwalk. In the years prior to 1947 it erupted regularly about every 3 hours, nearly always in concert with the East and North Triplets. Since then it has been much more irregular and changeable, but several eruptions are often seen during Grand Geyser's quiet interval. The bursting play reaches up to 10 feet high.

The nature of West Triplet's action relates directly to that of both Rift Geyser (73) and Grand Geyser (76). Periods of dormancy apparently occur only when Rift is also dormant. These times correspond to those when Grand is exceptionally regular and frequent and do not happen very often or for very long. It used to be said that whenever West Triplet had an eruption, that of Grand would be delayed by at least two Turban cycles (about 40 to 50 minutes) and sometimes much longer. (See the descriptions of Grand Geyser [76] and Turban Geyser [74] for an explanation of these cycles.) More recently, such a relationship has not been seen. Indeed, there have been times when rising water in West Triplet's crater has been taken as a good sign, indicating that Grand's time is near, and eruptions no longer seem to have a strong delaying effect.

One thing that is clear is that in addition to eruptions during the last hour or two preliminary to Grand, West Triplet almost invariably precedes eruptions by Rift Geyser. The relationship between Rift and Grand has recently changed, also. Overall, though, since activity by Rift is not considered beneficial to Grand, one must make the same assumption about West Triplet.

70. NORTH TRIPLET GEYSER was the closest of the Triplets to Grand Geyser (76). Before the advent of boardwalks, Park visitors were freer to wander about in the geyser basins, which caused tremendous amounts of damage. A great many rocks were thrown into the crater of Grand. Had such acts continued, Grand's vent might have become clogged, robbing us of what is now the tallest frequently active, predictable geyser in the world. To prevent this destruction, the Park Service removed numerous rocks from within and about Grand's crater. Grand was saved, but the surroundings were further altered. The water from Grand's eruptions was partially diverted into North Triplet's crater. Gravel completely filled it in and is now probably thoroughly sintered into place. Nothing is visible at the site except, perhaps, an occasional tiny string of bubbles when "the Sputniks" (72) are active.

71. PERCOLATOR GEYSER was felt by some to be an expression of old North Triplet's energy, but a photograph shows the three Triplets as well as Percolator in eruption during the 1880s. Evidently, it was simply too small to be considered important, because the name was not applied to this geyser until about 1970. Percolator is most commonly active for only a short period of time before Grand Geyser (76) erupts. Just how long before depends on the frequency of Grand — in years when Grand is highly frequent and regular, Percolator normally starts playing about 2 hours before; in off years, a preliminary on-and-off action can last more than 12 hours. So although Percolator is a sure sign of building "pressure" within the Grand Complex, it cannot be used as a predictive tool. The 1- to 2-foot eruptions usually stop shortly after

Grand begins its play, but they may resume for a short time after Grand has quit.

72. UNNG-CGG-2 and 3 ("THE SPUTNIKS") are two clusters of small spouters that are given two identification numbers based on separate locations. They behave more as a single unit, however. These geysers first appeared during the early 1980s. In some seasons they have been virtually invisible. In others, most notably 1984, 1989, and 1992, they have been vigorous enough to play several feet high and to develop rather prominent craters along the edge of the grass beyond the various Triplets. Additional sputtering spots develop in the gravel near Rift Geyser (73). If there is any meaning to these developments, it is not clear. The Sputniks do tend to be active in those years when Rift is having exceptionally short intervals — although in 1993 Rift had nearly record-setting activity, and the Sputniks were practically dead.

73. RIFT GEYSER is a very important geyser, yet one would little suspect that a geyser of any sort lies at its site. The crater is a slightly depressed, sandy area at the base of some rhyolite boulders. The vents, which may total more than two dozen, are actually nothing more than cracks in the rocks beneath the sand. The modern geyser was first seen in 1924 and in time came to be called "Six Fissures Geyser." Rift is completely dormant during some years. When active, intervals range from as little as 12 hours to several days. Most of the water jets are only a few inches high, but two of the central vents reach up to 4 feet. Throughout the eruption, which lasts from $1^1/_2$ to 4 hours, there is a copious discharge of water.

That, apparently, is the main "problem" with Rift Geyser. Because it is a member of the Grand Complex, this large volume of discharge must affect all the rest of the complex. Rift usually has a substantial delaying action on the start of the next eruption of Grand. An old rule of thumb said that one could expect a 2-hour delay in Grand's eruption for every 1 hour of action in Rift. Like the similar rule at West Triplet Geyser (69), this no longer seems to apply. In 1993 the activity of Rift Geyser seemed to have only a minor effect on Grand. Geyser systems are always changing, and the rules of the past may never again apply.

74. TURBAN GEYSER, lying as it does within a prominent sinter bowl, is mistaken by many new visitors as being Grand itself (76). Grand, however, is the large pool with almost no rim just to the right of Turban. Because of this it is often thought that Grand is starting, when actually Turban is undergoing its normal small eruption.

Turban is a very important part of the Grand system, however. Except for rare occasions, Grand will begin its eruption only about the time of the start of Turban's action. Turban normally erupts at intervals of 17 to 25 minutes, although so-called delayed intervals as long as 35 minutes are fairly common. The duration is about 5 minutes, throughout which the water bursts unimpressively to about 5 feet above the rim. During Turban's quiet intervals, the water level in Grand rises to overflow, then drops as Turban plays. Eventually, the rising water level in Turban acts as a trigger, sending Grand into play. Turban then erupts in concert with Grand and intermittently for 1 to 2 hours after Grand, with more powerful bursts 10 to 20 feet high.

75. VENT GEYSER is an unexpected bonus to an eruption of Grand (76). It issues from a small cracklike vent on the left side of Turban's massive geyserite shoulder. Vent erupts in concert with Grand, starting 2 to 3 minutes after Grand begins. At the beginning of the eruption the slightly angled water column slowly builds in force until it is as high as 70 feet — a major geyser in its own right. Thereafter, it dies down to about 35 feet. Vent continues to erupt in company with Turban (74) for an hour or more after Grand has stopped. Recently, it has also been realized that Vent often has eruptions about halfway through Grand's interval, near the time of Grand's first overflow. At these times, Vent simply joins Turban for the duration of its normal 5-minute eruption. The height of these plays is around 20 feet.

On a few known occasions during the 1960s, once in 1978, and once in 1982, Vent began erupting $1^1/_2$ to 2 hours *before* Grand. These eruptions were weak but steady. As the durations progressed, the water levels in both Grand and Turban slowly dropped about 1 foot. Then Grand and Turban went into normal eruptions.

76. GRAND GEYSER. If any geyser anywhere is worth seeing, it is Grand. Countless people have waited for hours, commenting later that it was well worth the time. With its massive water column sparkling in the sun, with a rainbow captured in its steam, and accompanied by the slender arching jet of Vent Geyser (75), Grand is a unique sight.

During the long quiet period, Grand slowly fills with water so that the first overflow is roughly 5 hours after the previous eruption. From then until the time of the next activity, the water slowly rises and falls in sympathy with the eruptions of Turban Geyser (74). Each cycle, from high water through low water as Turban plays and back to high water, takes the same amount of time as that particular cycle of Turban — most commonly about 22 minutes. It is this water level variation that allows the geyser gazer to tell how near Grand is to an eruption.

Stand where you can see the outermost part of the basin, where small pieces of sinter project through the water. Use these to gauge the level of the pool. If the water level drops rapidly and far enough to stop almost all overflow when the time for Turban to play is approaching, you know there will be at least one more cycle of Turban before Grand erupts. As Grand gets closer to the time of eruption, the water level generally drops less and more slowly, sometimes holding near full until only seconds before Turban plays. Finally will come a cycle when the water level doesn't appear to drop at all. Now is the time to watch closely. Waves, very small at first, waves begin to wash across the surface of the pool. Soon they become obvious as the water level continues to rise and discharge becomes heavy. In most years it is rare for the wave action to start without a consequent eruption; if that does happen there will probably be a substantial delay — at least two and perhaps several more Turban cycles — before there is another chance for an eruption. Remember, though, that

Grand Geyser is the tallest predictable active fountain-type geyser in the world, reaching 150 to 200 feet high about three times each day.

any prediction is only educated guesswork. Anything might happen, and appearances can be deceiving. Grand cannot erupt from a low pool, as some people have contended, but it can recover from a low water level in seconds; it can start with virtually no wave action; and sometimes there is no delay from a false start. This is what makes watching Grand so much fun.

The eruption begins when the water of the pool suddenly domes over the vent. The bubbling, frothing, and surging will continue for several seconds. It may even stop an agonizing time or two. But soon the geyser rockets forth, sending massive columns of water to tremendous heights. Some of the early bursts can reach 150 feet, but the best is yet to come.

Grand's eruption consists of a series of "bursts." The first normally lasts 9 to 11 minutes. During this time Grand averages less than 100 feet high, but the activity is continuous, and a great amount of water is discharged. Suddenly this burst ends, and the geyser is quiet. After a few moments of rapid refilling, Grand jets forth again. This and any succeeding bursts sometimes approach 200 feet high. If the second burst is short, there may be another pause leading to a third burst, and so on. Grand most often has two to four bursts; sometimes there is only one, but there may be as many as five and, very rarely, more. An exceptional eruption in 1983 had eleven bursts. Very approximately, the typical burst frequency in any given year is one burst 20% of the time; two bursts, 50%; three bursts, 25%; four bursts, 5%; and more than four bursts, none or few.

During most years since 1950, Grand's intervals have been very regular considering its many connections with other geysers. At these times the average is often near 8 hours, and the eruptions can be predicted with a great degree of accuracy. However, in some years, such as 1981, 1983–1986, 1989, and 1991, Grand is erratic and much less frequent. These are the years of vigorous action in other members of the Grand Complex, and Grand is then nearly unpredictable. As noted, however, these rules are not invariable; 1993 was a year of frequent action in Rift (73), West

Triplet (69), and other members of the complex, yet Grand was nearly as reliable as usual.

Whatever the nature of its current activity, Grand is the largest frequently active geyser in the world. Few geysers anywhere have consistently matched it in the combination of size, frequency, and predictability. Every geyser gazer has his or her favorite, but most agree that no geyser can match Grand in sheer beauty.

196. SHOE SPRING is normally a rather ugly feature right next to the boardwalk, shaped something like the sole of a shoe. It had no record of activity until August 21, 1988, when it underwent a series of eruptions. Although all durations were less than 1 minute long, Shoe sprayed muddy water up to 10 feet high and across the boardwalk. The moral to this story and that of Wave Spring (197) is that virtually any Yellowstone hot spring has eruptive potential, requiring only a slight change in the status quo to trigger activity.

77. ECONOMIC GEYSER was once a geyser of considerable interest and importance. It was named because of the economical manner in which the erupted water drained back into the crater. It erupted every few minutes and was one of those spouters that could always be counted on to perform. So it continued until sometime in the 1920s. Economic has been almost totally dormant since then. Five eruptions were witnessed one day in 1957, and it was active for a few weeks following the 1959 earthquake, when rather frequent eruptions reached up to 25 feet high. Now its water temperature is only 130°F (54°C), and the crater is lined with dark orange-brown cyanobacteria. Economic is at least indirectly connected to the Grand Geyser Complex, more than 400 feet away. When Economic was active during 1959, Grand (76) was completely dormant for the first time in decades. Grand reactivated within a few days of Economic's renewed dormancy.

78. EAST ECONOMIC GEYSER, located just 20 feet to the back-left of Economic (77), was a rather frequent geyser from

1888 through 1911, yet although nearby Economic was famous, this pool did not receive its name until after the 1959 earthquake. East Economic's postquake activity was closely tied to that of Economic — an eruption of one would result in a lowering water level in the other, and both returned to dormancy on the same day. The eruptions of East Economic were considerably more powerful than those of its neighbor, sometimes reaching 35 or 40 feet high. The lower branches of the lodgepole pines on the slope next to the crater were killed by those eruptions. Since those trees were old enough to have been there in 1888–1911, the implication is that the eruptions a century ago were quite small.

197. WAVE SPRING is normally a quiet, cool pool. Lined with a thick coating of orange-brown cyanobacteria, its surface pulsates slightly so as to produce a constant train of tiny waves outward from the center of the spring. In May 1989 it erupted. None of the eruptions was seen by any reporting witness, but some of the cyanobacteria lining the crater was blown out and landed several feet away. The height is inferred to have been as great as 10 feet.

79. UNNG-CGG-4 ("BUSH GEYSER GROUP"). In the open flat across the boardwalk from the Economics (77 and 78) and Wave Spring (79), extending as far as blue Calida Pool, is an assortment of small features, many of which are geysers. One of the larger of these, up to 4 feet high, has been called "Bush Geyser." Another has been known to exceed 10 feet in height. In general, activity is rare in any of these geysers.

80. CRACK GEYSER became active on September 21, 1959, the same day that Economic Geysers (77 and 78) went dormant, showing by inference that connections extend both north and south from Economic. The eruptions came from an earthquake-caused crack in the sinter platform. Through 1961 there were frequent eruptions from Crack. The 6-foot spout would last for several minutes. Except for slight occasional bubbling, there has been no activity since 1962.

81. BEAUTY AND CHROMATIC POOLS are not geysers, but no springs provide a better example of exchange of function. A periodic energy shift from one pool to the other causes one to overflow while the other declines, then the reverse. The time interval between the shifts ranged from a few weeks to a year or more before the 1959 earthquake. Since then the flow has most often been from Chromatic Pool, but Beauty has dominated since 1990. Aside from this interesting relationship, Beauty and Chromatic are among the most beautiful pools in the Upper Geyser Basin.

82. WITCHES CAULDRON lies right beside the Firehole River at such a level that high water will cover and drown it. At low water it roils and boils, seemingly toiling for the proverbial trouble, but the highest surges are only 2 feet tall. Witches Cauldron is nearly invisible from any trail, but it can be seen through the trees from the paved walkway on the west side of the river.

83. LIMEKILN SPRINGS is a set of small, perpetually spouting vents. Its cone is perched atop a large geyserite mound, which indicates a very long period of activity. Like Witches Cauldron (82) it is best seen from the paved trail running between Castle (48) and Grotto (111) Geysers. Limekiln's constant eruption is 1 foot high.

Table 2. Geysers of the Castle, Grand and Orange Spring Groups

Name	Map No.	Interval	Duration	Height (ft)
Bulger Geyser	67	frequent	sec–min	6
Castle Geyser	48	10 1/2–11 1/2 hrs	1 hr	30–100
"Chimney Cone's Spouter"	54	near steady	near steady	inches
Churn Geyser	57	minutes *	sec–1 1/2 min	3–15
Crack Geyser	80	[1962]	minutes	6
Crested Pool	51	frequent	seconds	boil–10
Crystal Spring	66	[1987]	seconds	2–20
"Crystal Spring's Geyser" ("Slurp")	66a	infrequent	1–3 hrs	1
Deleted Teakettle Geyser	56	minutes	1 min	1–2
Dishpan Spring ("Terra Cotta 'B' ")	52	hours	minutes	20

Table 2 continued

East Economic Geyser	78	[1959]	2–3 min	35–40
East Triplet Geyser	68	rare	minutes	5
Economic Geyser	77	[1959]	seconds	8–25
Grand Geyser	76	6–20 hrs	9–13 min	150–200
Limekiln Springs	83	near steady	near steady	1
North Triplet Geyser	70	[1947; vent filled, possibly dead]		—
Old Tardy Geyser	65	min–hrs	sec–hrs	5–10
Orange Spring	198	[1986]	seconds	15
Oval Spring	64	see text	seconds	1–20
Penta Geyser	62	6 hrs–days *	35 min–150 min	25
Percolator Geyser	71	hours	hours	1–3
Rift Geyser	73	12 hrs–days *	1–4 hrs	4
Sawmill Geyser	58	1–3 hrs	12 min–hrs	3–35
Scalloped Spring	55	induced only	unrecorded	unrecorded
Shoe Spring	196	[1988]	seconds	10
Spanker Geyser	53	steady	steady	6
Spasmodic Geyser	63	1–3 hrs	min–hrs	inches–10
Spatter Geyser	47	[1962]	minutes	10
Sprinkler Geyser	46	5–40 min	5 min–hrs	10
Tardy Geyser	60	min–hrs	sec–hrs	10
"Terra Cotta Geysers," vent 'A'	52	2 hrs	minutes	5–10
"Terra Cotta Geysers," vent 'E'	52	frequent	minutes	1
Tilt Geyser	50	45–100 min *	1 1/2–3 min	inches–6
Tortoise Shell Spring	49	steady	steady	2–6
Turban Geyser	74	17–35 min	5 min	6–20
"Uncertain Geyser"	59	hrs–days	2–5 min	10–15
UNNG–CGG–1 ("Twilight Spring")	61	see text	seconds	5
UNNG–CGG–2 and 3 ("Sputniks")	72	infrequent	minutes	inches–4
UNNG–CGG–4 ("Bush Geyser Group")	79	see text	—	—
UNNG–CGG–6	193	frequent	seconds	1–2
UNNG–CGG–7 ("Gizmo")	194	3–15 min	1–5 min	2–15
UNNG–CGG–8	195	minutes *	seconds	1–4
UNNG–OSG–1 ("Pulsar Spouter")	84	steady	steady	2
UNNG–OSG–2	199	see text	sec–min	1–15
UNNG–OSG–3 ("South Orange")	200	[1986]	1 1/2 min	2–6

Table 2 continued

Vent Geyser	75	with Grand	1–2 hrs	70
Washtub Spring ("Terra Cotta 'C' ")	52	infrequent	sec–min	10–15
Washtub Spring ("Terra Cotta 'D' ")	52	rare	5 min	20
Wave Spring	197	[1989]	unknown	10
West Triplet Geyser	69	hours	8–90 min	6–10
Witches Cauldron	82	near steady	near steady	2

* When active.
[ ] Brackets enclose the year of most recent activity for extremely rare or dormant geysers. See text.

Orange Spring Group and South Orange Spring Group

These two groups of related springs (Map D, Table 2) have previously been listed as parts of the Castle-Grand Group, in both this work and others, but they merit separate designations. Most of their features are quiet pools, and no geyser activity has ever been of long life.

The Orange Spring Group is the larger of the two, lying farther along the trail from Castle Geyser. Its largest single spring, Orange Spring, near the highest elevation in the area, has played as a significant geyser. The South Orange Spring Group consists of just two small pools with one geyser vent between them.

84. UNNG-OSG-1 ("PULSAR SPOUTER") is barely visible from the paved trail. Erupting from a vent on the far side of the highest geyserite mound in the group, it is only about 2 feet high.

198. ORANGE SPRING has had a few brief episodes of eruptive activity, most recently during 1986. The bursting eruptions were brief but reached up to 15 feet high. Another pool, between Orange Spring and OSG-1, has also acted as a geyser.

199. UNNG-OSG-2. A series of small springs lies near the paved trail. To the left are two that act together; one of these has a long fracture in addition to a deeper vent within the crater. These are frequently active, but the eruptions are less than 1 foot high. To the right is a cluster of springs dominated by a single pool of size. It had eruptions up to 15 feet high in the early 1970s and in 1988 and of up to 6 feet in 1993.

200. UNNG-OSG-3 ("SOUTH ORANGE GEYSER") is the only geyser ever recorded as part of the South Orange Spring Group, and it was active only during 1986. Throughout that one season, it played with remarkably regular 20-minute intervals and $1^{1}/_{2}$-minute durations. Early in the season some of the play reached 4 to 6 feet high, but the force very gradually declined so that the last observed eruptions reached no higher than 2 feet.

Giant Group

The Giant Group (Map E, Table 3), as handled here, includes everything near the Firehole River between the Grand Group and the Grotto Group. Although quite widespread, these springs are believed to comprise a single discrete group that includes two of the best-known geysers in the Upper Geyser Basin. Oblong, although not very high, discharges a tremendous amount of water. Giant, when active, can be the tallest geyser in both Yellowstone and the world, with the sole exception of Steamboat Geyser in the Norris Geyser Basin.

The Giant Group lies in the area where the two Upper Basin trails begin to merge into one. The best views are from the boardwalk, but nearly all of the springs can also be seen from the paved trail that runs directly between Castle Geyser and Grotto Geyser.

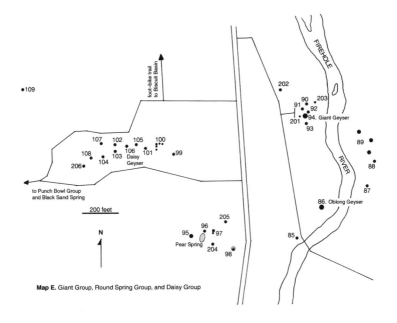

Map E. Giant Group, Round Spring Group, and Daisy Group

85. INKWELL SPRING sits on a small mound immediately next to the Firehole River. There are several craters that constantly discharge water, and two of them spout to about 2 feet. Although this is nearly a perpetual spouter, there is some variation to the play along with infrequent brief pauses. It is called Inkwell because of the black coloration in and about the vents, which is caused by deposits of manganese oxide minerals; the orange-brown colors here are caused by both iron oxide minerals and cyanobacteria.

86. OBLONG GEYSER is not a major geyser in terms of the sheer size of the eruption, but because of its tremendous water discharge it has always been high on the list of the Park's important thermal features. The actual amount discharged has never been accurately determined because it spreads out across a broad sinter platform and almost immediately cascades into the Firehole River, but it probably amounts to at least 10,000 gallons.

During many seasons Oblong is regular enough to be predicted (although in practice public predictions are not usually made), with intervals close to 8 hours. During the quiet intervals the water periodically rises and falls in the crater, resulting in light overflow. Each such cycle lasts about 20 minutes. It is during a period of overflow that the eruption begins. The water level rises a little more so that a sudden flood of water leaves the crater, and soon the ground begins to pound as steam bubbles deep within the plumbing system form and collapse. The boiling within the crater increases slowly until the entire pool is involved. The water is never really jetted into the air but instead is domed upward by a massive boiling that can reach 25 feet high. The entire play lasts between 5 and 7 minutes. Two to 3 hours are required for the system to refill.

Another form of activity has been seen at Oblong. Believed to be related to active periods of Giant Geyser (94), these involve longer intervals (as long as 20 to 50 hours) that culminate in series of eruptions at short intervals. Often, the first of these intervals will be around $2^1/_2$ hours; a second and third interval (if any) may be as short as 30 minutes. These secondary eruptions rise from an empty crater and, being unimpeded by a pool of water, can have bursts as high as 50 feet. Such activity is extremely rare, however.

Oblong has also undergone occasional dormant periods. The most recent of these began during December 1992. Oblong rejuvenated in late July 1993, with intervals of about 24 hours, but it returned to dormancy after only a few days. There have been few eruptions since, but on some of those dates there were other unusual occurrences in this part of the Upper Basin, including major eruptions by both Splendid Geyser (107) and Link Geyser (120). Sympathetic events such as these indicate that the deep plumbing system roots of the Giant, Daisy, Grotto, and Chain Lakes Groups are directly connected with one another or at least are close enough together to be simultaneously affected by deep-seated events.

87. "NEW GEYSER" didn't last very long, and the use of the name is considered objectionable by many — nothing is new

for very long in any case, and the term has been overused. Nonetheless, this name was used on U.S. Geological Survey maps and so is taken as "marginally acceptable." The first known eruption was on September 1, 1970, and lasted several minutes. Pieces of jagged sinter strewn about the crater indicated that an old vent had been enlarged by a small steam explosion. In the succeeding two months, several other eruptions were seen. The intervals could not be determined, but they might have been as long as several days. The maximum height of the eruptions was about 15 feet. No eruptions have occurred since 1970, but New Geyser does act as an intermittent spring at times. Note that its site and that of the next geyser described are practically impossible to see from the boardwalk, lying well down the river from Oblong Geyser (86).

88. UNNG-GNT-1 broke out in eruption on May 1, 1970, exactly 4 months before the first activity at nearby New Geyser (87). These two events are probably related, since the springs are near one another. This geyser plays from a small pool about 30 feet from South Purple Pool (89). It was probably active during 1951, too. When first seen in 1970, GNT-1 played as a perpetual spouter. After an early summer dormancy, the play resumed on a periodic basis. The eruptions were about 15 feet high. It is believed that the 1970 activity ended on September 1, the same day "New Geyser" (87) blew out and began to play. In 1987, when nearby South Purple Pool was active, GNT-1 had a few splashing eruptions in concert. GNT-1 is most commonly a cool pool with slight discharge.

THE GIANT GEYSER COMPLEX contains many springs. Most are small perforations in the sinter mound that is capped by Giant Geyser's massive geyserite cone. It includes the Purple Pools, 300 to 400 feet across the Firehole River. The complex is positively known to be connected with Oblong Geyser to the south and the Grotto Complex to the northwest and possibly with the Daisy Group to the west. Although largely inactive at present, the Giant Complex is a pivotal and highly important network of hot springs.

89. THE PURPLE POOLS, South, East, and North, are all directly connected with Giant Geyser (94). It has long been suspected that variations in the water levels and/or boiling action in the Purple Pools might serve as an indicator for Giant Geyser. No such relationship has ever been seen, but any activity in Giant can affect the Pools: as an eruption of Giant progresses, the water level in the pools subsides until it is about 3 feet below overflow.

The only known eruptions among the Purple Pools have occurred in 1971 and since 1986. The 1971 activity involved the East and North Purple Pools, which played frequently to about 2 feet high while South Purple Pool boiled vigorously. It was thought at the time that this activity might have been a precursor to renewed activity in Giant, but the eruptions soon stopped without anything out of the ordinary happening. Giant did return to active status during the 1980s. For some time before an eruption in 1986, the Purple Pools underwent limited activity similar to that of 1971. Then, in the few weeks following the Giant eruption of September 12, 1987, South Purple Pool had a series of powerful eruptions. Voluminous bursts as wide as they were high reached over 30 feet, killing trees on the nearby hillside. More recent eruptions by Giant have failed to produce true eruptions in any of the Purple Pools, but they often do boil and become murky.

90. BIJOU GEYSER used to be called "Young Faithful Geyser," apparently because of its frequent action. Bijou is by far the most active member of the immediate Giant Complex of springs. It is the highest cone on the left (north) side of the Giant Platform. For most of its history it has played almost constantly 5 to 15 feet high, wetting all sides of its cyanobacteria-covered cone, which is unlike any other. The only known lengthy pauses in the activity occur just after eruptions by Giant Geyser (94). During the 1980s it was discovered that the details of Bijou's action may serve as an indicator of "Giant hot periods," which are the only times at which Giant can start an eruption. Although Bijou's spouting is nearly constant, it does have brief quiet intervals. Usually,

these last less than a minute. When they extend to as long as 5 minutes, the rest of the group responds with higher water levels, and a hot period may result. See the description of Giant Geyser (94) for more details about these hot periods. Note also that long pauses in Bijou's action take place during and shortly after the long, "marathon" eruptions by Grotto Geyser (111). These pauses cannot be taken as signs of impending hot periods.

91. CATFISH GEYSER erupts from a ragged cone near the front base of Bijou Geyser's (90) cone and is another close member of the Giant Complex. At the time of Giant's (94) hot periods prior to the 1980s, Catfish would erupt violently to 15 feet high for several minutes. During 1951 the thermal energy within the Giant Complex shifted to the north, away from Giant and to Catfish, Mastiff (92), and Bijou (90) Geysers. During this activity, known as the "Mastiff function," Catfish became a major geyser, erupting for many minutes to heights ranging between 75 and 100 feet. Such activity ended during January 1952. In the 1980s and 1990s, some of Giant's eruptions have been during the Mastiff function, but Catfish has not played as it did in 1951.

92. MASTIFF GEYSER was known to be active just preceding eruptions of Giant during the 1870s, when it ejected large volumes of water to about 35 feet. Thereafter, though, Mastiff was so inactive that it was all but forgotten; some references even listed it as extinct. But in 1951 an exchange of function shifted the energy of the Giant Complex to the north side of the platform. Catfish Geyser (91) erupted to 75 feet. And quite unexpectedly, Mastiff joined in, with a massive column of water reaching well over 100 feet high and a smaller secondary column jetting at an angle to perhaps 75 feet. Such action was totally without precedent, for just a few minutes later Giant (94) itself began playing. Catfish stopped, but Mastiff continued on equal terms with Giant for fully 5 minutes; only when Mastiff stopped did Giant assume its usual stupendous eruption. When the Giant Complex behaves in this fashion, it is called the "Mastiff function." Some of the eruptions during the 1980s and 1990s have been Mastiff function plays, but in this case Mastiff has generally not exceeded 75 feet high and has not been joined by Catfish.

93. TURTLE GEYSER is little known. It possesses a highly eroded and somewhat detached cone on the far right (south) side of the Giant Platform. Apparently, Turtle is active only at the time of one of Giant's (94) eruptions and usually not even then. It might be the 20-foot geyser referred to in 1925 as having regular eruptions at intervals of 40 minutes, and it might also have been active in 1931 and 1933, but the first eruptions positively known took place in 1951. They reached 3 to 20 feet high for a few seconds. Only once has it been observed to erupt since 1951. In September 1956, during a hot period by the Giant Complex, a geyser believed to be Turtle played 20 feet high for about 4 minutes. During Giant's more recent activity, Turtle has had only light overflow.

201. "THE PLATFORM VENTS" are two clusters of geysers that are active only at the time of Giant's (94) eruptions or its preliminary "hot periods." A hot period takes place when, during an exceptionally long interval by Bijou Geyser (90), the water level rises within the entire Giant Platform. Very abruptly, small holes in the platform directly in front of Giant's cone begin to spout. The play by some of these can reach as high as 8 feet; historically, the tallest could hit 15 feet high and was known as the "Christmas Tree." During especially vigorous hot periods, a second cluster toward the far right-hand side of the platform will join the others, and as many as fourteen individual vents can be active simultaneously. It is a very impressive sight, even if it doesn't result in an eruption by Giant. It is known that Giant can begin an eruption *only* during a hot period. Unfortunately, most hot periods, which sometimes recur at intervals as short as a few hours, do not result in an eruption. Nevertheless, all are eagerly awaited because of their potential.

94. GIANT GEYSER was appropriately named. When in eruption there is nothing quite like it. A huge tower of water is
thrown far into the air, and, because it is a cone-type geyser,
this is a steady column rather than the intermittent bursts
seen in most of the other large, fountain-type geysers. In the
early references to Yellowstone, Giant is listed as erupting to
250 to 300 feet. During its more recent active cycles, it has
not approached that kind of height; most eruptions have
reached no more than 150 feet high. It is clear, however, that
Giant has two distinctly different modes of activity — the
"Normal function," when it may approach 200 feet, and the
"Mastiff function," when the play reaches far over 200 feet
high in concert with Catfish (91) and Mastiff (92) Geysers.
Giant was active on the Mastiff function during the 1870s,
leading to the high figures of those years and to some disappointment among observers ever since. The Mastiff function
did occur during 1951, and a few of the eruptions in the
period 1982–1992 were of this type, but most of the activity
of the last century has been on the weaker Normal function.

When active, Giant is characterized by well-defined hot
periods. Triggered by intervals of 5 minutes and longer in
Bijou Geyser (90), the water level rises in all parts of the
Giant Platform — that is, in Bijou, Catfish, Mastiff, the "Platform Vents" (201) and Giant itself. As the Platform Vents
begin to erupt, the other springs begin to surge violently.
When the group is operating on the Mastiff function, this
action is added to by a powerful steam phase in Bijou and
minor eruptions by Catfish and Mastiff. Most hot periods do
not trigger eruptions, but eruptions do begin *only* during
hot periods. Suddenly, the surging water within Giant's cone
lifts a few inches. Water pours through the open front of the
cone and floods the platform, and the eruption is on. Only
seconds are required for Giant to reach its maximum height.
A single eruption has a duration of at least 55 minutes, and
even when it is more than half finished, the height can still
be well above 100 feet. The total volume of water expelled
has been estimated at over 1,000,000 gallons.

During Giant's last episode of vigorous activity, from
1950 to 1955, the intervals ranged from 2 to 14 days; at one

point in 1953, the average was only 53 hours, and Giant was nearly predictable. But any geyser the size of Giant is adversely affected by exchange of function. Given that the Giant Complex is connected with the Purple Pools, Oblong Geyser, the Grotto Geyser Group, and possibly the Daisy Geyser Group and other hot spring systems, it is no surprise that Giant has not been frequently active. When it went dormant in 1955, many presumed it would reactivate within a few years. Indeed, during 1959 Giant did show signs of impending activity, and, perhaps more important, there was a decrease in activity in the Grotto Group. And then the Hebgen Lake earthquake struck. Giant hasn't been the same since. Neither has it been "dead."

Many references state or imply that Giant has been completely dormant since 1955. This is not so. As of December 1994, it had had nineteen eruptions since 1960. For the record, these took place on September 18, 1963; September 9, 1978; September 27, 1982; October 12, 1984; August 20, 1986; September 12, 1987; June 28, 1988; September 12, 1988; December 18, 1988; April 17, 1989; January 6–7, 1990; January 26–27, 1990; September 23, 1990; September 30, 1990; August 21, 1991; October 20, 1991; September 24, 1992; in late November–early December 1993; and September 29, 1994. Notice the preponderance of autumn eruptions. This is probably not some odd chance of probability. Many geysers and geyser groups are known to undergo increases in activity during the late summer–early fall seasons. The best-known case of this is in the Norris Geyser Basin, where it is commonly called the "seasonal disturbance." Although some have hypothesized about the role of cool surface water flowing from the hillside into the Purple Pools, Giant is one of the most persuasive points in favor of disturbance processes taking place in the Upper Geyser Basin.

It seems that the exchanges of function that affect Giant involve water volume more than they do heat. Giant is hot enough to have eruptions at all times. Indeed, it is among the very hottest geysers and isn't measurably cooler now than it was when it was so highly active during the 1950s.

Apparently, just too much water is lost from the system through the Grotto and other groups, and Giant isn't properly primed. Any geyser gazer prays for a 1950s-style reactivation of Giant and dreams of a true Mastiff function. Imagine if you can — Catfish begins splashing, then explodes to 75 feet. Mastiff joins in with a double column of water over 100 feet high, while Bijou goes into a roaring steam phase. And finally the Giant, reaching up to 200 feet and more. All of this within a complex of springs less than 100 feet from side to side. What a sight it must be. Unfortunately, a reflection of the known historical record of Giant Geyser's eruptions reveals that it has played much as it does now — a time or two per year — for most of Yellowstone's recorded history. To see Giant play is, and will probably remain, one of the rarest geyser-gazing treats.

202. UNNG-GNT-2 is a weathered hole near the boardwalk between the Giant and Grotto Groups. During Giant's activity of the late 1980s, when hot period activity was common, it was noticed that this low pool responded along with the rest of the group, its water level rising until the vent was nearly full. No eruptions were ever directly seen, but washed areas and killed plants indicated that GNT-2 did have a few eruptions, perhaps several feet high, several times between 1988 and 1991.

203. UNNG-GNT-3. In addition to all the miscellaneous geysers of the Giant Complex, a number of other geysers and perpetual spouters exist on the platform that, in spite of their very close proximity to the rest, seem to be a separate group of springs. Most of these are invisible from the boardwalk, hidden low on the back side of the geyserite mound. In total, there are at least an additional dozen springs here. Some are geysers with eruptions up to 4 feet high.

Round Spring Group

The Round Spring Group is a small cluster of springs of little overall significance. However, most have records of geyser activity, and Round Spring itself proved to be a major geyser during May 1990. The group is not threaded by any trail, but it is close enough to the paved Upper Basin Trail that most of its features can easily be seen from there. There has been considerable confusion over the years about the names within this group; it is hoped that the versions given here will set things straight.

95. WEST ROUND SPRING, along with North Round Spring (205) and several small, unnamed features within the group, started erupting the night of the 1959 earthquake. Little is known about that activity, but West Round continued playing into 1960. It was not known to erupt again until August 1971, when, for a brief period that month, eruptions were frequent and about 15 feet high. Splashes just 1 foot high were recorded in 1972. Again, it was (apparently) quiet until May 1990, when, at the same time Round Spring (204) was active, West Round was seen to have at least two eruptions perhaps 6 feet high. West Round Spring is located behind some trees in a position from which it is virtually impossible to see from any trail. It is possible that small eruptions are common and that the play seen in May 1990 was a "normal" sort of activity.

96. PEAR GEYSER (not to be confused with Pear Spring, the large pool visible in front of the trees just to the geyser's left) had its first known activity in 1958–1959, before the earthquake. In 1961 it was highly regular, erupting every 5 minutes to a height of about 12 feet. Additional brief episodes of similar activity were seen during the 1970s and 1980s, and Pear Geyser was active during the winter of 1989–1990, when it carved a wide and deep runoff channel without being actually witnessed, and in August 1990, when a single eruption 8 feet high was observed.

97. ROUND SPRING GEYSER AND UNNG-RSG-2 are located about midway between Pear Geyser (96) and North Round Spring (205). (Round Spring Geyser was referred to as UNNG-RSG-1 in the previous edition of this book.) Their history is quite confused. They probably played as small geysers or perpetual spouters in the 1870s and 1880s; they may have erupted in 1937 and are probably the "small geysers" referred to in reports written between 1940 and 1954. They were definitely active during 1956 and continued to play until an 8-year dormancy began in 1974. They have played frequently since their reactivation in 1982. Round Spring Geyser, the one to the north, is the larger and more active of the two, reaching up to 8 feet high at intervals and durations of only a few seconds. The smaller geyser plays only after an exceptionally long interval by the other and may in fact may be the trigger for the start of a new episode of short-term cyclic action. While Round Spring was active in May 1990, Round Spring Geyser and RSG-2 were both much more vigorous than usual, and one jetting eruption by Round Spring Geyser was easily 20 feet high.

204. ROUND SPRING lies near Pear Spring, to the left (south) of UNNG-RSG-2. That it played as a 5-foot geyser in 1895 had long been forgotten until it had a series of powerful eruptions in late May 1990. It was only active for about 30 hours, and the intervals were as short as a few minutes. Most eruptions had durations of only a few seconds, but they played to between 5 and 20 feet high. Some so-called major eruptions exceeded 30 feet, and one, which had an extraordinarily long duration exceeding 3 minutes, reached an estimated 50 to 60 feet. After this episode, Round Spring quickly returned to its usual dormancy in which it is a cool pool lined with cyanobacteria.

205. NORTH ROUND SPRING, once called Trefoil Spring because of its threefold shape, was a quiet pool until May 1990, when nearby Round Spring (204) was active. North Round was then seen to bubble vigorously, and on occasion the action broke the surface with splashes less than 1 foot high.

98. "EAST ROUND SPRING" (incorrectly identified in previous editions as "Round Spring") is the member of the Round

Spring Group closest to the trail. It had a single known eruption in 1941, when it reached 20 feet high for a duration of 3 minutes. It has probably not erupted since then, the belief being that other reports of an erupting "Round Spring" refer to Round Spring Geyser (97). East Round does act as a long-period intermittent spring.

Table 3. Geysers of the Giant and Round Spring Groups

Name	Map No.	Interval	Duration	Height (ft)
Bijou Geyser	90	sec–5 min	minutes	5–15
Catfish Geyser	91	with Giant	minutes	15–100
"East Round Spring"	98	[1961]	3 min	20
Giant Geyser	94	see text	55–80 min	150–250
Inkwell Spring	85	near steady	near steady	2
Mastiff Geyser	92	with Giant	5–10 min	35–125
"New Geyser"	87	[1970]	minutes	15
North Round Spring	205	[1990]	seconds	boil–1
Oblong Geyser	86	5–11 hrs *	5–7 min	25
Pear Geyser	96	infrequent	2–3 min	8–12
"Platform Vents"	201	see text	minutes	1–8
Purple Pool, East	89	[1986]	minutes	2
Purple Pool, North	89	[1986]	minutes	boil
Purple Pool, South	89	[1987]	minutes	30
Round Spring	204	[1990]	10 sec–3 min	5–60
Round Spring Geyser	97	sec–min	seconds	8–20
Turtle Geyser	93	[1956]	unknown	3–20
UNNG–GNT–1	88	[1970]	minutes	10–20
UNNG–GNT–2	202	with Giant	minutes	unobserved
UNNG–GNT–3	203	frequent	sec–min	1–4
UNNG–RSG–2	97	minutes	seconds	2–6
West Round Spring	95	uncertain	seconds	6

* When active.
[ ] Brackets enclose the year of most recent activity for extremely rare or dormant geysers. See text.

Daisy Group

The terms *Daisy Group* (Map E, Table 4) and *Daisy Geyser Complex* are nearly synonymous. Of all the geysers here, only two — Bank and Pyramid — are not known for certain to be connected with Daisy. Aside from the geysers and numerous sputs, the group includes only three cool, quiet pools. The group is thoroughly separated from other hot spring clusters at the surface, but there is some evidence that there is a subsurface connection with the Giant Group.

The Daisy Group lies to the west of the Firehole River and the Giant Group, up on a low hill. There are four approaches to the group. From the paved Upper Basin Trail are two smaller paved trails leading up the hill; passing on opposite sides of the springs, they then merge and head westward toward the Punch Bowl Spring Group. The trail to Punch Bowl Spring continues on the Black Sand Basin and therefore, if reversed, provides a third access to the Daisy Group. Fourth is a trail that leads through the forest between Biscuit Basin and the Daisy Group.

Daisy and Splendid Geysers are very large and are among most gazers' favorites. Splendid is seldom active, but when it is it may rival Grand Geyser in size and beauty. When Splendid is not active, Daisy usually is. During some years it has been among the most regular major geysers in Yellowstone.

99. BANK GEYSER might have been formed by a steam explosion in 1929 (at least it greatly opened up in that year), and for a time during 1933 it had spectacular eruptions up to 20 feet high. Even though it lies within a few feet of springs that are definitely members of the Daisy Group, Bank is an isolated spring apparently unrelated to any other. It lies in a small alcove down the slope toward the Giant Group. It presently erupts every 1 to 3 minutes. The play is a series of bursts over the course of a few seconds, a few of which reach 4 to 6 feet high. Bank has major and minor eruptions, distinguished by the height of the bursts, but there is no clear relationship between them. During some years the eruptions degenerate so that most are periods of mild boiling.

THE DAISY COMPLEX (numbers 100 through 108, plus 206). The Daisy Complex is a very interesting assortment of springs. It includes at least ten geysers, two of which are among the largest in the Park, and almost no other springs except for a miscellany of small sputs. All of the geysers are rather directly connected to one another at depth, and frequent exchange of function leads to great overall irregularity among them. Any description of one geyser almost demands a mention of others.

Daisy is, in spite of its many relatives, a highly predictable geyser most of the time. A sign giving predictions is maintained both at the Visitor Center and at the start of the southernmost of the two paved trails leading to the group.

100. UNNG-DSG-1 consists of two sets of several vents each between Bank (99) and Radiator (101) Geysers. Both of these sets appear to lie along fractures in the geyserite crust, and the point at which they cross one another is another spring crater. Although there is fully 20 feet between the two vents that are farthest apart, all are simultaneously active. Details about the activity are uncertain. Intervals can be as long as several hours. DSG-1 is somewhat more frequent and vigorous during active episodes by Splendid Geyser (107) than it is when Daisy Geyser (106) is active. Most of the vents sputter only a few inches high, but the largest splashes can reach up to 2 feet.

101. RADIATOR GEYSER is a geyser of historical origin. It sprang to life beneath a car within the old Daisy Area parking lot so that the people there thought the car's radiator was boiling. The eruptions involved little more than boiling until the time of the 1959 earthquake. Radiator has been active in company with Daisy (106) and Splendid (107) Geysers ever since, on most occasions playing a few minutes after the end of the larger nearby eruption. When Daisy is the active major geyser, Radiator's eruptions are mostly subterranean, but when Splendid is active Radiator can reach 10 feet above the ground. It has also had a few active episodes in which the action seemed to be completely indepen-

dent of the other geysers. At these times the play is just 2 feet high.

102. COMET GEYSER is located directly between Daisy (106) and Splendid (107). Its cone is the largest in the complex, yet the geyser is among the smallest — usually. The cone has been built to its present size by the nearly constant splashing of Comet over a long period of time. At best, this play reaches about 6 feet high. Every few minutes the surging becomes heavier, and large amounts of water are ejected, but even this discharge is never sufficient to form a surface runoff. The only time Comet seems to stop erupting is following full major eruptions of Splendid and, rarely, of Daisy. Even then, though, the play has not actually quit; instead, the water level has simply been drawn down so far that the eruption is confined entirely to the subsurface. Highly controversial are occasional reports of large eruptions by Comet. The vast majority of the time, these can be shown to have really been play by Daisy, but there are exceptions. One day in 1992, for example, reports of two separate 30-foot eruptions were turned in by people familiar with the Daisy Group. Thus, Comet might someday prove to be a third major member of the that group.

103. BRILLIANT POOL was historically never more than a calm spring prior to 1950. Until then it had ebbed a few inches at the time of Daisy's (106) eruptions, and the refilling was simultaneous with Daisy. In 1950 Brilliant Pool began to overflow heavily, but only on occasion. Whenever this happened, eruptive action in Daisy would stop. This interplay occurred many times during 1950 and was probably a prelude to renewed activity by Splendid Geyser (107) in 1951.

The response of Brilliant Pool to eruptions by Splendid is quite different. Following each eruption, the water level may drop by as much as 4 feet. After a series of several eruptions by Splendid, the crater may be completely empty. Only then can Brilliant Pool commence its own eruptive activity. This play, lasting as long as 2 minutes in 1951, is characterized by explosive jets of water 20 feet high and angled sharply away from Splendid. Brilliant Pool has played in similar fashion following more recent eruptive series by Splendid, except that the eruptions now come in sequences with short intervals and durations under 10 seconds.

104. DAISY'S THIEF GEYSER was known by the name "Dewey Geyser" (named for Admiral George Dewey, famed for defeating the Spanish fleet in the Battle of Manila Bay during the Spanish-American War) in 1898–1899. A reference to a "Daisy's Indicator" in 1932 might also be to this geyser. It only definitely appeared in 1936, however, and was seen a few times in most years during the 1940s. Moments before Daisy Geyser (106) was due to begin spouting, the Thief began jetting a steady column of water to 15 feet. The eruption lasted about 25 minutes without pause. Throughout, the water level in Daisy dropped slowly; at the end of the Thief's activity, it had been lowered to the same point as that following a normal eruption of Daisy. And, because Daisy finally did erupt after a normal interval following the eruption of Daisy's Thief, it appeared that the latter had discharged an amount of water and energy exactly equivalent to one eruption by Daisy. The origin of the name is therefore clear.

Following a few years of quiet, Daisy's Thief reactivated in 1953, but the manner of action was changed considerably. Instead of the 25-minute eruption, the spouting lasted several hours. It was less forceful than before, and when it ended Daisy erupted immediately. This type of function continued until the 1959 earthquake. Since then, there have been few eruptions. In July 1968 there was one that lasted more than 7 hours, during which Daisy had three brief, weak eruptions. Later in 1968, in the days following a swarm of small earthquakes, Daisy had a series of nine eruptions, seven of which were preceded by Daisy's Thief acting as an indicator rather than as a robber. Those were the only eruptions by Daisy during an 11-year dormancy. As Daisy rejuvenated from that dormancy in the early 1970s, the Thief had a few additional, very small eruptions. Because Daisy was having long and erratic intervals at that time, no clear relationship between the two geysers could be discerned. Daisy's Thief has now been dormant for more than 20 years, and the small round crater on a raised geyserite mound is difficult to see.

105. BONITA POOL was used as an indicator of Daisy's (106) eruptions until 1937 — the time of first overflow was related to the priming of Daisy. In that year the water level rose higher than ever before, and whenever overflow was achieved all eruptions of Daisy were stopped. Note the similarity between this and overflows by Brilliant Pool (103) during 1950. On one occasion the high water persisted for several months. Daisy was dormant for that entire period of time, to the extent that orange cyanobacteria was able to grow within the crater. This happened several additional times before the 1959 earthquake.

At first, following the big shock, Daisy continued with accelerated but normal activity. Then, in early 1960, Bonita Pool became very active, overflowing steadily and experiencing frequent small eruptions. Daisy became dormant, and Bonita did not stop overflowing until 1967. During that summer it would sometimes temporarily quit. Immediately, Daisy began filling and heating, but just when an eruption seemed imminent, Bonita would refill. Except for two occasions in 1968 when activity was initiated by Daisy's Thief Geyser (104), Bonita's action was enough to bring about complete dormancy in Daisy from 1960 into 1971. Only then did Bonita again stop overflowing. Often, as in 1967, Daisy tried to play without quite succeeding, but some eruptions did occur. The time required for a complete exchange of function back to Daisy was long, but by 1978 Daisy could finally again be predicted with confidence. Bonita has remained quiet and low. A little spray plays from "Bonita's Sputs" on the edge of the crater, usually near the time of Daisy's eruption, but Bonita seems finished for now, not even remotely meriting its name (Spanish for "pretty").

106. DAISY GEYSER is the most important member of the Daisy Complex. Although Splendid Geyser (107) is larger,

Daisy can erupt as often as and more regularly than any other major geyser in the Upper Basin, including Old Faithful.

Daisy is far more active. This has apparently been the usual case, for Daisy's runoff channels are wider, deeper, and more extensive than Splendid's.

Daisy erupts from a crater partially surrounded by a heavy sinter rim. At two points this margin is perforated by small vents, which have formed cones; these begin to spout shortly before an eruption. There are also several small vents within the main crater. When Daisy is predictably regular, the activity in the cones can be used to give an accurate time of eruption. Usually, the larger of the two begins to splash about 20 minutes before the eruption; the smaller begins 8 to 10 minutes later. Meanwhile, the water in the crater boils and surges constantly over the main vent. The eruption begins when this splashing suddenly becomes higher and stronger. Daisy rockets forth only moments later. The maximum height of 75 feet is reached within the first half minute of play, with the water column sharply angled from the vertical. The normal duration is $3^{1}/_{2}$ to 4 minutes.

When the activity of Bonita Pool (105) is such that it does not overflow and erupt, Daisy can be extremely regular. During most seasons it is among the most predictable of the major geysers. The average interval ranges between 85 and 110 minutes, varying from year to year, but during any one season the actual range between the longest and shortest intervals tends to be small. When Daisy is performing in this way, only two things can throw it off. One is a strong wind, especially out of the south — as is often associated with summer thunderstorms — which may delay Daisy's eruption by as much as half an hour. The other is Splendid Geyser (107).

During recorded history Daisy has been much more active than Splendid. But Splendid has had occasional active episodes, and these times are always periods of great irregularity in Daisy. The longest such period was during the years before 1900, and others occurred during the 1950s, 1970s, and 1980s. Among Splendid's best years were 1985 and 1986. At times, those same years were Daisy's worst. Yet Splendid plays a beneficial role in Daisy's activity, too. All of this can best be shown by the story of events during the 1970s.

Following the 1959 earthquake, Daisy was active as before. Indeed, as time passed it became more active until the average interval had shortened to only 48 minutes. Then, in February 1960, Bonita Pool began to overflow and erupt. Daisy declined rapidly and was soon dormant. Except for July 31 and September 18, 1968, when eruptions were triggered by Daisy's Thief Geyser (104), Daisy remained dormant until July 22, 1971. With two eruptions on that day came the first signs of a shift back toward Daisy, away from Bonita. By 1972 Daisy would have two or three eruptions during the course of a few hours, then lapse back into dormancy that lasted for several days. It soon became evident that these brief active phases were often initiated by eruptions of Splendid Geyser and that continuing action by Splendid was required to keep Daisy going. So it was until 1978. By then there had been such a complete shift of energy to Daisy that not only was Splendid no longer needed but it could seldom erupt at all.

From this it seems that perhaps eruptions by Splendid do not occur so much because of energy shifts to it but, rather, because of energy shifts away from Daisy. The two are not the same thing; exchanges of function away from Daisy allow not only Splendid but also many other members of the Daisy Group to come to life. It is only under these conditions that Daisy and Splendid can erupt simultaneously. Known as concerted eruptions, such plays were first seen during the 1880s but were not seen again until 1972. Never were concerted eruptions seen with such frequency as during 1985 and 1986, when single active phases of Splendid included as many as four concerts. When in concert, Daisy is usually much stronger than normal. Such eruptions may exceed 100 feet, and the measured record is 152 feet. Daisy is also increased in duration, playing for as long as 6 minutes. (It must be noted, too, that some in-concert Daisys are very weak, reaching less than 30 feet high for durations of less than 2 minutes.) Clearly, Daisy owes a lot to the existence of Splendid.

Situated on a hill, Daisy can be seen from much of the Upper Geyser Basin. It is always spectacular. It is best to see it erupt close at hand from a position where the sharp angle of the column is visible. Other geysers might be higher, more sharply angled, longer lasting, and so on, but somehow Daisy is a particularly special sight.

107. SPLENDID GEYSER has seldom been active during recorded times. It is possible that Warren Ferris saw and gave an accurate description of Splendid in 1834, and it was active through most of the early years of the Park. It entered a dormancy in 1898, and except for one eruption during 1931 and another in 1937, no other active episodes took place until 1951. Splendid then had a number of eruptions, often in series, during each year until the 1959 earthquake. Splendid rejuvenated along with Daisy Geyser (106) beginning in 1971, was dormant from 1978 until 1983, underwent many intense series of eruptions during 1985 and 1986, and has been nearly dormant since early 1987.

Splendid is on a hair trigger, requiring little to set off a series of eruptions. For years it has been known that Splendid is most likely to begin to erupt during a storm, when the barometric (atmospheric) pressure drops quickly as a front moves across the Park. This has the effect of slightly reducing the boiling temperature within Splendid's plumbing system. It appears that such falling pressure may be required for Splendid to be active, but surely other factors are involved as well. Once the initial eruption of an active episode has taken place, Splendid can continue to play regardless of further changes in the pressure.

The water in Splendid's crater is usually agitated, frequently boiling up several feet. The strongest action is usually about the time of or a few minutes after Daisy's eruption. If an eruption by Splendid is to occur, the surging will build abruptly to as much as 15 to 30 feet high. It would seem that such a tremendous output of water would have to trigger an eruption, but this is not so. "False starts" are common. Somehow, the sound of the start of an eruption is different from that of "only" a false start. This cannot be described, but anyone who has experienced both knows the difference well. When it is an eruption, the surging will hold its height for several seconds, then jet explosively to the full height. Few eruptions are less than 150 feet high, and nearly all the ones this small are in concert with Daisy. Some eruptions approach 200 feet high, and one was measured at 218 feet, making Splendid one of the handful of the tallest geysers in Yellowstone. Once started, an eruption may last from 2 to 10 minutes, and when there is a series of eruptions, the intervals range from just over 1 hour to more than 12 hours.

At times, the activity of the 1970s and 1980s was without precedent. Generally, if Daisy or Splendid has been active, the other has been dormant. Starting in 1972, there were probably more eruptions by Splendid than in all its previous active phases combined. During 1985 it played forty-four times; there were another ninety-nine eruptions in 1986 and twenty-six in 1987. Roughly 30% of these eruptions were in concert with Daisy. With only two known exceptions, every concert began with Splendid. Within the first 2 minutes of its start, Daisy joined in. The two geysers would nearly match one another for size, each reaching between 100 and 150 feet high. The spectacle cannot be adequately described. The refilling of the craters was rapid, and Daisy often erupted alone scarcely an hour after the concerted play. Unfortunately, no concerts have occurred since early 1987; in fact, Splendid has been nearly dormant. It played three times in 1988, none in 1989, and twice in 1990.

A new mode of activity appeared in September 1992. Taking place at the time of the usual false start activity a few minutes after an eruption by Daisy, this play reaches only 50 to 70 feet high for a duration of 1 to $1^1/_2$ minutes. Definitely not full eruptions but far more than just false starts, these are described as "post-Daisy minor" eruptions. During 1993 they seemed to occur once every 1 to 4 weeks.

That Splendid has not been frequently active is shown by the surrounding sinter platform. The recent cycles of activity have caused much erosion in the immediate area, yet the runoff channels are quite small and are shorter than Daisy's. Many eruptions would cause a considerable change in the crater and its surroundings. It may be that Splendid is of relatively recent origin and that much more can be expected of it in the future. For now, its eruptions are a rare treat.

108. MURKY SPRING, somewhere west of Daisy's Thief Geyser (104), was active during the 1950s and again during the 1960s. Quite regular, the eruptions recurred every 6 to 8 hours, lasted 10 to 15 minutes, and reached 15 feet high. It is amazing, then, that the descriptions do not allow a positive identification as to which spring is Murky. Near Splendid Geyser (107) and northwest of Daisy's Thief Geyser are two sinter-lined craters that show signs of having erupted in the past. They are definitely part of the Daisy Complex, as shown by their dropping water levels whenever Splendid erupts. Although the water of both is clear, one of these is probably Murky Spring.

206. "MUD POOL" is located within a stand of trees on the far southwest side of the Daisy Complex. Starting in 1982, it has been active as a perpetual spouter, the steady play being only 1 to 2 feet high. It is slightly possible that "Mud Pool" is identical to Murky Spring (108).

109. PYRAMID GEYSER is located at the base of the White Pyramid, also known as the White Throne, across the meadow northwest of the Daisy Complex. Little was known about this spring prior to the 1959 earthquake. Some eruptive episodes with intervals of 3 to 4 hours were recorded, but the balance of evidence shows that Pyramid was not very active. The quake caused a dormancy that lasted until 1971. Since then it has been continuously active, but on a cyclic pattern. During most years an inactive period of several hours' duration is followed by an eruptive episode consisting of several closely spaced eruptions. The eruptions occur at intervals of 3 to 8 minutes and at durations of around 1 minute; the height is 8 feet.

Punch Bowl Spring Group

The Punch Bowl Spring Group is a small collection of springs in the vicinity of Punch Bowl Spring, along the trail between the Daisy Group and Black Sand Basin. Punch Bowl itself is a boiling, intermittent spring. Vague reports say it was active as a geyser during the 1870s and 1880s. The spring immediately at the right-hand (eastern) base of the cone is also an intermittent spring, with periods that show no relationship to those of Punch Bowl.

110. UNNG-PBG-1 is the nearest of the pools west of Punch Bowl Spring. Eruptions are generally infrequent but of long duration — the boiling play up to 4 feet high may have durations of several hours. An exception to this pattern occurred during June 1990, when smaller, bursting eruptions recurred with both intervals and durations of a few minutes.

The two small pools north of PBG-1 also have histories of infrequent geyser activity, and they are probably active only when PBG-1 is also active. Both play 1 to 2 feet high.

207. BLACK SAND POOL. Farther down the trail from Punch Bowl Spring toward Black Sand Basin are two springs, which properly comprise a hot spring group of their own. Black Sand Pool alone was the original Black Sand Basin of the 1880s. (The present Black Sand Basin was then known as "Sunlight Basin.") Black Sand Pool has a history of infrequent eruptions. It may have been active when the Park was established, as its original name read "Black Sand Geyser," but the first eruptions specifically recorded were during 1895, when it played up to 20 feet high. It was not active again until 1950, when there were several eruptions about 12 feet high. The only other known activity, more of a vigorous intermittent boiling, took place during the first few weeks after the 1959 earthquake.

208. DEMON'S CAVE is located a short distance southeast of Black Sand Pool. It was originally named "Cave Geyser" in 1872 and was referred to as a "boiling cauldron" in 1881, both implying eruptive activity. The record is then blank, however, until the 1980s. Based mostly on signs of splashing and washing within the deep crater, occasional eruptions perhaps 3 to 6 feet high take place on an infrequent basis. Demon's Cave is a dangerous feature; the approach directly from the trail leads to a wide geyserite ledge that overhangs the pool. To view it, swing wide around the crater toward its back side.

Table 4. Geysers of the Daisy and Punch Bowl Spring Groups

Name	Map No.	Interval	Duration	Height (ft)
Bank Geyser	99	1–2 min	10–20 sec	4–20
Black Sand Pool	207	[1959, minor]	minutes	boil–20
Bonita Pool	105	[1978]	days–years	2
Brilliant Pool	103	with Splendid	10 sec	20
Comet Geyser	102	steady	steady	1–10
Daisy Geyser	106	85–120 min	3–4 min	75
Daisy's Thief Geyser	104	[1972]	min–hrs	8–15
Demon's Cave	208	infrequent	minutes	3–6
"Mud Pool"	206	steady	steady	1–2
Murky Spring	108	[1962]	10–15 min	15
Pyramid Geyser	109	3–8 min *	1 min	8
Radiator Geyser	101	irregular	sec–min	sub–10
Splendid Geyser	107	infrequent	1–10 min	50–218
UNNG–DSG–1	100	hours	min–hrs	2
UNNG–PBG–1	110	infrequent	hours	4

* When active.
[ ] Brackets enclose the year of most recent activity for extremely rare or dormant geysers. See text.

Grotto Group, with Riverside Geyser and the Chain Lakes Complex

The Grotto Group and the area a short distance to its north consist of three functional hot spring clusters — the Grotto Geyser Complex, Riverside Geyser, and the Chain Lake Complex (Map F, Table 5). Several of the geysers are large; usually, only Riverside receives much attention, but the over-all activity here is vigorous and, at least in part, is related to that of the Giant Group.

The two main trails through the Upper Geyser Basin merge at Grotto Geyser. This point is about 0.9 mile from the Old Faithful Visitor Center and 0.2 mile from the end of the main trail at Morning Glory Pool.

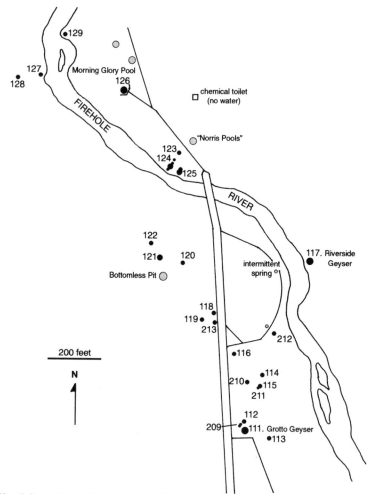

Map F. Grotto Group, Riverside Geyser, Chain Lakes Group, and Morning Glory Group

THE GROTTO GEYSER COMPLEX (numbers 111 through 115, plus 209 through 212) includes six geysers and several small sputs. Four of these are in closely related pairs; the others are more separated. Grotto Geyser is an almost never-ending source of pleasure for its visitors. Geologically, it is important in that it serves as a sort of pressure release for the Giant Complex. Any frequent activity by Grotto tends to result in the dormancy of Giant Geyser (94), as has been the case for much of recorded time. Should Grotto significantly decline, perhaps there would be a true reactivation by Giant. Grotto would be less active than it is now, but we would be blessed with both geysers.

111. GROTTO GEYSER was given its name by the Washburn Expedition in 1870. The interesting projections and caverns of the cone probably formed as siliceous sinter was deposited about a stand of dead trees. The remaining stumps are now thoroughly coated and petrified by the geyserite. An early picture shows a man sitting in one of the openings of the cone. One look at the steam that issues steadily from the hole would discourage anyone from doing so today. Obviously, Grotto was not as active then as it is now, and, in fact, the photograph was taken at a time when exchange of function had shifted much of the energy from Grotto to Giant.

The eruption of Grotto resembles a series of large splashes. At the very beginning of the activity these surges may reach over 40 feet high, but the play dies down quickly to about 15 feet, which is held for the remainder of the eruption. The duration of an eruption roughly controls the length of the following interval and is bimodal. Most eruptions, called "short mode" or "normal," last from 50 minutes to $3^1/_2$ hours and recur at intervals of roughly 7 hours. Interspersed among the normal eruptions every few days are "long mode" or "marathon" eruptions. Instrumental monitoring has shown that they have durations as long as 17 hours and are followed by intervals as great as 29 hours.

The discharge of water by Grotto is very great. A typical marathon eruption will spill at least 350,000 gallons of water, about as much water in half a day as Old Faithful erupts in half a week. Because of this high rate of water loss as well as its relationship to Giant, Grotto has always been numbered among the most important geysers.

112. ROCKET GEYSER almost always erupts in concert with Grotto (111). During most of Grotto's activity, Rocket

Grotto (right) and adjacent Rocket Geysers are not very tall, but their long and voluminous eruptions rank them as major geysers. Some of their geyserite formations have apparently grown on silicified tree trunks.

steadily churns and splashes about in its crater, most bursts reaching no more than 3 feet above the crater rim. It seems to be merely an additional vent for Grotto. On occasion, however, Rocket will take over the entire activity with a major eruption. Water jets in a steady stream to as much as 50 feet high, while Grotto falls nearly silent. Major eruptions usually begin about $1^1/_2$ to $2^1/_2$ hours after the start of Grotto. They last from 2 to 12 minutes, after which Grotto resumes its normal splashing action but then often stops within a few minutes. Interestingly, and showing that Grotto's normal and marathon eruptions are quite different phenomena, Rocket majors happen almost exclusively near the end of the short eruptions. They are uncommon during marathons but are sometimes seen at about the 13-hour mark of exceptionally long marathons. Extremely rare, observed only a handful of times, are eruptions that begin around half an hour after Grotto has completely quit. There is also a single known case in which Grotto's activity was initiated by a Rocket major rather than by the Grotto Fountain Geysers (114 & 115).

209. UNNG-GRG-2 ("THE CENTRAL VENTS"). Between the cones of Grotto (111) and Rocket (112) Geysers is an assortment of small vents that play throughout Grotto's activity. On occasion, these "Central Vents" erupt before Grotto starts, at about the time Grotto Fountain Geyser (114) appears ready to start playing. The most common result is a "Central Vent Delay" in which Grotto's start is postponed for at least 40 minutes; rarely, the "Central Vents" play the role of Grotto Fountain and trigger the start of Grotto.

113. UNNG-GRG-1 ("VARIABLE SPRING") is the first pool east of Grotto and the boardwalk leading toward the Giant Group. Eruptions by this spring, which were rare prior to 1983, are associated with marathon eruptions by Grotto Geyser (111) and are especially strong in the first few days after an eruption by Giant Geyser (94). Ordinarily clear, the water becomes murky to outright muddy as superheated boiling domes the water as high as 2 feet. When active, brief eruptions recur frequently for several hours.

210. (GROTTO'S) INDICATOR SPRING is a pool lying between Rocket (112) and Grotto Fountain (114) Geysers. During the last 2 or 3 hours before Grotto erupts, the spring fills intermittently to near overflow and then drops a few inches. The water level gets a bit higher with each 20-minute cycle, which is synchronized with similar changes in nearby Grotto Fountain Geyser (114). Around 1911 an Indicator Spring was said to "spurt up" just before the start of Grotto, but this was probably Grotto Fountain Geyser (114). Therefore, eruptions observed in 1988 are the only ones known for today's Indicator Spring. This activity, which reached as far as 6 feet above an empty crater, was associated with other "unusual" events within the Grotto Complex, such as an amazingly long, 53-minute eruption by Grotto Fountain.

114 and 115. GROTTO FOUNTAIN GEYSER AND SOUTH GROTTO FOUNTAIN GEYSER are difficult to describe separately. They are closely related to each other as well as to all other members of the Grotto Complex. Their histories are somewhat unclear. Many authorities have stated that Grotto Fountain was inactive until the late 1920s, but it was mapped as a "spouter" in 1872, and eruptions to 30 feet were clearly described in 1886. Major eruptions, said to have reached 100 feet high, were infrequently seen between 1922 and 1932, and Grotto Fountain was also active under the names "Strange Geyser" during the 1940s and "Surprise Geyser" during the 1950s and 1960s. It is probable that South Grotto Fountain has been active along with Grotto Fountain on all occasions.

The small cone of Grotto Fountain does not look like the source of a major geyser. Only a few inches high, it sits in the center of a broad, depressed runoff channel leading from Grotto (111) and Rocket (112). Yet when Grotto Fountain plays, the highest jets often reach between 30 and 50 feet high for most of the 7- to 17-minute duration. Grotto Fountain is capable of extraordinary eruptions, too — one in 1987 was measured as 83 feet high, and another in 1988 had a duration of 53 minutes. Its cone-type jetting is beautiful, especially when joined by South Grotto Fountain.

South Grotto Fountain's crater is about 30 feet south of that of Grotto Fountain (to the right when viewed from the main trail). When the two geysers are active, Grotto Fountain usually plays first, followed closely by its southern brother. If the reverse is true, Grotto Fountain may not play at all. South Grotto Fountain does not usually exceed 10 feet high but may last for more than 30 minutes.

Grotto Fountain serves as an indicator for Grotto in two ways. First, during the last hour or two before Grotto erupts, Grotto Fountain periodically fills, boils, and drops, completing one cycle in roughly 20 minutes in sync with the filling of Indicator Spring (210). The boiling becomes stronger with each cycle so that on this basis an experienced observer can quite accurately predict when Grotto will start. More precisely, Grotto Fountain can actually erupt only during the last few minutes before Grotto starts. Its head start ranges from less than 1 minute to more than 11 minutes, and, in general, the longer this lead time, the stronger will be both Grotto Fountain and the initial surges by Grotto. As noted, if South Grotto Fountain begins playing before Grotto Fountain, then Grotto Fountain may not play at all.

211. UNNG-GRG-3 ("STARTLING GEYSER"), previously referred to by the long-winded "South South Grotto Fountain," plays from two small holes immediately to the right-front of South Grotto Fountain's (115) crater. The vents are completely invisible from the trail, and to see such an impressive eruption rising from an apparent nothing is startling, to say the least. Startling is a rare performer and is not seen at all during most seasons. The eruptions take place about the time Grotto Fountain (114) would normally be expected to start and thus a few minutes before an anticipated Grotto (111) eruption. Rather than replacing Grotto Fountain, however, Startling plays a decidedly adverse role, usually delaying both Grotto Fountain and Grotto by at least 1 hour for each of what is sometimes a series of eruptions. When in series, the intervals are about 20 minutes, corresponding to the normal fill cycles shown by Indicator Spring (210) and Grotto Fountain Geyser. Startling is a pretty geyser. Both vents send steady jets of water up to 20 feet high throughout durations of 2 to 4 minutes.

116. SPA GEYSER looks something like a large oval bathing pool, but nearly every eruption by Grotto (111) results in overflow at near boiling temperatures in Spa. During most years eruptive episodes are relatively infrequent. Spa is almost exclusively associated with Grotto marathon eruptions, evidently requiring the greater discharge of water by the marathon versus a normal eruption to trigger its action. The activity consists of a series of brief eruptions, usually at intervals of 2 to 5 minutes, during episodes lasting as long as 3 hours. Very explosive, the play bursts large masses of water between 6 and 60 feet high. Close observation will show Grotto to weaken visibly while Spa is active. Also, Spa erupted powerfully after every eruption by Giant Geyser (94) during the 1950s, but such a relationship has not been seen since then.

212. UNNG-GRG-4 ("MARATHON POOL") is the circular spring located on the right (east) side of the trail leading between Spa (116) and Riverside (117) Geysers. Although it is now known that eruptions were seen during 1941, it was only named in 1988 because of its reaction to long duration ("marathon") eruptions by Grotto Geyser (111). Marathon's water level would slowly drop throughout the duration of the marathon. About the time Grotto finally quit, Marathon Pool would erupt as high as 6 feet. Most such activity was restricted to the first few weeks after Giant's eruption on June 28, 1988, and only a few eruptions have occurred since.

117. RIVERSIDE GEYSER is one of the least variable geysers in Yellowstone. On a statistical basis, Riverside is far more regular than Old Faithful and among major geysers is exceeded for accuracy only by Daisy and sometimes Castle. Its large cone proves a very long history of activity, but in fact it was probably dormant when Yellowstone Park was established and first thoroughly explored. Even after it became regularly active about 1881, it was seldom seen by Park visitors. It is largely out of sight from most of the Upper Basin, so less frequent geysers received more attention. Indeed, it was many years before maps and guidebooks were in full agreement as to which geyser really is Riverside — many used the name for what is now called Mortar Geyser (125).

Riverside is nearly an isolated spring, not connected with any others that can significantly alter its behavior. (In 1988 there seemed to be a correlation between Riverside and Grotto Group activity, but the indications were that the springs worked in harmony rather than in competition.) Therefore, the flow of water and energy into its plumbing system is nearly constant, resulting in extreme regularity. Only gradual, long-term changes in the flow rate can alter Riverside's performances. Over the years, average intervals have ranged from $5^1/_2$ to $8^1/_2$ hours.

Unlike those of most regular geysers (but in a fashion similar to Old Faithful), few of Riverside's eruptions occur at the time of the average interval. Instead, nearly all eruptions take place either about 25 minutes before or 20 minutes after the average time. It is the combination of this bimodal distribution of intervals that gives the net average. The predictions the ranger-naturalists make are based on the simple average, because one never knows whether the next interval will be long or short. Beyond that, though, eruptions seldom occur more than 30 minutes off of the average.

The setting of Riverside is superb. The crater rises directly out of the far bank of the Firehole River against a background of grassy meadowland and forest. The cone is shaped somewhat like a chair. The main vent is a shallow basin near the front part of the "seat." On the far side of the seat are two minor vents. The large hole on the chair "back" may once have been the main vent, and some play still issues from it during the beginning stages of an eruption.

Between $1^1/_2$ and 2 hours before an eruption, the main vent begins to overflow. The discharge is variable and is punctuated by boiling spells. About 1 hour before the play, the minor vents behind the main vent begin to bubble, spouting to a few inches. During this preplay, the old vent will occasionally splash directly into the river. A particularly heavy splash initiates the eruption. Boiling over the main vent becomes violent, and within a few seconds Riverside is arching out over the river, sometimes nearly spanning it. The maximum height of 75 feet is held for several minutes. Then the geyser slowly dies down. It doesn't stop spouting for 21 minutes, and that is followed by a short, weak steam phase.

The average interval of Riverside is practically the same now as it was in the 1880s; in early summer 1994 it was slightly over $6^1/_2$ hours. Riverside is a very stable geyser, and it will probably continue to play much as it does now for the better part of centuries to come. With its column arching over the river and a rainbow in its spray, Riverside Geyser is one of the beauties of Yellowstone.

While waiting for an eruption of Riverside, spend a few minutes watching the small pool just behind the benches on the paved trail. An excellent example of an intermittent spring with brief periods of light overflow every few minutes, the pool is known to have played as a geyser in 1950 and following the 1959 earthquake. No details were recorded on either occasion.

THE CHAIN LAKES COMPLEX (numbers 118 through 122, plus 213). The Chain Lakes and surrounding springs on the west side of the paved trail are all interconnected belowground. Geyser activity among the Chain Lakes themselves is rare but is major in size. The activity of the cluster can alter and be altered by that of the Grotto Complex a short distance away.

118. CULVERT GEYSER was hurt, then helped, by the hand of man. When the road was built through the Upper Basin, a number of small springs blocked the engineer's plans. Therefore, they were filled with dirt and forgotten. At this time a spring near Spa Geyser (116) was buried, and another had a retaining wall built around its crater. Now known as Culvert Geyser, the latter was not the boiling pool of today. Apparently, the energy of the buried spring was diverted here. Culvert rapidly enlarged its crater and began spouting to 2 feet. Such play is uncommon now, but Culvert still behaves weakly as an intermittent spring.

213. UNNG-CLC-2 ("PERSISTENT SPRING") might be another expression of the spring that was buried by the road construction and that apparently also led to the development of Culvert Geyser (118). It began to appear during 1988, when it broke out at the edge of the trail a few feet south of Culvert. The perpetual spouting, 1 to 2 feet high, rises from a break in a clay tile pipe.

119. SQUARE SPRING and the two smaller springs beyond it had an episode of eruptions during the 1950s, but no details beyond the fact that they were active were recorded. Square alone had a brief series of eruptions up to 10 feet high following the 1959 earthquake. Reactivating in 1982, it has been playing ever since. It performs mostly as an intermittent spring, but the times of high water are accompanied by bubbling and occasional splashes up to 4 feet high. The intervals are 5 to 10 minutes.

120. LINK GEYSER, so named when it proved to be an important link in the Chain Lakes, is truly a major geyser. Major eruptions are rare, however, much to the disappointment of geyser gazers but to the great delight of maintenance workers. The tremendous eruptions discharge so much water so suddenly that much activity might literally wash away the trail.

Link has had minor eruptions throughout recorded Park history. Recurring on intervals of several hours and lasting 15 to 30 minutes (although some have durations of many hours), these are little more than superheated boiling that is somewhat stronger than normal. Major eruptions probably begin during the minor play, although this is by no means certain.

The signs left by a major eruption are unmistakable, making it unlikely that any had occurred for many years before recorded history and making it certain that none had gone unnoticed more recently. In 1936 signs of activity were observed during the spring months, but no eruption was seen until early summer. Throughout the course of that season, eruptions were reported to the rangers with fair frequency. Sixty feet high and lasting less than 1 minute, they continued into 1937. Link also played in 1940, 1944, and 1946. No further major activity was seen until 1954, and during the next four years Link had a total of fifteen active episodes. In 1957 Link first showed that it could erupt in series, with several eruptions occurring in the course of a day. During such a series, the intervals would lengthen. This sort of action continued periodically through 1958. Then Link fell dormant, and no further major activity was seen until 1968, when there were two eruptions.

On August 8, 1974, Link had a series of eight eruptions. The first interval was 70 minutes, the last 197. Each play lasted less than 1 minute, but so much water was discharged that the Firehole River flowed muddy for a considerable time after each eruption. The play began with a doming of the water within the crater, sending a flood across the surroundings. Then the geyser literally exploded, with jets of water reaching 60 to 100 feet and carrying rocks with them.

A single eruption on September 4, 1983, proved to be a herald of Link's next and most intense active episode on record. Between October 13 and 18 it had forty major eruptions. These were distributed among six individual series, each consisting of as many as twelve eruptions, the starts of which were separated by about 24 hours.

Link has had only five major eruptions since 1983. There was one in April 1989. The play on January 1991 reached only 20 feet high and hardly deserves to be called "major." Link erupted three times during 1993. That on August 6 took place at night and is known only on the basis of washed areas. The eruption on September 11 was seen by many geyser gazers, as the muddy water reached 60 to 75 feet high; another on October 15 was similar.

Link is directly connected with the other members of the Chain Lakes Complex. On occasion the focus of energy may shift to any one of them, resulting in eruptions. Any such action is rare, however. The most frequently cited of these other members is "Bottomless Pit Geyser." There is a Bottomless Pit among the Chain Lakes, but it is a cool pool, and the geyser referred to is probably either Link or North Chain Lake Geyser (121). Indications are that Link has the potential for major activity whenever it is undergoing minor eruptions, but no one can say when or why the next spectacle will take place.

121. NORTH CHAIN LAKE GEYSER was active during 1931–1932 and again in 1953, when it played two or three times per week. A brief series of boiling eruptions 20 feet high followed the 1959 earthquake, but only one eruption has occurred since. Following Link Geyser's (120) intense series of eruptions in October 1983, the energy within the Chain Lakes shifted to North Chain Lakes. On March 25, 1984, it finally responded with a single eruption, bursting to 35 feet high.

122. UNNG-CLC-1 ("CLASP GEYSER") is the northernmost of the Chain Lakes, somewhat separated from the others. It was seen to have a single eruption during 1974, a few days after the active episode by Link Geyser (120) in August. The play was 20 feet high. Although it had a duration of only a few seconds, it seems to have thoroughly upset the system, as overflow, once common, now almost never occurs.

Table 5. Geysers of the Grotto Group, Riverside Geyser, Chain Lake Complex, and the Morning Glory Group

Name	Map No.	Interval	Duration	Height (ft)
Culvert Geyser	118	rare	minutes	2
Fan Geyser	124	2 1/2 days–months	45 min	100–125
Grotto Fountain Geyser	114	7–24 hrs	7–53 min	30–83
Grotto Geyser	111	7–24 hrs	2–15 hrs	15–60
Indicator Spring	210	[1988]	2–4 min	6
Link Geyser, minor	120	3–6 hrs	15–30 min	4
Link Geyser, major	120	[1993]	1 min	20–100
Morning Glory Pool	126	[1944 only]	unknown	40
Mortar Geyser	125	2 1/2 days–months	45 min	40–80
North Chain Lake Geyser	121	[1984]	sec	20
Riverside Geyser	117	5 1/2–8 1/2 hrs	21 min	75
Rocket Geyser	112	with Grotto	2–12 min	40

Table 5 continued

Sentinel Geyser, northwest vent	129	[1983?]	seconds	40
Sentinel Geyser, southeast vent	129	[1992]	12 min	15–20
Serpent's Tongue	128	steady	steady	2
South Grotto Fountain Geyser	115	7–24 hrs	5–30 min	10
Spa Geyser	116	2–5 min *	seconds	6–60
Spiteful Geyser	123	[1984]	minutes	10–30
Square Spring	119	5–10 min *	1–2 min	4
UNNG–CLC–1 ("Clasp")	122	[1974]	seconds	20
UNNG–CLC–2 ("Persistent Spring")	213	steady	steady	1–2
UNNG–GRG–1 ("Variable Spring")	113	minutes *	sec–min	2
UNNG–GRG–2 ("Central Vents")	209	irregular	minutes	1–3
UNNG–GRG–3 ("Startling")	211	[1991]	2–4 min	20
UNNG–GRG–4 ("Marathon Pool")	212	rare	20–40 min	1–6
West Sentinel Geyser	127	near steady	near steady	2–20

* When active.

[ ] Brackets enclose the year of most recent activity for extremely rare or dormant geysers. See text.

Morning Glory Group

Lying at the northwestern limit of the Upper Geyser Basin proper is the Morning Glory Group (Map F, Table 5). Named for Morning Glory Pool, the area contains seven geysers. A small collection of muddy springs known as the "Norris Pools," across the trail from Spiteful Geyser, are poor mud pots but are still among the best examples in the Upper Basin.

The developed Upper Basin Trail ends at Morning Glory Pool. Downstream from here it is about half a mile to the next cluster of springs, the Cascade Group. Between the two groups are a narrowing of the Firehole River and a hill, marking the end of the continuous open valley of the Upper

Geyser Basin. An unimproved trail follows the route of the old highway that traversed the Upper Basin through 1970 and leads past the Cascade and "Old Road" groups to Biscuit Basin.

123. SPITEFUL GEYSER occupies a deep and jagged crater right next to the trail. In 1884 tour guide G. L. Henderson wrote, "The Spiteful stones unwary heads, her water sources being dry." This is apparently a reference to the steam explosion that formed the crater at what had previously been a cluster of small geysers or spouters. It lies on a prominent fracture in the sinter that probably owes its origin to a prehistoric earthquake of considerable size. After some early eruptions, though, Spiteful was dormant until 1964. The new activity was very regular, with eruptions recurring every 15 minutes and reaching 10 feet high. The crater always remained empty between the plays. Following a brief dormancy, Spiteful rejuvenated in the early 1970s. The new activity was much more irregular than before. Always starting with the crater full, the geyser would rocket thin jets of water as high as 30 feet. This action slowly waned into another dormant period by 1974, which, with the exception of a single eruption in 1984, continues to the present.

124 and 125. FAN GEYSER AND MORTAR GEYSER cannot be discussed separately. With only a few minor modern exceptions, these two geysers always erupt in concert. Fan, with no fewer than eleven separate vents giving rise to as many as seventeen jets of water, lies along the same fracture that includes the crater of Spiteful Geyser (123). The two cones to the left, next to the Firehole River, are Mortar.

The large size of Mortar's cones and the great amount of erosion in the area prove that these geysers were very active in the past. But during most of recorded history, Fan and Mortar have erupted rather infrequently. During the first two decades of the Park, there was considerable confusion about which geyser was which. Mortar was often referred to as Riverside while at the same time other authorities called it Fan, and Fan was sometimes barely mentioned as "Perpetual

The fan-shaped nature of Fan Geyser's many separate water jets is most obvious when an eruption is seen backlit by a low sun.

Spouter." Numerous references, including the earlier editions of this book, state that Fan played as often as every 8 hours during the 1870s and 1880s. This is now known to be incorrect, the old records having apparently referred to today's Riverside. Instead, during those early years virtually all major activity here was from Mortar *without* Fan. Fan was rare and weak compared to how it is today. In essence, Fan and Mortar largely behaved as separate geysers during the 1800s. Only one concerted major eruption of the modern sort was described prior to 1925; that occurred in 1878. Somehow in the interim the two became so directly joined at depth that they are now effectively one very large geyser.

During the intervening years, minor activity occurred often. Even periods considered dormant were punctuated by such play. At these times Fan would spout about 3 feet high, ordinarily not accompanied by Mortar. On other occasions, especially in 1915, Mortar would have eruptions up to 30 feet high every 2 hours, not accompanied by Fan.

The first time they acted together as major geysers was in 1925, and there may have been some major eruptions during the early 1930s. It was not until late August 1937, however, that Fan and Mortar began comparatively frequent action. From that year through 1968, just a dozen or so individual eruptions were described among records that simply list them as "active." A rejuvenation in 1969 marked the start of the modern performances. Over 500 eruptions have taken place in the years since, and the only two years totally without major activity were 1975 and 1978. Through much of this time there were clear cycles to the performances. Following two to three years of frequent eruptions would be another one to two years with few or none. Since Fan and Mortar are not known to be connected with any other feature except Spiteful Geyser, why such cycles took place is unknown. They seem to have failed in the 1990s. In addition, Fan and Mortar tend to decline in frequency during the late spring and early summer months, in this case probably because of a quenching action by the spring thaw and high river levels.

When Fan and Mortar are active, they pass through a series of "hot cycles" prior to an eruption. Lasting between 1 and 3 hours, these cycles involve (1) a pause in which neither geyser is splashing, (2) surging in Mortar's lower vent, (3) jetting in three of Fan's vents, and (4) a return toward Mortar and another pause. These cycles are marked by very clear-cut stages that allow experienced observers to "guesstimate" when the next eruption might happen. Eruptions always begin while Fan is splashing. The force of the action increases, but there will be no eruption unless the play becomes steady jetting from all three vents. Within seconds to minutes, the water level lifts in both Fan and Mortar, and the eruption is on. The beginning is explosive and is virtually simultaneous in both geysers. The main vent of Fan arches up and out to as much as 125 feet high, the spray reaching well across the trail. During one extraordinary eruption, the horizontal throw of this column was over 200 feet. Meanwhile, several of Fan's other vents play as much as 60 feet high, each at its own angle, so the play does indeed resemble a fan. At the same time, Mortar is striving for and deserving of attention. Both of its vents can play over 50 feet high. Interestingly, some eruptions are dominated by the lower vent and others by the upper vent, either of which can reach 80 feet when the other temporarily shuts off. It is an indescribable spectacle.

The most impressive part of the eruption takes place during the first 10 to 15 minutes. During that time the eruption is steady, without any pause or diminishing size. Then the play stops almost without warning, only to resume moments later. After a few more minutes comes another pause. With each of these the renewed eruption is weaker. The last water jetting normally takes place after a duration of 45 minutes. Periodic steam bursts may persist for still another 45 minutes, giving a total duration as great as $1^1/_2$ hours.

When performing at their best, Fan and Mortar range between $2^1/_2$ and 5 days between eruptions. Since they resume their hot cycles within a few hours of an eruption, though, why they aren't more frequent is not clear. One speculation is that the Fan-Spiteful fracture extends into the Firehole River, allowing cold river water to flow into the plumbing systems. As it is, unless something more precise is learned, to see Fan and Mortar erupt requires either great luck or tremendous patience. It's worth a wait. As Dr. G. D. Marler, long-time Park Service geyser expert, wrote in his *Studies of Geysers and Hot Springs* in 1968, "To see eruptions of Fan and Mortar is to view some of the most spectacular activity in the Park. The infernal region would seem to have broken loose in full fury."

126. MORNING GLORY POOL is one of Yellowstone's most famous hot springs. Before the highway was removed from the area in 1971, it was visited by more people than any other spring or geyser except Old Faithful. There are many more beautiful pools, but this one, lying as it does at the entrance to the Upper Geyser Basin and next to what was the only access into the area, became a natural candidate for popularity.

That Morning Glory once was, and potentially still is, a geyser is shown by the deep runoff channels leading down to the Firehole River. Only one natural eruption has been recorded, and that occurred in 1944. The duration of the play is unknown, but the height was at least 40 feet, and a tremendous amount of water was thrown out.

Its popularity may have spelled the demise of Morning Glory Pool. In the past it was usually hot enough to prevent any growth of cyanobacteria within the crater. The color of the pool was a delicate pale blue, unlike that of any other. But people have thrown so much debris into the crater that the vent is becoming plugged. Hot water has smaller egress into the crater, and the temperature has dropped. Cyanobacteria can grow far down into the crater, and the color is much less beautiful than it used to be.

Because it was known to possess geyser potential, Morning Glory was artificially induced to erupt in 1950. The purpose was to empty the crater so it could be cleaned. The list of material disgorged is amazing. It included $86.27 in pennies, $8.10 in other coins, tax tokens from nine states, logs, bottles, tin cans, seventy-six handkerchiefs, towels, socks, shirts, and "delicate items of underclothing." Overall, 112 different kinds of items were recovered. Since 1950 several additional attempts to induce eruptions have been made, all without success. Many coins and rocks can be seen lining small benches on the crater walls. But Morning Glory Pool was not created to be used as a wishing well. If such action by Park visitors continues much longer, Morning Glory will become completely clogged. It would be a tragic loss.

127. WEST SENTINEL GEYSER and its companion across the river (129) were named because they seemed to guard the entrance to the Upper Geyser Basin. Now other, more northerly hot spring groups are included in the basin, and the two Sentinels go nearly unnoticed.

West Sentinel usually acts as a perpetual spouter. The eruption is a surging boiling of the water up to 2 feet high. True intermittent eruptions 4 feet high took place for a brief time following the 1959 earthquake, and a few more reaching 10 feet were seen in 1991 and 1992.

128. SERPENT'S TONGUE is a small, somewhat cavernous spring up against the hillside behind West Sentinel Geyser (127). It is a perpetual spouter, playing about 2 feet high. The name originated from the eruptive steam bubbles, which enter the crater in a darting fashion.

129. SENTINEL GEYSER, also known as East Sentinel, is actually two geysers within one crater. The large cone forms an island at the side of the Firehole River during much of the year and following heavy rains. At these times, river water pours directly into some associated vents, stifling any potential eruptions. When the river is low, Sentinel boils constantly but eruptions are rare, with active episodes being weeks, months, and even years apart.

Both of the Sentinel geysers erupt at an angle. One, which was especially active during the early 1980s, plays upstream toward the riverbank from the far northwest side of the crater. A shallow gully has been eroded by these eruptions, which reach up to 40 feet high but have durations of only a few seconds. The other geyser plays from the near, southeast side of the crater and arches its water jet into the river. Active in the late 1980s and into the 1990s, it can have series of eruptions. A series starts with a major eruption up to 20 feet high and reaching outward 15 to 20 feet for as long as 12 minutes; the follow-up minors are much weaker and last 4 minutes or less.

The pool on top of a large geyserite platform downstream and across the river from Sentinel is called "Green Star Spring."

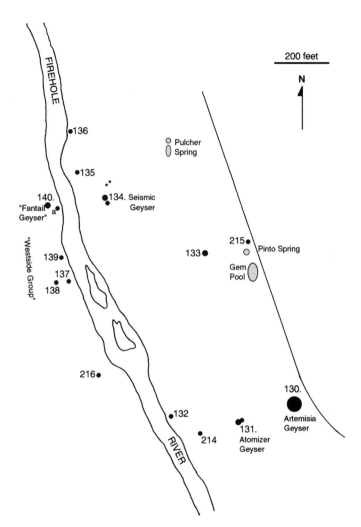

Map G. Cascade Group and "Westside"Group

Cascade Group

Historically, the Cascade Group (Map G, Table 6) has been nearly ignored. It includes Artemisia and Atomizer Geysers, both of which are among the more important geysers in the

Upper Basin, but because these springs lie over a hill from the Morning Glory Group and are hidden by dense stands of pines on the other sides, they have been observed comparatively infrequently.

No trail proceeds directly through the Cascade Group. The route of the old highway between Morning Glory Pool and Biscuit Basin is designated as a trail, and it affords the best views of the area. Across the river, running from the vicinity of Daisy Geyser to Biscuit Basin, is another trail, which provides better views of Hillside and Seismic Geysers as well as the members of the "Old Road Group." It must be emphasized that access to the Cascade Group is restricted to these trails. Wandering off the trail among the hot springs is illegal, and persons doing so are subject to arrest.

130. ARTEMISIA GEYSER was named because of the grayish-green color of some of its geyserite formations, which are very similar in color to the foliage of sagebrush (scientific name *Artemisia*). Artemisia has one of the largest craters of any hot spring in Yellowstone and is one of the more beautiful blue pools in addition to being a major geyser. During its long quiet period there is a steady overflow. Eruptions begin without any apparent warning when the water level suddenly rises to cause a spectacular flood across the geyserite platform below the pool. As the play slowly builds in force, a vigorous thumping underground can be felt and heard as steam bubbles repeatedly form and collapse within the plumbing. A minute or so is required for Artemisia to reach its full force, which is a massive boiling rather than bursting or jetting. Some of the surges can reach over 30 feet high. The eruptions last between 16 and 26 minutes, and although most of the larger surges occur near the middle of the duration, some often take place in the very last seconds of the activity. Following the eruption the water level drops slowly, requiring at least 30 minutes to fall about 18 inches. Refilling is extremely slow, taking about 5 hours before overflow is resumed. In recent years the intervals were predictably regular, almost always averaging between 9 and 12 hours. In 1992, with no known cause, Artemisia became much more

Atomizer Geyser plays a beautifully slender, pulsating jet of water from a low geyserite cone.

erratic. The intervals now range from 11 to 17 hours, with occasional gaps as great as 32 hours.

Minor eruptions were rare until 1985, but they have been quite common since then, sometimes occurring as often as once every two or three days. A minor eruption starts and progresses identically to a normal eruption, but it ends after a duration of only 5 minutes. The refilling of the crater is accomplished within 2 hours, and the following interval can be as short as 6 hours.

131. ATOMIZER GEYSER plays from two small cones, both about 3 feet tall, which lie directly beyond Artemisia Geyser (130) near a small stand of trees. Atomizer shows an interesting progression of activity through the cycle leading to its major eruption.

Following a major eruption, a few hours will pass before the plumbing system has refilled with water. Then there will be a number of brief episodes of overflow from the main vent (atop the southern, left-hand cone). Once these have begun, they recur every few minutes. Accompanied by bubbling, they inspired the geyser's original name, "Restless." It will usually be 6 to 8 hours after the major, and 2 to 4 hours after the first overflow, until the first of a series of minor eruptions takes place. Minors then recur about every hour, with six to eight usually occurring prior to the next major eruption. It is possible to tell approximately where Atomizer is within its minor series based on observing the duration and the height of a single minor. The first eruption of the series lasts less than 30 seconds and is only 20 to 25 feet high. Each subsequent minor is somewhat longer and stronger than the one before, and the last of a series often lasts well over 1 minute and reaches up to 35 feet high. In addition, whereas the minor intervals are about 1 hour, sometimes (not always) the *next to the last* minor interval will approach 2 hours instead. The final interval, from the last minor to the major, is usually 1 hour, too. Infrequent final intervals as short as 12 minutes are known, as are a very few as long as $1^3/_4$ hours.

The major eruption is indistinguishable from a minor until the end of its first minute or so. At that point, rather than quitting abruptly, the force increases. The height reaches between 40 and 50 (rarely, 60) feet. The water phase duration is 8 to 10 minutes. The play then gives way to a steam phase, which is loud enough to be heard from the trail as long as 50 minutes into the eruption. It is only at the time of a major eruption that the second (right-hand) cone joins the other. Nearly sealed in by internal deposits of geyserite, this is the actual "atomizer." During the steam phase, it sends steam and fine spray a few feet high.

Atomizer is regular enough to be predicted. The known range is from $12^{1}/_{2}$ to 19 hours between successive major eruptions, but almost all fall within a much tighter 14 to 16 hours. A 2-hour wait for Atomizer can be wonderfully rewarding.

214. RESTLESS GEYSER, recently more often called "Owl's Mask Spring," is a beautiful small spouter whose basin shares some of the sagebrush-gray color with Artemisia Geyser (130). The spring, with its 1- to 2-foot perpetual splashing, is visible only from near the Daisy Geyser–Biscuit Basin Trail on the west side of the Firehole River. Although the name "Restless" was first applied to Atomizer Geyser (131), confusion in interpreting early Yellowstone literature resulted in its official placement here.

132. "SLIDE GEYSER" is located on the high bank of the Firehole River below Atomizer Geyser (131). There is no record of activity from Slide prior to 1974. The vent opens directly onto a precipitous slope so that its erupted water seems to slide rather than flow to the river below. Slide is fairly regular in its performances. Intervals range from 5 to 20 minutes, with little variation at any given time. The water bursts out of the cavernous vent so that the play is almost horizontal, with jets sometimes reaching directly outward as far as 10 feet. Slide was dormant for part of 1991, and its intervals have generally been getting longer with each passing season. It can be viewed from the edge of the forest across the river, near the trail between Daisy Geyser and Biscuit Basin.

133. CALTHOS SPRING was clearly very active in the distant past. The deep crater sits in the middle of an extensive but highly eroded sinter platform, which is drained by a single, very wide and deep runoff channel. The present pool is perfectly quiet, however. Difficult to see from the trail, it is intensely blue in color. The only activity on record was triggered by the 1959 earthquake. For a few weeks Calthos underwent irregular eruptions, some of which reached 10 to 15 feet high but lasted only 1 minute. Although they were brief, the water discharged by these eruptions was prodigious, easily filling the runoff channel. During this active phase was the only known time when the water level in nearby Gem Pool was below overflow. For the next few years the two springs would alternately ebb and flow. Then Gem resumed the steady discharge that had characterized it since the discovery of the Park. The only further flow from Calthos occurred during 1970 and 1981–1982, and it was slight.

215. SPRITE POOL barely merits a place in this book. Its discharge flows down the trail, which passes right next to the pool. Sprite behaves mostly as an intermittent spring. During high water there is a steady bubbling over the vent, and on infrequent occasions this can be vigorous enough to cause a few splashes up to 1 foot high. Some authorities contend that such random splashing in what is otherwise much too weak to constitute a geyser eruption does not qualify the spring as a geyser. Suit yourself on this one.

134. SEISMIC GEYSER is famous for having been the most significant direct creation of the 1959 earthquake. A crack formed in the sinter and became the site of a small steam vent. Activity increased over the next $3^1/_2$ years until a steam explosion blew out the geyser crater. The force continued to increase even then, and the newly formed geyser became stronger and more explosive every year. By 1966 the eruptions were reaching from 50 to 75 feet high. But as the strength of the play grew stronger, the intervals between them also increased. When a small satellite crater was developed by a new steam explosion in 1971, most of the eruptive energy shifted to the new vent, which was called Seismic's Satellite. Eruptions soon became more constant and smaller in size. Ever so slowly, Seismic and Seismic's Satellite died out. The last true eruptions in Seismic were seen during 1974, and intermittent boiling has been rare in Satellite since about 1984.

Seismic Geyser is unquestionably connected with several other hot springs. The more important of these are Hillside Geyser (135) just downstream and the Pulcher Springs that lie among the trees a short distance up the slope. As Seismic increased in vigor, these other springs declined dramatically. Now that Seismic itself has declined, these related features have recovered to some degree. Seismic continues to pour out a heavy flow of water, however, making it unlikely that any of these other hot springs will ever resemble their pre-1959 states. It is interesting that the 1986 development of Fantail Geyser (140) directly across the river seemed to have no effect on Seismic.

135. HILLSIDE GEYSER was a boiling pool never seen in eruption prior to 1948. It was active with 20-foot eruptions throughout that year but then had few additional eruptions until a new cycle was initiated by the 1959 earthquake. Major eruptions, up to 30 feet high, occurred with great regularity every 26 minutes and lasted 4 minutes. Such activity lasted into 1961, then only minor play similar to that of 1948 was seen. These eruptions were just 3 feet high, and even they stopped in 1964, about the time nearby Seismic Geyser (134) began having its large, explosive eruptions. The water level is now about 10 feet below ground level.

Just up the slope from Hillside Geyser, two small geysers appeared during 1982. After just one year of action up to 3 feet high, they ceased to erupt. There is no other record of activity by them, either before or since.

136. UNNG-CDG-1 ("BROKEN CONE" OR "OCHEROUS GEYSER") plays from a decayed, iron oxide–colored vent immediately adjacent to the Firehole River, a short distance downstream from Hillside Geyser (135). The first eruptions of record were seen during the early 1980s. The intervals are very irregular, ranging from just 5 minutes to hours long; it could be that a cyclic pattern is at work here, but no real studies of the geyser have been performed. The height is usually not more than 3 feet, although some exceptional eruptions during 1983 reached at least 25 feet high. The duration is never more than a few seconds.

Table 6. Geysers of the Cascade Group

Name	Map No.	Interval	Duration	Height (ft)
Artemisia Geyser, minor	130	days	5 min	30
Artemisia Geyser, normal	130	9–32 hrs	16–22 min	30
Atomizer Geyser, minor	131	1–2 hrs	30–90 sec	25–35
Atomizer Geyser, major	131	12 1/2–16 hrs	50 min	40–60
Calthos Spring	133	[1959]	1 min	10–15
Hillside Geyser	135	[1964]	3–4 min	3–30
Restless Geyser	214	steady	steady	1
Seismic Geyser	134	[1974]	minutes	3–75
Seismic's Satellite Geyser	134	[1984]	long	boil–6
"Slide Geyser"	132	5–20 min *	1–1 1/2 min	10 horiz.
Sprite Pool	215	hours	1–2 hrs	1
UNNG–CDG–1 ("Broken Cone")	136	irregular	seconds	3–25

* When active.
[ ] Brackets enclose the year of most recent activity for extremely rare or dormant geysers. See text.

"Westside Group"

The name "Westside Group" was devised for the second edition of this book. The area (Map G, Table 7) contains a number of small hot springs and at least four geysers. Located directly across the Firehole River from the Cascade Group, these springs are probably physical members of that group (although there was no observable relationship between Seismic Geyser and Fantail Geyser during 1986). The groups are handled separately because of the clear topographical division caused by the river. The "Westside Group" is accessible by way of the trail that runs through the forest between the Daisy Group and Biscuit Basin.

In addition to the geysers and other hot springs in this area, an area of ground to the northwest of Fantail Geyser (140) began to heat up during 1984. It is believed that this phenomenon was triggered by the Borah Peak earthquake in 1983. By midsummer 1985 ground temperatures were as high as 205°F (95°C), hot enough to cause a distillation of organic matter in and on the ground. The sickeningly sweet odor of burned sugar can still be smelled when the wind is right (or wrong!), although the temperature of the soil has dropped.

216. "YM-210" (or "SOUTH POOL"), the southernmost feature of the "Westside Group," served as a numbered water sample reference point on the thermal-area maps produced by the U.S. Geological Survey in the years following the 1959 earthquake. It apparently had a few eruptions at that time, but so little was recorded that we had no idea as to the geyser's frequency, duration, height, and so on. It was exciting, then, when YM-210 proved to be a significant geyser during 1989. It had numerous eruptive episodes over several months that spring and summer. The play occurred as a series of eruptions, with a major eruption beginning each cycle. Up to 15 feet high, the water discharge was huge throughout most of the 10- to 15-minute duration. The major was followed by a series of minor eruptions over the course of at least 5 hours; these discharged little water, rising from a pool level several feet belowground. After a yearlong dormancy, YM-210 was active in a similar fashion during 1991. Additional minor eruptions, not in series and without any majors, took place in early 1992. When inactive, and between eruptive episodes, YM-210 is a pale greenish pool with only a trickle of overflow.

137. UNNG-WSG-1 is a slitlike vent at the top of the Firehole River bank. More forceful than it looks at first glance, the eruption does not seem impressive because its horizontal nature confines it almost entirely to within the slit itself. This

geyser is in eruption most of the time; periods of complete quiet never last more than a few seconds, and the durations can exceed 5 minutes.

138. UNNG-WSG-2 ("BIGFOOT GEYSER") plays from an oblong, foot-shaped crater. It is surrounded by several other hot springs, most of which act as small perpetual spouters. Bigfoot's vent is at its south end (in the heel of the foot). The intervals between eruptions are usually about $1^1/_2$ minutes long and are highly regular. Durations range from 30 to 40 seconds, and when Bigfoot is at its best, the splashing can reach over 6 feet high. This activity apparently began with the 1959 earthquake.

139. UNNG-WSG-3 ("CARAPACE GEYSER") is a cyclic and usually inactive geyser that can be very impressive in its time. Located immediately above the river, the cone's overall shape vaguely resembles the carapace of a tortoise. It is dormant most years. The most common form of activity is only a surging, bubbling intermittent overflow. When active as a geyser, as it was in 1993, Carapace can erupt as often as every 5 to 20 minutes. At other times intervals as long as 6 hours have been known. The eruptions come in two forms. Minor eruptions with durations of about 1 minute and heights of less than 3 feet are typical. Major eruptions are rare, but they may burst water up to 10 feet high for $2^1/_2$ to 5 minutes.

140. "FANTAIL GEYSER" was perhaps *the* geyser story of 1986. It had been a large, superheated pool during all of previous Park history. The water was clear most of the time but was occasionally murky because of suspended clay particles. That murkiness might imply that Fantail had infrequent eruptions, but none was positively known until 1985. No play was actually seen even then, but the surrounding sinter platform was washed clean of gravel, and the extent of the washed areas implied heavy overflow, perhaps accompanied by bursts several feet high.

Fantail became a major geyser in April 1986. From its very beginning, and persisting through most of summer

"Fantail Geyser" was powerful, beautiful, and extremely regular during 1986, when its only known active phase lasted less than six months.

1986, it was a highly regular and imminently predictable geyser, which allowed many people to enjoy its unique performances. The intervals were 6 hours. Following about 2 hours of intermittent boiling of increasing intensity, the eruption began with heavy surging that only gradually built up to the full force. Massive bursts and jets rose from both of the two craters, at their best reaching fully 75 feet high from one and perhaps 50 feet at an angle from the other. The play did not significantly decrease its strength until near the end of the 45-minute duration, when a powerful steam phase began. The show was truly amazing.

Very suddenly, in mid-August 1986, Fantail became erratic. The eruptions grew weaker, and the durations of only 10 minutes failed to result in a steam phase. Eruptions ceased completely before the end of October. Fantail had a few additional eruptions between 1987 and 1990. These were weak and probably random events. They were only a few feet high, and the intervals between them were on the order of months. There have been no eruptions since 1990.

140A. "OUZEL GEYSER" spends much of its time under the water of the Firehole River, like its namesake bird. The cold stream water usually quenches any potential eruptions, but it was active, along with Fantail (140) during 1986. Always an irregular and brief performer, some of the bursts of Ouzel's first eruptions reached over 50 feet high. It quickly died down, however, and was nearly dormant even before the decline in Fantail. Ouzel had a few more, independent eruptions 10 to 15 feet high during 1989 but has not been seen since.

Table 7. Geysers of the "Westside Group"

Name	Map No.	Interval	Duration	Height (ft)
"Fantail Geyser"	140	[1990]	10–45 min	40–75
"Ouzel Geyser"	140a	[1989]	seconds	2–50
UNNG–WSG–1	137	minutes	5 min	horizontal
UNNG–WSG–2 ("Bigfoot")	138	1–2 min	30–40 sec	2–6
UNNG–WSG–3 ("Carapace")	139	5–20 min *	1–5 min	1–10
"YM–210" ("South Pool")	216	infrequent	10–15 min	15

* When active.
[ ] Brackets enclose the year of most recent activity for extremely rare or dormant geysers. See text.

Biscuit Basin

The area traditionally included within the Biscuit Basin is more than half a mile long. The span covers two distinct groups of hot springs. One group lies parallel to the route of the old highway through the Upper Basin; this right-of-way does not enter among the hot springs, but it does provide the only reasonably close view of them. This group is referred to as the "Old Road Group" of Biscuit Basin. The Sapphire Group of Biscuit Basin, also referred to historically as the "Main Group" and "Soda Group," is on the west side of the Firehole River. It is traversed by a boardwalk, and a parking lot provides easy access.

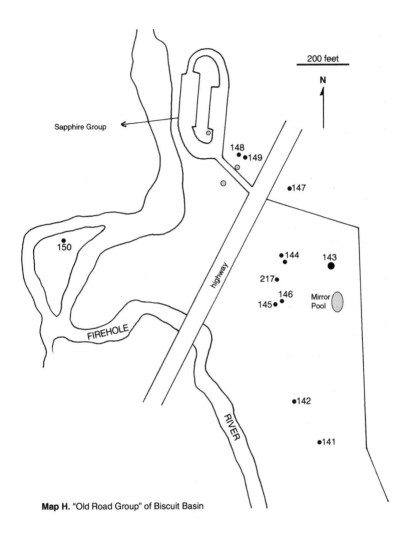

Map H. "Old Road Group" of Biscuit Basin

"Old Road Group" of Biscuit Basin

The "Old Road Group" (Map H, Table 8) occupies an old sinter platform. It is a wide-open area with little relief that can be reached only by following the trail along the old highway route. Many hot springs perforate this expanse, but the group contains only about ten, mostly small geysers. Note that some of the geysers are completely invisible from the established trail, but leaving the trail to wander among the springs is illegal.

141. BABY DAISY GEYSER was first observed to erupt during 1952. Along with it, seven other nearby springs erupted. None of these had ever exhibited any sort of previous animation. Baby Daisy was named because its eruptions were strongly reminiscent of those of the much larger Daisy Geyser (106). The play, 30 feet high at an angle, recurred every 105 minutes and was remarkably regular during 1952. In 1959, following the earthquake, additional eruptions occurred. This play was identical to that of before, except that the intervals were considerably shorter and were irregular. The runoff channels leading away from Baby Daisy were washed clean during 1980, and several times the pool was found to be a few inches below overflow. No eruptions were actually witnessed, however, and washed areas indicated that the play was nothing more than small splashes at the most.

142. BISCUIT BASIN GEYSER was one of the seven springs activated at the same time as Baby Daisy Geyser (141) in 1952. It was much larger, with bursting eruptions reaching 75 feet high. Always irregular, it had several eruptions on some days but none on others, each one lasting only 1 to $1^1/_2$ minutes. Because the crater is drained only by the shallow runoff channels created in 1952, it is believed that this was Biscuit Basin's first and only activity. The 1959 earthquake caused no change in the geyser's appearance.

143. CAULIFLOWER GEYSER has a large crater lined with cauliflower-like nodules of geyserite. Water continuously stands several inches below overflow in this aquamarine spring. The eruption begins with a sudden rise in the water level, accompanied by heavy boiling and copious discharge. The duration is 1 to 3 minutes. For years it seemed that the intervals were always either 20 *or* 40 minutes long, but they have become generally longer and more erratic in recent times. Beginning in 1980 and continuing into 1988, Cauliflower infrequently had large bursts during some eruptions. These reached an estimated 30 feet high, and at least two 1986 eruptions seen from distant Fantail Geyser (140) were probably double that.

144. UNNG-ORG-1 erupts from a small vent at the eastern corner of a shallow crater about 200 feet west of Cauliflower Geyser (143). Its activity began with the 1959 earthquake, and eruptions 5 feet high recurred every 5 minutes until the late 1970s. It was also active on occasion during the 1980s, but then the play reached only 1 foot.

At the northwestern edge of this same crater, another vent has also been occasionally active since 1983. Its eruptions do little more than cause a surface turbulence and slightly heavier overflow. Like ORG-1, the interval is about 5 minutes and the duration a few seconds.

145. UNNG-ORG-2 is hidden in some trees some 200 feet south of ORG-1 (144). The crater of this spring is solidly lined with beautifully beaded geyserite, much of which is stained a pale orange by iron oxide minerals. The eruptions, about 3 feet high, are small enough to be confined entirely to the crater so they are never visible from the trail. The play recurs every 2 or 3 minutes and lasts 10 to 15 seconds. Like so many others, this geyser apparently began its current activity at the time of the 1959 earthquake.

146. UNNG-ORG-3 ("DEMISE GEYSER"), just a few feet north of ORG-2 (145), is erratic and infrequently active. It received its informal name because the wash of the eruptions seems to be hastening the geyser's demise, severely eroding the crater and filling it in. The play is a steady jetting of steamy spray, some of which can reach more than 30 feet outward at a sharp angle. Demise is probably cyclic, erupting every few minutes over a stretch of several hours. These active episodes are days to weeks apart, so that Demise is rarely seen.

217. UNNG-ORG-5 had its best and practically its only activity during 1986 and 1987. Early in this activity a second vent was opened next to the original crater, and this often took over most of the action. Located at the edge of one of Cauliflower Geyser's (143) main runoff channels between ORG-1 (144) and ORG-3 (146), some of the bursts reached 10 to 15 feet high. When it was at its best, the intervals were as short as 40 minutes. The eruptions substantially enlarged the crater and eroded the plumbing system. Many of the last eruptions were nothing more than gushing overflow.

147. UNNG-ORG-4 ("MERCURY GEYSER") is located near the east side of the modern highway, opposite the entrance to the Biscuit Basin parking lot. It is highly irregular in its performances. Intervals of only a few minutes have been seen on some occasions, but a span of 1 to 2 hours is more common. The play reaches between 2 and 6 feet high, but there is little or no runoff. Mercury is essentially dormant during some seasons, when weak and brief eruptions are hours and even days apart.

148. RUSTY GEYSER is one of the most visible geysers in the Upper Geyser Basin. It is located just to the right (north) of the entry road to the Biscuit Basin parking lot. Before 1959 this geyser was cyclic in its activity, with dormant periods being the rule. At such times the rusty-colored crater would pass almost unnoticed. Since the quake, Rusty has been almost continuously active. Eruptions recur every 1 to 4 minutes (occasionally 9 to 13 minutes), last 10 to 45 seconds, and burst as much as 10 feet high.

149. "DUSTY GEYSER" erupts from a low sinter cone just a few feet east of Rusty Geyser (148). Because its geyserite lacks the iron oxide staining of Rusty, the duller appearance led to its name. When active during the 1970s and early 1980s, Dusty erupted several times per day. Each eruption lasted about 3 minutes and was up to 15 feet high. Dusty and Rusty could often be seen together, providing an impressive pair of eruptions. Unfortunately, Dusty has been nearly dormant since about 1987. Infrequent small splashes sufficient only to keep the surroundings wet are seen from it.

150. ISLAND GEYSER is somewhat separated from the other geysers of the group. Its crater is on a low, marshy island in the Firehole River. After the 1959 earthquake, numerous small springs developed on the island. About a dozen of these were geysers. In 1966 one took over the major function and began a steady spouting to 6 feet. After the 1983 earthquake, the play increased in size, with some jets exceeding 20 feet high. Island remained a perpetual spouter, however, until it began periodic action in 1986. Although now seldom playing more than 10 feet high, it is a true geyser with infrequent but fully quiet spells as long as 3 minutes separating durations of many minutes.

Table 8. Geysers of the "Old Road Group" of Biscuit Basin

Name	Map No.	Interval	Duration	Height (ft)
Baby Daisy Geyser	141	[1980]	2 min	30
Biscuit Basin Geyser	142	[1952]	1–1 1/2 min	75
Cauliflower Geyser	143	20 min–hrs	1–3 min	boil–60
"Dusty Geyser"	149	[1987]	3 min	15
Island Geyser	150	sec–3 min	5–20 min	10
Rusty Geyser	148	1–13 min	10–45 sec	3–10
UNNG-ORG-1	144	5 min *	5 min	1
UNNG-ORG-2	145	2–3 min	10–15 sec	3
UNNG-ORG-3 ("Demise")	146	minutes *	minutes	30
UNNG-ORG-4 ("Mercury")	147	irregular *	minutes	2–6
UNNG-ORG-5	217	[1987]	4–8 min	15

* When active.
[ ] Brackets enclose the year of most recent activity for extremely rare or dormant geysers. See text.

Sapphire Group of Biscuit Basin

Lying on the west side of the Firehole River is the Biscuit Basin proper. It received this common, modern name after

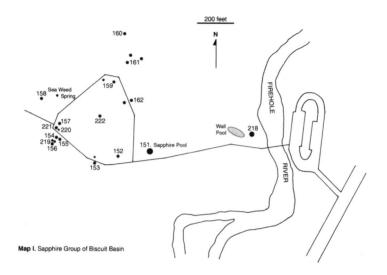

Map I. Sapphire Group of Biscuit Basin

the delicately formed nodules of geyserite that resembled biscuits. The best examples were at Sapphire Pool, but they no longer exist, having been blown away by powerful post-1959 earthquake eruptions. Sapphire Group is the officially approved name; "Soda Group" has also been used.

The Sapphire Group (Map I, Table 9) is traversed by a boardwalk, and every spring and geyser is easily visible. At the far west side of the basin, a dirt trail leads up the valley of the Little Firehole River to Mystic Falls, and a side trip half-way to the falls takes one up the bluff to an overlook view of the entire Upper Geyser Basin.

218. BLACK OPAL POOL occupies a rather large hydrothermal explosion crater that formed in 1934, apparently as a continuation of similar steam explosions that created nearby Wall Pool in 1912, 1918, and 1925. The large boulders of sandstone and conglomerate scattered around this area were blown out by these eruptions. Episodes of geyser eruptions, which were often single bursts 20 to 30 feet high, were then seen in 1937 and 1947-1948. The last known activity occurred during 1953, when rocks and sand were thrown as far as 50 feet.

151. SAPPHIRE POOL gained early notoriety as one of the more beautiful pools in Yellowstone. The crater is of great depth, giving the water an incredibly rich sapphire-blue color. Since discovery, Sapphire has been known as a geyser. Minor eruptions occurred every few minutes, doming the water to about 6 feet with resultant heavy overflow.

No spring in Yellowstone was more greatly affected by the 1959 earthquake than Sapphire. The day after the shocks the crater was filled with muddy water, constantly boiling with vigor. Four weeks later Sapphire began having tremendous eruptions. Fully 125 feet high and almost equally wide, these eruptions were among the most powerful ever known in Yellowstone. At first, the intervals were as short as 2 hours, and each play lasted 5 minutes.

The huge eruptions were short-lived. In time, Sapphire began to have short dormancies, and the periods of activity gradually grew shorter while dormant episodes became longer. In hand with this, during active phases the intervals between eruptions shortened, but the force of the play subsided. By 1964 no eruptions were more than 20 feet high. It wasn't until 1971 that Sapphire finally cleared all muddiness from its water, at about the same time true eruptive activity finally stopped.

Only time will tell whether Sapphire will ever again undergo major eruptions. There is plenty of evidence that the geyser damaged its plumbing system. Prior to 1959 the crater was circular and 15 feet in diameter; today it is oval, measuring 18 by 30 feet. The explosive activity that enlarged the crater also eroded substantial amounts of material from within the plumbing system. The frequent minor eruptions seen before 1959 no longer occur, and the only remaining trace of periodicity is a slight variation in the rate of boiling. Nevertheless, on August 9, 1991, Sapphire Pool had a splashing eruption about 20 feet high plus at least one other that sprayed people on the boardwalk. Clearly, some potential still exists.

152. JEWEL GEYSER is appropriately named, whether the term came from the beads of pearly sinter about the vent or

the sparkling droplets of water of its eruption. It was originally called Soda Geyser by the Hayden Survey, which considered this the most important geyser of its "Soda Group."

Jewel's eruptions are very regular. Although the known range is from 4 to 12 minutes, the average is usually near 8 minutes. Variations in the interval are dependent on the number of bursts:the more bursts there are, the longer the interval. Each eruption consists of from 1 to 10 bursts (usually 4 to 7) separated from one another by several seconds. The largest bursts are up to 20 feet high. Jewel was altered temporarily by the 1959 earthquake. The 1983 earthquake had a similar effect, and for the next few years some of the bursts reached as high as 40 feet and were strong and angled sharply enough to sometimes reach the boardwalk (which has since been moved farther away).

In early November 1992 the casing of the old "Y-8" research drill hole adjacent to the Biscuit Basin parking lot blew out. Interestingly, hot springs such as Rusty Geyser (148) near the well were entirely unaffected, but Jewel Geyser nearly 1,000 feet away was seriously impacted. Although there were still beautiful eruptions with perhaps more bursts than usual, the water level dropped so that there was little discharge during and none between the eruptions. Although the well was plugged within days of the blowout, Jewel's water level had not recovered as of July 1994.

153. SHELL SPRING lies within a yellowish crater that someone felt looked like a clam shell. Shell is a cyclic geyser whose total period has never been accurately determined. When it is in an active phase, each successive eruption of a series tends to last a little longer and raise the water level a little higher within the crater. The highest bursts reach about 6 feet above the pool level, however high it stands. Near the end of a cycle the crater begins to overflow, and one last eruption, with a duration of as much as an hour, fully drains the system. Shell then requires several hours to recover and begin the first weak eruptions of a new cycle. A second crater on the opposite side of the boardwalk erupts in concert with Shell.

THE SILVER GLOBE COMPLEX (numbers 154 through 157, plus 219 through 221). Few groups of geysers were affected more dramatically by the 1983 earthquake than this one. There was a great increase in activity. The complex was first recognized as a functional group in 1984, and something of the highly variable nature of the complex's activity was learned during 1985. Continuing observations indicate that probably no other group of springs anywhere shows such extensive cyclic behavior compounded by frequent exchanges of function. The descriptions that follow are confined to the most spectacular activity variations — to try to explain all varieties and exchange relationships here would be impossible. A few minutes spent at Silver Globe Complex is bound to be rewarding. Note that in 1990 the boardwalk was rerouted so that it now passes between, rather than around, these springs.

154. "SILVER GLOBE POOL GEYSER" was incorrectly identified as Silver Globe Spring (see # 221) in the previous edition of this book. It is the blue pool immediately below the boardwalk. This spring contains two vents. When active and at its best, the vent farthest from the walk plays the highest, spraying massive bursts up to 25 feet. The nearer vent may accompany the other by erupting up to 15 feet. Intervals can be as short as 5 minutes; all durations are only a few seconds. There are also frequent minor eruptions 1 to 4 feet high. Most of these rise from the vent nearer the boardwalk.

155. "SILVER GLOBE CAVE GEYSER" (identified as Silver Globe Geyser in the previous edition) plays from a cavernous opening in the cliff face immediately to the left of Silver Globe Pool Geyser (154). The eruptions are closely related to those of the pool. Constantly churning within the cavern, this geyser is likely to spray outward only in concert with or immediately following a major eruption of the pool. Typical eruptions are largely confined to the visible catch basin. So-called super eruptions are rare, but they send powerful jets of water as far as 50 feet outward away from the boardwalk.

219. "SILVER GLOBE PAIR GEYSER" erupts from two small craters between the Silver Globe Pool Geyser (154) and Slit Geyser (156). This was the most recent among the Silver Globe geysers to show major activity; no bursting eruptions of large scale had been reported before 1989. Some of the bursts now reach as much as 12 feet high. The spray is angled toward the pool geyser so that the hillside has been severely eroded. When this geyser is the focus of energy, eruptions can recur as frequently as every 5 minutes; most of the large bursts take place at the very beginning of the eruption, and the total duration can exceed 1 minute.

156. "SILVER GLOBE SLIT GEYSER" plays from a narrow rift in the sinter beside a circular geyserite basin, possibly a sealed-in pool. Slit is the most distant of the complex from the boardwalk. It is most active when the other Silver Globe geysers are not and when Avoca Spring (157) is having its weak but frequent mode of erupting. Intervals vary from 11 minutes to $1^1/_2$ hours but tend to be extremely regular at any given time. The duration is $1^1/_2$ to $2^1/_2$ minutes, during which a fan-shaped spray of water is jetted about 10 feet high. Slit often pauses for 10 to 30 seconds about halfway through its eruption.

220. UNNG-BBG-3 is a small crater across the boardwalk from the Silver Globe geysers. It has frequent eruptions at those times when Silver Globe Pool (154) and Cave (155) geysers are vigorously active. At other times the activity is far less frequent and is comparatively weak. Even at its best, only a little water is splashed above ground level.

221. SILVER GLOBE SPRING was long misidentified as one of the geysers, but it turns out to be the pool immediately next to Avoca Spring (157). The geyser was named by G. L. Henderson in 1888, and reading his description one would believe this is one of the most fascinating and gorgeous of the Yellowstone springs. Instead, it is a rather prosaic feature. The water level always lies well below overflow. The vent is at the far-back (eastern) side of the crater beneath a

thick, overhanging shelf of geyserite. When Silver Globe Spring is active as a geyser, Avoca Spring is dormant and the Silver Globe geysers exhibit minimal activity. Both intervals and durations are only seconds long. The play might reach several feet high if it wasn't for the underside of the overhang, which blocks the more vigorous splashes. When Silver Globe is dormant, the water level stands a few inches lower, and bubbling in the vent is slight.

157. AVOCA SPRING played as a small geyser during part of 1934 but otherwise was always a steadily boiling and overflowing, nonerupting spring prior to the 1959 earthquake. After those shocks it first became a powerful steam vent, then, by the end of the year developed into a geyser. Generally cyclic, there was a series of minor eruptions. Recurring at intervals of 1 minute, these were 4 to 6 feet high and lasted around 5 seconds. After a dozen or more minors, Avoca would have a major eruption. Up to 25 feet high, these had durations of 20 to 25 seconds and were followed by 6 to 25 minutes of quiet before the next series of minors began. Such performances continued until and after the 1983 earthquake.

At first, the Borah Peak earthquake seemed to have had little effect on Avoca Spring. When the Silver Globe geysers were active, Avoca was somewhat weaker and less frequent than normal. This difference was slight until 1986, when the Silver Globe geysers first had truly major eruptions. During those episodes, Avoca was nearly dormant, its play only a small splashing confined to within the crater. When Silver Globe Spring (221) was active, Avoca fell completely dormant, vigorous boiling occurring in some small side vents but virtually none taking place within the main crater. This relationship between the springs continues. As the activity shifts unpredictably within the Silver Globe Complex, Avoca frequently turns on and off. Active phases as short as half an hour have been seen, and during 1993 infrequent eruptions reached up to 35 feet high, the largest ever recorded for Avoca.

158. WEST GEYSER is the small pool near the trail leading to Mystic Falls, about 150 feet from Avoca Spring (157). It was active as a geyser within the first 2 weeks after the 1959 earthquake. No eruptions were witnessed by any reporting observer, but washed and splashed areas surrounding the crater indicated that the play might have reached 30 feet high. In similar fashion, West had some eruptions in both 1986 and 1988. Again, none was actually seen, and this time the splash zones implied heights of less than 5 feet.

The pool a few feet northeast of West Geyser is named Sea Weed Spring. Named for the thick, stringy cyanobacteria that grew within the crater in 1887, it boiled and possibly erupted during 1897. In 1988, at the same time West Geyser had unseen eruptions, the cyanobacteria was disturbed, and a rather large runoff channel was carved by Sea Weed. The true nature of the action that caused these changes is uncertain, but it was probably was heavy overflow rather than actual eruptions.

159. MUSTARD SPRINGS, East and West, are separated by 50 feet. The two were similar, nearly quiet pools until 1983. In the early part of that year, the water level rose in East Mustard and fell in West Mustard. Now East Mustard is active as a geyser. Bursts reach 6 to 10 feet high; the duration of 5 minutes is longer than the interval. West Mustard lies quietly at a low level. The rich yellow color of the geyserite caused by iron oxide minerals.

160. NORTH GEYSER was named because it is the northernmost of all of the Upper Basin hot springs. The vent is invisible; it is over the rise nearly 300 feet beyond the boardwalk. The only known eruptions followed the 1959 earthquake. The play was a vigorous splashing up to 15 feet high. North has been dormant since 1963.

161. UNNG-BBG-2. In the area north of the boardwalk but on the front side of the rise that hides the site of North Geyser (160) are several erupting springs. None has been named, and the activity them all changes frequently. They usually play as perpetual spouters, but they have histories as intermittent geysers as well. In 1993 the vent farthest to the right (east) sent noisy, steamy jets of spray 10 feet high at intervals of 25 to 40 seconds for durations of 5 to 10 seconds.

162. BLACK PEARL GEYSER AND CORAL GEYSER lie on opposite sides of the boardwalk. Which is really which is uncertain, but Black Pearl is *probably* the one to the west of the walk, Coral to the east. Both geysers have been dormant since 1967.

Black Pearl's best activity was in 1946, when eruptions up to 30 feet high were seen. The geyser is dormant most years, but the 1959 earthquake stimulated an active episode that lasted until 1967. The play was seldom more than 4 feet high; both intervals and durations were seconds to minutes.

Coral probably had episodes of small eruptions during the early years of the Park, but the only activity with known details again followed the 1959 earthquake. At intervals of 8 to 15 minutes, the play reached up to 10 feet high and lasted 5 to 8 minutes.

222. FUMAROLE GEYSER was one of the great many features throughout Yellowstone that had a brief episode of activity following the 1959 earthquake, first as a steam vent and then as a 10-foot geyser. No further action was seen until the mid-1980s. Most of Fumarole's activity is subterranean, but spray occasionally rises several feet above the ground.

Table 9. Geysers of the Sapphire Group of Biscuit Basin

Name	Map No.	Interval	Duration	Height (ft)
Avoca Spring	157	erratic	seconds	1–35
Black Opal Pool	218	[1953]	seconds	20–70
Black Pearl Geyser	162	[1967]	sec–min	4–30
Coral Geyser	162	[1967]	5–8 min	10
East Mustard Spring	159	1–3 min	5 min	6–10
Fumarole Geyser	222	frequent	seconds	6
Jewel Geyser	152	4–12 min	1–3 min	1–40
North Geyser	160	[1963]	minutes	15

Table 9 continued.

Sapphire Pool	151	[1991, minor]	sec–5 min	6–125
Sea Weed Spring	158	[1988]	unknown	unknown
Shell Spring	153	min–hrs	min–hrs	6
"Silver Globe Cave Geyser"	155	5 min *	seconds	4–50
"Silver Globe Pair Geyser"	219	5 min *	1 min	1–12
"Silver Globe Pool Geyser"	154	5 min *	seconds	25
"Silver Globe Slit Geyser"	156	11–90 min	1 1/2–2 1/2 min	10
Silver Globe Spring	221	seconds *	seconds	3
UNNG-BBG-2	161	see text	—	—
UNNG-BBG-3	220	frequent	seconds	1
West Geyser	158	[1988]	unknown	5–30

* When active.
[ ] Brackets enclose the year of most recent activity for extremely rare or dormant geysers. See text.

Black Sand Basin

Black Sand Basin (Map J, Table 10) is named for the obsidian sand and gravel that are found in many areas of this group. Originally, the name Black Sand Basin referred only to today's Black Sand Pool, whereas this area was the "Sunlight Basin." Black Sand Basin is a relatively small cluster of springs, well to the west of the rest of the Upper Geyser Basin. It is easy to reach and explore. A parking lot gives access to a boardwalk that approaches all of the important springs.

The best-known feature in the group is Emerald Pool. Not a geyser, Emerald is a deep green color because of the combination of the blue of its water and the orange-brown of the cyanobacteria lining the crater walls. The color was once much richer, but over the years the temperature has dropped several degrees, allowing darker cyanobacteria to live. Opalescent Pool, near the parking lot, probably had an explosive origin but now contains no hot spring at all and is only a catch basin for runoff from Spouter Geyser. The milky, opal-like color of the water is caused by suspended particles of colloidal silica that form in the cooling water.

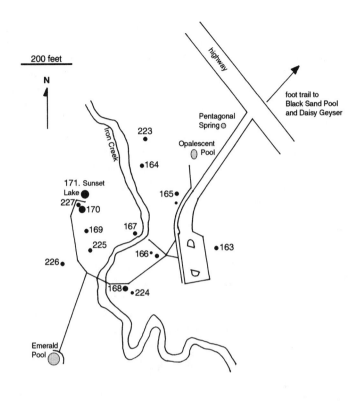

200 feet

N

highway

foot trail to
Black Sand Pool
and Daisy Geyser

Iron Creek

223

Pentagonal
Spring

Opalescent
Pool

•164

171. Sunset
Lake
227

•170

165•

•169

167

•163

•225

166•

226•

168• •224

Emerald
Pool

Map J. Black Sand Basin

163. WHISTLE GEYSER is very rarely active, although eruptions are now known to have occurred in far more than the 6
seasons noted in the previous edition of this book. Even so,
the grand total of known eruptions since the first was
inferred in 1878 is only thiry-six. The best year was 1957,
when seven eruptions were recorded. There was one in
1968, one in 1990, and two in 1991 (May and July). There is
little doubt that Whistle is an old geyser that has so nearly
sealed itself in with internal deposits that it has nearly lost its
water supply.

Whistle is capable of two kinds of eruption. Most of those observed have been steam phase eruptions; in these the 30-foot jetting of water lasts less than 30 seconds before a powerful steam phase lasting 2 to 3 hours sets in. The eruptions of 1990 and May 1991 were apparently this type. Water phase eruptions have perhaps happened only twice, in 1931 and July 1991. At first splashing water only a few feet high, Whistle does not begin the steam phase until at least 4 minutes into the eruption. Then, as the water gives way to steam, the jetting can reach at least 70 feet. This steam phase is possibly more powerful than that of the steam phase type of eruption, but it is also much briefer, decreasing significantly within an hour of the start.

164. CUCUMBER SPRING was a quietly flowing spring next to Iron Creek. The 1959 earthquake created a small steam vent on one shoulder of the crater, and it soon became a perpetual spouter a few feet high. Another explosion in 1969 enlarged the crater and merged it with Cucumber's. The combination now discharges a heavy stream of water, as the spouter still plays up to 2 feet high. It is best viewed from the high, bridgelike boardwalk next to Sunset Lake (171).

223. UNNG-BSB-5 lies within a cluster of springs beyond Cucumber Spring (164). At least one of these is a geyser. Activity is frequent, with splashes 3 to 10 feet high.

165. SPOUTER GEYSER was first believed to be a perpetual spoute — hence the name — and perhaps it was so for a time. It was recognized as periodic by 1887, but the durations are as long as several hours, and the quiet intervals are usually near 2 hours. The splashing play is 6 feet high.

Two additional vents erupt in concert with Spouter. One is a small crater on Spouter's shoulder that splashes 1 to 2 feet high. In a deep hole immediately next to the concrete sidewalk is The Grumbler; its noisy 4-foot splashing is mostly subterranean.

166. RAGGED SPRING (UNNG-BSB-1 in the previous edition of this book) occupies the jagged crater at the start of the boardwalk system. It lies on a prominent crack in the sinter. Nearby is a second vent sometimes called "Ragged Spring's Annex"; in fact, this might be the real Ragged Spring, with the jagged crater nearer the boardwalk still officially unnamed. Both are geysers that play in unison. Small splashing is nearly constant, with quiet intervals never longer than a few seconds. Every few minutes, however, brief eruptions send violent jets of water as high as 12 feet. There is evidence that these eruptions are more frequent when Cliff Geyser (167) is active with its modern version of a major eruption.

167. CLIFF GEYSER plays from a wide crater just across Iron Creek from the boardwalk platform. The geyserite on the stream side of the crater forms the cliff of its name. Cliff has gone through wide variations in its performances through the years. Dormant at times, during the 1960s it commonly had long eruptions separated by intervals of 12 hours. The play of the 1970s was more frequent, with typical intervals of a few hours, and by 1985 the frequency was as great as 30 minutes. During all of these times, the eruption would start with the crater empty, which allowed the bursts to spread widely. As the bursting continued, the crater slowly filled, and the deepening pool tended to focus the water into jets reaching up to 40 feet. Often, the eruption would end about the time the crater filled, but exceptionally long durations could continue play until well after the first overflow. During the later 1980s, Cliff abruptly changed its behavior. Most eruptions now have durations of only a few seconds to a minute or two, but they recur at intervals mostly less than 3 minutes. Major eruptions that fill the crater with water are now hours apart. Bursts higher than 20 feet are uncommon, but with the boardwalk spur ending only a few feet across the creek, Cliff is still one of the most impressive geysers.

168. GREEN SPRING was noted as "a bulger" during the 1880s, but its first certain year of intermittent activity did not come until 1934, when it had a few eruptions up to 20 feet high. Since then it has been active during only a few years, the most recent being 1975. The typical action is 12-foot bursting recurring every 30 minutes and lasting 3 to 5 minutes. On several occasions during the 1980s there were signs of heavy washing around Green Spring, but this was apparently caused by strong surging without actual eruptions. (As a historical note, Green Spring was reported as in eruption many times during the early 1980s. Eventually, it was realized that this was intended as a joke by some of the patrol rangers — an old "Green Spring" interpretive sign had been placed at the Old Faithful–area sewage treatment plant — but many such "eruption times" were entered into the logbook at the Visitor Center. Green Spring *was* active during some of those times, but it is impossible to separate the real eruptions from the fictional.)

224. UNNG-BSB-2 is a small vent just to the left (east) of Green Spring (168). During 1980 it was a highly regular geyser, with intervals of 40 minutes, durations of 5 minutes, and heights of 5 feet. Inactive by 1981, the crater quickly disappeared entirely, but it reappeared as a bubbler in 1987 and probably had some eruptions during the winter of 1992–1993.

169. HANDKERCHIEF POOL is the famous spring that once attracted nearly as many visitors as any other single hot spring. It was possible to place a handkerchief at one end of the spring and have convection pull it down a vent and out of sight. A few moments later it would reappear in another vent. Handkerchief Pool continued to work until 1926, when somebody jammed logs into one of the openings. Later, eruptions by Rainbow Pool (170) washed gravel into the spring, completely obliterating its site. However, in 1950 Handkerchief Pool began to reappear as a bubbling spot in the gravel. It was shoveled out and the logs were removed, but it is no longer accessible because of thick beds of cyanobacteria about its crater. On occasion, Handkerchief Pool acts as a perpetual spouter up to 3 feet high, and briefly, in August 1991, it was a geyser reaching 6 to 8 feet.

225. HANDKERCHIEF GEYSER was named after Handkerchief Pool. The geyser is about 150 feet south of the pool and much nearer the modern boardwalk. Active during the 1930s, with eruptions 3 feet high, the geyser was apparently dormant for most of the time thereafter until the 1980s. Eruptions were frequent during 1986 and 1987, often reaching 15 feet high. It declined after that and was dormant in 1993.

226. UNNG-BSB-3 broke out directly underneath the boardwalk (the walk has since been moved several feet). Nothing more than a sizzling hole at first, it has developed into a vigorous geyser that plays from a number of vents and cracks along a fracture zone. Some splashes reach 3 feet high. Both the interval and duration may be hours long.

170. RAINBOW POOL has a crater nearly 100 feet across. It is ordinarily a quiet spring with light overflow. A few eruptions during the early 1930s were a portent of the future, but not until 1938 was Rainbow known to possess powerful eruption potential. During that summer it erupted several times a day, the play often reaching 80 feet high. By 1939, although still active, it was much weaker. Rainbow was then an erratic performer through 1948, when eruptions were seldom more than 15 feet high. Beyond that the only other known major eruption was in 1973. The fact that it occurred at night and was apparently a single burst, yet was seen and reported by several people, indicates that this eruption was artificially induced. Minor splashing took place in 1981.

227. UNNG-BSB-4 plays from a symmetrical vent very near the bridgelike boardwalk next to Rainbow Pool (170). Eruptions are quite frequent, and durations can exceed 1 hour. The play is 2 feet high.

171. SUNSET LAKE, even larger than Rainbow Pool (170), has undergone small eruptions for many years. Because the high temperature of the spring causes dense steam clouds to form, it is difficult to observe the play except on the hottest days. The largest known eruptions occurred during 1981

and 1984, when some bursts were 35 feet high. More typical play, such as that of 1985–1987, recurred every 20 seconds to 5 minutes and consisted of a single burst ranging from 2 to 8 feet high.

Table 10. Geysers of Black Sand Basin

Name	Map No.	Interval	Duration	Height (ft)
Cliff Geyser	167	frequent	sec–min	20
Cucumber Spring	164	steady	steady	2
Green Spring	168	[1982?]	3–5 min	12
Handkerchief Geyser	225	minutes *	minutes	3–15
Handkerchief Pool	169	[1991]	min–hrs	6–8
Ragged Spring	166	frequent	seconds	12
Rainbow Pool	170	[1973]	sec–min	25–100
Spouter Geyser	165	2 hrs	hours	6
Sunset Lake	171	sec–5 min *	seconds	2–35
The Grumbler	165	with Spouter	hours	4
UNNG-BSB-2	224	40 min *	5 min	5
UNNG-BSB-3	226	hours	hours	3
UNNG-BSB-4	227	frequent	1 hr	2
UNNG-BSB-5	223	minutes	minutes	3–10
Whistle Geyser	163	[1991]	1–2 hrs	30–70

* When active.
[ ] Brackets enclose the year of most recent activity for extremely rare or dormant geysers. See text.

Myriad Group

The Myriad Group (Map K, Table 11) is the thermal area behind and to the west of the Old Faithful Inn. It is generally noticed by few people. Only the Three Sisters Springs Complex lies close to the road, and no trails penetrate the area. The Myriad Group is closed to public entry. True to its name, the area contains more than a thousand hot spring vents (a count done in 1959 came up with 1,113 features). The Myriad Group is extremely dangerous to explore, and unauthorized entry into the area is illegal.

The Myriad Group is the site of several important geysers, and some have been major in scale. In addition to the

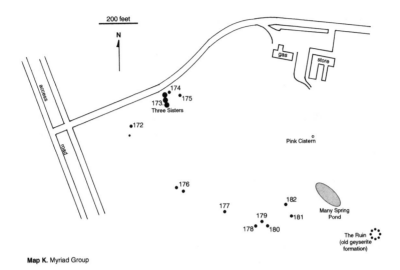

Map K. Myriad Group

geysers described here, the group contains dozens of other geysers and perpetual spouters that are too small to see from a distance. Among these are Bell, Pit, and Strata Geysers and Blue Lemon Spring, which were active as vigorous geysers following the 1959 earthquake but have been infrequent and small in size since then. Also located within the group are the largest and best mud pots within the Upper Geyser Basin, one of which is named Pink Cistern.

Every now an then an entire group of hot springs can undergo a sudden and dramatic increase in activity without any observable cause. One of these "energy surges" struck the Myriad Group during winter 1987–1988. Some of the resulting action continues.

172. BASIN SPRING was active as a geyser during 1984, undoubtedly as a result of the 1983 Borah Peak earthquake. The activity was somewhat erratic and perhaps cyclic. Most intervals were only seconds to minutes long, but some extended for hours. There were also some short dormant periods in which the pool would fill and quietly overflow, as it had during all of its previous history. When active, eruptions would last 3 to 10 minutes, during which a violent boiling domed the water as high as 6 feet. Basin Spring has not erupted since 1984. For a time the crater served as a drain hole for runoff from the Three Sisters Springs (173), but it is again filled with very hot water.

A few feet south of Basin Spring, a small vent played as a geyser during 1987. During its brief active phase the intervals were 3 minutes, durations 2 minutes, and heights 1 to 3 feet. Few eruptions have been seen since 1987.

173. THREE SISTERS SPRINGS sit next to the road leading from the main Old Faithful access route to the front of the Old Faithful Inn. The three craters, all filled with pale greenish water, are connected both above and below ground and incorporate at least five geyser vents. Only the vents within the North Sister, closest to the road, had any eruptive history prior to the 1959 earthquake. Most of this activity was referred to simply as "North Sister," but two of its three vents have historical names.

Three Crater Geyser (173a) is the far left (southeast) vent within the North Sister. The original "Mugwump" (173b), it was probably the geyser most involved in the postearthquake activity. Three Crater has also been very active in recent years, playing every few minutes up to 10 feet high. The start of its play is often accompanied by sharp, loud steam explosions that can be both felt and heard as distant as the gas station more than 400 feet away.

Mugwump Geyser (173b), the large vent in the right side of the North Sister, was named because of its brief but noisy eruptions in 1884. (The Mugwumps were Republican politicians who refused to support that party's presidential nominee, James G. Blaine, and voted instead for Grover Cleveland. Many people felt the Mugwumps complained loudly for little or no reason, accomplishing nothing. The geyser seemed similar.) It has had several active episodes since 1987. Bursts sometimes reach over 30 feet high. The intervals during 1992 were as short as 5 minutes, but Mugwump was largely inactive in 1993 and 1994.

The third vent within North Sister, **UNNG-MYR-1** (173c), is only infrequently active, bursting up to 3 feet high.

"**Middle Sister**" (173d) was active for a short time following the 1959 earthquake. Its play was frequent and up to 15 feet high, but it stopped erupting when Three Crater Geyser (173a) activated a short time later. Either Middle Sister or South Sister (173e) had a single 30-foot eruption observed in July 1993.

"**South Sister**" (173e) has rarely been active. It might have had a few small eruptions following the 1959 earthquake but otherwise has been a quiet pool.

174. LITTLE BROTHER GEYSER is closely related to the Three Sisters (173). It had eruptions in 1926 but gained little notice until 1950, when it briefly splashed to 3 feet every 5 minutes. The next year of activity was 1958, with eruptions to 12 feet. Following the earthquake, Little Brother reactivated along with the Three Sisters. These more erratic eruptions reached as high as 30 feet. The only recent active episode was during 1983–1984. Little Brother was very regular, most intervals being 15 to 17 minutes in length, unless Three Crater Geyser (173a) played; then Little Brother could be quiet for spans approaching an hour long. Those eruptions lasted 30 to 80 seconds and were up to 25 feet high.

175. "COUSIN GEYSER" is a more distant relative of the Three Sisters Springs (173). It underwent its first known active spell during July and August 1980. Lasting as long as 12 minutes, the eruptions shot a steady stream of murky water at an angle as high as 25 feet. At first the play recurred every $1\frac{1}{2}$ to 3 hours, then it slowly declined into dormancy. Cousin reactivated to a slight extent during 1985, when it had a few weak eruptions followed by several days of intermittent overflow. Erosion has now all but obliterated its vent.

176. TRAIL GEYSER and nearby **WEST TRAIL GEYSER** are small, shallow pools that were activated by the 1959 earthquake. For several weeks they underwent simultaneous, powerful eruptions. Playing hourly, Trail reached 50 feet and West Trail about 20 feet high. The play lasted 1 to 2 minutes. Dormant by December 1959, they were quiet, cool pools until an energy surge of unknown cause in 1987–1988. This time West Trail was the stronger of the two, with some bursts of 15 feet, and Trail often failed to join its companion. West Trail continues to act as a small perpetual spouter.

177. MYRIAD GEYSER was named because in its time it was the largest geyser ever seen in the Myriad Group. The only recorded eruptions were during 1954 and 1955. In those summers it erupted daily, with intervals ranging between 5 and 13 hours. The eruptions were between 80 and 100 feet high; shot out at an angle, they strongly resembled those of Daisy Geyser (106) during the 5 minutes of play. Exchange of function might have been at work during the activity of Myriad. While it and four small nearby spouters were active, the Three Sisters Springs (173), over 400 feet away, were completely dormant for the first time in their known history. It must be noted, however, that previous and succeeding dormancies by the Three Sisters did not result in the animation of Myriad and its neighbors, so this might have been a coincidence.

178. ROUND GEYSER, not to be confused with Round Spring elsewhere in the Upper Basin, ranks as the largest known geyser of the Myriad Group and one of the largest in Yellowstone. It erupts from an impressively deep crater, 4 feet in diameter and almost perfectly round.

That it had eruptions to rival those of Old Faithful in 1933 was forgotten until recently, and modern action did not take place until just after the 1959 earthquake. These eruptions were only 10 feet high. Following this brief period and another, even briefer one in 1961, Round was dormant until 1966. During the renewed activity the eruptions were more powerful, sometimes reaching 50 feet. With time they gradually gained strength so that by the mid-1970s some were fully 150 feet high. The intervals were quite regular, averaging around 14 hours within a 9- to 18-hour range.

During the quiet period the pool periodically boiled around the edges. It was during one of these hot periods that the water level suddenly rose, and heavy overflow accompanied a vigorous boiling up of the water to 2 feet. There were *always* three such surges, separated by about 10 seconds, before the eruption. A fourth surge suddenly rocketed the water, needing only a few seconds to reach the maximum height. The eruption itself lasted less than 1 minute but was followed by a series of equally short but impressive steam phase eruptions.

Round returned to dormancy in 1981. Only a few additional eruptions took place during the energy surge of 1987–1988, and three or four were seen in late summer 1989. Minor eruptions, just 30 feet high without the steam phases, were seen during the winter of 1989–1990. Round continues to boil and overflow, and more active phases unquestionably lie in its future.

179. ABUSE SPRING was named because of the vast amount of debris that was thrown into the crater by early Park concession employees. It was also once a source of hot water for the employee kitchens at the Old Faithful Inn. The crater still shows the abuse it received over the years. The first known eruption by Abuse was a result of the 1959 earthquake. Although that eruption was not observed, the amount of debris thrown out indicated that it was very powerful.

No further play occurred until 1974, when nearby Spectacle Geyser (180) also activated. At first there was frequent exchange of function between these two springs. Abuse would have one or two eruptions, then Spectacle would play over the course of several days. The eruptions by Abuse were massive domes of water 15 feet high. Both geysers returned to dormancy before the end of 1974. In May 1976 unprecedented eruptions took place, as both Abuse and Spectacle reactivated as truly major geysers. Intervals were as short as 90 minutes, and many of the eruptions were in concert. Abuse always reached 90 feet high and sometimes may have exceeded 125 feet, whereas Spectacle jetted simultaneously as high as 75 feet. For a one-week period, Abuse and Spectacle were among the most powerful geysers in the world. But it was nearly the end of the show. During the next few weeks Abuse had only a few more small eruptions, and it was dormant by the end of June 1976. The only action since then was a few eruptions just 5 feet high during the winter of 1989–1990.

180. SPECTACLE GEYSER has had an uncertain history. During an episode of construction at the Old Faithful Inn during 1928, Abuse Spring (179) was used as a hot water source by the workers' camp cook. The resultant lowering of the water level caused eruptions in a small, nearby hole. In order to stop the eruptions, the crater was filled with sand. The hole is now called Spectacle Geyser, but its crater is much larger than it was in 1928. Every episode of eruptions has enlarged the crater to a measurable degree, and it is now several feet across.

The first recorded eruptions of what is definitely Spectacle occurred during 1968, when it had a few small eruptions that gained little notice. Then in 1974, at the same time nearby Abuse Geyser (179) began erupting, Spectacle joined in. Of the two, Spectacle was usually the larger and more active. An active cycle was initiated by one or two eruptions by Abuse; then over the next several days Spectacle erupted about every 20 minutes. Each play lasted 1 to 3 minutes and was 25 feet high. The eruptions were vigorous and, jetted at an angle, quite pretty, with a resemblance to Daisy Geyser (106). After several months of activity, both Spectacle and Abuse were dormant until May 1976. Over a period of about a week, both became tremendous geysers. Erupting as often as every $1^1/_2$ hours, Spectacle would play at least 75 feet high, and Abuse joined it in concert at over 90 feet. Following these major eruptions, which ended on May 31, Spectacle continued minor activity through most of that summer, even though Abuse had fallen dormant. Since then, Spectacle has been dormant most of the time. Between 1978 and 1981, it would sometimes erupt shortly after eruptions by Round Geyser (178), but those plays ended with Round's dormancy in 1981. A few 30-foot eruptions were seen during 1983 and again in 1986, and occasional weak play still takes place.

181. WHITE GEYSER is the most visible geyser in the Myriad Group. It is active almost all of the time; eruptions recur at intervals of 2 to 15 minutes and last 30 seconds. The height

is about 12 feet. Dormant periods have been recorded, during which a small, subterranean spring nearby raises its water level and undergoes eruptions too low to be seen from the roadways. Usually, these dormancies are infrequent and brief, and White is the only geyser in the Myriad Group likely to be seen by a casual viewer.

182. LACTOSE POOL is a muddy, milky-white spring near White Geyser; in fact, it is probably the original "White Geyser" of the 1880s. It spends most of its time bubbling gently from a water level deep within its crater. On infrequent occasions, seemingly always in late summer, it enters active episodes that may persist for days. Some bursts of the muddy water reach 20 to 30 feet high over durations as long as 10 minutes.

Table 11. Geysers of the Myriad Group

Name	Map No.	Interval	Duration	Height (ft)
Abuse Spring	179	[1990]	1 min	15–125
Basin Spring	172	[1984]	3–10 min	6
Bell Geyser	—	min–hrs	2–5 min	1–6
Blue Lemon Spring	—	rare	minutes	1–2
"Cousin Geyser"	175	[1985]	12 min	25
Lactose Pool	182	infrequent	10 min	20–30
Little Brother Geyser	174	14 min–hrs *	30–80 sec	3–30
"Middle Sister"	173	[1993]	1 burst	30
Mugwump Geyser	173	minutes *	seconds	10–30
Myriad Geyser	177	[1954]	5 min	80–100
Pit Geyser	—	rare	unrecorded	3–20
Round Geyser	178	[1989]	1 min	50–150
"South Sister"	173	[1959?]	unrecorded	few feet
Spectacle Geyser	180	20 min–rare	1–3 min	2–75
Strata Geyser	—	frequent	seconds	2–4
Three Crater Geyser	173	minutes *	seconds	10
Trail Geyser	176	[1988]	1–2 min	5–50
UNNG-MYR-1	173	rare	seconds	3
West Trail Geyser	176	steady	steady	2–20
White Geyser	181	2–15 min *	30 sec	12

* When active.
[ ] Brackets enclose the year of most recent activity for extremely rare or dormant geysers. See text.

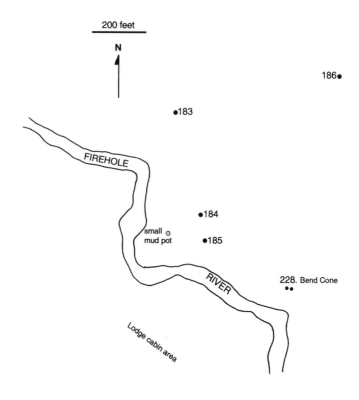

Map L. Pipeline Meadows Group

Pipeline Meadows Group

The Pipeline Meadows Group (Map L, Table 12) is located upstream from the main portion of the Upper Geyser Basin. No established trail leads into the area, which is visible directly across the Firehole River from the Old Faithful Lodge cabins. Only a few hot springs are located here, but five of them are geysers.

183. UNNG-PMG-1 ("DILAPIDATED GEYSER") is the first Pipeline Meadows spring encountered if one walks upstream along

the river. It plays from a badly weathered cone next to a crater with a considerable overhang. It was clearly active as a
geyser in prehistory, but no eruptions were witnessed until
late winter 1980. It was then active into 1981 and, more
briefly, in 1987 and 1988. Cyclic in its activity, Dilapidated
would experience a series of eruptions followed by a day or
more of quiet. Intervals were about 2 hours long. Throughout the 2- to 5-minute duration the geyser would burst from
the cone, some spray reaching 30 feet high. The size of
Dilapidated's cone and runoff channels indicates a great
deal of activity in its past, but the water level is now lower
than it was before 1980.

184. UNNG-PMG-2 erupts from a small vent surrounded by a
round geyserite platform. Leading from the platform are
several deep runoff channels that owe their existence to
eruptions since 1981. There is no certain record of activity
for any time before then. The fact that PMG-2 began erupting at about the same time Dilapidated Geyser (183) quit
might indicate a subsurface connection between the two.
The first activity was erratic. With intervals of minutes to
many hours, PMG-2 would squirt water about 10 feet high
for a duration of just 1 minute. Dormant in 1986, it renewed
activity in 1987 on a very different pattern that continued
through 1994. The intervals range from 9 to 14 hours. Small
splashing preplay, which starts with little variation about 4
hours before the eruption, serves as an indicator. Gradually
growing stronger, a series of heavy splashes triggers the
actual eruption. The initial play bursts from 2 to 5 feet high.
As it progresses, the action grows into a steady jet of steamy
spray reaching up to 15 feet. The duration of 10 to 12 minutes ends with a weak steam phase.

185. MIDAS SPRING (previously referred to as UNNG-PMG-3
and "Pipeline Meadows Geyser") is the most active geyser of
the group, playing every 3 to 8 minutes. Relatively infrequently, Midas has somewhat longer and more voluminous
eruptions that can be followed by intervals as long as several
hours. Mentioned in some early reports, it is not clearly

known to have ever had a dormant period. So, although the 30-second eruptions are not impressive because they are never more than 2 feet high, this is a remarkable feature. Simple math shows that it may have had 12 million eruptions since it was first recorded. (It is possible that there was a dormant period in the 1920s, when the name was first used. It was based on "golden algae" within the crater, which implies a water temperature too cool for eruptions.)

186. UNNG-PMG-4 was first observed in 1985; there is no known report about this spring even existing prior to then, yet it can be a significant geyser. The crater and its surrounding prove it has been active for a long time. Perhaps it was not noticed earlier because of its location well up the hillside and somewhat isolated from the other members of the Pipeline Meadows Group. PMG-4 is known to have both major and minor eruptions, both types occurring in erratic fashion. Minor eruptions are the only type seen during most years, and they are always the more common. They last only a few seconds and splash about 3 feet high. Major eruptions, when they take place at all, are usually hours apart but have durations of more than 2 minutes and reach 7 to 10 feet high. Dormant in 1993, PMG-4 was active, with minor eruptions only, during 1994.

228. BEND CONE is actually a pair of large geyserite cones merged together into a single feature at the upstream end of the Pipeline Meadows. At the top of each cone is a small spring. Both are active as perpetual spouters. The one to the northwest also occasionally plays as an intermittent geyser, with intervals only a few seconds to minutes long. Both springs splash just 1 foot high.

Table 12. Geysers of the Pipeline Meadows Group

Name	Map No.	Interval	Duration	Height (ft)
Bend Cone	228	sec–min *	minutes	1
Midas Spring	185	min–hrs	30 sec–min	2
UNNG-PMG-1 ("Dilapidated")	183	[1988]	2–5 min	30

Table 12 continued

| UNNG-PMG-2 | 184 | 9–14 hrs | 10–12 min | 15 |
| UNNG-PMG-4 | 186 | 2 min–hrs * | sec–2 min | 3–10 |

* When active.

[ ] Brackets enclose the year of most recent activity for extremely rare or dormant geysers. See text.

Other Upper Basin Geysers

Geysers are known to exist in at least four other hot spring groups within the Upper Geyser Basin, but in none of these is the activity common, spectacular, or persistent.

In the woods across the highway east of Black Sand Basin are the Pine Springs, which consist of two clusters of hot springs. Farthest to the south, and barely visible from the highway near the Old Faithful "freeway" interchange, is the "Mud Spring Group." **Mud Spring** itself is a small pool that has had a few eruptions since 1986, all of which are known only on the basis of washed areas and fresh runoff channels. Most active here is **UNNG-PIN-1.** It lies within a deep crater, and its activity is entirely subterranean, even though some bursts can reach 10 feet above the pool level.

The "Fracture Group" is the northern cluster of the Pine Springs. Numerous craters open along a series of fractures in an old sinter platform. A number of these were active as geysers following the 1959 earthquake, and three presently undergo infrequent, small eruptions. Near here is what appears to be the remains of a large geyserite cone; in reality, this is probably the eroded remnant of what used to be an extensive mound or platform rather than a cone.

Near the Pipeline Meadows, along the trail to Mallard Lake, is the Pipeline Creek Group. Most of its springs are mud pots and acid pools, but **UNNG-PIP-1,** which lies within an oval sinter-lined basin, often acts as an intermittent spring and sometimes has splashing eruptions as high as 4 feet. Nearby, both a small, subterranean pool and a tiny geyserite cone have also been known to erupt.

Along the Firehole River, toward the highway above Pipeline Meadows, is the "Upstream Group." There are several springs on geyserite platforms. One is a deep, blue pool that has infrequent episodes of eruptive activity. Some bursts by **UNNG-UPG-1** reached 3 feet high in 1991 for durations apparently hours long. A short distance upstream from the "High Bridge" on the highway is a small cone within the river, which was reported to have had intermittent eruptions 1 to 2 feet high in 1993.

Finally, the Hillside Springs lie northwest of Black Sand Basin, where they are visible as a series of colorful features on steep slopes below the cliffs. On the valley floor below them are some old spring craters. One of these held a small geyser during the early 1980s.

Chapter 5

Midway Geyser Basin

The Midway Geyser Basin (Map M, Table 13) is a relatively small area. The hot springs are mostly confined to a narrow band of ground paralleling a 1-mile stretch of the Firehole River. Additional springs, mostly small, cool, and muddy, extend up the Rabbit Creek drainage to the east, at the head of which is an assortment of mud pots, small geysers, and one exceptionally large pool.

Topographically, the Midway Geyser Basin is a part of the Lower Geyser Basin (Chapter 6), but it has always held separate status because it is separated from the Lower Basin by a forest of lodgepole pines. First known as the Halfway Group and Hell's Half-Acre, then as Egeria Springs, Midway contains only a few geysers of note. Possibly, dozens of other hot springs are geysers, too, but little is known about them. Two such areas are indicated on Map M.

Despite its small size, Midway is the location of some of the largest individual hot springs in the world. Grand Prismatic Spring is more than 370 feet across; possibly the only larger bona fide *single* hot spring anywhere is the lake in the Inferno Crater of New Zealand's Waimangu Valley. Excelsior Geyser discharges a steady stream of more than 4,000 gallons of water every minute. In fact, a large proportion of the springs at Midway are of extraordinary size.

The Midway Geyser Basin includes four named hot spring groups. The Rabbit Creek Group includes the springs in the lower Rabbit Creek drainage and along the Firehole River in that vicinity, at the southern end of Midway. Along the highway and river in the middle portion of the basin is

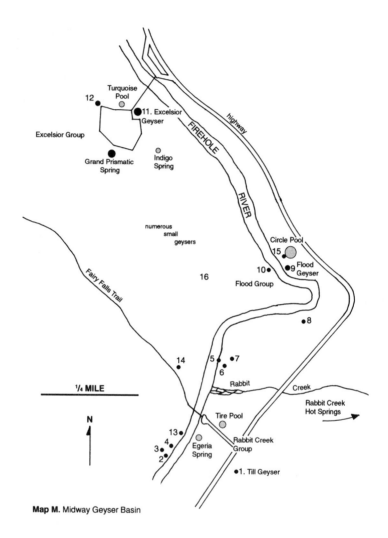

Map M. Midway Geyser Basin

the Flood Group, dominated by Flood Geyser. Most accessible, served by the parking lot and boardwalk at the Midway Geyser Basin signs on the highway, is the best-known area, properly known as the Excelsior Group. One of the best views of this area is from Midway Bluff, the hill across the highway from the parking lot. Only there is one high enough to get a good view of the pools and their coloration.

The hike is well worth the few minutes it takes. Finally, the Rabbit Creek Hot Springs are those at and near the head of Rabbit Creek. Although these springs are spectacular, the area is dangerous. Explorers should always be sure others know about any planned hike along Rabbit Creek and then check back in after the trip.

Rabbit Creek Group

The Rabbit Creek Group encompasses nine geysers, several large pools, and some mud pots. Although named for Rabbit Creek, which meets the Firehole River among these springs, the majority of the features hug the banks of the river rather than being scattered along the creek. None of the geysers is particularly large.

1. TILL GEYSER is named for the glacial gravel that composes the ridge it rises from. Active during the 1880s when it was named Rabbit Geyser (also an acceptable name), it seems to have been a forgotten feature until the time of the 1959 earthquake. Because of its location against the hillside, Till is readily seen by southbound travelers on the highway but is nearly invisible to those driving in the opposite direction.

Till erupts from a complex of vents. The two main craters are situated at the top and bottom of the cluster; between them are several smaller apertures that also jet water. The system fills slowly after an eruption and does not usually reach the first overflow until 30 to 50 minutes before the next play. Moments before the eruption begins, the overflow becomes periodic and then gushes as the jetting starts. The greatest height comes from the upper main vent, where some jets reach 20 feet. At the same time, the lower main vent sprays mostly horizontally outward as far as 10 (rarely, 30) feet. The smaller vents sputter a few inches to a few feet high. The entire operation lasts 30 minutes, with only a few brief pauses occurring near the end of the play. Although intervals are known to range from $5^{1}/_{2}$ to 10 hours, during most seasons Till is highly regular at about 9 hours.

In 1985 Till was observed to undergo at least two sequences of mid-interval eruptions. These occurred in series, with intervals of 11 minutes and durations of $2^1/_2$ minutes. Interestingly, there was no delay in the timing of the subsequent full eruptions.

2. UNNG-MGB-1 is located south of the steel bridge at the Fairy Falls trailhead; it is the vent farthest upstream within a small cluster of springs on the west side of the river. Very little is known about this geyser. During most seasons it is apparently dormant, or nearly so, but in others it is reported several times per month. The eruptions, either splashing 6 to 8 feet high or jetting more than 15 feet high, have durations that range from only a few minutes to as long as several hours.

3. UNNG-MGB-2 is located just up the slope from MGB-1 (2). A perpetual spouter, MGB-2 has a 1-foot eruption that issues from a low cone; cyanobacteria-covered and with grass growing on its sides, it is less than obvious from a distance.

4. UNNG-MGB-3 is the northernmost spring in this cluster. It is a true geyser, but the height of the eruptions is less than 1 foot. The play recurs every 1 to 3 minutes and lasts 1 to 2 minutes. A single report in 1988, apparently referring to this spring rather than to MGB-1, cited an eruption 10 feet high.

13. UNNG-MGB-5 is a small pool only slightly elevated above the river. Several times in the mid-1980s it was seen splashing 2 to 3 feet high. Nothing is known of its intervals; some durations were at least 30 minutes long.

14. SILENT POOL was always known as a quiet spring until 1989. For the next 3 years it erupted in cycles with considerable regularity. Several days to weeks would pass between active episodes. Then eruptions would recur every 2 to 3 hours for a day or more before Silent lapsed into another short dormancy. Durations were several minutes, with splashes up to 3 feet high. It was dormant in 1993 and 1994.

5. RIVER SPOUTER was apparently created by the 1959 earthquake when a crack formed in the sinter at the base of an old cone. (This cone is the original Catfish Geyser. The name was later transferred to a geyser in the Flood Group; it is also used for a geyser in the Upper Basin.) Because the vent is located beneath the water of the Firehole River, River Spouter is evident only when the river is low. Then the spout, steady during some years and frequently periodic during others, will sometimes reach 10 feet high. During these eruptions the old cone raises a commotion within its vent but seldom splashes any water onto its sides. Except for parts of 1989 and 1993, River Spouter has been weak or dormant since the mid-1980s.

6. PEBBLE SPRING is a small geyser located on the flat above River Spouter (5). Its small vent is centered in a round sinter bowl tinted a rich orange-brown by iron oxide minerals. Pebble undergoes continuous eruptions no more than 2 feet high, except that on infrequent occasions much larger bursting eruptions occur. Generally seen only once or twice a year, these spray 8 to 10 feet high and persist for about 1 hour.

7. UNNG-MGB-4 is a complex of related perpetual spouters. Some degree of eruption is always going on here, but the number and strength of erupting vents are always changing. Most often several vents are active at once, some of the play reaching 3 feet high, with occasional surges to 6 feet. The largest pool sometimes acts as a geyser, with intervals of 1 to 5 minutes and durations of a few seconds.

Flood Group

The Flood Group consists of just three geysers of any size, and only Flood is active on a frequent basis. There are also several pools and smaller springs. Best included as part of this group are the clusters of numerous small springs on the open flat to the west and southwest of the river. They include several little-known geysers and perpetual spouters of small sizes and infrequent performances.

8. CATFISH GEYSER is different not only from the Catfish in the Upper Geyser Basin but also from the spring originally given the name in the Midway Basin (see # 5). This Catfish is a large pool that has shown little variation in its activity over the years. About every 15 minutes the water rises. Along with heavy discharge, there is a vigorous boiling, which throws the water 2 to 3 feet into the air. The duration is near 5 minutes.

9. FLOOD GEYSER is perhaps the most important active geyser in the Midway Geyser Basin because it is frequent and discharges considerable water. Even so, it was largely ignored for much of its history; for years, the highway to Old Faithful crossed the river downstream from Flood, leaving it isolated. Now the road crosses the hillside directly above Flood, where a large turnout provides a wonderful view. Still, no systematic observations of Flood's performances were conducted until the early 1970s, and the full extent of its complex behavior was not revealed until 1985.

The vigorous activity of Flood consists of minor, intermediate, and major eruptions. The duration of an eruption is directly related to the length of the interval preceding it. (This is the inverse of almost all geysers, in which the duration controls the following interval.) The minor eruptions have durations of just 20 to 40 seconds following intervals of $1^1/_2$ to 4 minutes. The durations of the intermediates are 2 to 5 minutes after 15- to 25-minute intervals. And the majors last 6 to 8 minutes, the previous interval having been 27 to 45 minutes. These values change little from year to year, and eruptions with statistics outside these ranges are rare. The aspect that does vary is the relative proportions between the different kinds of eruption. Some years will have few minors; on other occasions it is the majors that are uncommon.

Regardless of the variety, all eruptions of Flood look about the same. Water is bulged upward by expanding steam bubbles rising into the crater, which burst large, globular splashes. The height ranges between 10 and 25 feet. There is a tendency for the bigger splashes to occur during major eruptions, but this is not an absolute rule. All eruptions have a heavy discharge of water, the total during the major play amounting to several thousand gallons. This may slosh well beyond the crater. Signs admonish visitors to stay away from Flood. Some people who failed to do so were seriously burned during 1994.

15. UNNG-MGB-6 ("TANGENT GEYSER") plays from a fracture that is tangent to the west side of Circle Pool, the large, round spring just northwest of Flood Geyser (9). Its best performances were during the early 1980s, when water could be jetted in a fan-shaped spray as high as 10 feet. Durations were 1 to 5 minutes. Tangent's intervals were quite erratic, ranging from a few minutes to several hours. Only rare, small eruptions have been seen since 1985.

10. WEST FLOOD GEYSER was named because of both its location near Flood Geyser (9) and its resemblance to Flood when in eruption. Although the two geysers are directly across the Firehole River from one another and thus not far apart, there seems to be no connection between them. West Flood was originally described as a quiet pool; no eruption was recorded until 1940, when there were bursts up to 40 feet high. During active phases, eruptions recur every 45 minutes to 4 hours. The splashes now are 3 to 12 feet high and last $1^{1}/_{2}$ to 6 minutes. West Flood has been dormant more often than not. Then its water level tends to stand quietly well below overflow; 1993 was different in that the pool was full and steadily overflowing without any observed eruptions.

16. UNNG-MGB-7 is this book's designation for the numerous hot springs in the grassy areas west of the Firehole River. Many of these have been known as geysers, but their small sizes and location make any detailed study difficult. Only one has been given an informal name. "Tentacle Geyser" has a series of fractures radiating away from the vent so that it

Excelsior Geyser, the only truly major geyser in the Midway Geyser Basin, last had a full, major eruption in 1890 (maybe 1901), when it played as high as 300 feet. Less activity, some of it up to 75 feet high, was seen in 1946 and 1985.

somewhat resembles a jellyfish, a fact not visible from the road. It can reach 10 feet high during its rare active episodes.

Excelsior Group

The Excelsior Group is the group served by the Midway Geyser Basin parking lot and a boardwalk loop. There are only two geysers, and both are rare performers, although they are very large. Other features here are Grand Prismatic Spring, Turquoise Spring, and Indigo Spring.

11. EXCELSIOR GEYSER is one of the brightest stars in the world of geysers — when it is active. The last of its truly stupendous eruptions was in 1890 (there may have been some activity in 1901, too). During the 10 years before that final great play it underwent many eruptions during several active episodes. Although most eruptions reached "only" 100 feet,

some were fully 300 feet high and were as wide as they were high. Considering the size of the geyser, the amount of activity was amazing. For example, during the 11 days of play from September 27 through October 7, 1881, Excelsior erupted 63 times, giving an average interval of only a little over 4 hours.

The present Excelsior is quite different although still impressive. The crater measures more than 200 by 300 feet. This entire volume was blasted out by eruptions, and the crater was relatively small prior to the eruptions of the 1880s; although it is impossible to know for certain, it might not have even existed in the 1830s. The huge, azure pool boils at numerous points, proving the existence of an abundant source of heat. The discharge is tremendous, too, amounting to a measured 4,050 gallons per minute. That is more than 5,800,000 gallons per day, enough to fill 300,000 typical automobile gas tanks. Old Faithful Geyser needs nearly 2 months to discharge as much water as Excelsior does in a single day.

This flow is constant, and that in itself tells us a lot. Excelsior was a geyser, a periodic hot spring. Thus the flow of the water might be expected to be periodic, too, even when no eruptions are occurring. The fact that Excelsior boils from many places other than the main vent indicates that the eruptions of the 1800s tore some of the crater and the plumbing system apart. In effect, Excelsior has been leaking, unable to generate the pressure needed for eruptions. Most observers felt Excelsior could not possibly erupt until it healed its wounds.

Boiling eruptions 10 to 15 feet high were recorded in 1946, but it was a big surprise when Excelsior had true bursting play during September 14–16, 1985. Eruptions were frequent during that 46-hour period. Most were minor in size, with the biggest bursts reaching perhaps 30 feet high. There were also a few "major" eruptions. Although not nearly of the scale of earlier times, some of the play sent jets of muddy gray water to as much as 75 feet. As before, the bursts were at least as wide as they were high, so it was a very impressive show. All of the eruptions lasted nearly 2 minutes, with

Opal Pool is a rare performer, but its eruptions are the tallest, other than Excelsior's, ever seen in the Midway Basin. (Photo by Genean Dunn.)

known intervals ranging from 5 to 66 minutes. During the active episode the water discharge was several times greater than at any other known time since 1890.

Unfortunately, the 1985 eruptions do not seem to have been a prelude to renewed activity on a major scale. Indeed, Excelsior now looks as it did before 1985. But the evidence is that Excelsior's eruptive history has been one of short series of sudden, explosive events. It may be its nature to experience brief periods of powerful eruptions followed by decades of relative quiet.

12. OPAL POOL is a significant geyser, but its eruptions are rare and exceedingly brief. No activity was known until 1947, when Opal played several times to as high as 50 feet. Similar action occurred in 1949, 1952, and 1954, but then nothing further was seen until 1979. The only seasons without known eruptions since then have been 1982, 1983, and 1990. Most modern eruptions are less than 30 feet high, although some estimated at 70 to 80 feet were reported in 1986 and 1993.

No matter what the size, the play is often only a single, virtually instantaneous burst of water. Sometimes there will be several successive bursts a few seconds apart, and then the duration may reach as long as 1 minute. During the minutes to hours before an eruption, the pool will gradually fill with strong convective upwelling visible over the vent. This sometimes happens without resulting in an eruption. Blind luck is about the only way to see Opal erupt.

Rabbit Creek Hot Springs

There is no trail into the Rabbit Creek Hot Springs. The distance from the highway to the main hot spring area is about 1 mile, with springs of lesser importance being scattered all along the way. Most people hiking into this area simply park at a roadside turnout and follow Rabbit Creek toward its source at the head of the valley. As noted before, this is a dangerous area — many of the springs have wide overhangs; mud pot areas can look solid but are actually only a dried crust on top of boiling mud. Always notify others of your planned departure *and* return if you go here. Do be careful — thermal burns are very serious injuries.

Most of the flow of Rabbit Creek originates in a single large pool. Rivaling any other for size and beauty, this pool has no name. Indeed, only one feature here has been named, and it is the only consistently active geyser in the group.

17. RABBIT CREEK GEYSER is located on the slope well to the south of the pool at the head of the stream. It lies within a deep, jagged crater, and most of its eruptions are confined to the subsurface. The play recurs every 15 to 25 minutes and normally lasts less than 10 seconds. Occasional major eruptions can jet several feet aboveground (so that the total height is actually 10 feet or more) over durations as long as 1 minute.

18. UNNG-MGB-8 is a pool north of Rabbit Creek Geyser (17), at the base of the slope. The vent is at the far eastern side of the crater. The activity is highly variable and usually consists of random splashes just 1 to 2 feet high. Vigorously jetting true eruptions as much as 10 feet high happen on intervals that are many minutes to hours long.

Table 13. Geysers of the Midway Geyser Basin

Name	Map No.	Interval	Duration	Height (ft)
Catfish Geyser	8	15 min	5 min	2–3
Excelsior Geyser	11	[1985]	2–4 min	30–300 [75]
Flood Geyser	9	1 1/2–45 min	sec–8 min	10–25
Opal Pool	12	hrs–days *	seconds	30–80
Pebble Spring	6	weeks–months	1 hr	8–10
Rabbit Creek Geyser	17	minutes	seconds	3–10
River Spouter	5	frequent *	sec–min	1–10
Silent Pool	14	2–3 hrs *	minutes	3
Till Geyser (Rabbit Geyser)	1	9 hrs	30 min	20
UNNG-MGB-1	2	infrequent	min–hrs	6–15
UNNG-MGB-2	3	steady	steady	1
UNNG-MGB-3	4	1–3 min	1–2 min	1–10
UNNG-MGB-4	7	near steady	near steady	3–6
UNNG-MGB-5	13	unknown	30 min	2–3
UNNG-MGB-6 ("Tangent")	15	min–hrs *	1–5 min	10
UNNG-MGB-7	16	see text	—	—
UNNG-MGB-8	18	irregular	sec–min	1–10
West Flood Geyser	10	45 min–4 hrs *	1 1/2–6 min	10–40

* When active.
[ ] Brackets enclose the year of most recent activity for extremely rare or dormant geysers. See text.

Chapter 6

Lower Geyser Basin

The Lower Geyser Basin (Map N) covers the largest area of any geyser basin in Yellowstone National Park. The hot spring groups are scattered across 5 square miles of a valley area that is more than twice as large. Most of these groups include geysers. Several of the spouters are as famous as those of the Upper Basin, and Great Fountain deserves its reputation as one of the most magnificent geysers in the world.

The majority of the individual geyser groups of the Lower Basin are readily accessible. Roads approach them in several areas. Boardwalks allow the visitor to further explore the most important clusters, and many of the more remote springs can be reached by way of primitive but maintained trails. A few groups, however, remain visible only from a distant highway or boardwalk. The geyser action in all of the areas is vigorous, and seldom is any group visited when some geyser is not erupting.

Most of the springs here are of the same clear-water type as those of the Upper and Midway Basins, but the Lower Basin is notable in that there are some large areas of muddy, acid activity. These are often closely spaced with the geysers, an unusual occurrence. The Fountain Paint Pot, within the Fountain Group of geysers, is the best-known example; it is the largest single cluster of mud pots in Yellowstone. The mud pots of Microcosm Basin and vicinity, near Pocket Basin in the River Group, require a hike to see but are more varied.

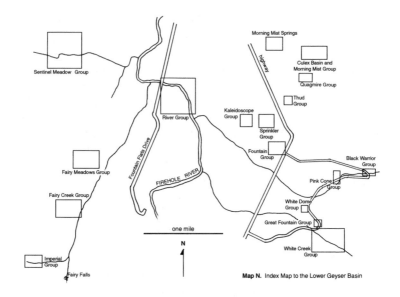

Map N. Index Map to the Lower Geyser Basin

Firehole Lake Drive

Firehole Lake Drive is a one-way loop road that leaves the main highway at the southern end of the Lower Geyser Basin and passes through several hot springs groups before rejoining the highway opposite the Fountain Paint Pot parking lot. Even to drive the road nonstop is worthwhile. To stop and explore the thermal areas is far better, of course, and one can easily spend days here without seeing the same thing twice.

Great Fountain Group and White Creek Group

Great Fountain Geyser should probably be assigned to a group consisting only of itself and one other small geyser. Its activity over the years has varied only slightly, and it is isolated from any other hot spring plumbing systems of importance. Along nearby White Creek there are many springs

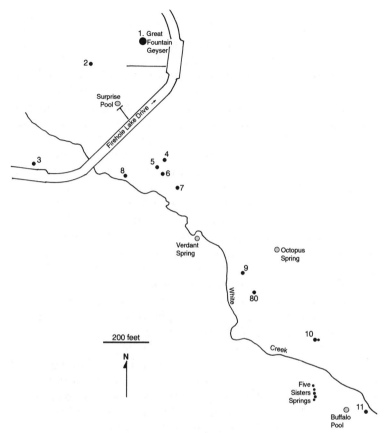

Map O. Great Fountain Group and White Creek Group

including at least ten geysers (Map O, Table 14). Some of the pools in this area are worthy of note in their own right: Surprise Pool is superheated and intermittent in its boiling overflow, Verdant Spring is a deep emerald green, Octopus Pool is crystal clear and pale blue, the Five Sisters Springs are pretty and occasionally support a unique chartreuse cyanobacteria growth along their runoff channels, and Buffalo Pool boasts wide, dangerous overhanging ledges of geyserite around its bone-littered crater. All in all, this group is well worth an extended visit.

Great Fountain Geyser is right beside Firehole Lake Drive (one-way north) where there is a small parking lot.

The White Creek area can be reached by following an old trail that winds upstream from the Great Fountain parking lot. Much of the pioneering work on thermophilic ("temperature-loving") life has been and still is being conducted along White Creek. The bacteria *Thermus aquaticus* was discovered in the White Creek Group. An enzyme called Taq polymerase — now used in DNA copying and amplifying, forensic DNA fingerprinting, and several medical diagnostic procedures — was recovered from this bacteria. DNA research based on Taq polymerase will soon be a billion-dollar industry, and biologists are presently studying other thermophilic Yellowstone bacteria for similar enzymes that may have unique uses. If you see experiments in progress, please look but do not touch. Remember to stay on the trail, as casual wandering among the hot springs is illegal.

1. GREAT FOUNTAIN GEYSER was observed and accurately reported on by the Cook-Folsom-Peterson party in 1869. It was their first geyser experience, and they were fortunate in arriving while Great Fountain was in eruption. Duly impressed, Cook later wrote, "We could not contain our enthusiasm; with one accord we all took off our hats and yelled with all our might" (quote in Haines, 1977; Marler, 1973; Whittlesey, 1989). After a long and dangerous search, they had finally found a source of the many rumors about Yellowstone. These would be rumors no more.

Great Fountain has always attracted much attention. The large crater is set into the middle of a broad, raised sinter platform. The exquisite catch basins, rims, and beadwork of this huge geyserite structure led to its first name, Architectural Fountain. The vent itself is about 16 feet across and is filled with clear, boiling water. The setting is impressive even when Great Fountain is not in eruption.

The eruptions of Great Fountain are regular enough to be predicted. Water slowly fills the crater and bubbles slightly during a long recovery period. It takes close looking, but the most significant time for a prediction is the time of first overflow from the crater onto the platform. This usually begins 70 to 100 minutes before the beginning of an

Great Fountain Geyser is the largest in the Lower Basin. Eruptions estimated as tall as 230 feet have been observed.

eruption. With this, gentle superheated boiling begins around the edge of the pool. The boiling becomes periodic and progressively stronger as the overflow continues. Eventually, a heavy surge known as the "1-meter boil" heralds the eruption. Often followed by a quiet pause a few minutes long, the boil leads to heavy surging, which becomes violent and domes the water several feet high. Then Great Fountain bursts into the sky. Many of the eruptions are "only" 100 feet high, but even these are spectacular since the water columns are very wide and are frequently jetted at an angle. Sometimes the bursting will reach 150 feet and splash onto the roadway. Superbursts are rather rare. They usually happen at the very beginning of an eruption, immediately following a massive, quiet doming of the entire crater volume in an amazing "blue bubble," and they have been carefully estimated to reach as high as 230 feet. (Not all blue bubbles result in a superburst, and the two may be separate phenomena.) The activity continues with bursts of widely varying heights for several minutes. Then Great Fountain pauses for a few minutes while leading up to a second eruptive period. This process is repeated three to seven times, so that the entire eruption lasts 30 to 90 minutes.

Every geyser, even one as intensely observed as Great Fountain, has something new to tell us. Only during 1993 was it realized that there is a very regular relationship between the duration of an eruption and the length of the following interval. Perhaps this had not been known before because the calculation demands that the duration be timed very accurately, requiring the observer to wait out the very last, weak bursts. The resulting mathematical relationship (probably varying some from year to year) indicates that the next interval (in minutes) will approximately equal $5\frac{1}{2}$ times the total duration (in minutes) plus 400; that is, I = 5.5D + 400.

During all of the pre-1959 earthquake years, Great Fountain's intervals averaged close to 12 hours. The tremors caused some sort of underground changes, for whereas Great Fountain continued to be regular, the intervals were cut to only 8 hours. Very slowly, the average has increased, but even now, more than 35 years later, it is only in the vicinity of 11^1/$_2$ hours within a range from 9 to 16 hours. On rare occasions, Great Fountain enters what is called "wild phase" activity. For many hours to several days it erupts almost continuously. Water is thrown from 10 to 50 feet high several times per minute. Although not nearly as high as normal eruptions, this play is impressive. What causes wild phase action is unclear, but it might be related to changes in the nongeothermal ground water level, since most occurrences have happened in the late summer and early fall months. The most recent wild phase happened in June 1994 — unusually early in the season but occurring in a year of severe drought. There have also been occasions of excessively long overflow before eruptions and a few instances in which Great Fountain failed to refill normally after an eruption. In both of these cases, which are rare, the resulting interval may be as long as 3 days.

Overall, Great Fountain is an extremely reliable performer. Being predictable and the only such major geyser in the Lower Basin, it performs for thousands of people every year. Few are disappointed by the display.

2. UNNG-GFG-1 ("PRAWN GEYSER") made its first known appearance during 1985. The name is in allusion to the geyser's small ("shrimpy") size compared to nearby Great Fountain (1). Located downstream and in the middle of Great Fountain's southern runoff channel, this geyser shows some relationship to Great Fountain's activity. Although intervals are known to range between 28 and 50 minutes, most are on the short side unless Great Fountain has just erupted; then the next one or two intervals will be longer. Lasting for several minutes, the eruption reaches a height between 1 and 6 feet. Long dormancies have been known.

3. FIREHOLE SPRING is immediately below the road at a pullout just before the White Creek crossing and before one gets to Great Fountain Geyser (1). A pretty, rich blue pool, it has functioned as a perpetual spouter throughout Park history. It is one of the very few hot springs to have completely escaped earthquake effects, and the bursting play reaches up to 6 feet high. Occasional seconds-long pauses in the activity lead some to call this a geyser; it's a close call. The name has nothing to do with the Firehole River or its valley; this "firehole" is so called because of the flashing flamelike appearance of steam bubbles as they enter the bottom of the pool. The same effect can be seen in several of the springs in the Black Warrior Group, farther along Firehole Lake Drive.

4. UNNG-WCG-1 ("A-ZERO (OR A-0) GEYSER") was named in allusion to its proximity to the somewhat more officially named A-1 (5) and A-2 (6) Geysers. A-zero is erratic in its performances. The first recorded eruptions apparently took place during the early 1970s. Intervals range from as little as 25 minutes to several hours, and it is easy to miss the eruption. Often consisting of only a few bursts over a duration of less than 10 seconds, the play reaches 5 to 10 feet high. Rare major eruptions, seen only a handful of times, last several minutes and reach as much as 20 feet.

5. "A-1 GEYSER" shows a clear relationship to nearby "A-2 Geyser" (6). If A-1 is active, A-2 is nearly dormant; if A-2 is frequent, A-1 is completely dormant. The crater is an irregular oval, largely filled with geyserite rubble, much of which has probably been tossed in by visitors. When active, A-1 plays every 30 to 40 minutes, bursting up to 6 feet high for 5 to 10 minutes.

A slightly altered pattern of activity was seen during 1993: A-1 was active even though A-2 was also playing. However, A-1's intervals were long and erratic, and the play was no higher than 2 feet. These eruptions, which were seen only a few times, had no apparent effect on A-2.

6. "A-2 GEYSER" lies 25 feet east of "A-1 Geyser" (5). It plays from a shallow basin containing three large and several small vents. The bulk of the eruption comes from just two of these openings. Except in 1970 and 1971, when A-1 was the dominant member of this group, A-2 has been the most important geyser along White Creek. There appear to be

both major and minor eruptive scenarios. Most common are the majors, in which intervals of 1 to 2 hours separate plays lasting 6 to 8 minutes. After an eruption, the crater drains and then slowly refills, the next play starting at about the time of first overflow. Minor activity recurs at intervals as short as 5 minutes, with durations of less than 1 minute. The crater does not drain during these episodes. The bursts are about 10 feet high during both modes of action.

7. BOTRYOIDAL SPRING erupts from a boiling pool about 100 feet east of A-2 Geyser (6). The crater is surrounded by thick, massive geyserite shoulders covered with botryoidal (grapelike) globules of sinter beadwork. Botryoidal is close to a perpetual spouter, the individual eruptions being separated by only a few seconds of semiquiet. Some of the larger bursts reach 7 feet high.

This part of the White Creek Group is dotted with numerous small hot springs in addition to A-1 (5), A-2, and Botryoidal. Several of those on the east side of A-2 and the northeast side of Botryoidal act as geysers. Typical intervals are only a few minutes, durations a few seconds, and heights less than 2 feet.

8. UNNG-WCG-2 ("LOGBRIDGE GEYSER") is so called because it lies near some cut logs that were placed across White Creek so many years ago that they have nearly rotted away. Logbridge was known for years but only as a small perpetual spouter. It attracted attention during 1985 when it began having exceedingly regular eruptions far larger than any seen before; the first intervals were very regular at 27 minutes. The play, which lasted 35 to 55 seconds, was as high as 15 to 20 feet. The discharge washed gravel out of old runoff channels, showing that similar activity had taken place long before. Since 1985 Logbridge has continued to play as a geyser, but the intervals are now 2 to 5 hours long. The duration is as great as 5 minutes, during which steady jetting reaches 5 to 8 feet high.

9. DIAMOND SPRING, named for the shape of the pool, always appeared to be a quiet spring until the 1959 earthquake. It apparently erupted powerfully that night, but no reasonably frequent eruptions were seen until 1973. These were brief and no more than 3 feet high. Washed and splashed areas showed that further strong action took place after the 1983 earthquake, but since then only a few small eruptions were seen in 1987. Diamond is otherwise active as an intermittent spring.

80. UNNG-WCG-4 occupies a deep crater on the sinter platform above Diamond Spring (9). Its 4-foot eruptions are confined to the subsurface, and the fact that it is a geyser was only discovered around 1980. The nature of the geyserite within the crater indicates that it has been active for many years, however. Eruptions are quite regular, usually falling on intervals of 40 to 50 minutes whenever checked. The duration is around 30 seconds.

10. UNNG-WCG-3 AND 3A ("TUFT GEYSER" AND "ECLIPSE GEYSER") are small geysers of which nothing was known prior to the 1970s. The more active is Tuft. It plays from a number of small openings next to a crescent-shaped deposit of geyserite only a few inches high (hence a second informal name, "Crescent"). The eruption is a sputtering out of the openings rather than a bursting or jetting, some spray reaching perhaps 2 feet high. Tuft's activity is such that it can be difficult to distinguish the interval from the duration. The sputtering begins before there is any overflow and continues after the last discharge, and sometimes it never completely quits before the next eruption begins. Taken on balance, most intervals are between 50 and 100 minutes, with overflow durations of 5 to 30 minutes.

Eclipse is rarely active. It erupts from a round hole, 6 inches in diameter, between Tuft and a bluish pool. When it is active, as it was most recently in 1984, it completely "eclipses" Tuft, rendering it dormant. The play recurs every 35 to 40 minutes, lasts 2 minutes, and sends a steady jet of water as high as 8 feet.

11. SPINDLE GEYSER is the most upstream of the geysers of the White Creek Group, lying in an orange-brown crater beyond the Five Sisters Springs and Buffalo Pool. (Walk widely around Buffalo. It has very wide and extremely dangerous overhangs around its edges, making it easy to see why skeletons lie in the bottom of the crater.) Few geysers illustrate the typical cycle of activity of a fountain-type geyser as well as Spindle does. Eruptions recur every 1 to 3 minutes. Steam bubbles can be seen rising into the crater, expanding as they go, then throwing the water 1 to 3 feet high. Following the eruption the water level drops several inches, far enough to stop all overflow. The pool then begins to rise again almost immediately, the flow becoming heavy just before the next eruption. Thus, the alternating buildup and loss of pressure within the system is readily seen. In 1985, during an episode of erratic action, eruptions 10 feet high were seen.

From Spindle Geyser, White Creek continues far up the canyon. Hot springs are scattered all along the way, but none are known to be geysers. The headwater areas were severely burned during the forest fires of 1988. Summer thunderstorms since then have produced several flash floods, and one in 1989 completely filled the crater of Spindle with mud. Spindle did not completely clear its crater and recover its previous mode of activity until 1993.

Table 14. Geysers of the Great Fountain and White Creek Groups

Name	Map No.	Interval	Duration	Height (ft)
"A–1 Geyser"	5	30 min–hrs *	5–10 min	2–6
"A–2 Geyser"	6	5 min–2 hrs	1–8 min	10
Botryoidal Spring	7	near steady	near steady	7
Diamond Spring	9	[1987]	seconds	3
Firehole Spring	3	near steady	near steady	1–6
Great Fountain Geyser	1	9–16 hrs	30–90 min	100–230
Spindle Geyser	11	1–3 min	seconds	1–10
UNNG-GFG-1 ("Prawn")	2	28–50 min *	minutes	1–6
UNNG-WCG-1 ("A–zero")	4	erratic	seconds	5–20
UNNG-WCG-2 ("Logbridge")	8	2–5 hrs	5 min	5–20
UNNG-WCG-3 ("Tuft")	10	frequent	minutes	2

Table 14 continued.

UNNG-WCG-3a ("Eclipse")	10	[1984]	2 min	4–8
UNNG-WCG-4	80	40–50 min	30 sec	4

* When active.

[ ] Brackets enclose the year of most recent activity for extremely rare or dormant geysers. See text.

White Dome Group

The White Dome Group (Map P, Table 15) is a tiny cluster of hot springs bisected by Firehole Lake Drive. It encompasses an area of little more than 300 feet square, yet it includes six geysers and one perpetual spouter. The most important is White Dome Geyser, one of the oldest hot springs in Yellowstone.

Across the marshy flat to the west of White Dome Geyser, another cluster of hot springs can be seen. Virtually nothing is known about the Tangled Creek Group except that at least eight of its springs have been active as geysers. Such action is rare, however, and this group is of little overall importance. In the opposite direction, in the fringe of forest across the grassland to the east, is another cluster of springs among which 10-foot "Toadstool Geyser" was briefly active during the 1960s. Neither of these groups is reached by a trail.

12. WHITE DOME GEYSER has been active for a long, long time. The massive geyserite cone built by the spray of its eruptions is over 20 feet high. The cone in turn sits atop a 12-foot-high mound of sinter formed by an even older hot spring. Yellowstone's only larger cone structures are at Castle Geyser and the nearly extinct White Pyramid Geyser Cone, both in the Upper Geyser Basin. Because some structural remains of the older crater can be seen, some believe it may have been a geyser of considerable power. White Dome, though, has apparently nearly sealed itself in with deposits of sinter inside the vent, for the remaining opening is only 5 by 7 inches. So, although the cone seems to hold promise of

The thin water jet of White Dome Geyser reaches 20 to 30 feet above the top of is 12-foot geyserite cone.

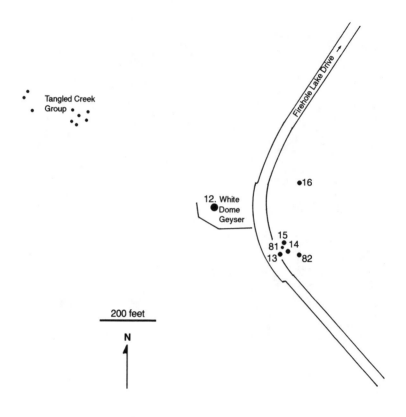

Map P. White Dome Group

big eruptions, the resultant display is disappointing to many viewers.

White Dome is nonetheless a fascinating geyser, so beautiful and symmetrical that it was selected as a symbol of the Yellowstone Association. The eruption begins after a few moments of splashing preplay. At first the action consists mostly of steam, but a steady jet of water soon makes up the bulk of the discharge. The maximum height of about 30 feet is maintained for most of the 2-minute eruption. White Dome shows a wide variation in its intervals. Although most are on the order of 15 to 30 minutes, some are as short as 9 minutes and others as long as 150. It is believed that intervals as long as 6 hours took place in 1992 and 1993. Also in 1993 were two known episodes of minor eruptions in series. The intervals were 8 minutes, durations a few seconds, and heights only 10 feet. Such action had never before been recorded. No way has been found to predict what the next interval will be. White Dome's erratic performance is probably a result of subsurface connections with the hot springs across the road, especially Cave Spring (82).

13. PEBBLE GEYSER is the small pool close to the road just across from the White Dome parking area. This spring was not known to erupt until August 1968, when it underwent several eruptions. Because the spring is located so close to the edge of the road, much gravel gets pushed and thrown into the crater. The first several of the 1968 eruptions scattered these pebbles across the road, giving the geyser its name. Those eruptions were brief but were over 20 feet high. Pebble continued occasional activity into 1969, when nearby Crack Geyser (14) became active. Since then, Pebble has had only infrequent and weak eruptions, most occurring in the few moments preceding those by Crack or Gemini (15). The exception to this occurred in 1988, when Pebble splashed up to 4 feet high for a few minutes after Crack had finished. These eruptions rose from a partially drained pool.

14. CRACK GEYSER developed along a fissure in the sinter platform. Formed by the 1959 earthquake, this break was initially the site of a fumarole. By 1960 it was erupting and became known as Crack Geyser. After a few months of activity, it went dormant when Gemini Geyser (15) rejuvenated, and it remained quiet until 1969. Renewed activity that year caused a corresponding dormancy in Gemini and Pebble (13). This switch in the location of activity also took place in 1983. During 1987-1988 an interesting pattern developed in which Crack and Gemini alternated having frequent eruptions. Crack would erupt for 3 to 4 minutes, sending a fan-shaped spray 10 feet high. About 20 minutes later would be an eruption by Gemini, and around 40 minutes after than would be another by Crack. This action was highly regular and persisted for about 10 months. Crack has been dormant since 1988.

15. GEMINI GEYSER plays from two small cones, each perforated by a tiny vent. At the beginning of an eruption, water begins to well from the cones, forming small pools. Progressively stronger bubbling builds the eruption in size. Splashing begins suddenly, and within moments the full height of 10 feet is reached. Both of the twin water jets are angled slightly away from the road. Except for 1987-1988, when Gemini and Crack Geyser (14) alternated eruptions, Gemini has been cyclic in its activity. During most active phases, eruptions recur every 5 to 25 minutes and last 1 to 3 minutes. As many as ten eruptions may take place. Several hours are then required before activity resumes. Sometimes individual eruptions not in series have intervals of hours and proportionally long durations of many minutes. Gemini was nearly dormant in 1994.

81. UNNG-WDG-2 is a small hole in the sinter between Gemini (15) and Pebble (13) Geysers. During 1987-1988 it would have brief play between the alternating eruptions of Gemini and Crack (14). Without a clear relationship to surrounding features, it was also weakly active during 1993, infrequently sputtering about 1 foot high.

82. CAVE SPRING lies deep within the large cavern to the northeast of Crack Geyser (14). The spring within is eruptive, probably as a perpetual spouter. Even for people illegally off the roadway, it is almost impossible to see.

16. UNNG-WDG-1, about 150 feet north of Gemini Geyser (15), is a small pool within a sinter-lined bowl. It was first observed during 1971. Intervals were 2 to 3 hours long, but durations of 20 minutes and splashes 5 feet high made it fairly obvious. Erratic activity continued through 1986, when both intervals and durations were only seconds to minutes long. WDG-1 has been essentially dormant *or* active as a perpetual spouter since 1986.

Table 15. Geysers of the White Dome Group

Name	Map No.	Interval	Duration	Height (ft)
Cave Spring	82	steady	steady	few feet
Crack Geyser	14	[1988]	3–4 min	10
Gemini Geyser	15	5–25 min *	1–3 min	10
Pebble Geyser	13	[1988]	seconds	4–20
UNNG-WDG-1	16	sec–min	sec–min	1–5
UNNG-WDG-2	81	rare	seconds	1
White Dome Geyser	12	9 min–hrs	2 min	30

* When active.
[ ] Brackets enclose the year of most recent activity for extremely rare or dormant geysers. See text.

Pink Cone Group

Pink Cone Geyser, for which this cluster of springs (Map Q, Table 16) is named, is by far the best-known geyser in the group, but all of the other members are geysers except Shelf Spring. The eruptions tend to be of considerable size, frequency, and regularity.

Wandering about in the Pink Cone Group is discouraged. There are signs warning you to stay on the roadway, and by positioning yourself properly it is possible to see all of the geysers from there. The area is perforated by many spring holes with overhanging rims. Shelf Spring is very deep and highly superheated. Its thin sinter rim projects far out over the water, making any approach very dangerous.

Perhaps no other hot spring group in Yellowstone was more dramatically affected by the Borah Peak earthquake of 1983. Most of the geysers increased their activity considerably, nearly doubling their frequency, and one arose from a long dormancy. This increased action has persisted with little evident waning through the decade-plus since.

17. PINK CONE GEYSER, with its brownish-pink cone, is colored by a trace of manganese oxide; if a bit more were present the color would be jet black. This same coloration

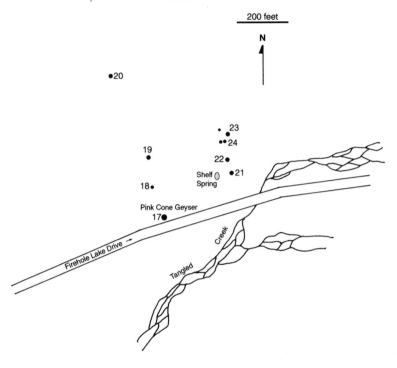

Map Q. Pink Cone Group

shows up in Pink (19) and Narcissus (20) Geysers. Because of this similarity and the fact that the three geysers lie along a line, they are undoubtedly connected by some sort of subsurface lineation — a long crack or perhaps a fault. The connection cannot be too direct, however, as none of these geysers' performances are affected by the others.

Pink Cone was named by one of the early surveys of Yellowstone. They recognized that it must have been a geyser, but no eruptions were seen, and, in fact, none were recorded until 1937. During this first known activity the intervals were as long as 50 hours.

The 1959 earthquake markedly increased Pink Cone's performance. For about 10 days the play was almost constant. In September the intervals varied between 40 and 55 minutes long, with durations of about the same length. Through time since 1959, the intervals have very slowly increased. The average is now about 16 hours. The eruptions begin abruptly, with virtually no preplay, and almost instantly reach the maximum height of 30 feet. The duration is 2 to $2^1/_2$ hours. Pink Cone's steady water jet pulsates some, and as the play continues these pulses become more extreme. Near the end of an eruption they begin to result in brief, total pauses; these in turn become progressively longer and merge into an indistinct end of the action.

Pink Cone Geyser lies immediately next to the road. When it was built, the route was cut right through the broad mound upon which the geyser sits. Some minor parts of the plumbing system were tapped into along the road cut, and these sputter a little water while Pink Cone is in eruption. The wonder is that Pink Cone wasn't altered or destroyed. But it did survive, and we now have an excellent cross section of a geyserite mound, built up layer after tedious layer by uncountable thousands of eruptions.

18. UNNG-PNK-1 ("DILEMMA GEYSER") plays from a small double vent about midway between Pink Cone (17) and Pink (19) Geysers. Tiny, very brief eruptions during 1984 were hardly worth noting, except that observations of the surroundings revealed old runoff channels leading from the vents. The "dilemma" was about the nature of activity that had produced the channels, since that of 1984 was not causing such erosion. Action during 1989 solved the problem. Although the eruptions were only about 3 feet high, they were preceded and accompanied by remarkably heavy discharge that thoroughly scoured the channels. Eruptions continue to take place infrequently.

19. PINK GEYSER lies about 235 feet beyond Pink Cone Geyser (17). The rose-colored sinter basin of this spring is 7 feet in diameter; the vent itself is only inches across and enters the ground at an angle. In most years eruptions do not take place more often than twice per day, but during other episodes intervals as short as 1 hour have been known. The

1983 earthquake stimulated Pink into a cycle during which intervals averaged about $5^1/_2$ hours, and this frequency has largely persisted since then. The jetting, which lasts from 11 to 17 minutes, reaches about 20 feet high and is angled in the uphill direction. It's a very pretty eruption, concluded by a steam phase as Pink runs out of water.

20. NARCISSUS GEYSER is located farthest from the road, nearly hidden behind a band of lodgepole pines. Therefore, it is seldom seen, either close at hand or from a distance. The geyser erupts from a soft-pink bowl filled with greenish-tinted water in a lovely setting.

Narcissus is quite regular in its activity. It is known to have both minor and major eruptions. The minors take place after intervals of 2 to 4 hours. Narcissus has not had time to fill its basin before the play starts, resulting in some jets of water over 20 feet high. Minor eruptions last 5 to 8 minutes. The major eruptions begin after Narcissus has been full and overflowing for more than an hour, the interval being between 4 and 7 hours long. These eruptions last longer than the minors — sometimes as long as 15 minutes — but because the crater is full, some of the eruptive force is lost, and the major eruptions seldom exceed 15 feet high. At times, and perhaps usually, major and minor eruptions alternate on a highly regular basis, the respective intervals then being 4 hours and 2 hours with little variation. After either type of eruption, the crater rapidly drains completely, often forming a large whirlpool.

21. BEAD GEYSER is known for its extreme regularity. It also used to be known for its fine collection of "geyser eggs" — small, loose $^1/_4$- to 2-inch spheres of geyserite that slowly form in the splash basins of most geysers. The geyser eggs of Bead are long gone, having been removed by Park visitors almost as soon as their existence was known.

Bead is one of the most — if not *the* most — regular geysers in Yellowstone. Although the length of the interval does vary as time passes, eruptions seldom occur more than 30 seconds off the average at any given time. This average has ranged between 23 and 38 minutes since 1959. The duration is equally regular, being just about $2^1/_2$ minutes with only a few seconds variation.

The eruption begins suddenly after water has slowly risen within its vent. Just when it reaches overflow level, the geyser suddenly surges. Within a few seconds, Bead is jetting up to 25 feet high. The bursting play is nonstop until it ends as suddenly as it began, and the remaining water is sucked back into the vent.

22. BOX SPRING was named during post-1959 earthquake studies, and in the successive years it had rare eruptions up to 5 feet high. The first consistent activity took place during 1984, possibly as a delayed result of the 1983 quake. Intervals were around 7 hours. The play was a vigorous bursting up to 10 feet high that decreased to minor bubbling by the end of the 1- to 5-minute duration. Box Spring continues to undergo occasional active phases, sometimes with series of eruptions over the course of a few hours. Most intervals are days to weeks long.

23. LABIAL GEYSER was a rather infrequent performer prior to the 1983 earthquake, the intervals being 12 and more hours long. The tremors doubled its frequency so that it now plays every 5 to 8 hours. From the road a viewer can see nothing of Labial except the eruption itself. That is unfortunate, because interesting preliminary activity takes place within Labial and some nearby vents. During the quiet interval the water level rises and falls every few minutes. This is most visible in a related spring a few feet away. The times of high water result in boiling and sloshing at depth within Labial. Each cycle brings the water level a bit higher, and the related vent begins to overflow about an hour before the eruption. During a final overflow Labial's own surging becomes violent, and the eruption is triggered. The play lasts less than 2 minutes, but the sharply angled water jet reaches as high as 25 feet. A second vent bursts to about 6 feet, and, rarely, the related spring splashes 1 to 2 feet high. Following the main eruption, Labial continues occasional

bursting, and this sometimes leads to a second and even a third briefer but full-force eruption during the next half hour or so.

24. "LABIAL'S SATELLITE GEYSERS," East and West, are related to Labial Geyser (23). The eastern of the two has a very ornate crater and is probably the original Bead Geyser rather than the spring that now bears the name. The Satellites are most active shortly before Labial plays and are essentially inactive for some time following Labial. At its best, the East Satellite may play at intervals as short as 2 minutes and have durations as long as 5 minutes. Discharge is considerable, as the play reaches 6 feet high. The West Satellite plays less frequently, but it is the larger of the two, sometimes topping 10 feet high.

During 1989 the Satellites underwent activity seemingly independent of Labial. Eruptions were consistently frequent in both geysers, recurring every 5 to 8 minutes, lasting around 30 seconds, and reaching 15 feet high. Unfortunately, since 1989 Labial's Satellites have been relatively quiet. Although they are still active, the majority of eruptions are confined to the subsurface so that much of the delicate geyserite deposit has decayed.

Table 16. Geysers of the Pink Cone Group

Name	Map No.	Interval	Duration	Height (ft)
Bead Geyser	21	23–38 min	2 1/2 min	25
Box Spring	22	hrs–weeks *	1–5 min	10
Labial Geyser	23	5–8 hrs	2 min	25
"Labial's Satellite Geyser," East	24	irregular	sec–5 min	6
"Labial's Satellite Geyser," West	24	irregular	seconds	10
Narcissus Geyser	20	2–7 hrs	5–15 min	15–25
Pink Cone Geyser	17	13–17 hrs	2 hrs	30
Pink Geyser	19	5 1/2 hrs	11–17 min	20
UNNG-PNK-1 ("Dilemma")	18	infrequent	minutes	3

* When active.

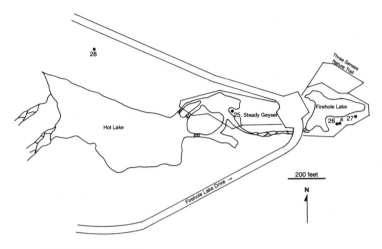

Map R. Black Warrior (Firehole Lake) Group

Black Warrior, or Firehole Lake, Group

The Black Warrior Group (Map R, Table 17) is an area of very high water output. The total discharge is about 3,500 gallons per minute, which flows from the area through Tangled Creek. Most of the hot springs are large, quiet pools. The biggest is Firehole Lake. Supplied with water through several vents, its temperature is about 160°F (70°C). Hot Lake covers a larger area, but it is not a hot spring as such, only a collecting basin along the runoff. Its temperature is about 100°F (38°C), yet occasional muskrats and families of Canada geese have been seen swimming in it. The group contains four geysers plus the well named Steady Geyser, a large perpetual spouter. The reason for the odd name "Black Warrior," first applied to Steady Geyser by G. L. Henderson in 1887, was never clearly explained but surely has to do with the mineral deposits within the group.

The springs around Firehole Lake have formed some unique deposits. Many are dark in color. Their craters are coated with a heavy, powdery deposit of black manganese oxide minerals. This is not so unusual in itself, but nowhere is as much being deposited as here. Also, this is the only geyser group in Yellowstone in which travertine, a form of the mineral calcite, is deposited along with siliceous sinter. Young Hopeful Geyser deposits crystalline calcite within its vent, Steady Geyser forms travertine geyser eggs, and Firehole Lake is bordered in places by low travertine terraces. There is no mystery as to how this travertine forms. The water here contains more carbon dioxide than usual, which allows the water to also transport more calcium. The two combine to form the travertine, calcium carbonate.

On the north side of Firehole Lake a short trail can be seen looping across the hillside. This is the Three Senses Nature Trail. The exhibits here emphasize sound, smell, and touch. They are designed for the blind, but they encourage everybody to experience the area without the use of vision. Try it.

25. STEADY GEYSER, also called Black Warrior Geyser, was for years the largest perpetual spouter in Yellowstone, but recently it has declined to a much smaller size. Steady has two vents, which alternate curiously between eruptive and dormant periods. The shifts of energy between these closely spaced openings are very slow, sometimes taking several years to complete. The top vent spouts straight up, in good times reaching 30 feet high. The other vent plays at an angle and may be 12 feet high. It is the lower vent that has been active for most of the past 20 years, with only a bit of splashing seen in the upper vent. Often, too, the current eruption is less than 5 feet high.

As is typical of the Black Warrior Group as a whole, Steady Geyser is forming some unusual deposits. The cone is tinted dark gray by the inclusion of small amounts of manganese oxide in the sinter. In the splash basins and runoff channels are some $1/4$-inch "geyser eggs" of rounded, pearly travertine (calcium carbonate) nodules; elsewhere, geyser eggs are composed of silica.

26. YOUNG HOPEFUL GEYSER, which name was applied in 1872 for uncertain reasons, used to erupt through eleven separate vents. Most of the time the play was only 2 to 6 feet high, but infrequently Young Hopeful erupted with considerably more force, hitting 15 feet in 1878 and as much as 20 feet during 1939. It also had frequent dormancies, lasting days to months. Around 1975 a steam explosion converted the vents into two larger craters. Most of the splashing, which is virtually perpetual, is just 1 to 2 feet high, sometimes surging briefly to 6 feet.

26a. GRAY BULGER GEYSER There has been considerable confusion as to which feature along the south shore of Firehole Lake should bear what name. A careful consideration of historical records leads to the following conclusions. The name Young Hopeful was originally applied to only some of its eleven original vents. Those nearer the break in slope and closest to the boardwalk separately comprise Gray Bulger. Spring #27, identified in the previous edition of this book as Gray Bulger, is really Artesia Geyser, which is how it was identified in this book's first edition in 1979.

Gray Bulger has been frequently active through most or all of Park history, playing sometimes as a geyser and otherwise as a perpetual spouter 1 to 3 feet high until 1975. In that year some small steam explosions enlarged the vents of it and its immediate neighbor, Young Hopeful (26). Gray Bulger began having explosive eruptions to heights as great as 25 feet. That kind of action continued through 1977. Gray Bulger has been generally weak since then, but play 6 feet high is still seen quite often.

27. ARTESIA GEYSER, frequently confused with Gray Bulger Geyser (26a), was named following the 1959 earthquake, when it began activity as a perpetual spouter. There is no record of it before then. In 1975, at the same time explosions and increased activity began in Young Hopeful (26) and Gray Bulger, Artesia also began series of powerful eruptions. Recurring every few seconds and lasting a few seconds so as to complete a full period in just about 1 minute, water jetted as high as 25 to 30 feet. A second vent, which had barely been noticed before, began playing almost horizontally, squirting outward as far as 20 feet. After a short dormancy in

1977, Artesia resumed activity, but the present play is usually less than 5 feet high. (See the Gray Bulger entry, #26a, for more about the confusion among these names. In 1975 a visitor walking along the boardwalk was severely burned by a 25-foot eruption. The official reports cite Gray Bulger. The event probably actually happened at Artesia, which has often been incorrectly identified as Gray Bulger.)

28. PRIMROSE SPRINGS' only known eruptive activity has been confined to short periods following the earthquakes of 1959 and 1983. In both cases the infrequent and brief eruptions reached as high as 10 feet. In 1988 and 1994 Primrose was marginally a geyser, with intermittent bubbling strong enough to be visible from the road. Primrose Springs is the second feature south of the road as it leaves the Firehole Lake area; note that the name is official in its plural form, even though Primrose is a single hot spring. The pool with wide shelves colored by cyanobacteria nearer the road is Fissure Spring.

Table 17. Geysers of the Black Warrior Group

Name	Map No.	Interval	Duration	Height (ft)
Artesia Geyser	27	30–50 sec *	10–30 sec	5–30
Gray Bulger Geyser	26a	erratic	sec–min	1–25
Primrose Springs	28	frequent *	min–hrs	bubbling–10
Steady Geyser	25	steady	steady	5–30
Young Hopeful Geyser	26	near steady	near steady	1–6

* When active.
[ ] Brackets enclose the year of most recent activity for extremely rare or dormant geysers. See text.

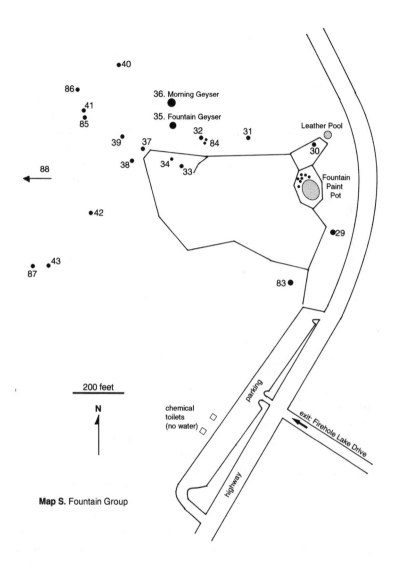

Map S. Fountain Group

Fountain Group

The Fountain Group (Map S, Table 18) is the largest single collection of geysers in the Lower Basin. Several are large, and most are connected as members of the Fountain Complex.

The activity is intense, perhaps more so than in any similar area of Yellowstone, but exchange of function also causes a high degree of irregularity among the geysers.

Geysers notwithstanding, the most popular attraction here is Fountain Paint Pot, the largest easily accessible group of mud pots in the Park. Since the 1959 earthquake increased their activity, the basin in which they lie has been considerably enlarged. At one time the expansion threatened to engulf walkways and roads, and remnants of the old concrete can be seen overhanging the mud at several points underneath the modern boardwalk.

The Fountain Group is traversed by a boardwalk with access from a large parking lot. Leaflets are available for self-guided tours of the half-mile loop trail, and they point out many fascinating aspects of the area in addition to the geysers and mud pots. During the peak of the summer season, a Park ranger-naturalist is often stationed here to answer questions or guide you about the area.

83. CELESTINE POOL is the closest spring to the parking area. A relatively large pool, it is ordinarily quiet, or nearly so, but it has had a few brief episodes of geyser eruptions. The play is then frequent, reaching 1 to 4 feet high. Celestine was active in July 1994.

29. SILEX SPRING fills a deep sinter-lined crater below the boardwalk. The overflow runs across a wide area and supports a profuse growth of multicolored hot water cyanobacteria. The name is derived from the Latin word for silica. Silex has often been observed to undergo occasional boiling periods with consequent heavier overflow. It was first known as a geyser in 1946 and 1947, when it erupted on several occasions. Following the 1959 earthquake the water level in Silex dropped several feet, and for several days it then surged constantly, tossing water 10 feet into the air. The steady activity died down as the crater slowly refilled, and it ceased when the first overflow was reached. No further eruptive action took place until 1973. Silex then began having intermittent eruptions rather often, and the activity persisted into 1979. After an eruption, it took between 2 and 4 hours for the crater to refill. Without warning and almost simultaneous with the first overflow, the pool would begin to surge and boil. Silex needed several minutes to reach full force, which at its peak could send some bursts as high as 20 feet for durations as great as 15 minutes. Silex has been dormant since 1979, but it remains one of the prettier pools in Yellowstone.

30. RED SPOUTER is a direct product of the 1959 earthquake. This was a flat, grassy area until two new mud pots formed following the shocks. After a while these became steam vents. Now, during the seasons of high water table, the vents act as perpetual spouters, throwing muddy, red water as high as 8 feet. At low water Red Spouter reverts to being a steam vent. In reality, then, Red Spouter is nothing more than a fumarole that is occasionally drowned by groundwater, and to call it a geyser is stretching the definition.

THE FOUNTAIN COMPLEX (numbers 31 through 41, plus 84 through 86) probably merits the term *complex* more than any other. It is an association of at least twelve formally and five informally named geysers. In fact, almost every spring in the area is a geyser, and the far-reaching subterranean relationships produce extensive exchanges of function. The activity of everything within the complex is dependent on the current behavior of the other geysers. Three — Fountain, Morning, and Clepsydra — are included in any list of Yellowstone's most important geysers.

On the hill above the Fountain Complex, a short boardwalk spur serves as the Fountain Overlook. From there nearly every spring in the complex can be seen in action.

There is often a well-established pattern of behavior in these springs. These patterns vary over the years, but the performances of 1985 will serve as an example. After Fountain Geyser had erupted, it took several hours for it to refill. During this time practically the only other geysers active in the complex were Twig and Clepsydra. FTN-2, Jet, and Jelly had only occasional plays. Eruptive frequency began to pick up as Fountain neared full, and once it began its next eruption things became exciting. Jet began playing frequently. Clepsydra lost the water supply to one of its vents, which then loudly ejected steam under great pressure. Spasm burst distinctly higher than normal, and even distant Sub could sometimes be seen playing aboveground. Such action would continue for a few minutes after Fountain ended, but then Clepsydra would stop and Twig would occasionally undergo a brief, steamy sort of play. Slowly, the group returned to the "normal" weaker activity typical of Fountain's quiet interval.

This description should only be taken as a guide to the kinds of relationships that exist here. That specific pattern was unique to 1985, and every other year has seen some other mode of behavior. The Fountain Complex is an extremely dynamic set of geysers. Dramatic change can happen overnight, and the reader should understand that the following descriptions relate only to the more typical activity of the past few years.

31. UNNG-FTN-1 plays from an old rift. Until eruptions began in 1985, the crack was filled with soil and grew grasses and wildflowers, aided perhaps by a bit of steam heat and moisture. The activity revealed a series of vents that were eventually enlarged into craters as much as 1 foot across. The play was small splashing, little of which reached more than 1 foot high. FTN-1 is apparently a member of the Fountain Complex, in that it is slightly more active near or during eruptions by Fountain Geyser (35). Its best activity was in 1986, when intervals were 10 to 15 minutes and durations were about 2 minutes long. FTN-1 has been largely inactive since then.

32. TWIG GEYSER lies near the foot of the stairway leading down from the overlook. North of the boardwalk, the shallow crater is about 4 feet in diameter and contains two vents. Both vents splash during the eruption, with bursts 2 to 5 feet high sometimes being topped with jets to fully 10 feet. Twig's intervals depend strongly on the activity of the rest of the Fountain Complex, especially on whether it is Fountain (35) or Morning (36) Geyser that is active. Intervals are commonly between 2 and 3 hours, and the durations range from 1 to $2^1/_2$ hours. During this form of activity, Twig is in eruption fully 50% of the time. However, in 1991, when there were some active phases by Morning, it was known to go as long as 14 hours between short series of brief eruptions. Twig has also been known to have steam phase jetting shortly after the end of some eruptions by Fountain.

84. UNNG-FTN-5 ("BEARCLAW GEYSER") consists of the three small vents a few feet southeast of Twig Geyser (32). As a member of the Fountain Complex, the activity by Bearclaw is strongly dependent on other members of the group. In general, it is most active while Fountain is in eruption and least active when Twig is playing. The intervals range from 10 to 55 minutes. The play lasts 1 to 5 minutes and reaches up to 3 feet high.

33. JET GEYSER is directly related to Fountain Geyser (35) and nearby "Sizzler Geyser" (34). Its elongated cone appears to have developed along an old fracture in the sinter, a break that also extends through Spasm (37), Clepsydra (39), and New Bellefontaine (41) Geysers and totals several hundred feet long. Jet has had a few known dormant periods, but it is normally active under the control of the nearby geysers.

During the first few hours following an eruption by Fountain, Jet is quiet, and it often remains so until Sizzler has played a time or two. Then Jet begins an active series in which eruptions recur every several minutes. Most durations are less than 1 minute, but some of the jets reach 20 feet high. Jet is at its most vigorous when Fountain is in eruption, and it normally stops about the time Fountain quits.

On the rare occasions when Morning Geyser, rather than Fountain, is active, Jet behaves in a very different fashion. There is no extended quiet period. Instead, Jet remains active throughout Morning's interval but with longer and more erratic intervals and durations as long as 2 minutes.

34. UNNG-FTN-2 ("SIZZLER GEYSER") is also known as "Super Frying Pan Geyser." Although that name has received much use, it is unfortunate in that a frying pan is a type of acid hot spring vastly different from a geyser. Sizzler plays from a series of small vents and cracks in the geyserite that probably formed at the time of the 1959 earthquake. The first activity was seen in 1960, with more in 1964, but the geyser did not break out in its present form until 1975. The play consists of sputtering and splashing from at least six distinct vents plus several cracks. The height is 3 to 8 feet for durations of 10 to 17 minutes.

Despite its small size, Sizzler is an important member of the entire Fountain Complex. Recent studies have shown that eruptive cycles in Jet Geyser (33) are strongly affected by Sizzler; Jet will not usually begin to play until Sizzler has had one or sometimes two eruptions. The relationships between Sizzler and the other geysers of the Fountain Complex were less evident while Morning Geyser (36) was active during 1991, when Sizzler had longer average intervals and durations.

35. FOUNTAIN GEYSER has long been considered the major geyser of the Fountain Group. Only Morning Geyser (36) can be larger, but it is seldom active. The pool of Fountain is the nearer of the two beyond the name signs. Broad and deep, it is a rich azure-blue color. The high sinter shoulders about the crater suggest that Fountain has been active for a *very* long time.

The pool is calm throughout the long quiet period. Roughly an hour before an eruption a few bubbles rise through the pool above the vent, but these are so small that they go unnoticed unless one knows exactly where to look or there is a wind. The eruption begins without further warning with a sudden rise in the water level. Huge steam bubbles propel water from the crater, sometimes appearing as gigantic "blue bubbles" that explode and throw water in all directions. The play is often as wide as it is high. Most bursts are 10 to 20 feet high, but some reaching 40 to 50 feet are common. Superbursts reaching over 80 feet are seen during nearly every eruption in some seasons. Fountain was at its very best in 1991 when it erupted in concert with Morning.

Concerted (that is, simultaneous) eruptions by Morning (right) and Fountain Geysers are extremely rare, having been seen only during the first two days following the 1959 earthquake and five times in 1991. (Photo by Lynn Stephens.)

Some of that play easily exceeded 100 feet high. The most typical duration is about 50 minutes.

Interesting patterns occasionally show up in Fountain's intervals. During many years it is regular enough that it can be predicted. At these times the intervals are usually about $5\frac{1}{2}$ hours *or* 11 hours. There are many exceptions to this, but it is curious that the duration and force are about the same whatever the interval and that these changes are not clearly associated with variations in nearby features. One recent study concluded that Fountain's time of eruption was controlled by "Sizzler Geyser" (34), but another analysis done a year later showed no evidence of any correlation.

36. MORNING GEYSER is one of the most powerful geysers in Yellowstone, and its eruptions are often more spectacular than anything seen in the Park since the days of Excelsior Geyser (see #11 of the Midway Geyser Basin). Tremendously explosive bursts can reach 150 to 200 feet high and may spread 60 to 100 feet wide. Unfortunately, though, Morning is seldom active.

The first recorded eruptions of Morning were in 1899, when it was called New Fountain Geyser. That active phase lasted about 3 months. The second period of action was even shorter, spanning 2 months in 1909. One eruption was noted during 1921 and another in 1922. Then nothing more was seen until 1945, when Morning began an active phase that ultimately saw a total of 62 eruptions through 1949. Curiously, the great majority of those eruptions occurred during the morning hours; hence, the renamed "Fountain Pool" became Morning Geyser.

After a dormancy, Morning was irregularly active from 1952 until the time of the 1959 earthquake. That jolt apparently caused a shift in the energy flow of the Fountain Complex. Clepsydra Geyser (39) became more and more vigorous, and the activity of Morning became weaker. By early September Morning was completely dormant. It did not erupt again until 1973, when there were several eruptions, some of which were only about 50 feet high. Additional active episodes, with eruptions approaching the power of old, occurred during 1978, 1981, 1982, and 1983.

None of this matched the unprecedented action seen in 1991. After 8 years of dormancy Morning had at least 5 eruptions in early May. Then on July 4 and 5 there were 2 eruptions. These were in concert with Fountain Geyser (35), an event previously seen only immediately following the 1959 earthquake. After another brief dormancy, Morning rejuvenated on August 9, and during a 21-day active phase there were at least 118 eruptions. Most of the time Morning was predictably regular, with average intervals of $3^3/_4$ hours. The first 1 and last 2 of these eruptions were in concert with Fountain, as had happened in July.

Morning was dormant from August 29, 1991, until March 30, 1994. On a few occasions during that time there were "Fountain stalls" in which Fountain Geyser had extraordinarily long intervals and the water level rose in Morning. The effect was that the system was "trying" to shift energy back to Morning, but it might have been years before it finally did so were it not for an earthquake. A tremor of magnitude 4.9 on March 26, 1994, was centered a few miles northwest of Madison Junction. Morning Geyser rejuvenated on either March 30 or 31. Reporters indicated that the activity resembled that of August 1991, with some intervals shorter than 6 hours. Unfortunately, this active episode was short-lived, lasting less than a week. As a major member of the Fountain Complex, Morning is severely affected by any other activity in the group. On most occasions too much water and energy are lost from the system through other hot springs, and as a consequence Morning is a rare sight.

37. SPASM GEYSER was named for a ragged, jerky pattern of eruptive play — except that the name was originally applied to today's Jelly Spring (38). This was the original "Jet Geyser." During its early history, Spasm sometimes reached as high as 40 feet, with an appropriately jetlike column of water. In 1963 a steam explosion occurred during an eruption. The old crater was enlarged, and a new vent was added to the system. The play now rises from the new, eastern vent, and the surging seldom exceeds 3 feet high. Because Spasm is a member of the Fountain Complex, it is irregular in its performances. The most direct connection is with Fountain Geyser (35). Spasm usually begins to play about halfway through Fountain's quiet interval, and it continues to play until quenched by Fountain's eruption runoff.

38. JELLY SPRING erupts from a crater measuring 16 by 30 feet, one of the largest in the Fountain Group. Prior to the 1959 earthquake Jelly was almost always active, with intervals as short as 10 minutes. Most play lasted only a few seconds and reached 3 to 12 feet high. For the last several years, though, Jelly has been mostly dormant. Showing its relationship to Morning Geyser (36), it erupted a number of times while Morning was active in 1991, had two known eruptions during "Fountain stalls" in 1992, and was seen but a handful of times during 1993. Many of these eruptions consisted of only two or three quick bursts less than 5 feet high. During the long dormant periods, the crater and runoff channels become lined with thick, jellylike masses of cyanobacteria; although the name was originally applied to another spring, it is perfectly fitting here as well.

39. CLEPSYDRA GEYSER was named after a mythical Greek water clock. For years it erupted for a few seconds at intervals of almost exactly 3 minutes. Although there had been some prior exceptions, the regularity came to a permanent end at the time of the 1959 earthquake. In the few weeks following the tremors, Clepsydra gradually grew stronger and steadier and entered what is called "wild phase" activity. This continued with few pauses into 1963. At that time Fountain (35) reactivated from a dormancy, and Clepsydra would then stop playing for a short time following each eruption by Fountain. When Fountain returned to dormancy in 1964, Clepsydra immediately resumed its nonstop wild phase. This kind of activity has characterized Clepsydra ever since:if Fountain is dormant, Clepsydra rarely stops playing; if Fountain is active, Clepsydra will often pause for a few minutes near the end of Fountain's eruption but seldom at any other time.

Clepsydra plays from several vents. The two largest open within a cone of geyserite stained a distinct yellow color. One of the vents jets as high as 45 feet, and the other, at a slight angle, reaches about 25 feet. A number of other openings splash a few feet high. The forceful wild phase activity shows no signs of abating nearly 35 years after the earthquake. It must now be considered Clepsydra's normal activity.

40. SUB GEYSER plays from a deep crater across the sinter flat northwest of Fountain Geyser (35). Most of its activity has been confined to levels deep within the crater, hence the name. Exceptional bursts can reach more than 10 feet above ground level and, therefore, perhaps as much as 20 feet above the actual subterranean pool level.

41. NEW BELLEFONTAINE GEYSER is located beyond Clepsydra Geyser (39), at the visible end of the rift that starts at Jet

Geyser (33). A very active geyser, it repeats its fountainlike play with never more than a few seconds between eruptions, which usually last much less than 1 minute. The height is as much as 20 feet.

85. FITFUL GEYSER lies on the near side of New Bellefontaine Geyser (41). It usually either passes unnoticed or is mistaken for a part of New Bellefontaine. Both intervals and durations are seconds long. The height is 5 to 7 feet. Fitful and New Bellefontaine are among a series of spouters and at least nine geysers that comprise the Gore Springs, a separately named part of the Fountain Complex.

86. UNNG-FTN-6 ("STALACTITE GEYSER") is the largest member of the Fissure Springs, a fracture-controlled group that lies hidden down the west-facing slope below the similar Gore Springs (see #85). Only on rare occasions does Stalactite play high enough to be visible from the boardwalk. Even then, only the top of the eruption is actually seen, and the full height is as great as 12 to 15 feet. The brief durations are separated by intervals of 1 to 8 minutes.

42. OLD BELLEFONTAINE GEYSER is not fitting of the name "beautiful fountain," which was originally applied to another member of the Fountain Group (probably Mask Geyser, #88). Active episodes are irregular, infrequent, and usually very brief. Intervals range from 10 to 60 minutes. Many eruptions consist of a single splash of water less than 6 feet high.

43. UNNG-FTN-3 ("FROLIC GEYSER") was first recorded in 1964. It has probably been active in every year since then but with much variation to its performances. Only a few eruptions are recorded in some seasons, but at other times the intervals can be as short as 5 minutes. The play always lasts less than 40 seconds. Most eruptions are 15 to 20 feet high, but exceptional jets can exceed 50 feet.

87. UNNG-FTN-4 plays out of a jagged crater a few feet beyond "Frolic Geyser" (43). The eruptions are rather uncommon and last only seconds, spraying up to 10 feet high. This area probably includes two (or more) other geysers among its complex of jagged vents, but their activity is rare, and little is known about them.

88. MASK GEYSER is a pool near the western base of the geyserite mound of the Fountain Group. The largest of the Pithole Springs, it is one of Yellowstone's more beautiful pools and is probably the original Bellefontaine Geyser. Unfortunately, it is visible only from the distant boardwalk. Mask's eruptions have shown much variation over the years. The intervals commonly range between 10 and 50 minutes, although periods of hours as well as long dormancies are known. The play lasts seconds to minutes and reaches 10 feet high.

Still farther out across the sinter flats west of the Fountain Group and Mask Geyser are some additional springs. At least two of these have been seen as geysers. The most vigorous known activity was in 1988, when a pool large enough to be quite obvious from the boardwalk played every 11 to 23 minutes. The duration was 5 minutes, and the height must have been at least 10 feet. The other geyser was more irregular and was probably only 4 feet high. No eruptions have been recorded in the area since 1988.

Table 18. Geysers of the Fountain Group

Name	Map No.	Interval	Duration	Height (ft)
Celestine Pool	83	frequent *	sec–min	1–4
Clepsydra Geyser	39	near steady	near steady	10–45
Fitful Geyser	85	seconds	seconds	2–5
Fountain Geyser	35	4–20 hrs *	30–50 min	20–100
Jelly Spring	38	infrequent	sec–min	3–12
Jet Geyser	33	7–30 min *	5 sec–2 min	7–20
Mask Geyser	88	minutes *	sec–4 min	1–10
Morning Geyser	36	[1994]	10–32 min	80–200
New Bellefontaine Geyser	41	seconds	seconds	3–12
Old Bellefontaine Geyser	42	irregular	minutes	2–6
Red Spouter	30	steady	steady	2–8
Silex Spring	29	[1979]	2–15 min	10–20
Spasm Geyser	37	with Fountain	hours	1–3

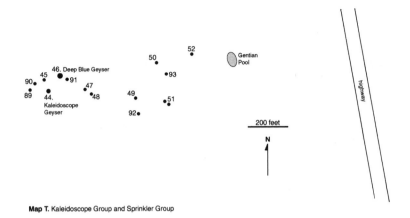

Map T. Kaleidoscope Group and Sprinkler Group

Table 18 continued

Sub Geyser	40	frequent	seconds	see text
Twig Geyser	32	2–3 hrs	1–2 1/2 hrs	5–15
UNNG-FTN-1	31	irregular	minutes	1–2
UNNG-FTN-2 ("Sizzler")	34	1 1/2–2 hrs	10–17 min	3–8
UNNG-FTN-3 ("Frolic")	43	5–60 min *	10–30 secs	20–50
UNNG-FTN-4	87	irregular	seconds	10
UNNG-FTN-5 ("Bearclaw")	84	10–55 min	1–5 min	1–3
UNNG-FTN-6 ("Stalactite")	86	minutes	seconds	12–15

* When active.
[ ] Brackets enclose the year of most recent activity for extremely rare or dormant geysers. See text.

Kaleidoscope Group

The Kaleidoscope Group (Map T, Table 19) is a relatively compact set of hot springs. Its location is especially marked by the large pool of Deep Blue Geyser, far across the sinter flats northwest of the Fountain Group. As of 1993 it contained at least twelve active geysers and numerous perpetual spouters. Since no trail leads into the area and the closest public approach and best view are from the boardwalk within the Fountain Group hundreds of yards away, only those geysers large and frequent enough to be easily seen and identified from a distance are described here. A number of the other geysers that are not included are important; for example, one known simply as "Kaleidoscope Group #12" can erupt as high as 80 feet, but it does so for durations of only a few seconds at intervals weeks to months long.

44. KALEIDOSCOPE GEYSER is the largest frequently active geyser of its group, but even it undergoes dormant periods. Kaleidoscope is cyclic in its performances, with several hours of quiet passing between the eruptive phases. Although not visible at a distance, the later stages of this time are marked by intermittent boiling in Kaleidoscope and small eruptions in a nearby feature. The initial eruption is always Kaleidoscope's largest. Without apparent warning, massive explosive jets of water are rocketed to between 50 and 120 feet high for as long as 2 minutes. Subsequent eruptions generally recur at intervals of only 2 minutes. These last less than 1 minute and reach 40 to 70 feet high. A complete Kaleidoscope cycle may consist of from just one (only the initial) to as many as thirteen eruptions. The concluding play of a series may last as long as 90 minutes but reaches only 1 to 20 feet high.

45. DRAIN GEYSER was named because most of the runoff from Kaleidoscope (44) runs into its crater. It is dormant on most occasions when Kaleidoscope is active. The overall activity is similar to Kaleidoscope's, being cyclic with pauses of several hours leading to series of eruptions with intervals of only a few minutes; unless one is familiar with the area, it is easy to mistake Drain for Kaleidoscope. Starting in 1991 Drain began to have occasional eruptive series during Kaleidoscope's cycle intervals. The net result was a complex double cycle of Drain-pause-Kaleidoscope-pause-Drain; the interval from first Drain to the next first Drain was 15 to 20 hours. Such action continued in 1994. Most of Drain's play reaches 40 to 80 feet high, but a few 1994 eruptions were estimated to top 150 feet.

89. UNNG-KLD-1 ("THREE VENT GEYSER") plays from one of three openings in a large crater a short distance beyond

Drain Geyser is one of several large pools in the Kaleidoscope Group that produces occasional spectacular eruptions. Unprecedented, though, were bursts estimated as high as 150 feet during 1994.

Kaleidoscope (44). The three vents are independent geysers, but only this one is frequent and large. At times, it has been the dominant geyser of the group, and when it is active the only time it pauses is for a few minutes after a series by Kaleidoscope. Three Vent's intervals are sometimes as short as 3 minutes, with durations fully as long. The height is usually 10 to 15 feet, but bursts as tall as 50 feet have been seen.

90. BLOWOUT SPRING is a rare performer. The crater is located beyond Kaleidoscope (44) and Drain (45), either of which it may be confused with and both of which are rendered dormant by its brief active phases. Blowout's eruptions consist of individual bursts of water several seconds apart distributed over a total duration of around 2 minutes. Some of the play is 40 feet high.

46. DEEP BLUE GEYSER, the largest spring in the Kaleidoscope Group, is very well named. The main crater measures 30 by 40 feet and is surrounded by an extensive area of more shallow water. Deep Blue has what have been called major

and minor eruptions. It used to be felt that the majors culmi-nated some kind of series and recurred about once a day, but it is now known that they are just random cases of extraordinarily large bursts. The intervals range from 6 to 90 minutes but are usually somewhat regular within a tighter span of 20 to 50 minutes. Over durations of 3 to 8 minutes, the eruptions involve individual splashes of water separated by several seconds each. Most splashes are 3 to 15 feet high; extraordinary "blue bubble eruptions" can reach over 40 feet. Deep Blue evidently can play much higher. Rare erup-tions known only from washed areas and gravel berms are implied to exceed 100 feet high.

91. UNNG-KLD-2 ("FIREHOSE GEYSER") is a controversial fea-ture. It developed during 1988 along a fracture created by the 1959 earthquake. When Firehose is active, the play is a steady jetting that reaches up to 45 feet high at an angle. At these times, which may last for several months, Firehose behaves as Yellowstone's largest perpetual spouter. But sometimes it has geyserlike pauses; the quiet spans have been observed to range from just 9 minutes to more than 53 days. This leads to the unanswerable question, "Is Fire-hose an 'intermittent perpetual spouter' or a 'long dura-tion geyser?' "

47. HONEYCOMB GEYSER, named because of the decorative form of the geyserite about its crater, is historically little known. It was named during the special studies that followed the 1959 earthquake, when it erupted 10 to 30 feet high about twice a day. It was mostly dormant, however, until 1987. The eruptions since then have generally been quite erratic in time but major in scale. Lasting about 12 minutes (rarely as long as 45 minutes), the play is a violent surging and boiling mass of water 50 to 70 feet high topped by some jets reaching over 100 feet. Honeycomb can also operate as a long-term cyclic geyser in which as many as 9 days pass between active phases, but this kind of action has not been seen since 1989. These episodes consisted mostly of minor eruptions, individual "lazy" bursts reaching 10 to 30 feet high and separated from each other by as long as 40 seconds. The culmination of these cycles was a major eruption.

48. HONEY'S VENT GEYSER was created by a steam explosion in 1960. During its first decade of life it behaved as a geyser, with both major and minor eruptions, but by about 1970 it had become a perpetual spouter. Most of the play was confined to the crater, but occasional surges produced jets as high as 12 feet. The only time it would pause was for a few minutes following the rare major eruptions by nearby Honeycomb Geyser (47). More recently it has again acted as a true geyser. Most intervals are between 15 and 60 minutes long. The durations range between 7 and 42 minutes, placing Honey's Vent into that category of uncommon geysers in which the durations are usually longer than the quiet period. The height reaches 3 to 15 feet above the pool, which normally lies several feet down inside the crater.

Table 19. Geysers of the Kaleidoscope and Sprinkler Groups

Name	Map No.	Interval	Duration	Height (ft)
Angle Geyser	49	frequent	sec–min	10–20
Blowout Spring	90	rare	2 min	5–40
Bridge Geyser	93	min–hrs	seconds	1–10
Deep Blue Geyser	46	6–90 min	3–8 min	3–40
Drain Geyser	45	minutes *	seconds	5–150
Earthquake Geyser	52	steady	steady	2
Ferric Geyser	50	steady	steady	1–8
Honey's Vent Geyser	48	15–20 min	7–42 min	3–15
Honeycomb Geyser	47	hours *	12–45 min	10–100
"Impatient Miser Geyser"	92	frequent	seconds	5–25
Kaleidoscope Geyser	44	2 min *	20 sec–50 min	1–120
Sprinkler Geyser	51	minutes *	minutes	8–15
UNNG-KLD-1 ("Three Vent")	89	3–30 min	3 min	10–50
UNNG-KLD-2 ("Firehose")	91	see text	near steady	5–30
UNNG-SPR-1 ("Vertical")	49	12–20 min *	5–35 min	12–20
West Sprinkler Geyser	51	1–2 min	5–10 sec	12

* When active.

Sprinkler Group

The Sprinkler Group (Map T, Table 19) contains literally hundreds of hot spring vents and at least twenty-one geysers as of late 1993. The Sprinkler Group includes the springs that lie to the north-northwest of the Fountain Group. As viewed from the boardwalk, the Kaleidoscope Group is to the west and Gentian Pool to the east. Gentian, 88 feet long, is among the largest hot springs in Yellowstone. As with the Kaleidoscope Group, no trail leads to these springs, and the identification of the individual geysers from a distance is difficult even for the most experienced viewer. Accordingly, only some of the larger geysers are described here.

49. ANGLE GEYSER plays from one of about a dozen vents within a single large crater complex. Actually, which of these vents is the original Angle is uncertain, as several of the openings have been active as angled geysers. The original played frequently and was about 20 feet high, but no such feature is active now. Another geyser within this complex, UNNG-SPR-1, has been called "Vertical Geyser." When active, it is cyclic in its performances. A series of minor eruptions, each lasting about 5 minutes and recurring every 12 to 20 minutes, is ended by a major eruption with a duration as great as 35 minutes. All of the plays reach 12 to 20 feet high.

92. "IMPATIENT MISER GEYSER" must have the strangest hot spring name. It came about because of nearly constant action that produced almost no external discharge. The geyser lies along the same fissure that includes the complex of Angle Geysers, and eruptions are frequent. Although they last only a few seconds each, some of the jets can reach over 25 feet high.

50. FERRIC GEYSER, surrounded by sinter heavily stained with iron oxide minerals, is the only geyser of the Sprinkler Group to have formed a raised, symmetrical geyserite cone. For a time following the 1959 earthquake, it played every hour as high as 25 feet. The activity has long since regressed

into a weak perpetual spouting just 1 foot high punctuated by infrequent, completely irregular surges that may send some spray up to 8 feet.

93. BRIDGE GEYSER is near Ferric Geyser (50) in an area dotted by myriad hot spring vents. Most of these craters are collapse features. At Bridge, a remnant of the original geyserite roof still arches across the opening. The intervals are extremely erratic, ranging from minutes to hours, perhaps on a cyclic basis. Most of the play is far too small to be seen at a distance, but some eruptions believed to rise from Bridge can reach 10 feet high.

51. SPRINKLER GEYSER lies within an iron oxide–stained crater of a rich red-brown color. Like many of the geysers in this area, it is cyclic in its action, with periods of relatively frequent eruptions separated by dormant periods of several hours. The play consists of sharp jets of water 8 to 15 feet high.

More impressive, perhaps, is "WEST SPRINKLER GEYSER." Rising from the same crater complex as Sprinkler, it erupts with a high degree of regularity and frequency. Most intervals are just 1 to 2 minutes long, water bursting 12 feet high for durations of 5 to 10 seconds. After an eruption the water level drops about 18 inches within the crater; it doesn't begin to rise again until a bare instant before the next eruption.

52. EARTHQUAKE GEYSER merits a place in this book because of its size. Its entire history as a significant geyser spans a few weeks following the 1959 earthquake. From a point along an old fracture, Earthquake Geyser began to erupt as high as 100 feet. A tremendous volume of water was discharged, but the eruptions ended when a steam vent developed just a few feet away on the same rift. Earthquake soon reverted to a perpetual spouter about 2 feet high, which it remains.

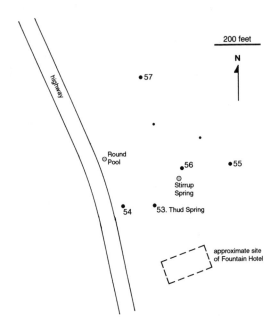

Map U. Thud Group

Thud Group

Once known as the Hotel Group because of the site of the old Fountain Hotel on the hill next to Thud Geyser, the Thud Group (Map U, Table 20) reverted to its original name when the hotel was razed during 1927. Although the springs of this group are generally of minor size, character, and activity, they have received much attention because of the former presence of the hotel. Also, nearly all have been active as geysers.

Many visitors to and employees of the hotel used these springs as trash receptacles. Especially damaged was Thud Spring, the closest member of the group to the building. In 1948 Ranger George Marler made an attempt to clean it; the results were later published in Marler's classic *Inventory of*

Thermal Features. The amount of material removed was astonishing. Here is the complete list of recovered trash: 3 1-gallon crocks, a frying pan, a duster, 7 soda pop bottles, 4 quart whiskey bottles, several beer bottles, a cog wheel, bones, 1 penny, 2 Colorado tax tokens, a 40-gallon drum, 2 wooden kegs, a bath towel, a bath mat, 1 rubber boot, a raincoat, some screen wire, 2 bricks, 1 horseshoe, 16 handkerchiefs, a copper plate, a pitchfork, 1 ladle, a large piece of canvas, a stew kettle, a gunny sack, 17 tin cans, 1 napkin, 1 pie tin, 1 window sash, 2 drawer handles, 1 cooking fork, 2 cake molds, 1 broom, 1 porcelain plate, 1 china plate, a surveyor's stake, 2 wagon braces, a blue dishpan, 2 knives, 1 fork, 1 spoon, a cigarette pack, a 1913 guidebook to Yellowstone, 2 marbles, 1 film box, 4 .22 caliber shells, 1 .45 caliber shell, 1 light bulb, 1 apron, a large piece of pipe, a mixing bowl, a set of men's outer clothing, 1 butter tub, 1 kerosene lamp, 1 large copper lid, an oak evener, a single tree, several barrel staves, 2 ear tags for cattle belonging to a Rexburg, Idaho, rancher, several pieces of window glass, an oven rack, a cotton coat, miscellaneous pieces of iron, copper, and aluminum wire, paper, 1 Mason jar, 1 Vaseline bottle, *and* 1 seltzer bottle. Enough? Let's hope so, for all of this was taken from a crater just 15 by 18 feet across and 12 feet deep.

Please throw your trash in the real trash cans. After all the abuse experienced by Thud Spring, it's a wonder it was able to survive at all.

The Thud Group contains no trails. It is possible to view the springs from pullouts along the roadway or from the site of the old hotel. As is the case with the Kaleidoscope and Sprinkler Groups, the intent is to keep this area inaccessible and, therefore, further untouched.

53. THUD SPRING, despite the treatment it received over the years, has rare active periods. However, because of confusing naming in this group (see Fungoid Spring, #54), the details are uncertain. When active, Thud Spring can play as often as every 3 to 4 hours, with most eruptions lasting 3 to 4 minutes and reaching 12 to 15 feet high.

54. FUNGOID SPRING has also been known as Thud Geyser, and it is likely that at least some reports of eruptions by Fungoid refer to Thud Spring (53) and vice versa. Fungoid received its present name because of the small, mushroom-like masses of geyserite about the rim of the crater. Its only certain years of activity were 1929, 1948, and 1972, when intervals of about 1 hour resulted in 5-minute eruptions up to 12 feet high. Weaker play, perhaps 2 feet high and lasting only a few seconds, was seen in July 1994.

55. GOURD SPRING undergoes such infrequent geyser activity that few details of its action have been recorded. As with Thud Spring (53), Gourd's crater was filled with debris from the old hotel. Much of this was expelled by a single powerful eruption following the 1959 earthquake. During the 1970s it was seen to have infrequent eruptions that splashed 2 to 20 feet high over short durations, and washed areas implied additional activity in 1988.

56. UNNG-THD-1 lies a few feet east of non-eruptive Stirrup Spring, about midway between Thud Spring (53) and Gourd Spring (55). During most years it behaves as a perpetual spouter 1 to 2 feet high. Infrequently, THD-1 acts as a geyser, with intervals of about 5 minutes and durations $1^1/_2$ minutes. Water jets up to 7 feet high have been seen at these times. Because of its location on the far side of Stirrup's geyserite mound, THD-1 is not visible from the highway except when it is having its strongest possible jets. Another unnamed geyser, THD-2, lies a few feet south of Stirrup Spring. It was known to be active only during 1988 and 1993, when eruptions 5 minutes long reached 5 feet high.

57. KIDNEY SPRING, the northernmost member of the Thud Group, is the only regularly active geyser here. The crater is roughly kidney shaped, about 34 feet long and 6 feet wide. Kidney is a very regular geyser. Intervals average about 25 minutes, and any variation of more than 2 minutes from the average is uncommon. Each eruption lasts 3 to 4 minutes, during which the play is mostly less than 4 feet high;

occasional random bursts may jet up to 10 feet. Kidney was inactive during the early years of the Park, but it has played without a known dormancy since the late 1940s or before.

Table 20. Geysers of the Thud Group

Name	Map No.	Interval	Duration	Height (ft)
Fungoid Spring (Thud Geyser)	54	rare	5 min	2–12
Gourd Spring	55	rare	1 min	2–20
Kidney Spring	57	25 min	3–4 min	4–10
Thud Spring	53	rare	4 min	10–15
UNNG-THD-1	56	5 min *	1–2 min	2–7
UNNG-THD-2	56	hours *	5 min	3–5

* When active.

Quagmire Group

The Quagmire Group (Map N, Table 21) is located in a small thermal pocket at the base of the Porcupine Hills along the east edge of Fountain Flat, about half a mile northeast of the Thud Group. Culex Basin and the Morning Mist Group are just beyond the same hills, which are a cemented thermal kame — rocky debris carried by Ice Age glaciers and dumped where the ice suddenly melted because of the hot springs. The Hayden Surveys of the 1870s often camped near the Quagmire Group, and several of the springs are named despite their small sizes and remote positions. Among them are Tree Spring and Lambrequin Spring in addition to Snort Geyser. The group has little to offer, but it does contain one geyser.

104. SNORT GEYSER, named for its hissing, rumbling steam discharge, was apparently a true geyser until the time of the 1959 earthquake. Eruptions were a daily occurrence and sent steamy spray as high as 12 feet for durations as long as a few hours. Since the earthquake, though, all observers have found Snort to be a perpetual spouter, sputtering about 2 feet high.

105. UNNG-QAG-1 plays from a small geyserite cone at the far-south side of the group. Its manner of play seems to have been quite consistent since at least the early 1980s. Intervals of 50 to 60 minutes separate durations that range from 13 to 17 minutes. The height is 2 feet.

Morning Mist Springs, Culex Basin, and Morning Mist Group

These three groups of springs lie along and near the Mary Mountain trail (Map N, Table 21), which departs the highway at the northern end of the Lower Geyser Basin. The first group, which is scattered about an open meadow area, is the Morning Mist Springs. It contains Porcupine Hill Geyser plus several small, infrequently active geysers. Continuing along the trail through a grove of trees, the valley opens out again into the Morning Mist Group, about one mile from the highway. Dominated by Morning Mist Geyser, it encompasses a number of other small geysers. This area is unmistakable because towering above the roadway (which is open only to Park Service vehicles and doubles as the hiking trail) is the face of a large rock quarry. It has been abandoned long enough to have trees growing among the loose boulders. Culex Basin is up and around the hill to the west (right) of the quarry. It boasts at least four unnamed geysers.

The hiking distance from the highway to Morning Mist Geyser is a bit more than one mile. Wildlife is abundant in the area, and since this is prime grizzly bear country, hikers should make some noise.

59. PORCUPINE HILL GEYSER is the first spring encountered as you begin the hike from the highway toward Morning Mist. Less than $1/4$ mile from the trailhead, the geyser is north of the trail at the summit of a broad geyserite mound. Whether Porcupine Hill Geyser has ever had a strictly natural series of eruptions is unknown. Activity was recorded during 1969-1970, shortly after the U.S. Geological Survey completed a nearby research drill hole that probably

induced the activity. The eruptions were as high as 30 feet but were brief, lasting much less than 1 minute, at intervals as long as a full week. An eruption in May 1985 was suspected to have been artificially induced illegally, and another in 1988 might have been induced, too. There are occasional reports of continuing eruptions, but these are generally discounted since the platform is well covered by animal droppings and other debris that would be carried away by any overflow. It is possible that there are occasional minor eruptions. That Porcupine Hill Geyser doesn't have major eruptions more often is curious, though, as the pool is highly superheated.

58. MORNING MIST GEYSER is the only large and truly important geyser in the Morning Mist–Culex Basin area. It lies between the trail and the quarry, about 75 feet south of the road. It is the only feature in the area to have a large runoff channel. The eruption of Morning Mist is not particularly high, reaching no more than 6 feet with its biggest bursts, but it is significant in terms of water discharge. Historically, a single eruption lasted about 12 hours. During that time, more than 100,000 gallons of water, double the volume discharged by Old Faithful in a comparable period, poured down the channel. Once the eruption ended, the water level in Morning Mist dropped about 12 feet within the crater. Refilling took place at about 1 foot per hour, and, once overflow was regained, from 12 to 36 hours of slight discharge took place leading up to the next eruption. Thus, the intervals ranged from 24 to 48 hours and were fairly easy to judge on the basis of water level, overflow rate, and strings of small bubbles that rose through the pool in the last few hours before the play. Unfortunately, Morning Mist has been known to have long dormant periods, and the intervals since 1991 have been at least as great as 5 days and perhaps much longer.

94. GEYSERLET is perhaps the smallest geyser given a name by the early surveys of Yellowstone. It is within a small cluster of springs just around the hill to the east (left) of the quarry. The play is frequent but is only 1 foot high.

Across the stream and meadow east of Morning Mist (58) and Geyserlet are a number of additional springs and pools. One on the valley floor and two on the steep slope above have been seen to erupt as geysers 1 to 3 feet high.

95. UNNG-CLX-1 is the largest and only reliably active geyser in Culex Basin. It can be a bit difficult to find since the rocky crater is in an unlikely position very close to the eastern brink of the steep drop down to Culex Creek. The intervals are usually 4 to 11 minutes long, and the 2-foot play, which lasts 1 to 2 minutes, often fails to fill the crater. Although there is a significant runoff channel, few eruptions produce any discharge. This clearly implies that greater eruptions (probably in terms of duration, not height) occasionally take place.

The other geysers in Culex Basin are more erratic and subject to dormant periods and are only inches to 1 foot high when active. *Culex*, by the way, is the scientific name for a genus of mosquitoes. During warm, moist weather Culex Basin is very well named, but usually more bothersome in the heat of summer are the deerflies, Genus *Chrysops*. Insect repellent provides little protection.

Table 21. Geysers of the Quagmire Group, Morning Mist Group, Morning Mist Springs, and Culex Basin, and Morning Mist Group

Name	Map No.	Interval	Duration	Height (ft)
Geyserlet	94	frequent	seconds	1
Morning Mist Geyser	58	days *	12 hrs	6
Porcupine Hill Geyser	59	[1988]	seconds	30
Snort Geyser	104	steady	steady	2
UNNG-CLX-1	95	4–11 min	1–2 min	2
UNNG-QAG-1	105	50–60 min	13–17 min	2

* When active.
[ ] Brackets enclose the year of most recent activity for extremely rare or dormant geysers. See text.

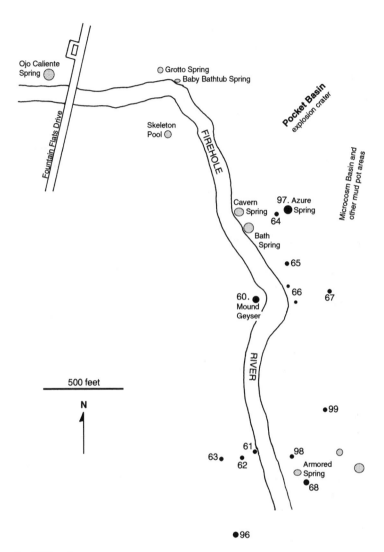

Map V. River Group

River Group

Of all the hot spring groups in the Lower Geyser Basin, only the River Group (Map V, Table 22) lies along the banks of the Firehole River. Thus, the setting of these springs is much like that of the Upper Geyser Basin. The geysers, however, are relatively small compared to those of other areas, and there are some rather wide spaces between some of the individual hot springs. Indeed, if this were a more heavily visited area, it would probably be considered to be several hot spring groups rather than just one.

Much of the lower part of the River Group is within an oval valley known as Pocket Basin. It formed during a large hydrothermal explosion shortly after the end of the last glaciation of the Ice Age, about 10,000 years ago. The ridge that forms the rim around the basin is composed of angular debris that was blasted out to form the valley. In terms of sheer power, the energy released during this explosion was about equal to that of the atomic bombs dropped on Japan at the end of World War II. Associated with this geological setting, over the ridge to the east, is an extensive area of mud pots. This is the largest assortment of mud pots in Yellowstone, and it alone is worth the hike to see. Several occupy impressively large, deep craters and are violently active. Two sometimes act as intermittently geysering mud volcanoes, spraying thick mud as high as 30 feet. Near the south end of the mud pot area, close to where it opens out into part of the River Group, are two clusters of mud volcano cones. The larger of these has the historical name Microcosm Basin. Interestingly, this mud pot area as a whole has no formal name.

There are no established trails in the River Group, but it is traversed on both sides of the Firehole River by paths worn into the ground by thousands of fishermen and geyser gazers. You can drive to the parking lot at Ojo Caliente Spring on Fountain Flats Drive. From there simply go to the appropriate side of the river and begin walking. As you go, remember the hazards of the geyser basins and stay well back from all hot springs.

Ojo Caliente Spring is a part of the River Group, but it is well separated from the rest of the group. It is a superheated pool and smells strongly of hydrogen sulfide gas. Ojo Caliente had a brief episode of eruptions during 1968, at the same time that a geothermal research drill hole was being sunk nearby. The eruptions ended as soon as the drilling stopped and the well was capped. The group contains many other large springs, most notably Grotto Spring, Skeleton Pool, Cavern Spring, Bath Spring, Armored Spring, and eruptive Azure Spring; many others are unnamed.

The geysers of the River Group are discussed geographically from north to south, first those on the west side of the Firehole River, then the ones on the east.

60. MOUND GEYSER is the most important named geyser in the River Group. Its crater measures about 25 by 10 feet and lies at the summit of a large sinter mound that was initially formed by a much older hot spring. Mound is quite regular in its activity. The intervals range from 11 to 35 minutes, but they usually average about 22 minutes and often show only a few seconds variation from that figure over considerable spans of time. The eruptions last 5 minutes. The play is in the form of a series of heavy boiling surges ranging from 6 to 12 feet high. On rare occasions Mound may have more powerful bursting, which was the case when a Park visitor was seriously burned at Mound in 1993. (You have read the warning before, but again: keep your distance from the hot springs. Any of them is capable of providing a surprise.)

Mound itself discharges almost no water, but a collection of related vents down the slope to the north gushes a heavy flow of water during Mound's play. These geysers also have independent eruptions.

61. UNNG-RVG-1 is a large pool near the level of the Firehole River about 800 feet south of Mound Geyser (60). At times of high water the river covers this spring and renders it dormant. Levels low enough to allow eruptions occur only during the driest seasons, most recently during the forest fire year of 1988. Then, after intervals generally only a few seconds long, the pool displays brief eruptions up to 5 feet high.

62. UNNG-RVG-2 had its first known activity during late 1985. After a year or two of play it fell dormant, only to return to action during 1993. The eruptions are very regular at any given time but are widely variable when a span of days is considered. The known range in intervals is from 20 to 50 minutes. Eruptions begin when the water level within the square crater abruptly begins to rise. First, a small subsidiary vent causes jetting 2 or 3 feet high; then the main vent bursts up to as much as 7 feet. Several minutes of minor boiling and splashing follow the 2-minute play. The 1993 activity was similar but weaker and sometimes occurred without action in the main vent.

A few feet north of RVG-2 is a small cone. It was active as a geyser in 1993, playing frequently about 6 inches high. About 15 feet down the slope from the cone was a small patch of gravel that sizzled every few minutes on its own independent intervals.

63. UNNG-RVG-3 is located in a grassy meadow area west of RVG-2 (62). Within this general area are two dozen or more hot springs, most of which show signs of having acted as geysers in the past. The only one of these with a known historical record of activity, however, is RVG-3. During 1973 it erupted frequently from a small pool atop a low geyserite mound. The play reached as high as 15 feet and occasionally had durations as long as 10 minutes.

96. "M-190-B" has come to be the accepted, although unofficial, name for a large pool at the far southern end of the River Group. The designation actually identified a water sample collected by the U.S. Geological Survey when the pool was active as a geyser. During the late 1960s up to 1972, M-190-B was a vigorous geyser. Although the intervals were erratic, ranging from minutes to many hours, the play was a spectacular bursting of water, some jets reaching easily 50 feet high. In 1993, although no eruptions were observed, the area immediately surrounding the crater appeared washed as if small eruptions had pushed waves of water out of the pool.

64. UNNG-RVG-4 is within Pocket Basin, on the east side of the Firehole River near Azure Spring (#97). There is no record of this geyser having erupted prior to the mid-1970s. It is highly variable in its performances, with periods of dormancy or quiet, intermittent overflow more common than episodes of geyser action. During the active phases, RVG-4 has intervals of seconds to a few minutes, the brief eruptions reaching 2 to 5 feet high.

97. AZURE SPRING is a large pool. Its irregularly shaped crater measures about 18 by 40 feet and is deep enough to produce a vivid blue color in the water. Azure is usually active as an intermittent spring. Periods of overflow are generally longer than those when the water level is low, but there is great variation as to how much time one of these cycles takes. On rare occasions, Azure has been known to have small eruptions at the times of high water.

The jagged edges and broken layers of sinter within Azure Spring's crater are proof of an explosive beginning. This happened sometime after the first mapping explorations of Yellowstone — the crater definitely did not exist in the 1880s, at least not in its present form — but prior to the 1959 earthquake, when it was named. In an interesting case of serendipity, a now unidentifiable spring in the River Group was called Azure Pool in 1878; the two are definitely different.

65. DIADEM SPRING is one of the larger blue-green pools in the River Group. Although never a geyser according to a strict definition, Diadem sometimes acts as an impressively voluminous intermittent spring. When active, the water level slowly rises. Just as overflow is reached, a surge sends water cascading over all sides of the crater. Although the height of the eruption is zero, the flood amounts to an estimated 500 gallons per minute for as long as 5 minutes. Just a few feet from the spring, the stream drops over a series of waterfalls and almost directly into the river. The steaming cascade is remarkable. The size of the runoff channels suggests that Diadem has had much activity in its history, but it has now been dormant since 1976.

66. CONE SPRING is at the top of a $4\frac{1}{2}$-foot-high cone perched on the steep bank of the Firehole River. A short distance farther upstream is Horn Spring, with an almost identical cone. Both of these springs bubble and spout slightly. It is doubtful that they have ever had large eruptions, as the slender cones would best be formed by seeping flow running down their sides. Both, however, do erupt intermittently to a slight extent, the bubbling producing splashes a few inches high. During the early 1970s Cone Spring was reported to throw steamy spray as high as 3 feet, but that would have been very exceptional behavior.

67. "POCKET BASIN GEYSER," as often as not known simply as "Pocket Geyser," lies near the natural drainage exit of the Pocket Basin mud pot area. It was not mentioned in any known report, including some written as recently as 1973, but it was vigorously active in 1976. The nature of its geyserite formations and its very deep runoff channel indicate that it is an old spring that reactivated rather than a new one. Pocket Basin Geyser is cyclic in its activity. It has been known to go as long as several days without erupting, yet at other times the intervals are regular and as short as 14 minutes. When it is active the water periodically rises and falls within the vent. Each rise brings the level a bit higher than before. Sometimes several preliminary overflow periods are needed to trigger the eruption; at other times there are none. The play starts with vigorous bubbling that quickly grows into a series of vigorous bursts, some jets reaching over 15 feet high. The entire play lasts about 45 seconds, no matter what the interval.

68. FORTRESS GEYSER, also officially known as Conch Spring, looks as if it should be a powerful geyser. The superheated pool lies within a massive geyserite cone rising more than 4 feet above its surroundings. Although periodic, the quiet intervals are typically only 2 to 4 seconds in length. The play is a violent boiling that sends occasional bursts about 5, rarely 10, feet above the rim of the cone. Wide and deep runoff channels lead away from Fortress, indicating that it did undergo major activity in the past. The only such play in recent history occurred the night of the 1959 earthquake. Although it wasn't seen, it was estimated from the area washed by the water to have reached around 40 feet high.

98. UNNG-RVG-5. The area extending downstream from Fortress Geyser (68) is studded with hot springs that range in size from large and deep pools such as Armored Spring to many tiny bubbling holes. Several of these have been known as geysers, but they all show highly irregular activity. The biggest is a blackish-green pool that has rare bursting eruptions as high as 6 feet.

99. UNNG-RVG-6 is this book's designation for the large area of hot springs on the muddy flats above and east of Fortress Geyser (68) and the RVG-5 (98) features. A number of these springs are vigorous perpetual spouters, and there are several large pools. Eruptive action here is extremely erratic, and appears to be subject to long-term waxing and waning cycles that simultaneously control the water levels. As many as eight or more geysers have been active at once, but often none are active anywhere in the complex. The most persistent is the northernmost geyser. A dark pool near an isolated pine tree somewhat separated from the rest of the cluster, it has a wide and well-used runoff channel. The infrequent eruptions are usually little more than heavy bubbling during surging overflow, but splashes as high as 4 to 6 feet have been seen.

Table 22. Geysers of the River Group

Name	Map No.	Interval	Duration	Height (ft)
Azure Spring	97	rare	sec–min	1–2
Cone Spring	66	near steady	near steady	inches
Diadem Spring	65	[1976]	minutes	see text
Fortress Geyser (Conch Spring)	68	seconds	seconds	5–10
"M–190–B"	96	[1972?]	minutes	10–50

Table 22 continued

Mound Geyser	60	11–35 min	5 min	6–12
"Pocket Basin Geyser"	67	14 min–days *	45 sec	15
UNNG-RVG-1	61	[1988]	seconds	5
UNNG-RVG-2	62	20–50 min *	2 min	2–7
UNNG-RVG-3	63	[1973]	10 min	15
UNNG-RVG-4	64	sec–min *	seconds	2–5
UNNG-RVG-5	98	unknown	1–2 min	6
UNNG-RVG-6	99	hours	minutes	4

* When active.
[ ] Brackets enclose the year of most recent activity for extremely rare or dormant geysers. See text.

Fairy Meadows Group and Fairy Creek Group

Along the broad valley of Fairy Creek, much of which is meadowland, are several small clusters of hot springs. There are few geysers of significant size within these two groups (Map N, Table 23). The easiest access to the area is by way of a trail that leaves the dirt portion of Fountain Flats Drive about 0.4 of a mile beyond (south of) the end of the pavement. This trailhead is not well marked. The route can also be used for access to the Imperial and Sentinel Meadows Groups (next sections).

69. COLUMN SPOUTER (previously identified as FCG-1) is a superheated pool just a few feet east of the trail, about $1/2$ mile from the road. Intervals of complete quiet are uncommon. When they do take place, the pool level drops $1^1/_2$ to 2 feet. As it refills, the water rises as fast as several inches per minute, accompanied by progressively stronger boiling. About when the first overflow following such a pause takes place is the only time Column Spouter can have true bursting eruptions. These may briefly reach 6 to 8 feet high. The play rapidly declines to a vigorous boiling, which may dome the water up to 4 feet but is more commonly a sizzling surface commotion because of the superheated water temperature.

70. UNNG-FCG-2. The Fairy Meadows Group proper lies directly west of Column Spouter (69). A trail to the Sentinel Meadows passes through this area, but the springs have never received extended study. Among them are several impressively large and deep pools, many perpetual spouters, and a few geysers. The eruptions are generally small, and often the largest active geysers will play only a foot or two high. One pool, informally named "Rhinoceros Spring," had a few 10-foot eruptions during 1992.

71. UNNG-FCG-3. Up the valley from the Fairy Meadows Group, isolated by several hundred yards of nonthermal meadow, is the Fairy Creek Group. It lies west of a stand of trees and extends onto the far hillside. FCG-3 is the closest spring to the trees. Eruptions observed during the early 1970s were as high as 30 feet with durations of 5 minutes. Since that time, however, this spring has dramatically changed its appearance: at some time, presumably around 1980, a steam explosion enlarged the crater. What was a vent only about 4 feet across is now a pool with an irregular diameter of 10 feet, surrounded by tilted, broken blocks of geyserite. No eruptions have been observed since the explosion was discovered.

72. LOCOMOTIVE SPRING (previously listed as FCG-4) lies a short distance up the hillside on the far western side of the Fairy Creek Group. It is nearly a perpetual spouter, with only the briefest of pauses interrupting its 6-foot jet. Water discharge is copious. Just down the slope from Locomotive is another spring that, based on extensive washed areas, had some powerful eruptions during the early 1980s, possibly at about the same time a steam explosion disrupted nearby FCG-3 (71).

Table 23. Geysers of the Fairy Meadows, Fairy Creek and Imperial Groups

Name	Map No.	Interval	Duration	Height (ft)
Column Spouter	69	minutes	very long	4–8
Imperial Geyser	73	sec–hrs *	sec–hrs	boil–80
Locomotive Spring	72	near steady	near steady	6
Spray Geyser	74	minutes	minutes	6–30
UNNG-FCG-2	70	see text	-----	-----
UNNG-FCG-3	71	[1980?]	5 min	30

* When active.
[ ] Brackets enclose the year of most recent activity for extremely rare or dormant geysers. See text.

Imperial Group

The most popular access to the Imperial Group (Map N, Table 23) is from the south end of the Midway Geyser Basin. The trail crosses the Firehole River at the "Steel Bridge," follows the old road along the west side of Midway, and then passes through the woods to Fairy Falls. Fairy Falls is one of the nicest waterfalls in Yellowstone, with a delicate, 200-foot sheer drop. It is unfortunate that this area was one of the most severely burned during the 1988 forest fires. From the waterfall the trail continues westward, joins the path that crosses Fairy Meadows, and passes near Imperial Geyser. The round-trip distance along either of the trails is about 7 miles.

73. IMPERIAL GEYSER was born in 1927. If there was a hot spring at the site before then, it had never been recorded. Imperial probably had some eruptions during 1927, but none were directly observed until the following July. Drs. Allen and Day of the Carnegie Institute of Washington conducted extensive observations on the development and behavior of Imperial for their classic work, *Hot Springs of the Yellowstone National Park*. They were instantly impressed with the geyser, and its fame spread rapidly outside the Park. It received its name as the result of a newspaper contest.

Erupting from near one side of a crater nearly 100 feet across, Imperial would continuously shoot bursts 30 feet wide to as high as 80 feet. A single eruption would last about 2 hours, throughout which about 3,000 gallons were discharged each minute (over 360,000 gallons during the entire eruption). "Quiet" intervals of 12 to 20 hours were periodically interrupted by brief splashing to 25 feet, and even then the discharge averaged 700 gallons per minute. In every way, Imperial was one of Yellowstone's most significant geysers. But after 15 months of activity, Imperial fell dormant in October 1929. Because of many apparent steam leaks in the floor of the crater, Allen and Day surmised that Imperial had ruined its plumbing system, never to erupt again.

The dormancy lasted 37 years. Throughout that time the high water discharge continued, and there were periodic episodes of small splashing, but major activity did not take place again until sometime in August 1966. Possibly a long-delayed effect of the 1959 earthquake, the first new activity was never more than 40 feet high, but it was nonstop. The new eruptions were also of different form from those of the 1920s, being rocketing jets rather than massive bursting. Through the succeeding years Imperial gained in strength. In 1973 measurements proved some eruptions to be more than 70 feet high. Although sometimes nearly steady, the activity was most often intermittent, with intervals of 60 seconds and durations of 40 seconds.

From the time of its 1966 rejuvenation through 1984, Imperial showed no signs of slowing down. It was therefore quite a surprise to find it barely active in 1985. Although still nearly constant in its play, the height was not more than 6 feet. Soon it was down to gentle boiling at the most. Imperial is now a beautiful pool. It still has very heavy discharge, but even tiny eruptions are uncommon.

74. SPRAY GEYSER has been known since the earliest days of the Park and is one reason an earlier existence for Imperial Geyser (73) is unlikely. When the first huge steam clouds of Imperial were seen at a distance, it was thought that the source was Spray. It sits back in the woods, up a small tributary a few yards from the runoff from Imperial, perhaps $^1/_4$ mile downstream from that geyser.

Spray was one of the few geysers whose intervals were consistently shorter than the durations. Although the length of these times could vary, the relationship between the two was always the same. In 1929 the quiet intervals lasted from 2 to 31 minutes, the durations from 12 to 38 minutes. During the 1950s the intervals were listed as 2 minutes and the durations as 5 minutes. More recently, Spray's eruptions have lasted 3 to 5 minutes, separated by intervals of less than 1 minute. These statistics show a gradual trend toward steadier activity, and since the mid-1980s Spray has been nearly a perpetual spouter. The eruption includes two main jets of water. One is nearly vertical and is 25 to 30 feet high; the smaller, angled column reaches about 12 feet. Several other openings play water between 2 and 6 feet. Unfortunately, the height of the modern perpetual action is seldom more than about 6 feet. Still, the entire cone complex and vicinity is covered with some of the lushest and most colorful cyanobacteria anywhere.

Sentinel Meadow Group

The hot springs of the Sentinel Meadow Group (Map N, Table 24) are scattered about a broad valley. Three of these have formed large geyserite mounds. Known as Flat Cone, Steep (or Sentinel) Cone, and Mound Spring, each is capped by a deep, boiling pool. The spring atop Flat Cone has been known as a geyser in recent years, and that on Steep Cone probably was in years past. A fourth major spring is Queen's Laundry. That name originated with Park Superintendent Norris in the early 1880s when bathers draped their colorful clothing on nearby trees. The same pool is also known as Red Terrace Spring because of the wide overflow terraces that used to be covered with orange-red cyanobacteria. Nearby is a wooden structure, the remains of a bath house built by Norris in 1881.

The Sentinel Meadow Group contains at least eight geysers. Little is known about them since this is a fairly remote area. From the trailhead on Fountain Flats Drive across the

Firehole River from Ojo Caliente it is 1.7 miles to Queen's Laundry. A second route, from the trailhead that leads to the Fairy Meadows Groups, is about the same distance.

75. BOULDER SPRING lies immediately at the base of a low, boulder-strewn hill about 300 yards southwest of Ojo Caliente. Not a part of the Sentinel Meadow Group, it is included here since access to it occurs from the Sentinel Meadows trail. Boulder Spring is a perpetual spouter, playing from two main vents within one pool. The height of the eruption constantly varies in a pulsating motion and it also waxes and wanes in overall force. The height ranges from less than 1 foot to more than 6 feet.

In 1991 another vent, among the boulders just outside the pool of Boulder Spring proper, was observed to have periodic eruptions. The play was frequent and was up to 4 feet high. It persisted for only a few weeks.

Northwest of Boulder Spring, between the hill and the Sentinel Meadow trail, is an area of old craters and sinter platforms. The activity here was vigorous once upon a prehistoric time but is now so dead that only slight wisps of steam can be seen on cold days. Near here, however, a short-lived mud pot at the base of the hill opened a 10-foot-wide crater full of boiling mud in 1985.

76. UNNG-SMG-1 is located on the northern flank of the wide, low mound of Mound Spring, the first of the large superheated pools encountered when entering the area on the trail from Ojo Caliente. The geyser plays from a beaded vent stained orange by iron oxide minerals. Somehow, I seem to be the only reporter to have seen it have large eruptions, which I did in the 1970s and again in 1993. The play is a series of distinct squirts of water, at first reaching up to 20 feet but quickly dying down to just 2 or 3 feet at the end of the eruption. From start to finish it lasts no more than 20 seconds. For several minutes following the eruption the water remaining in the vent boils violently before draining abruptly. The interval of this geyser is unknown but must be very long and erratic. SMG-1 also has long dormant periods during which the small runoff channels virtually disappear.

77. UNNG-SMG-2 ("CONVOLUTED GEYSER") lies down the slope toward the stream from Mound Spring and SMG-1 (76). It was named after the exquisitely ornate geyserite surrounding the crater, which looks much like the surface of a brain. The vent is about 6 inches in diameter. Convoluted is highly variable in its activity, sometimes erupting every few seconds for a few seconds and on other occasions going as long as hours between plays that last a few minutes. The height is always about 2 feet.

78. ROSETTE GEYSER is far to the northwest across the valley. It was not named for the shape of the crater, as previously reported, but because of the numerous rosettes of geyserite that decorate the platform surrounding it. Research has shown that during the first 14 years of Park history, Rosette was a well-known geyser. Eruptions were frequent and were up to 25 feet high. A long dormancy began in 1886. Rosette was not described again until 1929, when play lasting a few seconds reached 10 to 15 feet as often as every $1^1/_2$ minutes. Again, there is no further record of activity until the 1970s, when the intervals were 2 and more hours long and the play was just 2 to 4 feet high. Such activity continues, with one interval known to have exceeded 20 hours. Rosette may have been dormant in 1993; if it was active, the intervals were many hours long.

100. FLAT CONE GEYSER is, naturally, at the top of Flat Cone, the large geyserite mound across the valley toward Rosette Geyser (78). It is a superheated pool. A description written in 1878 seems to imply that there were no runoff channels on the cone at that time. Now they are deeply incised and extend down all sides, telling of extensive but unseen eruptive activity since 1878. Eruptions were finally observed during the 1980s. Intervals were generally a few hours long. The beginning of the play was marked by a sharp pounding of the ground that sometimes could be felt and heard at a distance of several hundred feet. The eruption consisted of a surging, bursting boil as high as 15 feet. Although still active, the frequency and force of the eruptions had decreased considerably by 1994.

101. THE BULGERS is a collection of small springs a short distance south of Steep Cone, which rises directly above Sentinel Creek. The Bulgers play so frequently that they come close to being perpetual spouters. The height is 1 to 3 feet.

79. IRON POT is a fascinating feature. The crater is oval, about 15 feet in diameter, and is lined with a smooth, tan geyserite. The crater tapers downward so that at a depth of about 20 feet it is a narrow opening measuring 6 by $1^1/_2$ feet. Iron Pot never overflows. During the interval, which is 6 to 14 hours long, the water level slowly rises within the crater. When it reaches about 6 feet below the rim, the eruption begins suddenly. A violently rolling boil domes the water as high as 6 feet and lasts as long as 1 hour. The play ends abruptly, and the crater drains almost completely within a few minutes.

102. UNNG-SMG-3 is a small spring southwest of Queen's Laundry. A buildup of sinter along its runoff channel has formed an interesting flumelike form. The spring itself usually only overflows a heavy but steady stream, but one time in 1993 it was seen splashing about 1 foot high.

"Marshall's Hotel Group"

The "Marshall's Hotel Group," so designated here, consists of the scattered springs near the entrance of Fountain Flats Drive. Two of the springs are named. Hygeia Spring, named after the goddess of health, is the cone on the left side of the road a short distance beyond Nez Perce Creek and the picnic area. Maiden's Grave Spring lies next to the river to the right of the road about halfway across the grassy flats. It was named in allusion to the grave of Mattie S. Culver, who died during winter 1889 at Marshall's Hotel. The grave is next to the Nez Perce picnic area, which is near the site of the hotel. Built in 1880, the hotel was Yellowstone's second commercial lodge.

103. "TWILIGHT GEYSER" lies several hundred feet out in the meadow across the river from Maiden's Grave Spring. Erup-

tions by this geyser were frequent but were only 1 to 5 feet high during the 1970s. After a dormancy, Twilight rejuvenated in 1985 but on a very different pattern. Eruptions are now uncommon, but they may last for several hours and burst the water 10 to 20 feet into the air during exceptional displays.

Table 24. Geysers of the Sentinel Meadow Group and "Marshall's Hotel Group"

Name	Map No.	Interval	Duration	Height (ft)
Boulder Spring	75	steady	steady	1–6
Flat Cone Geyser	100	hours *	minutes	boil–15
Iron Pot	79	6–14 hrs	1 hr	6
Rosette Geyser	78	hours	sec–min	2–25
The Bulgers	101	frequent	sec–min	1–3
"Twilight Geyser"	103	irregular	min–hrs	1–20
UNNG-SMG-1	76	rare	20 sec	20
UNNG-SMG-2 ("Convoluted")	77	sec–hrs	sec–min	2
UNNG-SMG-3	102	unknown	minutes	1

* When active.

Chapter 7

Norris Geyser Basin

The Norris Geyser Basin is very different from any other geyser basin in Yellowstone in several ways. Only the geyser eruptions themselves look the same. The casual visitor to Norris immediately notices that the scene is stark. The Porcelain Basin is a barren depression almost totally devoid of plant life, drab gray without the pastel shades of other areas. Runoff channels are only sporadically lined with cyanobacteria, bacteria, and true algae, and the few other visible colors are dominated by the rich orange-brown of iron oxide minerals.

Norris's unique appearance is a result of the presence of acid water, which is not common in the other geyser basins. Large amounts of sulfur are being brought to the surface. In the springs it is oxidized to form sulfuric acid. The siliceous sinter deposited in the acid water is spiny and does not form the thick masses so common in the alkaline areas such as the Upper Geyser Basin. Norris does have some springs of alkaline water, and they tend to deposit geyserite at rates much greater than those elsewhere.

Norris is also the hottest geyser basin in Yellowstone and, in fact, is one of the hottest in the world. The water temperatures are higher and, consequently, the geyser activity is more vigorous, whereas quiet pools are less common than elsewhere. One research drill hole here reached a temperature of 459°F (237°C) at a depth of only 1,087 feet below the surface.

One curious aspect of the activity at Norris occurs during the summer or fall of most years. Popularly known as the "seasonal disturbance," its exact cause is still uncertain but apparently includes the following conditions. There is evidence that the hot springs at Norris are served by two separate geothermal reservoirs at depth, one deep and hot and the other more shallow and somewhat cooler. Because of the lack of extensive geyserite deposits, which might otherwise seal the upper part of Norris's geothermal system from inflowing surface water, there is an inflow of cold groundwater as well as some recycling of hot spring water back into the shallow parts of the geothermal system. As summer progresses, the decreased supply of cold surface water allows a higher temperature to develop in the upper reaches of the regime. The result is that quite suddenly, often within a few hours, many of the Norris springs and geysers become muddy. Pools that are normally quiet spring to life as geysers; existing geysers become more frequent in their activity. Usually, the disturbance occurs just once a year, commonly during August or September. In 1984, however, a series of localized small-scale disturbances was distributed between May and October. In any situation in which an individual spring is especially affected by the seasonal disturbances, the fact is noted in the following descriptions.

As with geysers anywhere, those at Norris are also affected by earthquakes. There is little information about specific changes in 1959, but the shock of 1975 caused both immediate and long-term alterations in many of the geysers. That of March 1994 may have caused some alterations, but any 1994 adjustments are difficult to determine since significant changes were already underway at Norris when the quake took place.

The only public facility at Norris is a small museum. It contains displays about the different kinds of hot springs, their mineral deposits, and the life of the geyser basins. An information desk and book sales area are found in the Museum, and rest rooms and vending machines are located at the parking lot. A trail guide is available. Norris has a small naturalist staff whose members lead occasional guided walks, rove the trail system, and present evening talks at the campground.

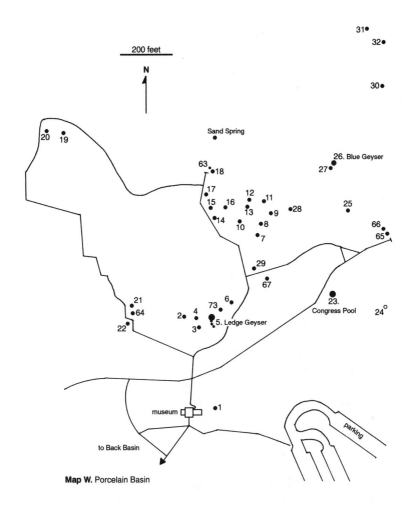

Map W. Porcelain Basin

Porcelain Basin

The Porcelain Basin (Map W, Table 25) comprises the northern portion of the Norris Geyser Basin. It was named for one of the few masses of alkaline sinter found at Norris. Porcelain Basin is a relatively small area, but the geyser and other hot spring activity is highly concentrated. A single glance from the Museum overlook might easily take in a dozen or more erupting geysers.

Porcelain Basin is also an extremely changeable area. The larger, long-lived geysers — most of those that have names — are never quite the same from one year to the next. Most of the geysers are small and very short-lived, and many act as perpetual spouters rather than as true geysers during their brief existence. Because of the internal deposition of minerals (mostly silica with some clay), they quickly seal themselves in. The hot water they give off soon finds exit through new geysers and spouters. Such features, possibly numbering fifty or more at any given time, obviously cannot be included in the descriptions here. Look for them in the central part of Porcelain Basin, especially on the wide flats east of Pinwheel Geyser, and below Porcelain Terrace at the far eastern end of the area.

For reasons that are not known, the southwestern and central portions of Porcelain Basin underwent a substantial decline in vigor during the 1980s. There was, however, a nearly simultaneous increase in the action of the eastern part of the basin. One surmise is that this was caused by a large-scale exchange of function that might have been started by the earthquake of June 30, 1975, a magnitude 6.1 shock with its epicenter only a few miles from Norris. Preliminary indications are that this same area was benefited by the magnitude 4.9 earthquake of March 26, 1994.

The Porcelain Basin trail is a combination of dirt, asphalt, and boardwalk paths. The entire system covers about 1 mile.

1. HARDING GEYSER probably had some eruptions during the late 1910s, but it wasn't named until 1923, the year President Harding visited Yellowstone. The vent is almost invisible from the trail, hidden within a gully a few feet east of the Museum building. Harding Geyser rarely erupts. The best seasons on record are 1975 and 1982, with several eruptions each. The play lasts about 5 minutes, and the 50-foot water jet is concluded by a short steam phase.

2. DARK CAVERN GEYSER is usually a faithful and frequent performer. It issues from a cavelike opening in a pile of

boulders coated with dark gray geyserite. The water jet would be higher and more pronounced if it didn't strike an overhanging rock. Deflected as it is, the maximum height is still as much as 20 feet. Dark Cavern is known to have both minor and major eruptions. In general, eruptions recur every 17 to 25 minutes. Sometimes, when nearby Valentine Geyser (3) is active, there is a clear progression of gradually stronger and longer eruptions, leading to a major that ends the series. It is followed by a somewhat longer interval at about the same time Valentine erupts.

During the winter of 1993–1994, Dark Cavern began having eruptions of unprecedented force. Durations were highly variable and were as long as 45 minutes. Water jets more than 45 feet high would periodically yield to powerful steam phases whose roar could be heard nearly a mile away. The intervals between these eruptions ranged from 12 hours to 5 days. When Ledge Geyser (5) erupted, the interval could be as long as 9 to 14 days, proving for the first time a subsurface connection between the two geysers. This activity was continuing as of July 1994.

3. VALENTINE GEYSER was named because of an eruption on St. Valentine's Day, 1907, but either it or an adjacent vent erupted as Alcove Spring in 1890–1891. Its history since 1907 has been highly erratic. In good years the intervals are as short as a few hours. At other times days to weeks may pass between eruptions, and Valentine is dormant much more often than it is active. The most recent vigorous cycle took place during 1989, when series of minor eruptions at intervals of 8 to 20 hours led to major eruptions 3 to 5 days apart. A few additional eruptions took place in the days following a minor earthquake swarm in June 1990. Valentine apparently was *not* affected by the March 1994 tremors.

Located in a wide, deep alcove below the trail, Valentine's 6-foot-high cone is the largest at Norris. The major eruptions are strangely quiet. Little more than the hissing sound of falling water can be heard. Near the beginning of the play, the steady jet may reach 75 feet high, although 20 to 50 feet is more typical. The water rapidly gives way to steam, and the remainder of the play is an impressive cloud of steam and fine spray shooting to 40 feet. Most durations, water plus steam phase, are in the range of 5 to 22 minutes.

4. GUARDIAN GEYSER is generally a rare performer. It lies at the narrow exit of the alcove containing Valentine Geyser (3) and spouts from a small pile of iron-stained rocks. It has shown several different modes of activity. It sometimes acts as a precursor to Valentine, preceding that eruption by a few moments. The play is 8 to 25 feet high and lasts only a few seconds. When Valentine is dormant, Guardian shows a different manner of play. These independent eruptions are infrequent but have been observed to last as long as 4 minutes and reach up to 30 feet. This kind of action may be more common when Ledge (5) is active, and, indeed, Guardian was playing about daily in April and May 1994. Finally, Guardian has also been known to undergo noisy steam phase eruptions with little or no preliminary water ejection. In the long run, it is dormant more than it is active.

First seen during 1984 and only rarely since is another geyser, just outside the alcove opening a few feet from Guardian. Its activity coincided with steam phase eruptions by Guardian. The play recurred every 9 to 26 minutes, lasted as long as 19 minutes, and much resembled the action of a squirt gun. The height was about 6 feet.

5. LEDGE GEYSER is, aside from Steamboat (36), the largest geyser at Norris, but it is highly irregular in its activity and is dormant during most years. Its best year on record was 1974, when eruptions occurred every 14 hours with predictable regularity. It continued such action until the earthquake of June 30, 1975; less frequent activity then continued into 1979. Ledge was completely dormant from then until the last week of 1993.

When active, there is an extraordinary amount of preplay from Ledge. It erupts from five vents that are aligned so that the activity somewhat resembles the human hand. Three of the central vents jet water a few feet high; they are known as the "finger vents," and their activity is almost constant during

Ledge Geyser is the most powerful in Porcelain Basin. Dormant for more than 15 years, it reactivated in late 1993.

the buildup to an eruption. At the point nearest the trail is a deep cavity with a small vent at the bottom. This "little finger" slowly fills with water during the preplay. When Ledge was frequent and regular, as in 1974, the water level in this "pressure pool" could be used to predict the time of an eruption. The main vent is difficult to see from the trail. It lies to the far right, it the area where the bench containing the finger vents drops off to lower ground. This opening, the "thumb," penetrates the hillside at an angle. During the preplay, water occasionally splashes out of this vent. When Ledge is ready to erupt, one of these splashes becomes a steady surge and then suddenly bursts into a tremendous eruption. It is one of the most impressive anywhere, reaching full force in a matter of seconds. The water shot from the thumb reaches a height of 80 to 125 feet, and, because of its 40-degree angle, it falls as far as 200 feet from the vent. (The known record, tape measured in 1974, was 220 feet. However, sometime between 1978 and 1993 a rock that projected over the vent fell off. The eruptions of 1994 described here are at a steeper angle and have a somewhat shorter horizontal throw.) Meanwhile, the fingers are playing slender columns of water to 30 feet and more, and the pressure pool may burst to more than 60 feet. The booming and roaring spectacle cannot be matched anywhere. The major activity of Ledge lasts about 20 minutes, throughout all of which the maximum height is maintained by the main vent. Thereafter, the eruption slowly subsides. After about 2 hours it is finished, although Ledge never falls completely silent.

Whatever caused the 1979 to 1993 dormancy in Ledge was probably what also started a long-term dormancy in Valentine Geyser (3) and a general decline throughout the southwestern and central portions of Porcelain Basin beginning in 1978. This might ultimately have been triggered by the 1975 earthquake, since the activity went into a gradual decline shortly thereafter. In 1989 and the early 1990s there were some signs of recovery. Jetting by Ledge's finger vents was sometimes quite strong, and there was occasional overflow from the main vent. However, because a number of noisy steam vents had developed on the slopes near Ledge, some observers felt they were robbing Ledge of eruptive energy. But during the last week of December 1993, Ledge did erupt. All of the vents of old were active about as before, and one of the new openings joined in by arching 100 feet high up and over the asphalt walkway. Eruptions at intervals of about 9 to 14 days were continuing in July 1994. They began after as much as 3 days of nearly steady overflow and ended with hours-long steam phases the equal of any other geyser. The March 1994 earthquake had no clear effect on Ledge's performances.

73. JETSAM POOL is a few feet northeast of the main vent of Ledge Geyser (5). It had small, bursting eruptions in 1970–1971, probably in conjunction with nearby Ledge, so it was a geyser gazer's delight but not a historical surprise when it joined the early 1994 play by Ledge with erratic bursts up to 65 feet high. It apparently had only a few eruptions before lapsing back to the murky, quiet pool of before.

6. BASIN GEYSER used to erupt from the center of its pool. The play was frequent but small. Near the time of the 1975 earthquake some new vents developed at the left end of the crater, and most of the eruptions issued from them, reaching 6 feet high. In the late 1970s the crater drained, and all eruptive activity stopped. Basin again contains a bubbling pool, but a lack of eruptions has allowed wildflowers to grow deep within the crater.

7. UNNG-NPR-1 ("GEEZER GEYSER") erupts from an unimpressive little hole among some jagged rocks. It is active essentially only at the time of a seasonal disturbance, but even then activity is rare. The play can last as long as 15 minutes and reach up to 15 feet high.

8. ARSENIC GEYSER poses some mystery. Through the years the name has apparently been variously applied to the geysers now known as Pinto (11), Fan (12), one of the vents of the Lava Pool Complex (9), and perhaps others. Accordingly, many historical references to "Arsenic" do not apply to today's geyser. It plays from a small, conical, sinter-lined vent slightly to the south of the others. This modern Arsenic has also recently been known as Moxie Geyser. Sometimes, Arsenic is nearly dormant, the "eruptions" being little more than intermittent bubbling. At other times true bursting plays up to 20 feet high recur several times a day and last as long as 20 minutes. During the disturbance events, Arsenic is much more active, and durations as long as 3 hours with heights of fully 35 feet are known.

9. LAVA POOL COMPLEX is a group of vents at the base of the low hillside beyond Arsenic Geyser (8). There are at least seven vents, and there is nearly always some spouting action among them. Their nature changes rapidly, but typical is splashing a few feet high. Infrequently, especially during the seasonal disturbances, all of the vents can be active for durations several hours long and heights as great as 10 feet.

10. AFRICA GEYSER developed during 1971 in a previously inactive crater shaped somewhat like the continent of Africa. The eruptions were 45 feet high and very regular, with almost clockworklike intervals of 90 minutes. As time progressed the intervals shortened and the force weakened. By 1973 Africa had become a perpetual spouter perhaps 20 feet high. Change continued. The water gave out in the late 1970s, and a steady steam phase ensued. At times, the roar could be heard from the far end of the Back Basin, over the hill and more than a half mile away. But even that was temporary. Africa quit playing shortly after the sinter sheet ruptured nearby, and it is now only one among many holes in the ground.

In January 1994, just a few days after the rejuvenation of Ledge Geyser (5) and Jetsam Pool (73), a "new" geyser was reported a short distance north of Africa. It played from an old crater with no previous record of activity. The eruptions were frequent as first, but the geyser quickly died down and was not seen during postearthquake observations in April 1994. It is possible that this was actually Fireball Geyser (13), but not all observers agree.

11. PINTO GEYSER spends most of its time as a calm, blue pool, although it did have early records of activity under the names Twentieth Century and Arsenic (see #8). At the time of the seasonal disturbances Pinto can become a geyser of considerable power. Muddy water is thrown to 40 feet in eruptions that last as long as 30 minutes. The irregular intervals range from 5 minutes to several hours during the few days of the disturbance.

12. FAN GEYSER is located a few feet beyond Fireball Geyser (13). The pearly, orangish vent is almost impossible to see from the boardwalk. Fan is often dormant for long periods but sometimes becomes a very regular geyser. Then it may have 10-minute eruptions as high as 10 feet several times a day. During the disturbance episodes Fan develops a nearly perpetual bubbling and splashing punctuated by frequent, brief eruptions 15 to 25 feet high.

13. FIREBALL GEYSER shoots out of several small vents among a low pile of red, iron-stained rocks about 100 feet beyond Little Whirligig Geyser (14). Each of the openings jets water at a different angle and height. The largest is vertical and is 12 feet high. Eruptions by Fireball are normally frequent, with durations of around 5 minutes. During the early 1990s the intervals were as long as several hours, but the play lasted as long as 20 minutes and reached up to 25 feet. As with many other geysers in this part of Porcelain Basin, Fireball becomes more frequent at the time of the seasonal disturbances; during 1984, when a series of minor disturbances was recorded, it was in eruption about half the time.

There has been discussion as to which geyser, #12 or #13, is Fan and which is Fireball. The play of #13 is distinctly fan shaped, whereas that of #12 certainly is not. There is little doubt that the names were inadvertently switched sometime in the past so that we now have a nonfan-shaped geyser named Fan and a fan-shaped geyser named Fireball.

14. LITTLE WHIRLIGIG GEYSER erupts from a crater colored bright orange-yellow by iron oxide minerals. It is one of the more colorful spots in the Porcelain Basin. Although known to have been active in 1887 and 1922, Little Whirligig rarely erupted prior to the early 1930s. During that decade nearby Whirligig Geyser (15) declined in activity until it seldom played. By then, Little Whirligig was nearly a perpetual spouter. The eruptions were a squirting sort of action, jetting water as high as 20 feet at an angle toward the boardwalk. It wasn't until 1973 that it began taking occasional rests, pausing for about 20 minutes just two or three times a day. These pauses gradually grew more extreme, and by 1975 Little Whirligig was nearly dormant. The earthquake of June 1975 might have sealed its fate for the time being. It has since had only a few, very brief active phases of frequent but small bursting eruptions.

15. WHIRLIGIG GEYSER, also known as "Big Whirligig," was named because of the way the water swirls about the crater during the eruption. After many years of dormancy, Whirligig

rejuvenated in summer 1974, corresponding with a decline in vigor in nearby Little Whirligig (14). Eruptions were frequent and regular, lasting between 3 and 4 minutes. This action persisted into the 1980s, but it is now more erratic, with intervals as long as 24 hours. The play begins with a sudden, rapid filling of the crater. The largest portion of the activity comes from the central vent, where the water is thrown 6 to 15 feet high by a series of closely spaced bursts. This is joined by the "rooster-tail vent" in a crack on the far side of the crater. It shoots water in a series of puffs, looking much like the bird's tail plumes and sounding like an old steam engine. This chugging sound can easily be heard from the Museum.

16. CONSTANT GEYSER has never seen anything approaching constant eruptions, but at one time it had such a high degree of regularity and frequency that it was the one reliable "constant" at Norris. That has certainly changed. On most modern occasions the action has been erratic, with infrequent eruptive episodes interspersed among long dormancies. Constant is clearly related to the two Whirligigs: it is most active when Whirligig (15) is also active and is nearly dormant while Little Whirligig (14) is playing. When it is active, Constant often has eruptions in series, with cycle intervals ranging from minutes to a few hours. One sign to look for is a pulsation of the surface of the shallow pool, which is located a few feet beyond Whirligig. Watch closely! After only a few seconds of such warning, the entire play lasts just 5 to 10 seconds. The height can be between 5 and 30 feet. Sometimes, a few small splashes take place about 3 minutes before "major" eruptions, which were about 45 minutes apart in early 1994.

17. SPLUTTER POT, once known as the "Washing Machine," plays from a small crater in the middle of the runoff from Pinwheel Geyser (18). The rim of the crater often forms an island in the middle of the stream, but it only partially blocks inflowing cool water so that Splutter Pot has had many long dormancies. When active, the intervals are normally about 4

to 6 minutes. The play is a chugging splashing 2 to 6 feet high that lasts 1 to 2 minutes. Splutter Pot becomes a perpetual spouter during some seasonal disturbances.

Along the runoff between Splutter Pot and Pinwheel Geyser are two other vents that occasionally play as small, irregular geysers.

18. PINWHEEL GEYSER was once one of the stars at Norris. Its eruptions were frequent and were over 20 feet high. In allusion to Grand Geyser in the Upper Basin, it was known as "Baby Grand." During the late 1960s the ground on the far, upstream side of the crater settled a few inches. Cooled runoff from other springs, which formerly flowed away from Pinwheel, was able to run directly into the pool. This water lowered the temperature of Pinwheel enough to stop almost all eruptive activity. During the late summer disturbance of 1974, this inflow decreased markedly, and Pinwheel had minor eruptions 1 to 2 feet high. This play was often accompanied by a vigorous pulsating of the pool. It appeared that Pinwheel was about to explode with the power of old, but nothing happened. There is a feeling that enough sediment has now washed into the crater to effectively seal Pinwheel off. If so, it may never again erupt as it did in the past.

63. "PEQUITO GEYSER" (misspelled from the Spanish *poquito*, for small one) was named because of its tiny vent near the left edge of Pinwheel Geyser's (18) sinter shoulders. Seen during only a few seasons, most recently in 1992 and 1993, the irregular eruptions squirt water several feet high over the course of a few minutes.

About 50 yards beyond Pinwheel and Pequito, right at the base of the hillside, is Sand Spring. Most often active as a perpetual spouter, it has been known to act as a frequent periodic geyser. The splashes are 1 to 3 feet high. Sand Spring was dormant in 1994.

19. BEAR DEN GEYSER has been dormant for several years. The vent is a narrow defile among some boulders of welded volcanic ash and has been thoroughly clogged by debris eroded from above. Bear Den came as a complete surprise to many who managed to see an eruption. Its site attracted little notice, as it is partially hidden by trees below the trail and because there was no pool to emit steam. The eruptions, though, were very impressive. Water was squirted by a series of distinct pulses to heights as great as 70 feet, the jets angled so the water fell far downhill from the vent. A single eruption consisted of just 1 to as many as 35 individual bursts. Typical intervals were between 3 and 7 hours. Bear Den's dormancy came suddenly, and there has been no indication of a recovery by it or any nearby feature.

Bear Den came into existence during the 1950s, after the vent of nearby Ebony Geyser (20) was nearly choked by debris thrown by visitors — it may have developed as a new outlet for Ebony's blocked energy. However, Bear Den might have eventually formed even without the vandalism. Extending through the forest west of Ebony, on a line that includes Bear Den, is a chain of old hot spring craters. It appears that over a long span of time the focus of energy has progressed from west to east along a subsurface fracture, with Bear Den being the most recent development in the series.

20. EBONY GEYSER erupted from a yawning crater lined with dark gray geyserite. Until the mid-1950s Ebony was one of the largest and most faithful geysers at Norris, but a constant throwing of debris by Park visitors into the ready target below the trail apparently spelled its demise. Even though the vent appears to be clear of rubble, it is probably thoroughly choked at depth. Major eruptions, 75 feet high, have not been seen for many years. The most recent eruptions of any note occurred during 1974, when a few surges 10 feet high were recorded.

21. "GLACIAL MELT GEYSER" was named because of the opalescent appearance of the water. This is caused by a high content of suspended, colloidal silica particles that produce a milky-blue color similar to that of glacial meltwater. This geyser is most active during the seasonal disturbances, when individual splashes several seconds apart reach 5 feet high.

Although additional eruptive episodes are known, Glacial Melt is usually a quiet pool.

64. "CAT'S EYE SPRING" is just a few feet northeast of "Glacial Melt Geyser" (21). Like Glacial Melt, it is most often active at the time of a seasonal disturbance, when play can reach 2 feet high. It was also active during most of 1986.

22. "TEAL BLUE BUBBLER" is a sometimes spouter, sometimes geyser that plays from a small pool perched on the hillside. The boardwalk stairway passes immediately next to it. Although Teal Blue is not active during most seasons, eruptions as high as 6 feet have been seen.

The large body of water along the base of the hillside west of Teal Blue Bubbler is called Crackling Lake. Slightly elevated within a geyserite formation on its hillside shore is Crackling Spring, which is variably active as a small perpetual spouter or geyser.

23. CONGRESS POOL began life as a steam vent, then a mud pot before it became a geyser in 1891. Within weeks it had become a large and regular performer. Because of a visit to Yellowstone that year by members of the International Geological Congress (which led to the geyser's name), it gained considerable attention and fame. Much to everybody's disappointment, though, it soon stopped erupting and became a quiet pool. From that time into the 1970s there apparently was little activity from Congress. In 1974 it began some almost eruptive behavior. Constantly roiling, it would sometimes burst muddy water as high as 20 feet. As this activity continued, the water level dropped lower and lower until it was down fully 5 feet. After about two weeks, Congress began to decline in force, the crater refilled, and the pool was soon back to normal. This activity began earlier than, but otherwise coincided with, that year's late season disturbance. Since then, Congress Pool has often drained entirely, and it then acts as a weak steam vent. It also continues to show disturbance-related behavior but never to the degree seen in 1974.

24. CARNEGIE DRILL HOLE. Across the flat, barren area to the back-left of Congress Pool (23) is what looks like a conical rock pile. Water spurts from a small pool at the base of the mound. What you cannot see from the trail is that the entire area — rocks, pool, and all — pulsates up and down as much as half an inch every second or so. Actually, the rock pile is cemented together, marking the site of a drill hole sunk for research purposes. The work was done in 1929 by Dr. C. N. Fenner of the Carnegie Institute of Washington. The project was part of one of the earliest efforts to do deep drilling in a geothermal basin; such drilling had never been done before in an area as active as Norris. The purpose of the drill hole was to gather data about the alteration of the rocks in a geothermal system and to learn something about the subsurface temperatures. The results were surprising. First, all notable rock alteration was confined to the upper few feet of the hole, showing that Norris's strongly acid condition is a surface phenomenon. Second, the hole had to be abandoned at a depth of only 265 feet — the steam pressure was so great that it threatened to blow up the drilling rig. At that shallow depth the temperature was 401°F (205°C). After abandonment, the hole was filled with cement, but the hot water soon found a way around the plug. The pool that developed is now a perpetual spouter. It was briefly dormant after the earthquake of March 26, 1994, but by the following July even the rock pile was spouting a foot or more high. The ground pulsations indicate that this could someday be the site of a steam explosion.

Numerous perpetual spouters of great variety lie along the base of the hillside behind Congress Pool and the Carnegie Drill Hole. Some have names, such as Vermilion Spring and Locomotive Spring, and these all act as intermittent geysers at times.

25. FEISTY GEYSER was once one of the finest geysers of Porcelain Basin, but if it still exists it cannot be distinguished from the many other geysers and spouters that have developed in its vicinity. Feisty's site was on the sinter shield below the Porcelain Springs, which flow alkaline water and are depositing geyserite at the fastest rate ever measured in Yellowstone. New formations sometimes grow four inches per year (compared to the more typical 1 inch per century). As a result, existing springs change rapidly. Feisty was always somewhat irregular but usually played a few times per hour. Lasting several minutes each time, the play was as hgh as 25 feet. No such geyser exists in the area now, but at least a dozen vents are known to play up to about 10 feet. One of them may be Feisty.

65. UNNG-NPR-4 ("INCLINE GEYSER") made its first appearance during February 1990. It behaves as a now dormant, now active geyser near the base of Porcelain Terrace. Located at the bottom of the hillside below the old road near the end of the trail, its huge eruptions have caused obvious erosion of the slope. Incline's jagged crater is filled with vigorously boiling and surging water even when eruptions are not taking place. The eruptive activity is usually cyclic, with a long series of eruptions taking place over the course of several hours separated by quiet periods days to weeks long. The play, which may last several minutes, reaches 30 to 70 feet high; some of the first eruptions hit at least 110 feet. Played at an angle, Incline inundates the hillside and sometimes completely spans the old roadway. Given that Incline is one of the Porcelain Springs, it will probably have a short lifetime.

66. UNNG-NPR-5 came to life in 1990, about the same time as did "Incline Geyser" (65) just a few feet away. In early 1994 it was still jetting vigorously, often as high as 20 feet, but as with all the Porcelain Springs, NPR-5 is probably a temporary feature.

26. BLUE GEYSER lies far out on the barren flats in the north-central part of Porcelain Basin. The only large pool in that area, it is active most of the time, sending up periodic large domes of water as high as 15 feet with still taller spike jets. Blue's activity is complex. Eruptive periods may be as short as 15 minutes, but some last several hours. Shortly after the

March 1994 earthquake, intervals ranged between 7 and 14, minutes with durations from $^1/_2$ to 5 minutes. The name sometimes seems to be a misnomer, as Blue is often gray in color, especially during disturbances.

27. IRIS SPRING occupies a small crater immediately southwest of Blue Geyser (26). It is usually a perpetual spouter. Most of the splashes are quite small, but jets reaching 15 feet are frequently seen.

28. THE PRIMROSE SPRINGS lie along a shallow "valley" extending from below the trail northward toward the main flats of Porcelain Basin. Within this group are several perpetual spouters. The largest, Primrose Spring, has been known to act as a geyser, splashing up to 3 feet high.

The area between the Primrose Springs and Blue Geyser (26) used to be occupied by numerous large pools. Given informal names such as "Green Apple Cider" and "Norris," they had massive bursting eruptions, especially during the seasonal disturbances. They have now largely been filled in or covered over by geyserite deposited from the runoff of the Porcelain Springs, but they could reappear at any time.

67. HURRICANE VENT is a deep hole on the uphill side of the boardwalk near Sunday Geyser (29). The reason for the name was the cyclonelike whirling of the water in the crater during early eruptions. It formed during the winter of 1885–1886, probably as a result of an earthquake. Hurricane Vent became quite a tourist attraction in 1886, with frequent eruptions up to 30 feet high. It was even stronger the next summer, when the viewpoint of the previous year was frequently inundated by the bursts. Since then, though, Hurricane Vent has been almost completely inactive. A few small, erratic splashes were seen during 1991.

A steam vent that is sometimes intermittent, located high on the east wall of the crater, is often mistaken as Hurricane Vent.

29. SUNDAY GEYSER got its name because it had its first spectacular eruptions on Sunday, July 12, 1964. It is dormant nearly all the time. The last episode of large eruptions was in 1981-1982, when it was a frequent performer. Eruptions 30 feet high recurred every 15 to 20 minutes. The vent is a rather small hole at the south end of a shallow, bluish pool just below the boardwalk. This pool, which often becomes muddy gray during disturbances, has rarely had small eruptions of its own.

30. "RAGGED SPOUTER" was a 1968 development in the far northeastern part of Porcelain Basin. The vent was a wide spot along an old fissure. In 1981 it was described as having "Echinus-like" bursts approaching 50 feet high (see Echinus Geyser, #38). That action rapidly died down, and now, as is common with the features of the Porcelain Springs area, its crater cannot be identified.

31. "GRACEFUL GEYSER" became active in late 1981 or early 1982. At first, the eruptions played from a small cone. Being old and badly weathered, the cone did not last long. The original slender, graceful jets were replaced by a bursting action out of a jagged crater. Some of the spray of the infrequent eruptions reaches 20 feet high.

32. UNNG-NPR-3 ("COLLAPSED CAVE GEYSER") is another little-known, recently reactivated geyser in the far corner of Porcelain Basin. It erupts within a large, cavernous opening, from which part of the roof collapsed in the 1980s. The eruptions, although lasting no more than 10 seconds, play up to 20 feet high at intervals as short as 5 minutes. Since its first known action in the early 1980s, Collapsed Cave has undergone several dormancies.

Note: Many other geysers are known to have existed within Porcelain Basin. Most have been active only one known time, and that occurred during a disturbance event, but some have been more persistent. Those that have had active phases as long as a year or two have often been given informal names. For the record, some of these names are "Junebug Geyser, Ramjet Springs, Blowout Geyser, Christmas Geyser, and Green Apple Cider Pool." Whether any of these geysers will be active again in the future is, of course, unknown. As stated in the introduction to Norris Geyser Basin, this is an extremely changeable area.

Table 25. Geysers of the Porcelain Basin

Name	Map No.	Interval	Duration	Height (ft)
Africa Geyser	10	dormant	90 min–steady	20–45
Arsenic Geyser **	8	irregular	5–20 min	1–35
Basin Geyser	6	dormant	near steady	6
Bear Den Geyser	19	dormant, vent choked by debris	sec.min	10–70
Blue Geyser **	26	frequent	min–hrs	15
Carnegie Drill Hole	24	artificial	steady	1–4
"Cat's Eye Spring" **	64	disturbance	steady	2
Congress Pool **	23	rare	min–hrs	4–20
Constant Geyser	16	irregular	seconds	3–30
Dark Cavern Geyser, normal	2	17–25 min	seconds	5–20
Dark Cavern, steam phase	2	days	to 38 min	40–50
Ebony Geyser	20	[1974]	3–5 min	10–75
Fan Geyser **	12	irregular	10 min	10–25
Feisty Geyser	25	dead?	minutes	25
Fireball Geyser **	13	5 min–hrs	5–20 min	12–25
"Glacial Melt Geyser" **	21	disturbance	steady	5
"Graceful Geyser"	31	infrequent	minutes	20
Guardian Geyser	4	irregular	sec–4 min	8–25
Harding Geyser	1	rare	5 min	50
Hurricane Vent	67	dormant	unknown	30?
Iris Spring	27	steady	steady	5–10
Jetsam Pool	73	with Ledge	sec–min	65
Lava Pool Complex **	9	frequent	min–hrs	1–10
Ledge Geyser	5	days–years	hours	80–125
Little Whirligig Geyser	14	[1991]	min–hrs	15–20
"Pequito Geyser"	63	irregular *	minutes	2–5
Pinto Geyser **	11	disturbance	2–30 min	20–40
Pinwheel Geyser **	18	dormant	5 min	20
Primrose Spring	28	steady	steady	3
"Ragged Spouter"	30	may no longer exist	minutes	10–50
Splutter Pot **	17	4–6 min *	1–2 min	2–6
Sunday Geyser **	29	[1982]	5 min	30–50

Table 25 continued

"Teal Blue Bubbler"	22	infrequent	near steady	1–6
UNNG-NPR-1 ("Geezer") **	7	disturbance	15 min	15
UNNG-NPR-3 ("Collapsed Cave")	32	minutes	seconds	20
UNNG-NPR-4 ("Incline")	65	min–hrs *	minutes	20–110
UNNG-NPR-5	66	frequent	minutes	10–12
Valentine Geyser	3	hrs–days *	5–22 min	20–75
Whirligig Geyser	15	hours *	3–4 min	6–15

— When active.
** Indicates geysers that show more frequent and/or more powerful activity at the time of a seasonal disturbance. In interval column, "disturbance" indicates geysers that are active essentially only at the time of a disturbance.
[ ] Brackets enclose the year of most recent activity for extremely rare or dormant geysers. See text.

Back Basin

Hot spring activity in the Back Basin (Map X, Table 26), the southern part of the Norris Geyser Basin, is much less concentrated than that in the Porcelain Basin. Pine trees separate small groups of hot springs from one another, often even isolating individual springs. Because of this, the Back Basin is a more popular place to stroll on a hot summer day. These springs are perhaps more strongly affected by the late season disturbances than are those of Porcelain Basin, but they are also more stable, with fewer thermal features appearing and disappearing over the years. In addition to abundant geyser activity, visitors sometimes encounter wildlife such as elk, moose, sandhill cranes, and even bear. Before you leave the Museum area be sure to check the status of Echinus Geyser, usually the only predicted geyser at Norris.

Tantalus Creek is the name of the hot water stream that drains Norris Geyser Basin. The name is after the Greek god Tantalus, one of the sons of Zeus.

The loop trail around the Back Basin is about 0.9-mile long. For those who do not wish to walk the entire distance, a cutoff reduces the round-trip by half.

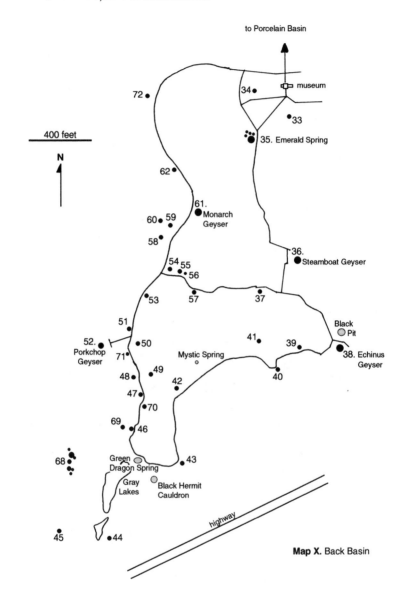

to Porcelain Basin

72

34

museum

33

35. Emerald Spring

400 feet

N

62

61.
Monarch
Geyser

60 59

58

36.
Steamboat Geyser

54 55

56

53

57

37

51

Black
Pit

52.
Porkchop
Geyser

50

41

39

38. Echinus
Geyser

71

Mystic Spring

49

40

48

42

47

70

69

46

68

Green
Dragon Spring

43

Gray
Lakes

Black Hermit
Cauldron

highway

45

44

Map X. Back Basin

33. STEAMVALVE SPRING was known during the early days of the Park, but a dormancy of many decades left it all but forgotten except as a "dead" crater within an abandoned parking area. During the late 1970s Steamvalve suddenly reappeared as a geyser. For several years its activity was fairly predictable. About $1^{1}/_{2}$ hours before an eruption, bubbles began to rise through the water in the crater, which was slowly filling. The play began well before overflow was reached. Some of the bursts were as high as 12 feet, the biggest usually occurring near the end of the 15-minute eruption. A gradual decline in the activity returned Steamvalve to dormancy by the mid-1980s.

34. BATHTUB SPRING is usually an acid-water spring splashing from a crater lined with massive geyserite formations. The sinter probably formed at times when Bathtub held alkaline rather than acid water. It has been known to switch back and forth several times. Bathtub is apparently identical to a geyser of the 1800s known as the "Schlammkessel." In more recent years, Bathtub has acted as a perpetual spouter, most play reaching 3 feet high.

35. EMERALD SPRING is generally a beautiful yellow-green pool. The color is from the combination of the blue of the deep water and the yellow of sulfur lining the crater walls. The color is intense and is very different from that produced by yellow cyanobacteria. The name is fitting.

Most of the time, Emerald Spring calmly bubbles above its vents. The bubbling is not boiling — the temperature is usually several degrees below boiling — but instead is caused by mixtures of steam, carbon dioxide, and other gasses. At the time of a seasonal disturbance Emerald commonly becomes turbid gray-brown, and then it does boil and sometimes acts as a geyser. Most such eruptions are 3 to 6 feet high. In 1931 it had an extraordinary episode of activity; it was in eruption at least 87% of the time with bursts reaching 60 to 75 feet.

Around the northern sides of the shallow alcove that includes Emerald Spring is a series of depressions. These mark the vents of several ephemeral springs and spouters. First active in the 1930s, they were not reported again until some brief action in 1971. Then, in 1974 they became active again. It was remarkable how within 30 minutes the area went from having no springs at all to featuring more than a dozen vigorous spouters. Their development was the first sign of the onset of a seasonal disturbance, one that proved to be basinwide in effect and one of the most intense ever. Although some of these springs played as high as 10 feet and their total water discharge was large, most completely disappeared within weeks. Two or three continued their action into 1975. None of these springs has been active since then.

36. STEAMBOAT GEYSER is the tallest and probably physically the largest geyser in the world — when it is active. The only geyser on earth known to have played higher was New Zealand's mighty Waimangu, but it has been dead since 1904. Most of the time the only eruptions seen are a series of minor splashes every few minutes. Actually, the boardwalk is farther from Steamboat than it looks, and the minor eruptions are as high as 40 feet. For Steamboat, such bursts are almost insignificant.

Steamboat has an interesting history. According to some descriptions there was no spring of any kind here before 1878; it is more likely that something did exist but was inactive. In any case, 1878 is the year of Steamboat's first known series of major eruptions. The new geyser was called both Steamboat and New Crater. (Both names are officially approved for use, but Steamboat is the name that stuck.) The destruction the eruptions brought to the surrounding forest was unmistakable: trees were killed, huge rocks were thrown about, and plants were covered with sand and mud by eruptions well over 100 feet high. Through the next three decades Steamboat mostly showed only minor action; major eruptions are known only in 1890, 1891, 1894, and 1902, although others may have occurred. The next year in which there was a series of major eruptions was 1911. The height was said to be over 250 feet. Steamboat again fell quiet, with only minor activity for almost exactly 50 years. Starting in 1961 and continuing into 1969, Steamboat had its best active period on record. All told, there were ninety major eruptions during those 8 years, twenty-nine in 1964 alone.

It is difficult, if not impossible, to adequately describe a major eruption of Steamboat. Even photographs do not do it justice; the cover of this book seems to impart a sense of beauty rather than violence. With the proper study, Steamboat's minor eruptions go through a relatively clear-cut progression of types of play, defined mostly on the basis of which one of the two vents initiates the eruption, whether there is simultaneous action, the duration, and so on. To those not familiar with this sequence, a major eruption seems to begin with a normal-looking minor, except that the action persists and continues to build in height. More often than not, even these "superbursts" and "silver bullets" fail to trigger a full eruption. But there is simply no describing the scene when a superburst proves to be the start of a major. The height continues to grow, almost beyond belief. One eruption was measured at about 380 feet high, more than three times the average height of Old Faithful, and none is less than 250 feet. The water phase of the eruption lasts from 3 to 20 minutes, during which several hundred thousand gallons of water are discharged. Then comes the steam phase. The roar is tremendous and may last several hours. There is a rumor that one eruption, on a cold, crisp, and windless winter day, was heard in Madison Junction, 14 miles away. That is highly unlikely, but at times it is impossible for people nearby to yell at one another and be heard — as if anybody had anything sensible to say.

After its major eruption on March 20, 1969, Steamboat failed to play again for years. There is no chance that any eruptions were missed in the interim, because every eruption by Steamboat leaves abundant signs. So it was hoped that the eruption of March 28, 1978, presaged a new series of activity. And so it did, although eruptions were sparse until 1982. There were twenty-three eruptions that year, the third best on record; twelve more occurred during 1983, but there were only five in 1984. Since then, Steamboat has had just five additional eruptions: three in 1989, one in 1990, and one in 1991.

In addition to the joy of seeing eruptions by Steamboat, the geyser's activity has revealed some things about the water circulation of the Norris hydrothermal system. A geyser as large as Steamboat must be served by an abundant supply of very hot water. It seems likely that Steamboat's deeper plumbing taps rather directly into a second, hotter and deeper thermal aquifer than do many of the other hot springs at Norris. At the times of the seasonal disturbances, however, there is a mixing of the two waters. Recently, the onset of a disturbance has first appeared in Steamboat, sometimes as long as 2 days before it is evident elsewhere. Often this has happened when Steamboat's minor play appeared to indicate the approach of another major eruption. The disturbance ends any such possibility until well after its effects have passed. Known as the "zap," the effect is also seen in Echinus Geyser (38), Emerald Spring (35), and Steamvalve Spring (33), suggesting that these geysers may be associated along some sort of subsurface fracture system.

For both geyser gazing and geothermal research, Steamboat is a very important geyser. It is not likely that you will get to see it have a major eruption. Then again, somebody will be there. Maybe it will be you.

37. CISTERN SPRING is (amazingly) the only spring known to be directly connected to, and therefore affected by, an eruption of Steamboat Geyser (36). Every major eruption causes Cistern to drain by as much as 12 feet; Steamboat's superbursts have also been observed to have a slight effect on Cistern. As a geyser, though, Cistern has been known to erupt on just two occasions. Both followed majors by Steamboat, in 1978 and 1982. The height was about 20 feet.

Cistern Spring is building a sinter terrace about its crater at a very rapid rate. The deposit is growing upward at the rate of about $1\frac{1}{2}$ inches a year. Additional trees are entombed each year, and the trail has had to be moved a few times.

38. ECHINUS GEYSER is a favorite of nearly everybody. Regular and predictable, it is also large and beautiful. Nowhere else can you get so close to a major geysers.

The name "Echinus" comes from the Greek word for spiny. The same root gave the sea urchins and starfish their

collective name of "echinoderms." The name was applied to
the geyser because an early visitor thought some of the
stones about the crater resembled sea urchins. Indeed they
do. They are rhyolite pebbles that have been coated with the
spiny sinter typical of acid water conditions. This is one of

the better examples of such geyserite. The prominent reddish and yellow-brown colors are caused by iron oxide minerals that are deposited along with the sinter. This is also one of the rare cases in which arsenic compounds are being deposited by the hot water — the sinter at Echinus contains about 5% arsenic pentoxide. Don't worry about the water if you happen to be sprayed. The arsenic content of the water itself is far too low to be harmful.

Echinus's activity begins with its large crater slowly filling with water. The water level is easy to gauge by watching some specific point within the basin. As the filling progresses and the eruption time nears, the filling becomes faster. In some years the crater must fill completely and even overflow for some time before the eruption begins, but more often the play starts with the level still a few feet below the rim. Either way, the bubbling above the vent becomes a boiling and the boiling a heavy surging, and the eruption is on within seconds. Echinus is a typical fountain-type geyser, throwing its water in a series of closely spaced bursts. Each burst is different from every other — some small, others well over 80 feet tall, some straight up, and others so sharply angled that they can soak people on the benches with warm water. (It's only warm, not hot, after the flight through the air. How long has it been since you took a geyser shower? Some viewers get to enjoy this unique and harmless experience with nearly every eruption. Do protect and immediately dry your camera and eyeglasses if it happens to you, though. If allowed to dry, the water will leave permanent spots on the lenses.)

After the eruption, the water remaining in the crater slowly recedes. In some years it drops no more than 4 feet, and in others the crater empties entirely. Then it begins the steady refilling toward the next eruption. The average interval varies through time, but it generally ranges between 40 and 80 minutes. The durations also vary, from just a few minutes to as long as 70 minutes. The longer eruptions have been growing more common in recent years. Most are followed by a complete draining of the crater and then a weak steam phase, yet succeeding intervals are sometimes much shorter than average.

Echinus is at its most variable at the times of the seasonal disturbances. Then, it may undergo what has been termed a "super eruption," during which the water turns from nearly clear to very muddy during play that will be of considerable power and very long duration. As with the "zap" at Steamboat (36), the super is often one of the first signs of the onset of a disturbance. Echinus also rarely has series of minor eruptions, in which the play reaches only a few feet high and fails to fill the crater over a duration of only about 1 minute.

Prior to 1948 Echinus was often dormant, and the best of its infrequent eruptions reached only 35 feet high. Now it is the one large geyser you can count on seeing at Norris. Regardless of the specifics of its action, Echinus is one of the finest geysers in Yellowstone, one that should not be missed.

39. CRATER SPRING has also been called "Collapse Crater Spring," for reasons that should be clear to the observer. Sometime in the rather distant past the entire undercut rim of the crater collapsed inward. The rubble still lies there. For most of Crater Spring's known history, a steady eruption jetted above the boulders. During an exceptionally early disturbance in May 1983, Crater Spring began playing as a true geyser. Eruptions, lasting as long as 10 minutes and recurring as often as every 30 minutes, threw water as high as 20 feet. The main jet was angled to the north, reaching over the trail so that a new route had to be constructed on the other side of the pool (where it remains). By midsummer 1983, Crater Spring had regressed to a pool, but unlike before it was full and overflowing and of a rich blue color. Gradually, it returned to its previous state, and it now generally resembles the pre-1983 spouter.

40. ARCH STEAM VENT undergoes very rare major eruptions. This is positively known from splashed areas, runoff channels, and killed vegetation, but apparently no reporting observer has ever seen one of the plays. The greatest number known for any single year is four, in 1974, and none have probably taken place since then. The evidence is that the eruption is jetted at about a 45-degree angle away from the slope, reaching perhaps 40 feet high. Deep runoff channels just below the vent imply that Arch had considerable eruptive activity in the past.

41. TANTALUS GEYSER had important eruptive activity only during 1969, and in fact it is probably no different from the many other disturbance-related geysers and spouters so common to Norris, except for its size. During its few days of activity in 1969, Tantalus played as high as 35 feet, with massive, widely spraying bursts of brown, muddy water. It is usually a quiet pool, which still tends to become muddier and splash weakly during most disturbances.

42. MUD SPRING is, contrary to its name, clear most of the time. If it is eruptive, however, it will be muddy. Most eruptive periods are associated with disturbances, when some bursts have reached 30 feet high. More typical is a steady surging to just 1 to 2 feet. During 1984 Mud Spring performed as a small but regular geyser for most of the summer. Intervals were 40 to 60 minutes, durations 12 to 20 minutes, and the height about $1^{1}/_{2}$ feet. It is unfortunate that the name Chocolate Fountain, which predates Mud Spring, failed to gain acceptance.

43. "PUFF 'N STUFF GEYSER" is right next to the trail. The dissected cone constantly rumbles and gurgles violently at depth, sending a fine spray of water a few feet high. Puff 'N Stuff looks and acts as if it could do more at any time, but it never has.

The next three geysers lie away from the trail system and are difficult to see from there. They are described here because they are of size and importance. The requirement is that you stay on the trail. Since the 1988 forest fires cleared much of the growth in the southern part of Norris, Big Alcove Spring (44) and Medusa Spring (45) are visible from the highway at a point about $^{1}/_{2}$ mile south of Norris Junction. The Hydrophane Spring Complex can barely be seen from that same point as well as from the trail near Blue Mud Spring (46).

44. BIG ALCOVE SPRING is, as seen from the highway, near the front-right side of the large pools known as the Gray Lakes. It plays from a crack in the volcanic bedrock within a deep, alcovelike crater. The pulsating jet is nearly steady and has been known to reach over 25 feet high, although most bursts hit only 10 feet or so. Big Alcove is never completely quiet, but the strong jetting occasionally pauses for a few seconds.

45. MEDUSA SPRING varies among being a geyser, a perpetual spouter, and a quiet pool. Viewed from the road, it lies south of the Gray Lakes next to the forest on the far side of the thermal tract. Medusa is a round pool about 10 feet in diameter that can erupt as high as 12 feet.

68. HYDROPHANE SPRINGS is a complex of pools, spouters, and geysers largely hidden from view from any trail or road access. When standing at Blue Mud Spring (46), they are the features across the stream and beyond a low ridge with scrubby trees. The activity within the Hydrophane Complex is extremely variable. Often, but not exclusively, active at the time of a disturbance, a number of the vents may act as perpetual spouters or geysers, sometimes of substantial size. Most often, all that can be seen is a bit of blue in the deeper pools.

46. BLUE MUD SPRING is a constantly active spouter immediately below the trail. More often than not it does not, send any water above ground level, but sometimes the play will briefly spray as high as 10 feet.

69. UNNG-NBK-4 is on the flat between Blue Mud Spring (46) and the stream. Its crater is shaped like an arrowhead, but that, as a seemingly good name, has been applied elsewhere in Yellowstone. This geyser erupts frequently. Most plays last between 20 and 30 seconds, bursting as high as 4 to 6 feet.

NBK-4 and the other features here are members of the "Muddy Sneaker Complex." These springs began to appear in previously inactive ground during 1971, when a small mud pot opened right in the middle of the old trail. Since then, the individual springs other than NBK-4 have come and gone frequently, and a few additional temporary geysers have been observed.

To the north a few feet from Blue Mud Spring, occupying the bottom of a shallow draw, is the "Tangled Root Complex." It also appeared during the early 1970s, and, again, some brief geyser activity has been observed. Often, these small pools are a beautiful opalescent blue color because of an extremely high silica content in the water. More commonly, the craters are empty.

70. YELLOW FUNNEL SPRING deserved its name into the 1980s. Now, it is usually a quiet murky-brown pool with very slight bubbling above the vent. It becomes muddy and more vigorous during the seasonal disturbances, and eruptions 1 to 2 feet high are then common if the water level drops. In 1989 and 1992 it had some vigorous disturbance eruptions while still full. No known observer witnessed any of size, but splashed areas implied spraying eruptions several feet high.

47. UNNG-NBK-1 ("SON OF GREEN DRAGON SPRING"). This unofficial name has caught on, although the pool bears little resemblance to the much larger, cavernous, muddy Green Dragon Spring a few hundred feet away. Son of Green Dragon is generally active as a perpetual spouter, so weak that the biggest splashes are usually only a few inches high. Occasionally, and often when it becomes muddy during disturbances, it bursts up to 2 feet. In 1993 it was acting as a geyser, with both intervals and durations of around 5 minutes, as was "Grandson of Green Dragon" a few feet down the runoff channel.

48. "ORBICULAR GEYSER" (sometimes called "Orby Geyser") plays from a shallow, round (orbicular) crater about 100 feet west of the trail. During most of its known history it has been an insignificant spring, sometimes even empty or filled with cold water. When active, though, as it has been most of the time since the late 1970s, it has frequent and vigorous eruptions. Most intervals are around 3 to 5 minutes in length.

Water is splashed 3 to 6 feet high over durations of several seconds. At the times of the seasonal disturbances, Orbicular often approaches perpetual activity, being in eruption more than 90% of the time, with intervals of seconds and durations as long as 10 minutes.

49. "DABBLE GEYSER" is most active during the summer disturbances, although it can play at other times as well. Its action is highly variable. At its uncommon best, intervals as short as 30 minutes may result in vigorous 8-foot splashing for as long as 4 minutes. When inactive, it is a quiet and rather cool pool.

71. UNNG-NBK-5 ("BASTILLE GEYSER") made its appearance during the seasonal disturbance that began on July 14, 1992, France's Bastille Day. The crater developed right next to the boardwalk, covering it with sandy debris and leading to a temporary closure of the area as it grew from a 2-inch hole to a 3-foot crater over the course of 8 hours. (Whenever a new vent opens in this way, it is always possible that a substantial steam explosion might ultimately result.) Unlike most hot springs that appear during disturbances, Bastille has persisted. By 1993 the crater was lined with pale gray geyserite punctured by several openings. The spring would quickly drain with a whirlpool after an eruption. Refilling began almost immediately and was quickly joined by small sputtering from some of the tiny vents. The culmination was splashing 1 to 3 feet high from the two larger openings at the bottom of the crater. With bursting durations of about $1\frac{1}{2}$ minutes, the entire period of eruption was 4 to 5 minutes long. This is one of the best geysers to watch through its entire activity cycle. If it is permanent, it will be a wonderful addition to Norris.

50. DOUBLE BULGER is now only half alive. The larger of the two vents usually acts as a murky perpetual spouter. The second, smaller opening probably used to perform in a similar manner, but it self-sealed itself with geyserite and then became filled with rocks and gravel. Recently, another

opening, at the base of the small cliff between the boardwalk and Double Bulger, had some eruptive episodes, and this now appears to be the focus for some of Double Bulger's energy.

51. PEARL GEYSER is one of the few hot springs at Norris to resemble those of the other geyser basins. The wide crater of smooth, gray geyserite is centered by a symmetrical vent filled with a pool of clear water. Pearl is highly variable, though. In many years the water level is well down inside the vent, where nearly constant bubbling gives rise to frequent but erratic splashes 1 to 2 feet high. Only on rare occasions will Pearl completely fill and overflow, but then it tends to act as a regular geyser. During such episodes, cyclic activity produces intervals ranging from seconds to minutes in length, and some bursts are 8 feet high. Pearl is also known to drain completely and behave as a weak steam vent.

52. PORKCHOP GEYSER used to play from a crater that was indeed shaped like a porkchop. The vent was a 2-inch hole at the narrow end of the crater. It was a vigorous geyser, sometimes highly regular in both its intervals and durations. The typical play sounded like an old steam engine, with several chugs per second sending jets of water 15 to 20 feet high. Through the years Porkchop showed a tendency toward progressively steadier, stronger, and steamier eruptions. By the late 1980s it had become a perpetual spouter, with nonstop steamy spray reaching over 30 feet high.

The culmination happened on September 5, 1989. During the seasonal disturbance, Porkchop literally exploded. Its beautiful crater was replaced by a ragged pile of broken geyserite boulders tumbled around a pool measuring 6 by 12 feet. The blast threw rocky debris as far as 220 feet away. It continued to have superheated boiling eruptions up to 6 feet high into 1991 but is now a quiet, opalescent blue pool.

53. VIXEN GEYSER plays from a reddish vent close to the trail and tends to attract a considerable crowd when active. It has two types of play. Minor eruptions are generally the rule.

They last only a few seconds but recur every few minutes and reach up to 10 feet high. Major eruptions tend to occur during brief episodes months to years apart. Most have durations of several minutes, although play lasting as long as an hour has been seen. This jetting reaches 35 to 40 feet high, and it is only during these major eruptions that Vixen discharges enough water to produce a runoff stream away from the vent. The channel leading to Tantalus Creek is very shallow, an indication that major eruptions have always been rare. Unfortunately, during most recent seasons even minor play has been uncommon, with Vixen only weakly churning and splashing down inside the vent.

One of the displays at the United States Centennial Exposition in Philadelphia in 1876 included a beautiful geyserite cone. It is possible that this cone belongs to Vixen, summarily chopped off as a special exhibit from America's then-new national park. The cone now resides in the archives of the Smithsonian Institution. Some feel the cone had another source, but either way it is a sad commentary.

54. "RUBBLE GEYSER" first erupted in 1972. Before then there was no evidence of any spring having existed at the site, but its coming was foretold by the small lodgepole pines within the area. In 1970 they began dying as the ground warmed up and exceeded their temperature tolerance. The ragged vent formed when Rubble broke out with vigorous boiling. At first, the geyser played frequently and regularly. The eruptions began after 1 to 2 minutes of heavy overflow. Lasting about 6 minutes, some of the bursts reached 10 feet high. Rubble rapidly declined in frequency and force. Eruptions are now rare, but brief episodes, such as that of 1988 when eruptions were as frequent as every hour, will probably occur in the future. Quiet overflow is still common.

55. CORPORAL GEYSER hardly merits either attention or the name geyser, whether active or not. It is a fairly cool pool containing much silt and debris and decidedly is not a pretty feature. The eruptions consist of nothing more than intermittent overflow that is sometimes accompanied by a few splashes perhaps 1 foot high. During active years the intervals tend to be regular at about 20 minutes. The duration is around 3 minutes.

56. UNNG-NBK-2 ("DOG'S LEG SPRING") is located at the break in slope a few feet east of Corporal Geyser (55). When active as a geyser, it far overshadows Corporal. It has been known to play up to 3 feet high and to do so for durations of several hours. More often, its water level drops when Corporal erupts, and it refills as quickly as Corporal stops.

57. VETERAN GEYSER is a spellbinder. People have been known to sit here for long periods, waiting for an eruption that always seems about to happen. Often, they are not disappointed, but Veteran is a long-term cyclic geyser that can go many hours to several days between major eruptions.

The main vent of Veteran is the large opening on the far side of the deep crater. Connecting the main vent and the crater is a hole. A third vent is outside the crater, within a jagged cavern next to the trail. Subsurface churning and splashing within the main vent is almost constant and causes water to gush intermittently through the hole into the crater. When it is time for an eruption, the turbulence becomes violent. Water is shot through the hole, rapidly raising the water level in the crater while bursts spray out of the main vent. Once the pool is high enough to thoroughly cover the hole, the action is forced largely to the main vent. Most of the play is as minor eruptions, which tend to stop at about this point in the activity. The less common major eruptions continue, jetting water at an angle away from the trail. The best reach as much as 25 feet high and 40 feet out. Only during a full, major eruption does the third vent join in, shooting across the trail at a very low angle. The eruption ends abruptly after a duration of just 10 seconds to $2^1/_2$ minutes. During Veteran's long cycles there is a gradual increase in the frequency and force of the minor eruptions, which in turn leads to a greater frequency of major eruptions. A cycle often ends with a series of frequent and powerful majors.

A few feet east of Veteran's pool is another crater with a similar appearance. This is known as "Veteran's Auxiliary

Vent." As Veteran approaches the start of a new cycle, this spring undergoes a simultaneous rise in water level. Seldom is the water actually visible within the small vent, but on rare occasions the Auxiliary has its own, mostly subsurface eruptions.

58. PALPITATOR SPRING is a geyser. It apparently had some rather strong eruptions during the 1880s, but in modern times it was not known as a geyser until 1974. Since then, its action has stabilized, and it is now a fairly regular performer. As a quiet spring prior to 1974, and now during the quiet intervals, the pool constantly bounces (palpitates) over the vent, sending small waves over the rim of the crater. The eruptions consist of splashes up to 3 feet high. The crater slowly drains during play that lasts as long as 3 hours. Most intervals are in the vicinity of 7 hours.

59. FEARLESS GEYSER has a confused history. It probably had some eruptions, perhaps as high as 30 feet, during the 1880s, but it is also possible that those early reports were referring to some other hot spring in this area. A few decades ago the intervals were listed as "several per day" with a height of 3 feet. The present Fearless is a perpetual spouter that domes and surges the water about 1 foot high.

60. UNNG-NBK-3 is a set of perpetual spouters that initially appeared during the 1970s. Spouting muddy brown water, some of the play reaches 6 feet high. The activity, which frequently shifts among several vents, is most vigorous during seasonal disturbances.

61. MONARCH GEYSER, as the name implies, was a major geyser. Its play reached as high as 200 feet. Lasting around 10 minutes, the eruption would throw out so much water that the old road through Norris had to be closed each time the geyser played. The last few eruptions threw out muddy water, an indication that Monarch might have been damaging its plumbing system at depth. It has been conjectured that the "death" of Monarch in 1913 was related in some way to the dormancy of Steamboat Geyser (36) that began in 1911. The two geysers are actually quite near one another, so there could be a relationship, but Monarch underwent minor activity in 1920, 1923, and 1927 without any reported changes in Steamboat.

In recent years, the low-temperature acid pool was so unlike a geyser in its appearance that most people felt Monarch was truly dead. That word should never be used for geysers. In fall 1993 it began having occasional "hot periods" in which heavy overflow accompanied episodes of superheated boiling. In early March 1994 there was an unseen eruption. The earthquake of March 26, 1994, did not trigger any other eruptions, but continued hot periods finally resulted in fairly frequent play by the end of April. In May it was evident that the play was in series, with intervals as short as 1 hour and active episodes separated by as much as a few days. The eruptions were primarily a superheated boiling with some bursting that could throw water as high as 15 to 20 feet. Although this is a far cry from the action of a century ago, it shows that there is no such thing as a "dead" geyser.

62. MINUTE GEYSER received its name because of the very regular but brief nature of its eruptions many years ago. Some of the eruptions were reported to be as high as 60 or more feet. The geyser later changed so thoroughly that its name appeared in literature as "mi-NUTE," meaning something very small. What happened is that a vandal threw a large boulder into the vent — the rock could not have gotten there any other way. Unable to remove it, Minute shifted its activity to another opening a few feet away. The play became almost constant and only 4 feet high. Further, natural changes have led to some improvement. Although often still a small perpetual spouter, Minute sometimes shows intervals of about 20 minutes, with 5-minute eruptions reaching 10 feet high. True major eruptions as high as 50 feet have also been seen a few times in recent years.

72. UNNG-NBK-6 ("REDISCOVERED GEYSER") was hidden in the woods well away from the trails until 1993, when a new path

was opened along the old roadway between Minute Geyser (62) and the Museum area. It lies a few feet below the trail through some small trees. Rediscovered is mostly active as a perpetual spouter only about 1 foot high. During some years it becomes intermittent, and then, with both intervals and durations of several minutes, it erupts up to 4 feet high.

Note: As is the case with the Porcelain Basin, a great many other geysers have been observed in the Back Basin. Most of these have been of small size, with their temporary existences related to the seasonal disturbances.

Also to be noted is the One Hundred Spring Plain. This is the northwestern portion of the Norris Geyser Basin. Not accessible by any trail and, because of the great number of hot spring vents and extensive mud flats, a dangerous area to explore, it is the site of a few small perpetual spouters and ephemeral geysers.

Immediately adjacent to a highway pullout in Elk Park, about 1 mile south of Norris Junction, are the small, sinter-lined "Elk Park Springs." Properly a part of the Norris Geyser Basin, two of these have records of infrequent, small eruptions. In the forest near the still visible route of the old highway leading north from Elk Park is large and hot Big Blue Spring. Named around 1920, this spring is not described in early reports about the Park, so it may have formed since the 1800s. Maps in some old guidebooks identify this as Cupric Cauldron, but the real spring of that name is a nondescript feature still farther north through the trees.

Table 26. Geysers of the Back Basin

Name	Map No.	Interval	Duration	Height (ft)
Arch Steam Vent	40	[1974?]	unrecorded	30–40
Bathtub Spring	34	steady	steady	3
Big Alcove Spring	44	seconds	seconds	6–25
Blue Mud Spring	46	steady	steady	1–10
Cistern Spring	37	rare	minutes	20
Corporal Geyser **	55	20 min *	3 min	1
Crater Spring **	39	[1984]	minutes	10–15
"Dabble Geyser" **	49	erratic **	4 min	8
Double Bulger **	50	steady	steady	1

Table 26 continued

Echinus Geyser **	38	20–80 min	1–70 min	10–125
Emerald Spring **	35	disturbance	steady	3–75
Fearless Geyser	59	steady	steady	boil
Hydrophane Springs **	68	irregular	sec–min	1–30
Medusa Spring **	45	irregular	1–15 min	2–12
Minute Geyser	62	20 min	5 min	10
Monarch Geyser, minor	61	hours *	5–15 min	3–20
Monarch Geyser, major	61	[1913]	5–10 min	100–200
Mud Spring **	42	40–60 min *	10–20 min	1–30
"Orbicular Geyser" **	48	minutes	seconds	3–6
Palpitator Spring **	58	4–7 hrs	2–5 hrs	3
Pearl Geyser **	51	erratic	sec–min	1–8
Porkchop Geyser **	52	see text	—	—
"Puff 'N Stuff Geyser"	43	steady	steady	1–3
"Rubble Geyser"	54	rare	3–6 min	5–10
Steamboat Geyser, minor **	36	minutes	seconds	20–100
Steamboat Geyser, major	36	5 days–50 years	hours	250–386
Steamvalve Spring **	33	[c. 1986]	15 min	12
"Tantalus Geyser" **	41	disturbance	minutes	3–35
UNNG-NBK-1 ("Son of Green Dragon") **	47	erratic	sec–min	2
UNNG-NBK-2 ("Dog's Leg")	56	infrequent	min–hrs	1–3
UNNG-NBK-3	60	steady	steady	1–6
UNNG-NBK-4	69	minutes	20–30 sec	4–6
UNNG-NBK-5 ("Bastille") **	71	4–5 min *	1 1/2 min	1–3
UNNG-NBK-6 ("Rediscovered")	72	minutes	minutes	1–4
Veteran Geyser	57	min–hrs	sec–2 1/2 min	3–40
Vixen Geyser	53	sec–min *	sec–1 hr	1–35
Yellow Funnel Spring **	70	disturbance	sec–min	2–10

* When active.

** Indicates geysers that show more frequent or more powerful activity at the time of a seasonal disturbance. In interval column, "disturbance" indicates geysers that are active essentially only at the time of a disturbance.

[ ] Brackets enclose the year of most recent activity for extremely rare or dormant geysers. See text.

Chapter 8

West Thumb Geyser Basin

Compared with the other areas of clear, alkaline water, the activity at West Thumb Geyser Basin (Map Y, Table 27) is limited and generally weak. Only about a dozen geysers have ever been observed within the developed part of the basin, which is properly known as the Lower Group. The three geysers currently of the greatest importance lie to the north, near one another in the Lake Shore Group, squeezed between the lake and the highway. Still farther to the north is the Potts Hot Spring Basin, in which there are numerous small geysers but seldom eruptions of significant size.

West Thumb may be better known for its pools. Some are among the largest in Yellowstone, and two of them, Abyss Pool and Black Pool, have undergone powerful eruptions since the previous edition of this book. The Thumb Paint Pots were first described by Daniel T. Potts back in 1826. Well-known in the early days of the Park because of their variety of pastel colors, these mud pots are far less active than they used to be. Within their limited depression are a few low, gray mud cones but little else.

For unknown reasons, much of the Lower Group underwent a sudden and drastic decline in water levels during the late 1970s, and geyser activity decreased in hand. Except for brief and infrequent recoveries known as *energy surges*, there is still rather little geyser action there.

Numerous hot springs and extensive geyserite deposits lie a few tens of feet off the lakeshore. These sinter shields

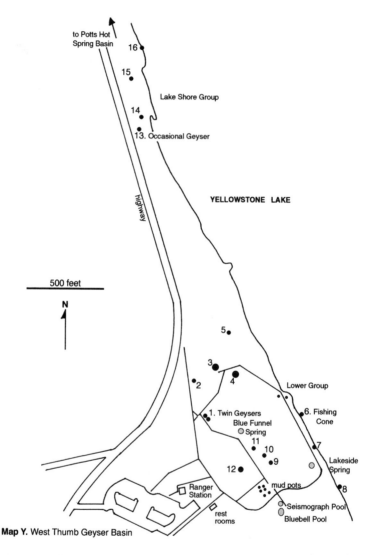

to Potts Hot
Spring Basin

16

15

Lake Shore Group

14

13. Occasional Geyser

highway

YELLOWSTONE LAKE

500 feet

N

5

3

2   4

Lower Group

1. Twin Geysers
Blue Funnel
Spring
11
10
12
9

6. Fishing
Cone

7

Lakeside
Spring

8

Ranger
Station

mud pots

rest
rooms

Seismograph Pool

Bluebell Pool

Map Y. West Thumb Geyser Basin

and cones could not have formed underwater, as they are
now. In fact, they have only recently been submerged.
Because of a shallow intrusion of volcanic magma in the
north-central part of the Park, east of the Grand Canyon of
the Yellowstone, the entire basin of Yellowstone Lake is

periodically being tilted toward the south. The north shore is getting higher, whereas forests — and the hot springs at West Thumb — are being progressively inundated. These hot springs are still active, and bubbles can be seen rising from their vents when the lake is calm. Several springs near the shoreline, including Lakeshore Geyser and Beach Geyser, are now exposed only at times of extremely low lake levels, and only then are they able to erupt.

The Lower Group is serviced by a boardwalk system. The Lake Shore Group and Potts Basin are not accessible but are sometimes visited by ranger-led walking tours. The full range of visitor services — including a hotel, store, gas station, campground, and visitor center — is available at Grant Village, about $2^1/_2$ miles south of West Thumb.

Lower Group

The Lower Group is, as noted earlier, the "main" portion of the West Thumb Geyser Basin and is the only part traversed by a boardwalk system. Geyser activity has been an on-again, off-again affair here, and on most occasions only a few small geysers are active. At generally long and unpredictable intervals, there is a temporary increase in water levels and temperatures, and then there may be several active geysers. In late 1991 and early 1992, first Black Pool and then Abyss Pool underwent episodes of explosive eruptions, among the largest ever seen at West Thumb.

1. TWIN GEYSERS is the largest and most spectacular geyser at West Thumb, when it is active. During most of its history, however, it has been dormant. When in such a state the water often boils in the northernmost of the two craters; the other basin is active only just before and during a major eruption. The first recorded activity in Twin was probably during 1910, when a single eruption described as being 200 feet high was recorded. It also played in 1912, and nineteen individual eruptions 75 to 100 feet high were recorded during 1916. Twin was again active in the late 1920s and early

Twin Geysers, though seldom active, is the most important geyser in West Thumb's Lower Group, the only portion of the geyser basin threaded by boardwalk trails. (Photo by Ron B. Dent.)

1930s and from 1948 into 1952. It was then dormant once more until 1970, when it began its best recorded active episode.

The intital activity was only 40 to 60 feet high, but by 1973 many of the eruptions exceeded 100 feet, and a few were estimated at fully 120 feet. As early as 1932 the geyser was known as "Maggie and Jiggs" after the old cartoon characters. First one crater would erupt, and as its water jet reached 50 feet the other would begin spouting. The two columns converged far above the ground, and just as Maggie often ended the great plans of Jiggs, the second column would take over the eruption, reaching the maximum height as the other died down to just a few feet high.

There were at least ninety-nine eruptions during 1973. Much of the action was erratic, but on some days eruptions recurred every 4 to 8 hours and were regular enough to be predicted. The play lasted 3 to 4 minutes. Since August

1973, Twin has been active only for 8 days in September 1974 and the first 2 days following the earthquake of June 30, 1975. There have been no eruptions since then, and even the boiling stopped when Abyss Pool (3) was active in 1991-1992.

2. ROADSIDE STEAMER is a pool at the base of the slope immediately below the old highway route. It began having eruptions during 1948, some of the first of which reached 30 to 40 feet high. Never regular, and dormant much more often than active, Roadside Steamer continues to have occasional active phases. Recent eruptions have seldom exceeded 3 feet high.

3. ABYSS POOL is one of the larger, deep-blue pools in the Park. That it was active as a major geyser in 1904–1905 was one of those points of almost forgotten history until recent research turned up some old U.S. Army reports. Active in July 1904 to 20 feet, Abyss (then called Elk Geyser) began an episode of large, explosive eruptions in early 1905. Bursts reached 80 to 100 feet high over typical durations of 20 to 40 seconds. It was common for chunks of geyserite weighing up to 30 pounds to be thrown out of the crater. Between April 1 and May 31, 1905, fifty-seven eruptions were recorded. There the records stop, because the Army sergeant who made them was arrested to face court-martial. The action undoubtedly continued for some time, but there are no further records.

Abyss Pool did not play again until a single eruption occurred in 1987, perhaps a prelude to a substantial active phase that began in September 1991. Over a 1-month period it had a few eruptions up to 100 feet high. These initial plays lasted 45 seconds. After a brief dormancy, Abyss renewed activity in December and continued to play for 6 months. At its best, during the 1992 winter season, the intervals ranged between 45 minutes and 5 hours. Over durations of 1 to 3 minutes, the rocketing bursts reached 50 to 70 feet high. Unfortunately, by the summer season of 1992 the activity had declined in frequency and force. The last known eruption took place on June 7, 1992. For several weeks thereafter, Abyss continued to boil around the edges of the crater, but it had soon returned to the beautiful but quiet pool of before.

4. BLACK POOL usually had a water temperature low enough for dark orange-brown cyanobacteria to grow throughout its crater; the color was never really black, but it was an exceptionally dark green. During 1991 an exchange of function transferred energy from the central part of the Lower Group toward Black and Abyss (3) Pools. A small spring at the edge of Black Pool gradually heated up and began having small eruptions. With this, Black also warmed up until the cyanobacteria had been killed and the spring assumed a rich blue color. Then, on August 15, 1991, the small spring exploded and merged with Black Pool. The explosion was not witnessed by any reporting observer, but it must have been impressive, as blocks of geyserite several feet in dimension were blasted loose. Over the next few hours Black Pool had frequent boiling eruptions that domed the water 1 to 3 feet high and produced heavy runoff. The activity was confined to that 1 day, but only about 3 weeks later eruptions began at nearby Abyss Pool. Two more brief episodes of small eruptions took place the following winter while Abyss Pool was still active. Black Pool remains very hot, and it is now one of Yellowstone's most beautiful blue pools.

5. KING GEYSER played as a major spouter in 1905, at the same time that Abyss Pool (3) was active. Intervals were a few days long, and the eruptions lasted only a few minutes, but some bursts were fully 60 feet high. At that time it was called Lake Geyser. The modern name is probably a result of the visit to Yellowstone by the future King Gustaf of Sweden in 1926. This implies that there were some eruptions during that year, but no others were specifically recorded until 1933. King played erratically through the rest of the 1930s, generally lasting 5 to 10 minutes and reaching 6 to 8 feet high. Only a small number of similar eruptions have been recorded since 1940.

It has been many years since Fishing Cone erupted as a geyser, and now it could hardly be used to cook fish.

6. FISHING CONE is one of the most famous hot springs in Yellowstone. As the story goes, it was possible to stand on the cone while fishing in the lake, and the catch could be cooked in the boiling hot spring without having to be removed from the hook. At times, this actually could have been done, but Fishing Cone is usually too cool to cook in efficiently. However, it has had two recorded episodes of vigorous geyser activity. In 1919 the play reached as high as 40 feet, and in the late 1920s it was not more than 4 feet tall. More recently, Fishing Cone has sometimes splashed weakly as a near perpetual spouter. During the exchange of function that caused eruptions in Black (4) and Abyss (3) Pools in 1991-1992, Fishing Cone drained to a low level, and a small hole in its side acted as a weak steam vent. This condition still existed in July 1994.

North of Fishing Cone are two smaller cones, respectively Big Cone and Little Cone by formal name. Although usually cool, completely quiet, and with only seeping discharge, Big Cone has been known to undergo rare eruptions 1 foot high or less. Eruptions are not known in Little Cone.

7. LAKESHORE GEYSER has a cone much like that at Fishing Cone (6). It sits within the lake, too, but unlike Fishing Cone its vent is usually covered by water. It can erupt only when the lake is low enough to completely expose the crater. Even then, Lakeshore is usually dormant. When in an active phase it erupts every 30 to 60 minutes. The play usually lasts about 10 minutes, reaching 25 feet high. Lakeshore's last known activity was during the winter of 1992-1993, when minor eruptions less than 1 foot high were seen.

8. UNNG-WTL-1 ("BEACH GEYSER") lies along the lakeshore a short distance south of Lakeshore Geyser (7). It is active only when the water level of Yellowstone Lake drops to exceptionally low levels, which occurs late in the season or during drought years. Even then eruptions are uncommon. The bursting play reaches 4 to 6 feet high for durations of several minutes.

9. SURGING SPRING is the southernmost of three similar springs that have developed along a line that probably represents a subsurface fracture that might extend as far as Twin Geysers (1). On rather infrequent occasions, the central portion of the Lower Group undergoes an "energy surge" during which several springs are able to erupt. These include Surging Spring, Ledge Spring (10), Percolating Spring (11), and Thumb Geyser (12) plus numerous smaller features. The most recent energy surge lasted for about 2 months during 1987. In an opposite fashion, exchanges of function such as that toward Abyss (3) and Black (4) Pools during 1991–1992 will cause these springs to cool and drop to low water levels.

When active, Surging Spring fits its name. The eruptions consist of strong pulsations of the pool, with heavy surges doming the water and producing very voluminous overflow. Some bursting may occur, splashing water as high as 3 feet. Most commonly, Surging Spring is a quiet pool barely at or just below overflow.

10. LEDGE SPRING is drained by a very wide runoff area. It was first witnessed as a geyser in 1928 and has been seen during only a few years since, most recently in 1991. During its rare episodes of activity, eruptions can occur as frequently as every few minutes. The action produces a huge discharge, and the bursting 2 to 6 feet high may continue for as long as 3 minutes.

11. PERCOLATING SPRING was probably named because of the steady streams of bubbles that usually rise from several small vents at the bottom of the crater. At the times when an energy surge leads to eruptions in the nearby hot springs, Percolating infrequently joins in with splashing eruptions 1 to 4 feet high. The only known year of consistent activity was 1987.

Just north of Percolating Spring is PERFORATED POOL. Small eruptions rose 1 to 2 feet high from two of its several vents during 1992.

12. THUMB GEYSER can have very impressive eruptions. During 1925 it played fairly regularly, every 6 to 12 hours, bursting up to 20 feet high for as long as 15 minutes. More typically, when it has been active during recent energy surges, the intervals have been long and erratic. The play lasts 4 to 5 minutes and reaches 6 to 10 feet high.

Lake Shore Group

The Lake Shore Group includes West Thumb's most active geysers. The group extends northward from the Lower Group along the shore of Yellowstone Lake. The hot springs are confined to a narrow tract of ground mostly less than 100 feet wide between the lake and the highway. Unfortunately, there is no trail here and direct access is not permitted, but most of the geysers can be seen from the edge of the road or, even better, by boat.

13. OCCASIONAL GEYSER is, in spite of its name, a frequent and regularly active geyser. It plays from a complex of vents, one of which is an extraordinarily smooth and perfectly round crater lined with tan, beaded geyserite. It is a beautiful sight. Eruptions generally recur every 20 to 30 minutes. The water rises steadily in the craters and begins to bubble during the few minutes before an eruption, which begins abruptly. Eruptions last 4 to 5 minutes, and the height is about 10 feet. The crater of Occasional sits atop a high sinter platform, and the runoff flows only a few feet before dropping over a fall into the lake.

During the 1890s observers described a "Lake Geyser" in this area; this was definitely different from the "Lake Geyser" now known as King Geyser (5). The eruptions were 100 to 200 feet high. Later reports from the 1920s and again as recently as 1958 have a geyser listed as "Occasional" playing up to 60 feet. These almost unquestionably all refer to the present Occasional.

14. LONE PINE GEYSER is currently the largest active geyser in the West Thumb Geyser Basin. It received its name in 1974, the year of its first modern action. The round crater lies near a small peninsula of sinter that extends into the lake; this land projection is decorated by a single, small pine tree. The 1974 activity consisted of eruptions recurring every 20 minutes. The duration was 5 minutes, and the height was 25 feet. As time progressed the eruptions came less frequently, but they also grew in strength. Since the early 1980s there has been little further change in the action. Most intervals are longer than a day — usually 26 to 32 hours — but are often predictably regular. There is little warning of the initial, major eruption. A sudden, heavy overflow leads quickly into strong, steady jetting that can exceed 75 feet high. This play lasts as long as 30 minutes, about half of which is a steam phase. The major eruption is followed by a series of minor eruptions. These occur at intervals of a few minutes and last only a few seconds but still reach 25 to 40 feet high. There may be as many as five such follow-up eruptions in the series. Lone Pine then falls silent and begins to refill. Slight overflow occurs for several hours before the next eruptive sequence begins.

15. BLOWHOLE SPRING is not visible from the highway and is only barely so from the lake. It is usually a slightly bubbling spring but has rarely been known to play as a small geyser. It was last observed in 1988. The eruptions send steamy spray 4 to 6 feet high. Although the duration can be as long as several minutes, there is little runoff.

16. OVERHANGING GEYSER is so named because erosion caused by waves on Yellowstone Lake has undercut the crater so that it is actually perched out *over* the water. It is a miracle that the erosion did not tap into any part of the plumbing system. Although Overhanging has shown widely variable intervals over the years, it most often plays quite regularly about every 2 hours. The eruptions last 3 to 25 minutes and burst the water 3 to 6 and, rarely, 10 feet high. The runoff drops in free fall over the edge of the overhang, a unique sight when the geyser is in eruption.

Potts Hot Spring Basin

The Potts Hot Spring Basin is named after Daniel T. Potts, an early trapper who described his 1826 visit to the West Thumb area in a letter to his brother the next year. The highway north from the main West Thumb area used to pass directly through these springs, but even then they received little attention. Now that the road has been moved, they are almost never visited. In fact, geyser activity has evidently been rather uncommon here, in spite of the large number of hot springs. A series of detailed studies during the 1980s revealed that the area goes through episodes of energy surges similar to those that sometimes affect West Thumb's Lower Group. Then, for short periods of time as many as two dozen springs act as geysers. The Potts Basin naturally divides into two parts.

THE "EMPTY HOLE GROUP" encompasses the southern portion of the Potts Hot Spring Basin. Until the early 1970s the main highway passed directly through these springs. It's good that it was moved — sometime in the early 1980s a rather large steam explosion excavated a good-sized crater here, and part of the old roadway was involved. Additional smaller explosions in 1983 and 1984 further enlarged this crater, which is now about 50 feet in diameter. The group received its name because of the many "empty holes" that perforate a sinter platform between the old road and the lake. Several of these are small geysers of generally frequent but erratic performances. A total of eight geysers have been seen in this group.

17. UNNG-POT-1 ("RESURGENT GEYSER"), just west of the old road, is the largest member of the Empty Hole Group. Its activity is highly irregular and possibly cyclic. Intervals are known to range from as little as 30 minutes to as long as a day; it also has long dormant periods. The play is a steady jetting as high as 15 feet that lasts as long as 5 minutes.

THE "MERCURIAL GROUP" of the Potts Basin lies at a lower elevation and comprises the northernmost part of the West Thumb Geyser Basin. Visible from a large highway pullout on the hill above, it contains several dozen hot springs, many of which are aligned along a series of fracture zones. It received its name because of the highly variable nature of its geyser activity. Usually, few if any of these springs are active as geysers, and then they are of very small size, but during the infrequent energy surges as many as at least a dozen have been animated at the same time. Such eruptions are frequent and vigorous. All are less than 10 feet high, but their net discharge is easily several hundred gallons per minute. None of these springs has been given a formal name.

18. UNNG-POT-2 ("MERCURIAL GEYSER") is generally the largest of the geysers within the Mercurial Group. It plays from a pool of moderate size. Essentially inactive except during the

energy surges, it then has series of frequent minor eruptions punctuated every 7 to 13 minutes by major eruptions. Lasting 25 to 65 seconds, these produce very heavy overflow while bursting up to 8 feet high.

Table 27. Geysers of the West Thumb Geyser Basin

Name	Map No.	Interval	Duration	Height (ft)
Abyss Pool	3	[1992]	1–3 min	50–100
Big Cone	6	rare	unknown	1
Black Pool	4	[1992]	minutes	1–3
Blowhole Spring	15	[1988]	minutes	4–6
Fishing Cone	6	[1928?]	minutes?	1–40
King Geyser	5	rare	10 min	6–8
Lakeshore Geyser	7	30–60 min *	10 min	25
Ledge Spring	10	8–50 min *	3 min	2–6
Lone Pine Geyser	14	26–32 hrs	17–30 min	25–75
Occasional Geyser	13	30 min	4–5 min	10
Overhanging Geyser	16	2–4 hrs	5–25 min	3–10
Percolating Spring	11	[1987]	sec–min	1–4
Perforated Pool	11	[1992]	seconds	1–2
Roadside Steamer	2	erratic	seconds	3–15
Surging Spring	9	infrequent	minutes	1–3
Thumb Geyser	12	infrequent	4–5 min	6–10
Twin Geysers	1	[1975]	3–4 min	60–100
UNNG-POT-1 ("Resurgent")	17	min–hrs *	5 min	15
UNNG-POT-2 ("Mercurial")	18	7–13 min *	25–65 sec	8
UNNG-WTL-1 ("Beach")	8	rare	minutes	4–6

* When active.
[ ] Brackets enclose the year of most recent activity for extremely rare or dormant geysers. See text.

Chapter 9

Gibbon Geyser Basin

The Gibbon Geyser Basin (Map Z, Table 28) includes the hot spring clusters that lie around the perimeter of Gibbon Meadows, about 5 miles south of Norris Junction. For various reasons, these hot springs contain elements of interest even though geysers are comparatively few. True geysers exist in four of the five important groups. The fifth group is the Chocolate Pots, located along the road in the small canyon at the north end of the basin, where relatively cool springs are forming unique sinter deposits.

The main highway runs through Gibbon Meadows near the middle of the Gibbon Basin. Trails proceed to the hot spring areas, although some of them have not been maintained for many years.

Artists' Paintpots

The Artists' Paintpots is the best-known thermal group in the Gibbon Geyser Basin. The trail to the group is well marked, heading east from a parking area next to the highway near the south end of Gibbon Meadows. The path is well maintained and incorporates some boardwalks where it passes among the hot springs. The round-trip around the area is about 1 mile.

The group was named for the numerous bright colors that characterize the springs at the bottom of the hill. Brilliant oranges and reds are created by iron oxide minerals. Clay minerals form pastel pinks and blue-grays, and hot

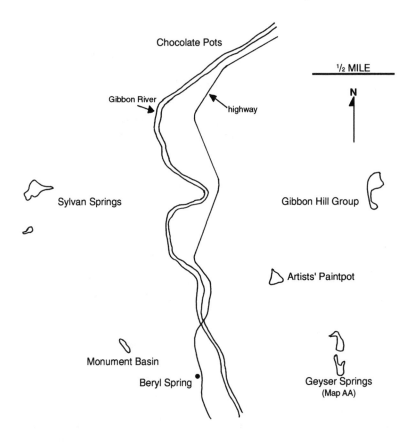

Map Z. Index Map to the Gibbon Geyser Basin

water cyanobacteria and algae contribute other oranges plus browns and greens. Add to these the usual blues of the pools, abundant wildflowers, and the forest. The overall effect is striking. Like an artist's palette, it is one of the most colorful places in Yellowstone.

The Artists' Paintpots themselves are a pair of mud pots located up the hillside, somewhat separated from the other hot springs. Although restricted to just two small basins, they tend to be very active. At times, the gray mud is tossed as high at 20 feet. Despite their proximity to one another, the two sets of mud pots always have different thicknesses.

The clear-water springs, including two geysers, are located at the base of Paint Pot Hill. Several other springs in the area appear to be geysers but actually are not. Their spouting is virtually perpetual and is largely caused by the evolution of carbon dioxide in water that is well below boiling. The best known of these is Flash Spring, immediately next to the easternmost point of the trail just where it begins to climb up the hillside. The first of the geysers is to its southwest (right).

1. BLOOD GEYSER plays from a shallow basin near the far east end of the group. First described as a perpetual spouter in 1882, it has only a few brief pauses to the play. Most such quiet intervals last less than 1 minute and fall as long as several hours apart. The bursting is up to 6 feet high.

The water discharge of this one spring amounts to about 150 gallons per minute, half that of the entire group. The small alcove surrounding the spring is highly colored by iron oxides, and, in fact, the water contains a far greater than normal concentration of iron in solution. A sample, allowed to cool and sit quietly, will develop a precipitate of reddish iron oxide within a few minutes. This is what led to the name Blood Geyser. The only other Yellowstone springwater known to do this comes from the Chocolate Pots, elsewhere in the Gibbon Basin.

2. UNNG-GIB-2 is difficult to see from the trail. Its vent is nothing more than a crack in a large rhyolite boulder near the base of the hillside a short distance to the right (west) of Blood Geyser (1). A small pool at the base of the rock constantly pulsates and splashes a few inches high. The geyser's activity is irregular, but every few minutes a brief squirting rises from the crack, reaching as high as 4 feet.

Geyser Springs (Geyser Creek Group)

The maintained trail ends at Artists' Paintpots. Signs admonish the visitor to stay on the trail, so continuing onward can be a bit tricky. What appears to be a good trail beyond the signs rapidly deteriorates to nothing. There used to be a maintained trail, on through the forest another $1/2$ mile to the Geyser Springs — traces of it still show in the form of cut logs — but there is a tremendous amount of downed timber along the route, some of which burned in the 1988 forest fires. The hike is strenuous but well worth the effort.

Geyser Springs (Map AA) is the site of the most vigorous geyser activity in the Gibbon Basin. Ten geysers are described here, and at least as many other small, irregular geysers have also been observed. Dozens of additional springs, ranging from clear pools to mud pots and sulfurous cauldrons, make this a dangerous area. Perhaps no place in Yellowstone contains more fragile crust, and the temperatures are high. Any exploration of the area should be confined to the hillsides as much as possible.

The Geyser Creek area naturally divides into three sections. First is an open valley in which most of the larger springs are found. Farther upstream, separated from the "Lower Basin" by a forested ridge, is the smaller "Upper Basin" that includes several pools and at least three geysers. The uppermost set of hot springs is on the precipitous slopes of a narrow canyon, where there are no geysers but one does find several mud pots and some of Yellowstone's most spectacular perpetual spouters. Another reason for caution: this canyon was the residence of a grizzly bear during 1992.

Geyser Springs is one of those Yellowstone areas in which you should definitely notify somebody of your planned trip and then check back in afterward. As always in the backcountry, your safety is in your own hands.

3. UNNG-GIB-7 ("BULL'S EYE SPRING") is a large pool near the bottom end of the "Lower Basin," near where the old trail leaves the forest. Within a massive geyserite rim, this pool is

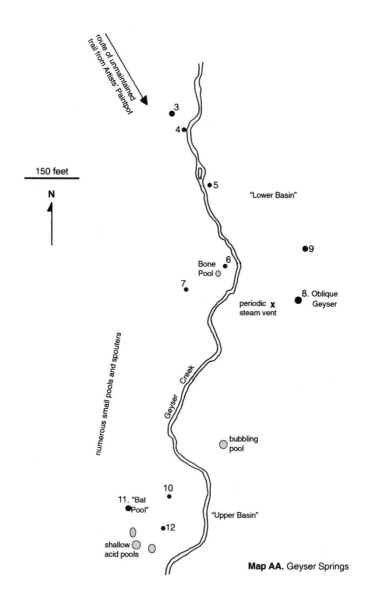

Map AA. Geyser Springs

most commonly active as a small perpetual spouter. The water is acid and rich in free sulfur, but it clears occasionally. At such times Bull's Eye may have periodic eruptions with substantial overflow. Both the intervals and durations are typically a few seconds long. The bursting may reach 4 to 6 feet high.

4. UNNG-GIB-3 ("ANTHILL GEYSER") is next to the creek a few feet southeast of "Bull's Eye Spring" (3). It erupts from a complex of vents dominated by a small, symmetrical geyserite cone that looks something like an anthill. Its vent is less than an inch across. Anthill is quite variable in its activity. Although dormant periods are known, it most often is fairly regular in its performances. Both the duration and quiet period are commonly in the range of 2 to 9 minutes, but one eruption seen in 1994 lasted well over 20 minutes. The play is a mixture of steam and spray splashed about 1 foot above the top of the cone. Sometimes it develops into a partial steam phase that jets 4 feet high and may be loud enough to be heard from a considerable distance. A small pool below the cone commonly splashes to about 1 foot in company with Anthill, but sometimes, too, its greatest degree of action happens during Anthill's quiet interval near the time of the next eruption. When the geyser is dormant, this pool acts as an intermittent spring.

5. UNNG-GIB-8 is a large, muddy pool almost at creek level a short distance upstream from "Anthill Geyser" (4). A pile of sandy gravel on the north side of the crater has been produced by the muddy water of eruptions and implies considerable frequency and force, but eruptive episodes have seldom been witnessed. During such episodes the play repeats every few minutes. Black, muddy water is burst as high as 10 feet for as long as 2 minutes. Most commonly, the pool bubbles and pulsates slightly.

There are several small springs out on the wet geyserite flats east and southeast of GIB-8. At least three have been seen as geysers 1 to 3 feet high, but it is unusual to see them playing.

Oblique Geyser at Geyser Springs is the most vigorous geyser in the Gibbon Basin. It jets water in all directions from at least seventeen separate vents.

6. UNNG-GIB-4 is near Bone Pool, the only clear blue pool in the lower portion of Geyser Springs. First observed in 1985, it erupts from a jagged crater that appears to have been formed by a relatively recent steam explosion. The play splashes about 4 feet high for a few seconds. Nothing is known of the intervals, and GIB-4 is often dormant.

7. "SUBTERRANEAN BLUE MUD GEYSER" is unique among Yellowstone geysers. It is located up a narrow draw west of Bone Pool, a few feet above some small mud pots. Its vent is pipe-like, about $1^{1}/_{2}$ feet across and plunging vertically downward to a water level probably 10 feet below the ground surface. Eruptions begin with subterranean surging, which pounds the ground and creates a deep echoing sound. The play builds up rapidly until a fine spray of water charged with blue-gray clay is jetted out of the opening. The duration is less than 1 minute, but eruptions recur as often as every few minutes.

8. OBLIQUE GEYSER has also been referred to under a long series of other, informal names, including Rockpile, Ava-

lanche, Talus, Marvelous, Geyser Creek, and Spray Geyser. The name Oblique might actually have first been applied to a geyser in Gibbon Canyon, but it was attached to this geyser at least as early as 1884. Any of the other names would also be applicable, providing good descriptions of the setting and activity. Oblique spouts from not less than seventeen separate vents, and the play from each has its own character. All of the vents open among a pile of boulders that have been coated by a spiny, pale brown geyserite.

Oblique is a frequent and highly regular performer, a geyser that would do justice to any geyser basin. Active at all known times, it has shown a gradual increase in the intervals through the years. During 1928, for example, the 25-foot play recurred every 6 minutes. By 1974 the intervals had increased to 7 to 8 minutes, and since 1985 most observers have found averages of around 9 or 10 minutes. The duration is $2^1/_2$ to 3 minutes. No dormant period has been recorded.

The eruption begins with sudden puffs of steam from the two main vents. With a series of rapidly stronger gushes, the steam is quickly followed by water, and, before many seconds have passed, Oblique is in full eruption. The two main vents shoot water at slight angles to 25 or 30 feet high. A third important vent erupts out away from the others, at a low angle with the water falling fully 30 feet from the opening. Most of the other vents play only 2 to 5 feet high, but much steam is discharged along with the water. Finally, several other openings emit only steam under pressure. The display is very impressive, roaring and spraying water in all directions. The end of the eruption is sudden. The water abruptly gives out, and Oblique falls quiet, with two or three dying gasps of steam. Occasional gurgling interrupts the quiet interval.

Near a huge boulder on the hillside west of Oblique is a periodic steam vent. At times it seems to play in sympathy with Oblique, starting near the end of Oblique's eruption. This happens too frequently to be sheer chance, but the steam vent also has independent activity and is sometimes dormant.

9. "BIG BOWL GEYSER" is about 150 feet north of Oblique Geyser (8), near the base of the slope at the eastern side of the valley. The crater and its surroundings are decorated exquisitely with pearly geyserite beadwork. Activity in the deep basin is nearly constant. Highly superheated, the water boils continuously, and this is punctuated by truly periodic eruptions. The intervals are usually only 5 to 15 seconds long, and the durations are perhaps 5 seconds. Most of the play is less than 10 feet high, but occasional heavy surges send sharp jets of water as high as 30 feet.

10. UNNG-GIB-9 is a pair of small connected pools among the "Upper Basin" springs, down the gentle geyserite platform from "Bat Pool" (11) and near the creek. It is usually observed only as a weakly intermittent spring, but eruptive periods in which splashing 2 feet high repeats every few minutes are known. In addition, the runoff channels are sometimes found to be extensively washed, showing that larger eruptions and gushing discharges sometimes take place.

11. UNNG-GIB-6 ("BAT POOL") is a deep-blue, superheated spring next to a rocky outcrop at the edge of the upper area. The boiling is steady but normally rather gentle. Every few seconds to minutes it increases in vigor, and bursting action can then throw water up to 3 feet high.

One of the boulders near Bat Pool was fractured in its fall from the hillside above. A colony of bats usually nests inside the crack. Take a close look. They'll scurry about, twitter complaints, and glare at you with beady eyes. These bats are insectivores, harmless to people. Obviously, though, the crack is not a place for fingers.

12. UNNG-GIB-5 ("TINY GEYSER") is among a dense cluster of springs a few feet southeast of "Bat Pool" (11). It can be difficult to find except when actually erupting. Tiny is extremely small, perhaps the smallest true geyser known in Yellowstone. The vent is marked by a shallow depression in the geyserite platform and is surrounded by beaded, yellowish geyserite. Water rises within the 1-inch hole, sputters a bit of fine spray a few inches high, and then drops following about 5 seconds of play. Eruptions usually recur every 2 to 3 minutes. Tiny has had some known dormancies, but the solid geyserite and repeated rejuvenations indicate that it is a long-term fixture despite the minuscule size.

Gibbon Hill Group

Gibbon Hill lies east of Artists' Paintpots and northeast of Geyser Springs, respectively about 1 and $^1/_2$ mile from those groups. No trail leads to the area, so access is gained by cross-country bushwhacking through dense forest and wet meadows. The hot springs of the Gibbon Hill Group are scattered along the base of the hill, and they include two or three geysers.

13. GIBBON HILL GEYSER will be difficult to find for anybody who has not been to it before. It used to be a significant geyser whose steam cloud would lead the hiker to it. The 25-foot bursts were vigorous and continuous throughout durations of 20 to 50 minutes. Eruptions ended without warning, and the crater drained, often with a loudly sucking whirlpool over the vent. Slow refilling usually began before the crater was completely empty. At times like these the intervals were regular, with an average of 5 hours. Occasionally, as during the early 1980s, Gibbon Hill acted as a perpetual spouter. Such play was much weaker, with few splashes more than 6 feet high.

Large portions of the Gibbon Geyser Basin, including Gibbon Hill, burned in the forest fires of 1988. The barren hillsides were subject to severe flooding and erosion until new plants gained a foothold. Thunderstorms in August 1989 produced a number of muddy debris flows, some of which can be seen at Geyser Springs. Here, one of the floods completely inundated Gibbon Hill Geyser. The crater remains all but obliterated. What seems remarkable is that the large volume of water and energy once emitted by Gibbon Hill Geyser seems to have been thoroughly sealed in.

The geyser has not been able to clear its crater — indeed, only the barest trace of steam is visible on cold days — but no nearby spring has shown any increase in activity or temperature, not even a crater just a few feet to the north that was active as a geyser in the 1920s.

14. UNNG-GIB-10 is the largest member of a cluster of springs about 250 yards north of Gibbon Hill Geyser (13). Near it are several vigorous perpetual spouters, one of which sometimes reaches over 10 feet high. The pool of GIB-10 is about 20 feet in diameter and is very deep. It lies atop a large sinter mound and has massive but badly weathered geyserite shoulders. The spring bubbles at several points, and on what are probably very irregular intervals this can develop into true splashing 1 to 2 feet high.

15. UNNG-GIB-11 is a gorgeous spring up the slope and on top of a conical mound northeast of GIB-10 (14). The intricate scalloping of geyserite around the crater is a silvery gray. The basin is filled with shimmering, absolutely crystal clear-water, and some of the surrounding catch basins are tinted various pastel shades of blue, green, and yellow. The spring, though, is a perpetual spouter of rather low temperature. The 1-foot splashes are primarily a result of gasses other than steam, mostly carbon dioxide.

Monument Geyser Basin

High on the hill above the south side of Gibbon Meadows, 600 feet above the valley floor, sits the Monument Geyser Basin. It is a long, narrow area of limited activity. Most of the springs are acid mud pots, sulfurous pools, and steam vents. The thermal activity extends from Monument down the precipitous slopes to the southeast, where it includes Beryl Spring, right next to the highway in the bottom of Gibbon Canyon.

Monument was named for the weird sinter cones that are scattered along the southwestern margin of the basin.

This "monument" is typical of the geyserite cones in the Monument Geyser Basin, one of several hot spring groups in the Gibbon Basin.

Built up by geysers with spraying eruptions, they are totally unlike the cones of other areas. Only one of these — Monument Geyser — is still active. No other spring in the group contains alkaline water. Were it not for these strange formations, the Monument Basin would have attracted little attention.

A 1-mile trail leads to the basin. It starts next to the highway bridge across the Gibbon River, between Beryl Spring and the Artists' Paintpots trail. The entire 600-foot climb is accomplished in the second half mile. It is a rigorous hike but well worth the effort. Monument is a unique area, and the view from the mountaintop is terrific.

16. MONUMENT GEYSER, also known as Thermos Bottle Geyser, spouts from one of the largest cones in the Monument Geyser Basin. Unlike the others, it has not quite sealed itself in by the internal accretion of sinter. That time is not far off. During the 1930s and before, Monument played most of the time, with fine spray being jetted as high as 15 feet. Now it steams gently, hissing under slight pressure, but almost no liquid water is ejected.

17. BERYL SPRING is next to the highway about 1 mile south of the Artists' Paintpots trail. It is served by a remarkably large parking area. Beryl Spring is superheated, constantly boiling and surging so as to perpetually throw water as high as 3 or 4 feet. Beryl has appeared in some lists as a geyser, but there is no evidence that it has ever had intermittent activity as a true geyser.

18. UNNG-GIB-12 is located within a cluster of hot springs on the hillside just across the highway bridge from the Monument Geyser Basin trailhead. All of these springs are small, but most have high temperatures and act as perpetual spouters. One of the closest to the highway reached 6 feet high during 1985. In 1991 it was much smaller but truly periodic.

Sylvan Springs Group

Sylvan Springs is the most visible hot spring group in the Gibbon Geyser Basin. It is the large, barren, steaming area at the far-western end of the meadows. The hot springs are almost entirely acid, relatively cool, and often muddy. The more important springs here have undergone frequent and rather drastic changes.

Evening Primrose Spring was once regarded as one of the more beautiful pools in the Park, and it was probably the one reason a maintained trail used to lead here. In shape and color it was comparable to Morning Glory Pool in the Upper Geyser Basin. At some point (just when does not seem to have been recorded) the water changed from alkaline to acid. The surface became covered with a thick froth of pure elemental sulfur. Then, during 1972 Evening Primrose was invaded by *Sulfolobus*, an archaeobacteria that metabolizes sulfur. Today's pool has become one of Yellowstone's ugliest, with a murky yellowish-green or brown color. The temperature in recent years has been recorded as low as 106°F (41°C), and the pH was measured at 0.95, the highest acid value ever determined in any Yellowstone spring.

Another important Sylvan Spring is Dante's Inferno. Although it is not a geyser as such, the shocks of the 1959 earthquake caused it to erupt violently to more than 100 feet high. The activity has not yet completely died down. The pool, milky-blue because of suspended particles of colloidal silica, churns and boils vigorously while building extensive geyserite terraces.

Within the small gorge at the center of the group are several perpetual spouters, some of which are gas powered, with temperatures below boiling. Just over a small ridge west of these is Sylvan Spring, a vigorously boiling-bubbling pool that was named after the group as a whole. A mud pot near the northeastern limit of the area is called Coffin Spring.

What is sometimes called the "South Group of Sylvan Springs" lies about $1/4$ mile through the forest to the south. These springs are much more fitting of the term *sylvan*, and in fact they probably comprise the original Sylvan Springs. One of these pools is a geyser.

18. UNNG-GIB-13 was active in 1974, 1984–1985, 1992, and probably in all the years in between. It is a large, oval pool, 30 by 7 feet in dimensions. It evidently developed along a fracture because there are several vents along the length of the bottom. Eruptions have been regular on all of the rare occasions when GIB-13 has been visited. Intervals of 10 to 12 minutes lead to durations of 8 to 9 minutes. The play reaches 5 feet high.

Table 28. Geysers of the Gibbon Geyser Basin

Name	Map No.	Interval	Duration	Height (ft)
Artists' Paintpots				
Blood Geyser	1	near steady	near steady	6
UNNG-GIB-2	2	minutes	seconds	4
Geyser Springs				
"Big Bowl Geyser"	9	5–15 sec	5 sec	10–30
Oblique Geyser	8	9–12 min	2 1/2–3 min	25–30
"Subterranean Blue Mud Geyser"	7	2–30 min	10–60 sec	see text
UNNG-GIB-3 ("Anthill")	4	frequent *	3–20 min	1–4
UNNG-GIB-4	6	unknown	seconds	4
UNNG-GIB-5 ("Tiny")	12	2–3 min *	seconds	inches
UNNG-GIB-6 ("Bat Pool")	11	sec–min	seconds	1–3
UNNG-GIB-7 ("Bull's Eye Spring")	3	seconds *	seconds	4–6
UNNG-GIB-8	5	infrequent	sec–2 min	10
UNNG-GIB-9	10	minutes *	seconds	2
Gibbon Hill Group				
Gibbon Hill Geyser	13	[1989]	20–50 min	6–25
UNNG-GIB-10	14	irregular	sec–min	1–2
UNNG-GIB-11	15	steady	steady	1

Table 28 continued

Monument Geyser Basin

Beryl Spring	17	steady	steady	1–3
Monument Geyser	16	steady	steady	spray
UNNG-GIB-12	18	near steady	near steady	2–6

Sylvan Springs

| UNNG-GIB-13 | 19 | 10–12 min * | 8–9 min | 5 |

* When active.
[ ] Brackets enclose the year of most recent activity for extremely rare or dormant geysers. See text.

Chocolate Pots

Next to the highway in the small canyon between Gibbon Meadows and Elk Park are the Chocolate Pots. The highest temperature in these small springs is only around 130°F (54°C), but the deposits being formed are unique. Rich red-brown, they are more than 50% iron oxide, 5% aluminum oxide, and 2% manganese oxide; their silica content is only 17%. A sample of the clear water allowed to sit for a few minutes will become a cloudy brown as iron oxide spontaneously precipitates from the water.

Chapter 10

Lone Star Geyser Basin

In the early days of Yellowstone National Park, most of the attention paid to geysers was given to the basins along the Firehole River. The Lone Star Geyser Basin (Map BB, Table 29) is one of these, lying about 5 miles upstream from Old Faithful. For a time the present Upper Geyser Basin was known as the Great Geyser Basin, and the Lone Star area was either the Upper Geyser Basin or the Third Geyser Basin. In terms of the number of geysers, the Lone Star Basin is Yellowstone's smallest.

The basin was named for Lone Star Geyser, which in turn was named not after the state but because of its isolated position. Until 1973 it was the only geyser of note here. One of the more obvious benefits of having a large cadre of geyser gazers has been the increase in knowledge about the previously all-but-ignored Lone Star Basin. Enough is now known about ten geysers for them to be described in this book.

The Lone Star Basin naturally divides into five parts, all of which contain at least one geyser. These groups, with their informal names, are shown on Map BB. Continuing another mile along the Shoshone Lake trail beyond the "Campsite Group," the hiker enters the large Firehole Meadow area. There, between the trail and the hillside to the east, are a number of hot pools and, up one small canyon, some mud pots.

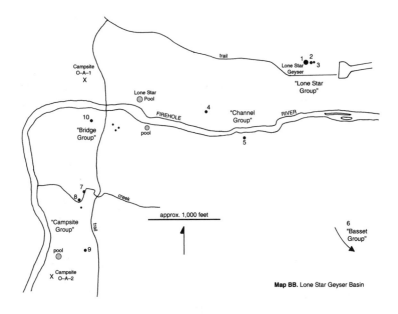

Map BB. Lone Star Geyser Basin

The Lone Star Basin is reached by way of a wide trail beginning from the main highway near the Kepler Cascades of the Firehole River. An old road open to traffic until 1971, it is mostly paved and is recommended as a bike trail. It is about $2^1/_2$ miles from the highway to Lone Star Geyser. Worth noting is a small cluster of springs along this trail, not far beyond the bridge over the river. The largest feature here, playing from a sinter crater on the hillside, is "Halfway Spring." Usually active as a variable perpetual spouter, it has been known to act as a geyser, with intervals and durations of a few seconds; its height is up to 3 feet.

Lone Star Group

The Lone Star Group is a compact cluster of hot springs, most of which are small, acid features of little importance on the hillside. Separated slightly from them, though, is a geyserite mound topped by three alkaline springs, each of which is a geyser. The star attraction is Lone Star Geyser. To help the visitor better anticipate when Lone Star might erupt, the National Park Service maintains a logbook. It is hoped that visitors who see Lone Star or the other geysers erupt will write the time in the book. That way later observers will know when it last played, and the Park Service will be able to gather the data needed to better understand the area.

1. LONE STAR GEYSER gained early fame because of its very large geyserite cone. Over 9 feet tall and very steep-sided, it is one of the biggest cones in Yellowstone. Lone Star erupts from one main and several minor vents at the summit of the cone. (The minor vents are known collectively as The Pepper Box.)

The cone was built to its present height by the frequent splashing of the geyser during its quiet phase. This activity generally starts 60 to 90 minutes after an eruption. With gradually increasing force, the preplay leads into a minor eruption. Lone Star usually has just one minor preceding the major eruption; on relatively rare occasions there may be a second and even a third minor, each followed by a few minutes of quiet. Sometimes, too, there is very little preplay before the minors. The usual single minor play lasts about 5 minutes and reaches as high as 45 feet. After a rest of 25 to 35 minutes, renewed splashing builds into the full, major eruption. It also jets water to 45 feet, and the eruption lasts fully 30 minutes. In the waning stages the water gives out, and the final part of the play is a powerful steam phase, loud enough to be heard more than a mile away. No matter what the nature of the preplay and minor eruptions, Lone Star's major intervals are always very close to exactly 3 hours; in fact, the average of more than 100 intervals in the 1982 logbook was 2 hours, 59 minutes, 48 seconds. No dormant period has ever been recorded.

2. UNNG-LST-1 ("BLACK HOLE GEYSER") is just a few feet from the base of Lone Star's (1) cone. Its vent is a symmetrical funnel penetrating the geyserite of a broad mound that predates the modern activity of the area. This geyser probably

Lone Star Geyser is one of the most regular geysers anywhere, repeating its major eruptions every three hours with little variation. Its cone is one of Yellowstone's largest.

had some activity during the early years of Yellowstone, but it was not reported in modern times until 1973. The activity of Black Hole is variable. Regular intervals as short as 10 minutes with durations of 3 to 4 minutes are known, but so are periods as long as several hours with durations longer than 15 minutes. The better eruptions jet rockets of water as high as 25 feet, but only 3 to 4 feet is more typical. Sometimes, too, there seems to have been a relationship between Black Hole's activity and the buildup of pressure within Lone Star, with Black Hole playing only near the time of Lone Star's major eruption. During the quiet interval, bubbling water may be visible within the vent, and this will start to burst outward and produce runoff before the real eruption begins. This preliminary bubbling can continue for several hours. The bursts of the full eruption begin abruptly with no other warning.

3. UNNG-LST-2 ("PERFORATED CONE GEYSER") is located within a low, rounded geyserite cone directly on the opposite side of "Black Hole" (2) from Lone Star (1). The cone is punctured by numerous small holes. The eruptions are erratic and infrequent, and consist of nothing more than steamy sputtering out of the holes. This is enough to keep the mound decorated with spiny sinter, but there is little or no actual runoff.

"Channel Group"

Along both banks of the Firehole River, starting roughly $1/4$ mile upstream from Lone Star Geyser, are numerous hot springs. Collectively, these make up the "Channel Group." The majority are in the grassy meadow on the south side of the river. Most of the springs are small and of little importance, but a few are geysers. At the west end of this group, near the Shoshone Lake trail bridge across the river, is "Lone Star Pool," which behaves as a long-cycle intermittent spring and has one report of small eruptions. Another pool and a perpetual spouter lie in the woods across the river from Lone Star Pool.

4. **UNNG-LST-3** is an assortment of small springs surrounded by meadow on the north side of the river. They include one pool about 3 feet in diameter plus several geyserite cones a few inches high. The springs of LST-3 are closely related to one another, as they are all active at the same time. Usually dormant or with tiny perpetual sputtering, these springs infrequently erupt as geysers, with some of the play reaching 2 to 3 feet high. A large runoff channel drains this cluster, implying that greater discharge takes place on rare occasions.

5. **UNNG-LST-4** is across the river and slightly downstream from LST-3 (4). The small pool only a few inches above the stream level constantly surges and bubbles. Its eruptive activity may be cyclic. It is often seen to play with short intervals but sometimes goes for long periods without bursting action. The eruptions last only a few seconds, sending splashes 1 foot high.

All along the river on both sides of LST-4 and up the hillside to the south are many other hot springs. Most of these possess runoff channels, yet few discharge more than a trickle of water, and the channels are filled with vegetation. Evidently, these were once active as geysers, but it has been several decades since they last played.

"Basset Group"

The "Basset Group" was named for the large rock faces exposed in the cliffs near its largest geyser; *basset* is French for a jagged, rocky outcrop. Well separated from the other Lone Star Basin springs, the group is easiest to locate from Lone Star Geyser, from where the steam of the one large geyser, "Buried," can be seen. Hike in that direction, either by fording the Firehole River near Lone Star or by crossing on the Shoshone Lake trail bridge about $1/2$ mile upstream and backtracking through the springs of the "Channel Group." The geyser is the first hot spring encountered in this group, at the base of the cliffs above a wide, barren drainage area.

Beyond the geyser, up and over the ridge, are several additional springs, some of which erupt out of beautiful craters as perpetual spouters. At the summit of the steep slope above them is a fine mud pot.

6. "BURIED GEYSER" is probably more significant as a geyser than Lone Star (1). Although not as high, its eruptions are frequent and powerful and often have great water discharge. Buried was so named because its crater was once partially covered by a sinter ledge; that is now virtually gone, removed by the erosion of the bursting activity of the past 20 years. Buried was apparently a quiet spring before the first perpetual spouting was reported in 1973. It became a geyser in 1983 and now has minor, intermediate, and major eruptions. Usually, about two-thirds of the eruptions are minors. Their duration is $3^{1}/_{2}$ minutes, followed by intervals of 7 to 9 minutes. The play is 3 to 9 feet high and ceases abruptly just as the first overflow is reached. The water level then quickly drains down as far as 2 feet, only to immediately begin to rise again. Intermediate eruptions are distinct from the minors because the water level rises much more rapidly during the eruption so that there is considerable overflow before the play stops, again after a duration of about $3^{1}/_{2}$ minutes. This play is somewhat more vigorous, and the bursts may reach as high as 12 feet. The major eruptions begin in the same fashion as do the minors, with a slow rise in the water level. But rather than stopping at the first overflow, the play becomes violent. Bursts fully 20 feet high are accompanied by a gushing overflow that floods the formations down the slope below the crater. Most major eruptions have durations of 4 to 5 minutes and are followed by intervals of 11 to 15 minutes. In the long run, Buried has been quite consistent in its performances. Times have been known when all the eruptions were minors, and for a while in 1990 nearly half were majors. Since 1973, only one short dormant period, in which the water lay quietly about 1 foot below overflow, is known.

"Bridge Group"

The "Bridge Group" includes a compact cluster of hot springs next to the Shoshone Lake trail just south of the footbridge that crosses the river. Mostly of no account, two of these springs were seen to have small eruptions in 1989. Along the fringe of forest in the upstream direction is a scattering of larger springs, at least one of which can be a significant geyser.

10. UNNG-LST-8 is a strange feature. It plays out of a small, conelike buildup of geyserite within a more open, saucerlike crater. Most of the time the play is perpetual spouting about 1 foot high confined to the cone, but LST-8 has been seen to fill its outer crater and burst as high as 8 feet. Such eruptions are brief but may occur as a series of plays every few minutes. There is never any overflow. The frequency of the major activity is unknown.

"Campsite Group"

About 1 mile from Lone Star Geyser along the Shoshone Lake trail, starting several hundred feet beyond the "Bridge Group," is the "Campsite Group." A backcountry campsite is located at the southern end of this group. This is a fairly extensive set of hot springs. Most are small and many are muddy, but the area includes at least three geysers plus the largest blue pool (which, surprisingly, is unnamed) in the Lone Star Geyser Basin.

7. UNNG-LST-5 plays from a shallow crater lined with spiny, yellow geyserite. It is just downstream along a small creek the trail crosses on a low boardwalk bridge. This geyser has long dormant periods during which the crater is only about half full of water. When it is active, the intervals are apparently several hours long. The play lasts as long as 30 minutes but is only 1 foot high.

8. UNNG-LST-6 is almost identical to LST-5 in every respect. It also has long dormant periods and, when active, undergoes small eruptions at intervals of several hours. The one difference is that the eruptions may also have durations as long as a few hours.

Just west of LST-5 and LST-6 is an assortment of vents and fractures in a geyserite platform. Although no eruptions were witnessed, these apparently played in some fashion in 1988 and 1989, when washed areas and small runoff channels were formed. Just across the small creek from LST-6 is a muddy pool with a unique red-orange color.

9. UNNG-LST-7 is, by size at least, the most important geyser in the "Campsite Group." It is a small pool that constantly bubbles and splashes weakly. Active periods as a geyser are rare. During the mid-1970s a number of eruptions were seen. They lasted about 10 minutes and reached 3 feet high. A few eruptions, known mostly on the basis of washed areas, have taken place since then. Several small vents near LST-7 are also known to act as rare, tiny geysers.

Table 29. Geysers of the Lone Star Geyser Basin

Name	Map No.	Interval	Duration	Height (ft)
"Buried Geyser"	6	7–15 min	3 1/2–5 min	3–20
Lone Star Geyser	1	3 hrs	30 min	45
UNNG-LST-1 ("Black Hole")	2	10 min–hrs	3–15 min	3–25
UNNG-LST-2 ("Perforated Cone")	3	erratic	minutes	inches
UNNG-LST-3	4	frequent *	minutes	2–3
UNNG-LST-4	5	minutes *	seconds	1
UNNG-LST-5	7	hours *	30 min	1
UNNG-LST-6	8	hours *	hours	1
UNNG-LST-7	9	rare	10 min	3
UNNG-LST-8	10	minutes *	seconds	8

* When active.

Chapter 11

Shoshone Geyser Basin

The Shoshone Geyser Basin (Map CC) is one of the most important thermal areas in the world, even though its major portion measures only 1,600 by 800 feet. The basin may contain as many as eighty geysers, perhaps more than any single place on earth other than the remainder of Yellowstone and the Valley of Geysers on Russia's Kamchatka Peninsula. Many of these geysers are small and infrequent performers, to be sure, and since the Shoshone Basin is a remote area, little is known about most of them. Accordingly, only forty-six are described here. Some of the spouting at Shoshone can be of considerable size, and one geyser — Union — is of truly major proportions. Extensive areas of acid mud pots, frying pans, and pools surround the hills between the geyser basin proper and Shoshone Lake.

The Shoshone Geyser Basin in general resembles the Upper Basin. The hot springs form compact, closely spaced groups along the course of Shoshone Creek. But Shoshone has its own special attributes as well. The deposits are often brightly colored by iron oxide minerals, and substantial amounts of mercury have been reported in some of the formations. Yellow crystalline sulfur forms at some springs, and small amounts of arsenic sulfides spot the ground with brilliant orange-reds and yellows in a few places among the acid springs around the perimeter of the basin. There are colorful growths of cyanobacteria along the runoff channels and in some of the cooler pools.

The first written description that can be ascribed to a particular geyser at Shoshone was penned by trapper

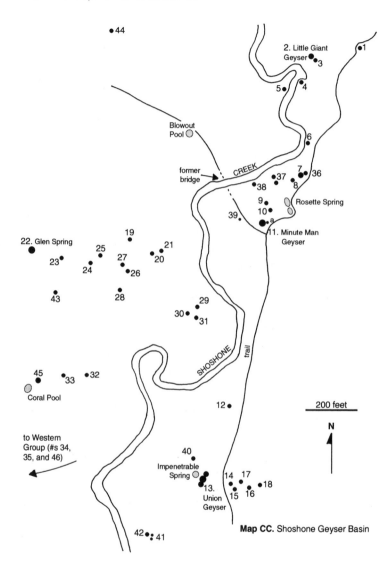

Map CC. Shoshone Geyser Basin

Osborne Russell in 1839. Calling it "Hour Spring" because of its regular activity, he was probably describing either Minute Man Geyser or the adjacent "Minute Man's Pool." Some people feel either Union Geyser or Little Giant Geyser is a more likely candidate. We will probably never know for sure. Nothing now active at Shoshone closely resembles the geyser Russell described. During the 1870s the Shoshone Basin was only slightly more remote than any other area of Yellowstone, and it was studied extensively by surveys in 1871, 1872, and 1878. Most of the recognized names were given to the springs in those years. From that time on, no detailed studies or maps were made of the area until the late 1960s and subsequently. Probably only the Heart Lake Geyser Basin has been as ignored over the years. It is likely that geyser activity is more extensive than that recognized here.

The Shoshone Basin is reached most easily by way of the same trail that passes Lone Star Geyser (see Chapter 10). The total distance from the highway at Kepler Cascades is about $8^{1}/_{2}$ miles each way. The route is well maintained and generally easy. The basin can also be reached by way of other, longer trails that lead along both shores of Shoshone Lake from the east or by canoe. There are several backcountry campsites nearby.

It is easy to imagine yourself as being the first person ever to see Shoshone's geysers. Most of the basin seems nearly untouched. Unfortunately, not everybody appreciates the natural world. Some of the formations have been severely vandalized, one even being chopped out with an ax. When in the area please do everything you can to avoid damaging any of the springs and geysers or their deposits. As always, remember the dangers of the hot spring basins. Even a small thermal burn is a severe injury in a place as remote as this.

Little Giant Group

The Little Giant Group (Table 30) is the first collection of hot springs encountered when entering the basin along the Lone Star trail from the north. It is a small area with most of its springs near Shoshone Creek. Little Giant Geyser can be the third largest in the basin, but it rarely has major eruptions now. The group contains several small pools in addition to the geysers, and most of these have also been known to erupt.

1. "TRAILSIDE GEYSER" is located at the base of the hill immediately to the left of the trail as you enter the basin. The trail here is a bridgelike affair made of cut logs. It was constructed to avoid damage to the geyserite formations that were exposed by the first recorded eruptions during the late 1970s. The sinter of the shallow crater is lightly stained by iron oxides. During the quiet intervals, which range from 6 to 16 minutes in length, the crater is about half full of water. Eruptions begin with a sudden filling of the basin. Water is splashed 1 to 5 feet high for durations of 20 to 60 seconds.

At the base of the slope just behind Trailside is another geyser, first observed in 1981. Its eruption is little more than intermittent superheated boiling recurring every several minutes, although small splashing is sometimes seen. In the opposite direction, within the fanciful geyserite drainage area from Trailside, is a tiny hole that sometimes has sputtering eruptions of its own.

2. LITTLE GIANT GEYSER plays from a heavily iron-stained vent in the middle of a round sinter platform. In the early days of Yellowstone it was a significant geyser, spouting as high as 50 feet about twice a day. There is no record of when such eruptions ceased; indeed, there is no mention of Little Giant in any twentieth-century reference — other than to repeat the data of the 1800s — until after the time of the 1959 earthquake. A survey of the Shoshone Basin two months after the shocks found Little Giant to be active, with eruptions 15 to 20 feet high. It is very interesting that this report noted the eruptions as being more frequent than they had been before the quake. Although Yellowstone's backcountry thermal areas were practically ignored in those years, it is puzzling that a geyser this large could (apparently) have been active without being mentioned in any known thermal report of the previous few years.

In any case, the 1959 activity was evidently brief, and Little Giant has had mostly minor eruptions since sometime before 1970. This play is an erratic bursting 1 to 6 feet high that takes place while nearby "Double Geyser" (3) is having its eruption. There is a single report of a 20-foot eruption being seen in 1988, and some sort of major eruption might have occurred in late 1991 when a long-unused runoff channel was found cleanly washed. Over the long run, Little Giant has had an irregular and a largely mysterious history. Major eruptions clearly can still take place, and more probably lie in its future.

3. "DOUBLE GEYSER" jets two columns of water into the air. There is actually only one vent, but a piece of sinter above it splits the stream. Double has also been called The Pirates because of the near certainty that it is the cause of Little Giant Geyser's (2) weak activity. Double apparently did not exist during the early years of Yellowstone, when Little Giant was a regular and major geyser. Now a very regular performer, its average interval is near 1 hour, with only a few minutes variation. The play begins with a progressively more vigorous welling of water out of the vents. It takes several minutes to build to the full height. Of the twin jets, the vertical one is the highest, reaching about 10 feet; the other shoots at an angle and is 6 feet high. The total overflow duration is 10 to 15 minutes; the actual jetting lasts 5 minutes.

4. "MEANDER GEYSER" was first observed in 1974, when it was active as a perpetual spouter. More recently, it has generally acted as a periodic geyser but with tremendous variability. Intervals as short as 3 hours leading to 12-minute durations were known in the early 1980s, but now both the interval and duration are many hours, perhaps even days, long. Meander rises from a small cone just below a meander in Shoshone Creek and reaches 1 to 3 feet high.

Of nearly as much interest as Meander are two independent vents nearby. One is a small, weak steam vent in Meander's sinter shoulder; when Meander is active this vent is periodically drowned, and then it sputters its own fan of water about 1 foot high with great commotion. The second vent is at the stream's edge so that a periodic withdrawal of its water causes a loud gurgling.

5. LOCOMOTIVE GEYSER was originally described in 1947 when its water jet was periodically cut off by a puff of steam. The resulting sound resembled that of a steam locomotive. The action shown by Locomotive has changed considerably since then, but there is still a pulsating action to the eruptions. These occur very irregularly. Over the years, intervals have been known to range from as little as 4 hours to more than 24 hours. Eruptions last as long as 2 hours, and the slender water jet squirts as high as 15 feet. Every few seconds there is a brief pause in the play, but the eruption never stops completely until the entire active period has ended; then it quits abruptly. The vent and surrounding sinter platform at Locomotive are colored a very dark gray, possibly because of the presence of manganese oxide minerals.

Minute Man Group

The Minute Man Group (Table 30) contains many hot springs, and most have histories as geysers. Minute Man Geyser is dominant. It is cyclic but plays very frequently during active phases only a few hours apart. Either the hillside above Minute Man or the rock outcrop south of Little Bulger Geyser is a wonderful place to take in the view that encompasses most of the geyser basin. Rosette Spring, just south of the outcrop, sometimes acts as an intermittent spring. It was well publicized during Yellowstone's early days because of its delicate sea-green color and perfectly formed examples of geyserite rosettes around its rim. As a mark of backcountry vandalism, these rosettes are long gone.

6. BLACK SULPHUR SPRING is a perpetual spouter that plays out of a vent within the steep sinter embankment above Shoshone Creek. The water is jetted by a series of rapid pulses about 6 feet outward at a 45-degree angle. The black color is probably a result of manganese oxide, not sulfur, incorporated into the geyserite.

36. UNNG-SHO-10, a spring within a cavernous crater next to the trail near the northeast base of Soap Kettle's (7) sinter

Locomotive Geyser is typical of the small but vigorous geysers in the Shoshone Basin. Unfortunately, in recent years it has tended to long and erratic intervals between eruptions.

mound, underwent some eruptions during 1986. None was witnessed, but the overflow washed out a wide and deep runoff channel, and muddy spray coated vegetation and the trail as far away as 15 feet. Minor eruptions were seen during several seasons since 1986, most recently in 1993.

7. SOAP KETTLE is a superheated spring within a massive sinter cone near the trail that, in most years, exhibits true geyser activity. The intervals generally range between 9 and 21 minutes and are very regular at any given time. Eruptions begin when the boiling water starts to rise within the crater. When it nears overflow the boiling increases in force, and some bursts throw water as high as 6 feet above the rim. The duration is 1 to 3 minutes. Severe erosion around the base of the cone indicated that some exceptionally voluminous eruptions took place during 1987. When Soap Kettle is not eruptive, the water level stands higher within the crater and boiling is more constant.

8. LITTLE BULGER GEYSER used to be one of the nicest geysers at Shoshone, with eruptions 10 feet high recurring every 8 to 13 minutes. But in 1985 a subsidiary vent, known as "Little Bulger's Parasite," developed at the northeast edge of the crater. Active at about the same intervals Little Bulger used to show, it has brief, erratic bursts up to 3 feet high. This new vent is between Little Bulger and Soap Kettle (7). Some have surmised that its evolution was related to the general increase in Soap Kettle's action and the blowout of SHO-10 (36) 2 years later in 1987. If so, Little Bulger may have met its demise. Although it still splashes on occasion, no regular eruptions have been seen since these developments.

37. UNNG-SHO-11, known to most geyser gazers as "USGS #11," is a very deep, oval spring along the runoff channel leading from Shield Geyser (10). Its activity depends on the volume of flow from Shield. When Shield is active, which is a great deal of the time, much of its water flows directly into the crater of SHO-11. The play then consists of only a gushing, bubbling overflow. However, when Shield is inactive and

there is no runoff, SHO-11 can burst as high as 3 feet. Perched as it is within a massive formation right at the brink of a steep slope, it is a fascinating feature.

At the base of the slope below SHO-11 is another pool, mapped by the U.S. Geological Survey as #12. It is also a geyser whose erratic play can splash as high as 5 feet, but #12 is most often either dormant or active only at long intervals.

9. GOURD SPRING is the first of the four members of the Minute Man Complex. Its low sinter cone is occupied by a crudely gourd-shaped crater; the massive geyserite shoulder is punctured by numerous minor vents. As with nearby Shield Geyser (10), Gourd is cyclic in its action. The intervals between active phases range from a few minutes to several hours. Their length is dependent on the previous duration, which is known to vary from 15 to 70 minutes. When it is active, the play is an almost continuous splashing 2 to 3 feet high.

10. SHIELD GEYSER erupts from a somewhat squarish cone a few feet from Gourd Spring (9). An open, flat-bottomed crater centered by a small vent occupies the top of the cone. Like Gourd, Shield is also cyclic. It is usually active when Gourd is in eruption, but it is also known to undergo independent, albeit short, active phases of its own. Shield will erupt only when its crater is full of water and overflowing. The bursting play reaches 10 feet high, lasting a few seconds and repeating every minute or two until the crater drains at the end of the active phase.

11. MINUTE MAN GEYSER erupts from a prominent cone 5 feet high and 12 feet long. Most of its sinter is exquisitely beaded, unlike any other formation that can be seen close at hand elsewhere in Yellowstone. Minute Man is cyclic, like the other members of its complex, but its cycles bear no discernible relationship to those of Gourd Spring (9) or Shield Geyser (10).

During active periods Minute Man jets water every 1 to 3 minutes, with the intervals generally getting longer as the active phase progresses. The play lasts just a few seconds. The steady jetting reaches as high as 40 feet near the start of an active period, then drops to as little as 10 feet as the intervals grow longer near the end. The cycle interval, start to start, is usually about 7 hours; the eruptive periods commonly last 3 to 5 hours so that Minute Man tends to be active more than it is not.

11A. "MINUTE MAN'S POOL." During the 1870s the pool sandwiched between Minute Man's (11) cone and the hill was reported to "sometimes spout." No details as to the frequency or height were given. A photograph taken in 1930 shows a small eruption, perhaps 4 feet high. Similar eruptions were seen in 1974, and such eruptions took place several times during each of Minute Man's active phases throughout that summer.

Beginning in 1975 and increasing in power and frequency through 1977 "Minute Man's Pool" began exhibiting unprecedented major action. The eruptions were so strong and persistent that they became the major part of Minute Man's activity. At times Minute Man itself was practically dormant. During an active period the bursts would recur as often as every 6 minutes. They were brief, most lasting less than 20 seconds, but throughout the play jets of water were propelled at least as high as 35 feet. Some eruptions had bursts of more than 50 feet, and heights in excess of 75 feet were estimated by some observers. The explosive concussions could be felt and heard throughout Shoshone Geyser Basin. These eruptions washed out a section of the trail, eroded some of the adjacent hillside, and considerably widened the runoff channels. This erosion makes it all but certain that such eruptions had never happened before.

Unfortunately, the major activity declined after 1975 and ended completely in 1978. Now the pool quietly rises and falls in synchrony with Minute Man's eruptions. Splashes 6 to 10 feet high are sometimes seen, usually near the end of Minute Man's active phase.

"Minute Man's Pool," a vent between the cone of Minute Man Geyser and the hillside, underwent eruptions of unprecedented power between 1975 and 1978. Of all the geysers in the Shoshone Basin, only Union Geyser has been known to play to a greater height.

38. UNNG-SHO-12 is a small hole within Minute Man's (11) westward runoff channel. Eruptions were first observed in 1992, when it frequently sputtered up to 1 foot high.

39. FIVE CRATER HOT SPRING lies near the level of Shoshone Creek down the slope from Gourd Spring (9). The complex crater system contains numerous highly convoluted and decorated ridges and projections of geyserite. These structures produce the "five craters," which are really just separate openings above one vent below. Five Crater is mostly active as a pulsating intermittent spring. The action rocks the water about within the crater, occasionally causing squirts to rise as much as 2 feet above the openings. There may be a relationship among Five Crater, Gourd Spring, and Shield Geyser (10), in that the more vigorous action, perhaps including true eruptions, tends to take place during exceptionally long cycle intervals of the other springs. Then the play is regular, repeating every 5 to 7 minutes and lasting 2 to 3 minutes.

Table 30. Geysers of the Little Giant and Minute Man Groups

Name	Map No.	Interval	Duration	Height (ft)
Black Sulphur Spring	6	steady	steady	3–6
"Double Geyser"	3	55–63 min	5 min	6–10
Five Crater Hot Spring	39	5–7 min *	2–3 min	1–2
Gourd Spring	9	cyclic	near steady	*2–3
Little Bulger Geyser	8	8–13 min *	3–5 min	8–10
Little Giant Geyser	2	see text	sec–min	2–8
Locomotive Geyser	5	[1982?]	45 min–2 hrs	6–15
"Meander Geyser"	4	hours *	hours	2–3
Minute Man Geyser	11	1–3 min *	seconds	10–40
"Minute Man's Pool," minor	11a	with Minute Man	seconds	1–10
"Minute Man's Pool," major	11a	[1978]	10–30 sec	35–75
Shield Geyser	10	cyclic	seconds	6–10
Soap Kettle	7	9–21 min	1–3 min	4–6
"Trailside Geyser"	1	6–16 min	20–60 sec	1–5
UNNG-SHO-10	36	[1986]	see text	—
UNNG-SHO-11 ("USGS #11")	37	5–30 min	sec–min	0–3

Table 30 continued

UNNG-SHO-12	38	frequent	sec–min	1

* When active.
[ ] Brackets enclose the year of most recent activity for extremely rare or dormant geysers. See text.

Orion Group

The Orion Group (Table 31) contains at least seven geysers of note plus several perpetual spouters, small, flowing springs, and pools. Union Geyser is the largest of all the geysers at Shoshone. It is believed that its three cones, which have a fancied resemblance to the three stars in the belt of the constellation Orion, are what gave the group its name. That the group also includes Taurus Spring supports the astronomical connection. For reasons that are unclear, the Orion Group underwent a drastic decline in water levels during the late 1970s, and since then there has been little activity in the area. This might be the result of an exchange of function, but none of the neighboring spring groups showed a corresponding increase in activity.

12. TAURUS SPRING is a small but very deep pool located just where the basin begins to open out into the north end of the Orion Group. Superheated, Taurus boils constantly and vigorously, and this is usually the only activity noted. Taurus erupted as high as 50 feet for an unknown but probably short time following the 1959 earthquake. Other eruptions occurred during the early 1970s. These 4-foot splashes were seen at times when Union Geyser (13) was in actual eruption. Often taken as an indication of a connection between the two, this was probably a chance of the observations, especially since a few additional eruptions of the same size were seen in 1991 when Union was completely dormant.

13. UNION GEYSER is a spouter of the first rank. Unfortunately, it alternates between periods of extreme activity and

Union Geyser, playing powerful jets of water from three separate cones, is one of the tallest geysers in Yellowstone and is the star performer in the Shoshone Basin. During recorded history it has been dormant much more than it has been active.

others of very little activity. It was first seen in 1872 and was reported by every geological survey and numerous tourist guidebooks until 1911. The frequency of those reports implies that Union was continuously active during those years. It was then dormant for almost 40 years with the sole exception of two eruptions noted in 1934. Rejuvenated in 1949, it apparently survived the 1959 earthquake without change and continued playing into 1977. It has been dormant since then.

Union erupts from three distinct geyserite cones. About 4 feet tall, the center cone is the largest and shoots the highest water jet. When Union is active, during the quiet period all three cones are nearly full of water. On occasion, an increase in the superheated boiling will splash some water out of the cones. An eruption begins with a series of heavy surges. It is a sight to behold. The water column rapidly climbs to its maximum height. The jet from the central cone will be well over 100 feet high, and its play will last for 12 minutes with diminishing power. The northern, second-largest cone begins spouting within seconds of the first. It plays its own water jet to at least 60 feet. The longest lasting of the three cones, it persists for over 20 minutes. The southern, smallest cone delays its start for as long as 2 minutes after the others and then briefly shoots a double stream of water to about 30 feet. As each jet gives out, a steam phase takes over; when the third spout dies, the entire eruption briefly becomes violent. The roar can be heard throughout the Shoshone Basin. The entire eruption, including the steam phase, lasts about an hour.

Union has been known to have infrequent single eruptions, but it usually has distinct active periods separated by about 5 days of inactivity. Once an active phase begins, there will usually be three, but sometimes four or only two, eruptions in the next few hours. The second normally follows the first by about 3 hours; the next interval is near 7 hours and the next, if any, around 10 to 12 hours. All of the eruptions are of equal force, but each in succession has a shorter total duration.

When Union is inactive for long periods, as it has been since 1977, the water level remains well below overflow. It is always superheated, so the inactive periods are apparently caused by an exchange of function that draws water volume away from Union. Where it goes is unknown; many other springs in the Orion Group are similarly affected at the same time as Union, but a corresponding increase in the activity of other groups is not seen. Since dormant periods have been known to last for decades, the eruptions of the 1970s are apt to have been the last for a long time.

The hot, sometimes boiling pool in a deep crater next to Union Geyser is Impenetrable Spring.

14. UNNG-SHO-1 ("SEA GREEN POOL") was observed as an active geyser only during 1976, at a time when Union (13) was in active eruption. The eruptions lasted only a few seconds but recurred as often as every 2 or 3 minutes. The height was about 10 feet. It is interesting to note that this was both the first and the last known active period of this geyser, and since 1976 it has never even been known to fill its pool as it did before. What was a beautifully beaded geyserite crater is now severely weathered, and the remaining small pool of water stands several feet below ground level.

15. WHITE HOT SPRING has a cavernous vent that opens out into a broad, shallow pool. Records of its geyser activity date to 1872, but apparently at no time was it a frequent or regular performer. During the last active episode of Union Geyser (13), White Hot erupted fairly often for long durations. The water burst from the vent, reaching well out into the pool and about 2 feet high. Since the 1977 dormancy of Union, White Hot has had a low water level. The pool area is dry except for the slight spray of erratic eruptions that are largely confined to the vent.

16. UNNG-SHO-2 ("FIFTY GEYSER") was located just a few feet east of the crater of White Hot Spring (15). First observed during the early 1970s when its interval was extremely regular at 50 minutes, it actually proved to be an irregular performer. However, whatever the interval, the eruptions always lasted 5 minutes, splashing water about 2 feet high. With

declining frequency through the 1970s, "Fifty" entered dormancy before 1980, and its site is now only a slight depression filled with gravel.

17. UNNG-SHO-3 was active only for a short time during the late 1970s. The eruptions came from a symmetrical vent at the apex of a triangle formed with White Hot Spring (15) and "Fifty Geyser" (16). Few details about the eruptions of SHO-3 are known, except that they reached 4 feet high.

18. UNNG-SHO-4 might be a recipient of some of the energy lost by the other members of the Orion Group. Prior to the first known activity in 1978, the site was a depression sometimes containing a bit of tepid water. Now, there is a large crater lined with spiny geyserite. It is clear that it is an old spring that had been buried by erosion during a very long dormancy and that it has simply been reopened by the current activity. The geyser plays murky water in bursts as high as 12 feet. The play lasts around 2 minutes and repeats every 15 to 30 minutes. Dormant periods are common, increasingly so as the years pass.

40. UNNG-SHO-13 is a small spring over the ragged geyserite mound northwest of Union Geyser (13) and Impenetrable Spring. It is better known to geyser gazers as "USGS #86a." It apparently formed since the 1968 mapping by the U.S. Geological Survey. Although small, usually less than 1 foot high, SHO-13 is regular and persistent. The intervals are 1 to 2 minutes and the durations generally 20 to 50 seconds.

Camp Group

The Camp Group is a cluster of small springs near the base of the hill south of Union Geyser. Rather decayed in appearance, most of the springs have little or no overflow and are at relatively low temperatures. Two or three besides those described here have had geyser eruptions, but their active episodes have been brief and scattered. One of these is Lavender Spring. Across Shoshone Creek in an area studded by numerous small cones and one good-sized pool is the Island Group. Several of the cones have recorded histories as small, irregularly active geysers.

41. GEYSER CONE was named in 1878, probably because of its appearance since no actual eruptions were described. It reactivated in 1974 and now plays frequently. The intervals are around 30 minutes. Water rises within the vent and bursts vigorously enough for outward spray to moisten the cone.

42. UNNG-SHO-14 is a small pool next to the formation of Geyser Cone (41). Its activity is apparently independent of Geyser Cone's. The splashing is frequent, throwing water 1 to 4 feet high for several seconds.

Table 31. Geysers of the Orion and Camp Groups

Name	Map No.	Interval	Duration	Height (ft)
Geyser Cone	41	minutes	seconds	1–3
Taurus Spring	12	[1977?]	seconds	4
Union Geyser	13	[1977]	40–60 min	100–125
UNNG-SHO-1 ("Sea Green Pool")	14	[1976]	seconds	10
UNNG-SHO-2 ("Fifty")	16	[1980]	5 min	1–2
UNNG-SHO-3	17	unrecorded	minutes	4
UNNG-SHO-4	18	15–30 min *	2 min	6–12
UNNG-SHO-13 ("USGS #86a")	40	1–2 min	seconds	1–2
UNNG-SHO-14	42	minutes *	seconds	1–4
White Hot Spring	15	frequent	minutes	1–2

* When active.
[ ] Brackets enclose the year of most recent activity for extremely rare or dormant geysers. See text.

North Group

The springs and geysers on the west side of Shoshone Creek were separated into the North Group and the South Group by the 1878 researchers. There is actually only a slight natural divide between them on the surface, but they are clearly separate units at depth.

The North Group contains the greatest number of hot springs at Shoshone. Fourteen are geysers important enough to have been given names. A branch of the trail used to cross Shoshone Creek by way of a bridge near Minute Man Geyser, but the bridge was removed in 1976. Now, to reach this area one must either ford the stream or cross it over downed logs at the south end of the basin near the Camp Group.

Next to the route of the old trail across the creek from the Minute Man Group is an exceptionally deep pool. Blowout Pool apparently formed through a steam explosion in the winter of 1928–1929 and had some early geyser action. As it quit playing, another nearby spring began erupting during 1930, but it soon quit, too. No additional eruptions have been known among these springs.

Most of the spring names in this group were applied during the 1870s, but in the intervening years many were inadvertently shifted to other springs. Corrections have now been made, and the following descriptions place the names where they belong.

44. UNNG-SHO-16 lies well to the northwest of Blowout Pool, where it is isolated from other hot springs by a surrounding meadow. Also known as "USGS #110," it was a late addition to the map prepared in 1968, and nothing is known about it prior to that time. It has sometimes been identified as the Yellow Funnel Spring of the 1870s, which was active as a geyser but was probably closer to Blowout Pool. A vigorous geyser, SHO-16 generally erupts every 2 to 5 minutes. The play lasts as long as 3 minutes and reaches 2 to 4 feet high.

19. MANGLED CRATER SPRING (identified first as Grotto Spring and later as SHO-5 in earlier editions of this book) was named in 1872 because of the numerous complex vents and projections of geyserite formations within the large crater. The real Grotto Spring is a small, noneruptive pool about 100 feet to the east. Mangled Crater does not discharge any water during its eruptions, but a nearby pool does overflow quietly at those times. The activity is erratic. Intervals are known to range from just 30 minutes to as long as several hours. The duration varies accordingly, being as short as 5 minutes on some occasions but as long as 30 minutes when the intervals are hours long. Bursts from the main vent can reach over 10 feet high.

20. FRILL SPRING as a name was long thought to belong to a wide, shallow, orange pool near this geyser, previously identified as both "TB Geyser" and SHO-6. It apparently got its name because of the decorative sinter about the edge of the teardrop-shaped crater. The vent, at the narrow end of the pool, extends downward vertically to a considerable depth. Frill is probably cyclic in its action, going long periods (perhaps weeks) between brief active phases. Then, eruptions may recur as frequently as every 5 minutes. The play lasts as long as 4 minutes and jets water up to 30 feet high. More commonly, the geyser is in a relatively dormant condition in which intermittent overflow may be punctuated by occasional splashes 1 foot high.

21. PEARL SPRING is little more than an intermittent spring, but its periods of overflow may include some bursting 2 feet high. These eruptions last as long as 2 hours. Following the play the water level of the pool drops very slowly, requiring about 2 hours to drop 12 inches. Refilling takes another 2 hours, and a long period of intermittent overflow is needed before another bit of splashing occurs.

22. GLEN SPRING is situated in a deep alcove in the hill, largely out of sight from the rest of the basin. It is a geyser but is only seen to play on rare occasions. Away from the vent the wide, shallow pool is colored a strange mixture of oranges and yellow-greens. Along the front of the pool is a

series of logs, which appear to have been placed there purposely long ago. The infrequent eruptions are a series of individual bursts of water, separated from one another by as much as 30 seconds. Some reach 5 feet high. The duration of such action is believed to be several hours.

23. BROWN SPONGE SPRING was named because of a brown mineral stain on the inside of the crater, which is composed of a porous-looking geyserite. Brown Sponge probably plays rather frequently, but little attention has been paid to it because of the small size of the play and lack of significant runoff. The height of its boiling eruption is less than 1 foot.

24. YELLOW SPONGE SPRING erupts from a water level well below the surrounding ground surface. The geyserite is tinted a pale, pure yellow by a trace of iron oxide. One of the more vigorous geysers in the area, Yellow Sponge plays every few seconds. Each eruption lasts just 2 to 4 seconds and jets spray to between 4 and 8 feet high. It is very close to being a perpetual spouter.

25. SMALL GEYSER has evidently changed its behavior considerably since the 1870s. Back then, it erupted frequently and as high as 20 feet. No geyser of that sort exists in the vicinity now. A number of craters, all with water levels well below the surface, lie in the area, and any of them could be the original Small. The name is presently applied to the crater among these that does erupt. There are nearly always steam bubbles rising into the bottom of the crater, causing a flickering, flamelike appearance. These bubbles produce the nearly constant eruptive activity. There is some periodicity to the splashing, but the flickering never stops. Most splashes are less than 3 feet high, but an exceptional few reach 8 feet.

26. KNOBBY GEYSER is cyclic in its action and is also known to be affected by activity in Velvet Spring (28). Although mapped in 1878, no eruptions were reported until the mid-1970s. The crater of Knobby is square in general outline and

is decorated entirely with exceptionally ornate geyserite. The vent is at the uphill corner of the crater. Knobby's best performances take place when Velvet Spring is dormant, as has been the case since 1982. Then, Knobby is clearly cyclic in its activity. Quiet periods without eruptions are generally 1 to 4 hours in length. Active periods are highly variable. Some consist of just two or three eruptions within a few minutes, but others have dozens of eruptions and last as long as 3 hours. Most plays are minor in scale and duration, reaching less than 10 feet high for a few seconds to $1^1/_2$ minutes. Major eruptions have been known to be 35 feet high for durations in excess of 7 minutes. At times, there is a clear progression of gradually stronger minor eruptions leading to a major play that ends the cycle.

The cyclic behavior of Knobby has only been clear since the 1982 dormancy of Velvet Spring. Before then, Knobby was comparatively inactive. Most eruptions were weak and fell at intervals as long as 24 hours.

27. BEAD GEYSER was an impressive 20-foot spouter during the 1870s. What happened to Bead during the years between then and now is uncertain. Indeed, exactly which spring was Bead is unknown. It may have played from a crater — now mostly filled and eroded — betweeen Knobby Geyser (26) and a symmetrical vent a few feet upslope from Knobby, or it could be that symmetrical vent with considerably changed activity. This latter spring is a geyser, but its eruptions are infrequent, brief, and not more than 3 feet high.

28. VELVET SPRING was not a geyser during the early days of Yellowstone, but it was active from some early date until 1982. Based primarily on the size of its eruptions, it was long believed to be Bead Geyser (27) until a comparison of an 1878 illustration with the modern crater revealed the error. The eruptions by Velvet were remarkably regular, with only a few seconds variation, making it one of the most regular geysers in Yellowstone. The play recurred every 12 to 14 minutes and lasted $2^1/_2$ minutes. Velvet has two vents. The main crater contains a deep, blue pool. Its bursting eruption would

spray water up to 20 feet high. The smaller vent to the west would play with more of a jetting action, at an uphill angle, to as high as 25 feet. Since the current dormancy began in 1982, Velvet has generally behaved as an intermittent spring. The times of overflow correspond to a few seconds of increased, superheated boiling in the main vent. The decline in activity is apparently a result of an exchange of function with Knobby Geyser (26). Velvet had brief active phases during 1985 and 1987. Each apparently lasted only a few days, but, as expected, Knobby had simultaneous dormancies.

43. FISSURE SPRING consists of an elongated fissure vent plus three other openings a few feet to its east; directly associated with it are two additional pools nearby. Fissure has become much more active during the past few years. Eruptions recur at intervals of 2 to 6 hours, last about 10 minutes, and reach 3 feet high. One of the nearby pools splashes along with Fissure while the other slowly drains.

29. LION GEYSER is one of the most regular geysers in the Shoshone Basin, except that it is subject to rather frequent and long dormant spells. When active, which might be as little as one year out of three, the intervals usually range from 50 to 70 minutes, although some as great as 2 hours were recorded in 1993. The eruptions last 4 minutes. Most of the bursts are only 2 to 4 feet high, but because Lion's vent is slitlike and penetrates the ground at an angle, some bursts squirt water to the south at a sharp angle. These may reach as much as 12 feet high and 25 feet outward, the water falling well beyond the crater rim. At the end of the eruption the crater drains, forming a sucking whirlpool over the vent. Very little refilling takes place until immediately before the next eruption.

The use of the name Lion for this feature is mysterious since neither the geyser's behavior nor its crater bear any resemblance to the animal. In 1991 a previously inactive vent a few feet away began to play. Interestingly, in time it revealed an old crater similar in size to that of Lion, and it also played at an angle to a distance as great as 25 feet. One time, these two geysers erupted at the same time, and their water jets collided in midair. This "Old Lion Geyser" was very likely the original Lion of 1878. Unfortunately, its development did nothing to answer the question about the name. Old Lion has been inactive since 1991.

30. BRONZE GEYSER was evidently a frequent performer during the 1870s and 1880s, but it rarely erupts now. Located a short distance south of Lion Geyser (29), the most notable thing about it is the color of its geyserite rim. The sinter has incorporated iron oxide in such a way as to give it an almost perfect metallic, bronzelike luster. When Bronze does erupt, the play lasts only a few seconds and reaches 2 to 3 feet high.

31. IRON CONCH GEYSER forms the third point of a triangle, along with Lion (29) and Bronze (30) Geysers. The crater is even more heavily stained with iron oxide than is Bronze's; the result is a brilliant red-orange vent surrounded by bumpy, bronzy mounds of geyserite. Iron Conch is a regular geyser. Intervals range from 9 to 30 minutes but usually average near the lower figure. The play lasts 1 to $1^1/_2$ minutes and reaches 2 to 3 feet high.

Table 32. Geysers of the North, South, and Western Groups

Name	Map No.	Interval	Duration	Height (ft)
Bead Geyser (symmetrical vent)	27	infrequent	unknown, brief	3
Boiling Cauldron	35	near steady	near steady	6
Bronze Geyser	30	rare	seconds	3
Brown Sponge Spring	23	minutes	minutes	1
Fissure Spring	43	hours *	minutes	1–6
Frill Spring	20	infrequent	1–4 min	1–30
Glen Spring	22	erratic	sec–hrs	1–5
Iron Conch Geyser	31	9–30 min	40–90 sec	2–3
Knobby Geyser	26	1–35 min *	sec–8 min	3–35
Lion Geyser	29	50 min–2 hrs *	3–4 min	2–12
Mangled Crater Spring	19	30 min–hrs	5–30 min	10
Pearl Spring	21	hours	2 hrs	1–2
Small Geyser	25	near steady	near steady	1–3

Table 32 continued

Three Crater Spring	45	irregular	seconds	1–2
UNNG-SHO-7	32	seconds *	seconds	4
UNNG-SHO-8 ("Outbreak")	33	28–36 min *	2–3 min	5–15
UNNG-SHO-9 ("Pectin")	34	3–7 min	sec–2 min	1–6
UNNG-SHO-15	46	10–15 min	1–2 min	1–3
UNNG-SHO-16 ("USGS #110")	44	2–5 min	2–3 min	2–4
Velvet Spring	28	[1982]	2 1/2 min	20
Yellow Sponge Spring	24	10–15 sec	3–5 sec	4–8

* When active.
[ ] Brackets enclose the year of most recent activity for extremely rare or dormant geysers. See text.

South Group

The South Group springs are located over a slight ridge of old geyserite about 100 yards south of the North Group. Eight of its 15 springs are known to have been geysers, but most of these have had only brief episodes of small eruptions. Among these are the well-named Blue Glass Spring (also known as Ornamental Spring), named for its color; Flake Spring, named after the nature of its geyserite deposits; and Coral Pool, farthest to the southwest against the hillside.

32. UNNG-SHO-7 is a narrow spring surrounded by smooth geyserite deposits. Although dormancies are known, it is usually a frequent performer, with intervals and durations of a few seconds. The height is 2 to 4 feet.

33. UNNG-SHO-8 ("OUTBREAK GEYSER") might be an old, rejuvenated feature that reappeared following a steam explosion in 1974. At first the eruptions were extremely erratic, but Outbreak has settled down into a very reliable behavior. At times almost stopwatch regular, the intervals range between 28 and 36 minutes. The play lasts 2 to $2^{1}/_{2}$ minutes and bursts water 5 to 15 feet high. It often has a number of false start minor eruptions in the last few minutes before the full play. Outbreak was dormant in 1992 but was active again in 1993. The renewed play was usually on the pattern of before, but it sometimes regressed into small perpetual spouting.

45. THREE CRATER SPRING actually contains several vents, but there are three large ones within the wide, shallow basin. One of these vents has had several short episodes of small but frequent eruptions since the 1970s. The action is always irregular.

Western Group

The Western Group, also known as the Fall Creek Group, is isolated from the rest of the Shoshone Geyser Basin It is located through the woods and around the hill southwest of the South Group. The springs are near Fall Creek, which flows into Shoshone Creek just downstream from the Camp and Island Groups. It is an area of many large and very active hot springs. In addition to the two geysers and one large perpetual spouter described here, it includes numerous small spouters, beautiful pools such as Cream Spring and Great Crater, and mud pots.

34. UNNG-SHO-9 ("PECTIN GEYSER") is an interesting geyser in that most of the time, although it is unquestionably active as a true geyser, its surface water temperature is well below boiling. The eruptions are apparently triggered by the evolution of gas other than steam (probably carbon dioxide), but there is still boiling at depth once the play has started. Pectin plays frequently. The intervals usually fall within the range of 3 to 7 minutes. Over the course of a few seconds to 2 minutes, water is splashed 1 to 6 feet high. The name came about because of a gelatinous bacterial growth along the runoff channel.

46. UNNG-SHO-15 is a new geyser. The U.S. Geological Survey mapping of the Shoshone Basin was completed in 1968, and

this spring was not shown. Its vent is a jagged opening in the sinter that indicates an explosive origin. Eruptions were first seen in 1987. They recur every 10 to 15 minutes but show a wide variation in the durations, sometimes lasting only a few seconds but usually more like $1^1/_2$ to 2 minutes. The splashing play of 1 to 3 feet is largely confined to the crater, and eruptions usually end just as the pool reaches the verge of overflow.

35. BOILING CAULDRON produces most of the large stream of scalding water that flows past Pectin Geyser (34) and SHO-15 (46). Boiling Cauldron is a perpetual spouter, jetting from several vents. One plays almost constantly about 6 feet high but has been known to have brief pauses. Another opening jets high-pressure steam, producing a hissing roar that can be heard for several hundred feet.

Chapter 12

Heart Lake Geyser Basin

The Heart Lake Geyser Basin (Map DD) lies in a setting rather different from those of the other geyser basins. Instead of the hot springs being found in nearly contiguous groups, here they occur as a series of distinct, widely spaced clusters. Hiking into the area after having walked through $5^1/_2$ miles of dense lodgepole pine forest (now open in places following the forest fires of 1988), one suddenly emerges from the trees to find oneself at the edge of a deep valley. With the muddy hot springs of White Gulch just below, the view from the overlook is down the valley of Witch Creek toward Heart Lake, still $2^1/_2$ miles away. Spotting the length of the green valley are white patches, the sinter deposits of the hot spring groups. Beyond is the lake and, farther still, the snowy peaks of the Absaroka Range. The view is of one of the prettiest in Yellowstone.

The Heart Lake Geyser Basin is divided into five groups of importance, separated from one another by extensive nonthermal ground. Geysers have been known in each of the groups, although those of the Middle Group were active only during the period 1986–1988. Most of the geysers are small; even the largest, at a maximum of 60 feet high, is quite small compared to what can be seen in most other geyser basins. Overall, though, the activity at Heart Lake is intense.

Perhaps because its geysers do tend toward small sizes, the Heart Lake Geyser Basin has seldom attracted much

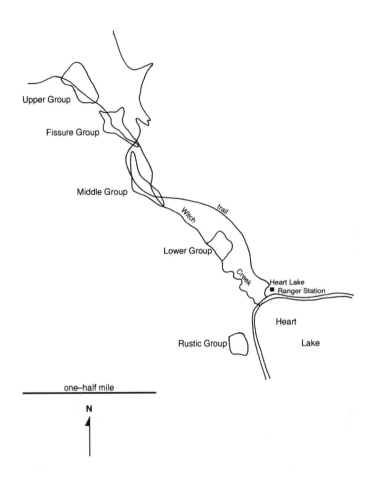

Map DD. Index Map of the Heart Lake Geyser Basin

attention. A detailed but ridiculously small-scale map was published in 1883, thorough descriptions without a map appeared in 1935, and a cursory, unpublished study by the U.S. Geological Survey was compiled in 1973. It was not until 1988 that truly accurate maps, tables, and descriptions were completed through the extraordinary personal efforts and research of geyser gazer Rocco Paperiello. The following descriptions extract much from his work.

As with all the other geyser basins described in this book, the serial numbers of the individual geyser descriptions of the earlier editions have been maintained. Few of the geysers have ever had names applied to them, and most that appear here are unofficial. The previous editions of this book gave the unnamed geysers numerical designations based on the 1973 USGS paper. That system was awkward since the report had almost no distribution, so the old designations are being dropped in favor of a new numbering system based on Paperiello's 1988 descriptions and maps. In an effort to further clarify the difference between the old and the new designations, modified group abbreviations have also been adopted. For example, what appeared before as UNNG-HLR-G2 is now UNNG-HRG-P7. Paperiello's work has not been formally published, but it is available through the nonprofit Geyser Observation and Study Association, and copies have been placed in the Yellowstone Research Library. It is hoped that the Paperiello designations will be adopted by future researchers at Heart Lake so that this numbering system will become standard.

As a historical aside, the name of the lake and geyser basin really should be Hart. It was named after an early prospector, Hart Hunney, who explored throughout the Yellowstone region. The spelling was changed inadvertently during the 1870s but is official in its "incorrect" form.

Heart Lake is one of the least impacted areas of Yellowstone. The heavy foot traffic to the lake is mostly that of fishermen who have little or no interest in the hot springs. The trail leaves the South Entrance highway at a point about 6 miles south of the Grant Village junction and just north of Lewis Lake. From the trailhead it is $5^1/_2$ miles to the overlook at the head of the valley. It is another $2^1/_2$ miles from there to Heart Lake, where there is a series of backcountry campsites along the shore. The Heart Lake Ranger Station is often staffed during the summer months and, if so, will provide assistance and outside communication in the case of an emergency. Such help cannot be counted on, however. In

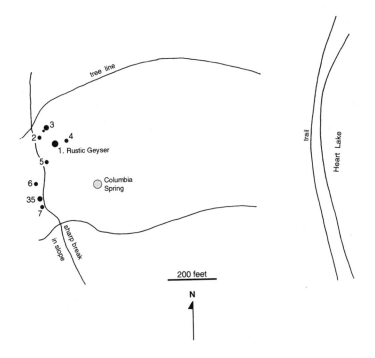

Map EE. Rustic Group

this backcountry area, as in all others, your safety is your own responsibility.

Rustic Group

The Rustic Group (Map EE, Table 33), named after Rustic Geyser, is the closest hot spring group to Heart Lake. Set against the base of Mt. Sheridan, it is about $^1/_2$ mile south of the Heart Lake Ranger Station and 1,000 feet from the lakeshore. The best approach is to take the shortest route possible from the lake. The meadow outside the tree line is normally very soggy, and it is often impossible to find a completely dry route to the springs.

Rustic Geyser was considered to be the most important geyser in the Heart Lake Geyser Basin until it entered a dormancy during 1984. Its replacement by way of exchange of function is not as high, but it is perhaps more spectacular as a performer. In addition to these, the group contains at least five other geysers. Columbia Spring is among the most beautiful pools in Yellowstone. It cannot be approached closely because of extensive overhanging geyserite rims.

1. RUSTIC GEYSER is a spectacular geyser. For most of its known history it was the only large and frequent geyser in the entire Heart Lake Basin. Although not named until 1878, it was first seen and described in 1870 and again in 1871. From that time until 1984 Rustic was never known to undergo a dormant period, and there was relatively slight change in its performances. The intervals ranged from 10 to 90 minutes. The play began with little warning. Water slowly rose in the crater. When it was still about 6 inches below the rim the water suddenly surged, filling the crater to overflow within a few seconds. Bursts came in rapid succession, with perhaps 100 of them during the usual 40- to 60-second eruption. The water was thrown into the air as steam bubbles exploded within the shallow pool, and the pop could be heard with each explosion. The bursts varied in their forcefulness. Although most were only 10 to 20 feet high, every eruption also included a few reaching 35 to 50 feet. The play ended as abruptly as it began.

There was some evidence that the length of the interval was dependent on the level, temperature, or volume of subsurface groundwater — quite persistently, as the summer season progressed and the environment dried out, Rustic developed shorter intervals. For example, during June 1974 the average interval was nearly 25 minutes; by August it had decreased to just 14 minutes, and it lowered still further in September to only 10 minutes (the shortest running average ever recorded). Whatever the average, the intervals were highly regular at any given time, and intervals of 26 minutes seemed typical. Similar changes were seen in some of the other Rustic Group features. This has been less evident since Rustic fell dormant.

Rustic Geyser, reaching up to 50 feet high, was the only frequently erupting geyser of considerable size in the Heart Lake Basin until it fell dormant during the winter of 1984–1985.

The cause of Rustic's dormancy, which began in late 1984 or early 1985, is clear: an exchange of function shifted the energy flow to nearby UNNG-HRG-P6 (3). HRG-P6 changed simultaneously from a very infrequent and weak geyser into one with powerful and regular eruptions. How long Rustic's dormancy might last is unknown, of course. The lack of well-defined runoff channels leading away from HRG-P6 implied that it had seldom, if ever, erupted prior to 1984. But there is no indication of a decline in its action. Rustic's water temperature varies slowly through time, occasionally dropping low enough for cyanobacteria to grow in the crater, and a complete lack of runoff has allowed such substantial disintegration of the geyserite deposits that grass is growing in some of the catch basins.

That is unfortunate. At some time in the distant past Rustic was altered by man. Logs were placed around the crater, giving it a squarish outline. Long completely covered by pale brown sinter, the logs appeared virtually unchanged from the early days of the Park. Given that time span, it is probable that the logs were placed by Indians as long as 200 or 300 years ago. Why they would do such a thing is a mystery, but it does indicate that they did not shy away from the geysers. Now, the geyserite is spalling off of the logs (aided by vandals), revealing the silicified wood. In time, a unique archaeological treasure might be lost because of an exchange of function.

2. UNNG-HRG-P7 lies at the base of the grassy slope a few feet from Rustic Geyser (1). About 10 feet across, the crater is coated with a pale brown geyserite identical to that at Rustic, and, indeed, there are direct connections among HRG-P7, Rustic, and HRG-P6 (3). When Rustic was active prior to 1984, HRG-P7 was very regular in its activity. Most of the time the average interval was near 25 minutes but some as short as 5 minutes were seen. The bursting play reached 5 to 15 feet high for durations of $1^{1}/_{2}$ to 5 minutes. Since the dormancy of Rustic, HRG-P7 has operated on a very different cyclic pattern directly related to HRG-P6. A series of minor eruptions, each somewhat more vigorous than the one

Unnamed geyser "P6" of the Rustic Group began having vigorous erup
tions sometimes more than 30 feet high around 1984, probably because of
an exchange of function with nearby Rustic Geyser, which fell dormant at
about the same time.

before, takes place during HRG-P6's quiet interval. A major
eruption then occurs about 2 minutes following the end of
HRG-P6. This 10-foot play lasts 1 to 4 minutes and ends with
a brief but loud steam phase.

3. UNNG-HRG-P6 ("COMPOSITE GEYSER") is a few feet from
Rustic (1) and HRG-P7 (2), forming the third apex of a triangle. It received its informal name because the larger of
the two vents acts as a bursting fountain-type geyser while
the other, a small hole a few feet away, jets with steady cone-
type play. Composite was a rare performer prior to the 1984
dormancy of Rustic. There was evidence of some large eruptions during 1974, when a runoff channel was carved into
the loose gravel surrounding the crater. It can be surmised
that that unobserved activity also resulted in a brief dormancy in Rustic. The modern activity of Composite is cyclic.
A series of minor eruptions, usually lasting only a few seconds and reaching 2 to 6 feet high, takes place as the "quiet"
interval progresses. Major eruptions usually occur at intervals of $1^{1}/_{2}$ to 3 hours. The play from the main crater is a

massive bursting as high as 20 feet that persists throughout the 5-minute duration. It is only during the major eruptions that a small hole in the geyserite a few feet toward HRG-P7 joins in, sending a steady jet of water as high as 30 feet. It is an amazing spectacle, especially given that it is followed within 2 minutes by the major steam phase eruption of HRG-P7.

4. UNNG-HRG-P3 is a rare performer that erupts within a deep hole about 50 feet from Rustic Geyser (1). It did not benefit from the 1984 exchange of function. The only record of major eruptions was in 1973, when jetting play reached as far as 10 feet above the ground. The intervals were about $1^1/_2$ hours long. At most times since then, P3 has acted as a subterranean perpetual spouter, splashing 1 to 3 feet high from a boiling pool.

5. UNNG-HRG-P9 ("TRAPEZOIDAL SPRING") was incorrectly added as geyser HLR-S4 in the previous edition of this book on the basis of reports that it had undergone an explosion. In fact, the new activity took place in another, previously quiet spring (UNNG-HRG-P12, #35). Trapezoidal remains the pretty, gently bubbling pool it has always been. It is not a geyser.

6. PROMETHEUS SPRING has behaved as a nonerupting flowing spring, as a perpetual spouter, and as a geyser during its known history. Just how dominant each of these kinds of action was is unknown. When it was a perpetual spouter, the play was usually about 6 feet high. When acting as a true, periodic geyser, Prometheus was more spectacular. Intervals ranged from 8 to 15 minutes. The jetting eruption lasted less than 1 minute, sending spray as high as 15 feet at an angle away from the hillside. Sometime during late 1977 or early 1978, Prometheus lost its water supply to nearby features, especially HRG-P12 (35). It is now so completely dormant that the once beautiful geyserite formations have almost entirely weathered away, and only the barest trace of steam is visible even in cold weather. It is possible that Prometheus Spring is truly dead.

35. UNNG-HRG-P12 formed in 1977-1978, apparently because of an exchange of function from Prometheus Spring (6). It should be noted that this exchange is apparently unrelated to the one between Rustic Geyser (1) and HRG-P6 (3) that happened about seven years later. This spring had previously been a pair of small, murky pools that barely overflowed and had occasional periods of weak perpetual spouting. The new activity was initially reported as resulting from a steam explosion and was incorrectly cited as having occurred at HRG-P9 (5). In fact, there was no explosion. Instead, the new eruptions, clearly the first ever by these springs, quickly eroded a large crater complex in the hillside. Eruptions now recur at intervals of 2 to 12 minutes. Most of the play is splashing from the rear of the two vents. It reaches 4 to 10 feet high. Sometimes the front vent is also known to play, bursting violently as high as 25 feet. Typical durations are 5 to 20 seconds. Given the previous minor nature of HRG-P12 and the vigor and volume of these eruptions, the subsurface plumbing system connection between HRG-P12 and Prometheus has likely been thoroughly changed. HRG-P12 is probably a permanent addition to the Rustic Group, and Prometheus Spring is unlikely to ever be resurrected, at least in its previous form.

7. UNNG-HRG-P15 is almost a perpetual spouter. The eruption is only 1 foot high. Just in front of the crater is an old geyserite cone within which the water level slowly rises and falls. It may have small eruptions at times. Just in front of the cone is yet another spring whose rate of overflow varies in sympathy with the eruption of HRG-P15.

Table 33. Geysers of the Rustic Group

Name	Map No.	Interval	Duration	Height (ft)
Prometheus Spring	6	[1978]	1 min	15
Rustic Geyser	1	[1984]	40–60 sec	35–50
UNNG-HRG-P3	4	[1973]	seconds	10
UNNG-HRG-P6 ("Composite")	3	10 min–3 hrs	sec–2 1/2 min	6–33
UNNG-HRG-P7	2	minutes	1–4 min	5–10

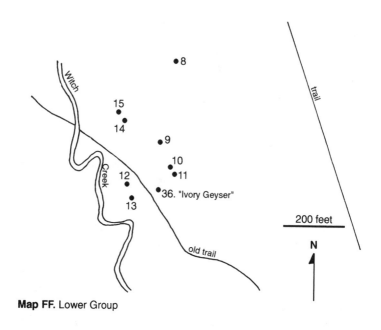

Map FF. Lower Group

Table 33 continued

UNNG-HRG-P12	35	2–12 min *	5–20 sec	10–25
UNNG-HRG-P15	7	steady	steady	1

* When active.

[ ] Brackets enclose the year of most recent activity for extremely rare or dormant geysers. See text.

Lower Group

Until the early 1970s the Heart Lake trail passed through the center of the Lower Group. Now, it runs across the hillside through the forest about 300 feet away from the nearest of the springs. The Lower Group (Map FF, Table 34) is a compact cluster containing at least six geysers and several perpetual spouters among its thirty hot springs.

8. UNNG-HLG-P1 splashes out of a 2-foot-high cone. The activity of the geyser is weakly cyclic. Most of the time the eruption is confined to within the cone and is nearly perpetual. Some spray rises above the rim, but nearly all of it falls back inside. During such periods there are infrequent surges when the splashes reach 3 feet above the top of the cone, and then there can be some runoff. Very rarely, HLG-P1 has more powerful eruptions. For a few seconds water is thrown to over 10 feet, with enough discharge to create a considerable but short runoff stream. Such eruptions have not been witnessed since the 1970s. The extent of the runoff channels indicates that large and voluminous eruptions were frequent during prehistoric times.

9. UNNG-HLG-P19 is one of the smallest known geysers anywhere. Although dormant periods are known, it is a persistent feature. Centered in an unobtrusive splash zone covered with beaded sinter, the 1-inch-wide vent spatters a fine spray of water a few inches high; some droplets may occasionally reach 1 foot. The eruptive activity is doubly cyclic. Several hours of complete quiet may pass between active phases. Then, during an active phase minor eruptions recur every 60 seconds and last only about 5 seconds. These are irregularly punctuated by "major" eruptions, identical to the others except for durations of 20 seconds. Following a major eruption, HLG-P19 will lie quiet for around 5 minutes before another sequence of minor eruptions begins.

10. UNNG-HLG-P32 is a very pretty little pool. The rim of the crater is beautifully beaded and scalloped with pearly gray sinter. Nearby are two tiny vents surrounded by "geyser eggs." Until these holes began erupting as true geysers in the 1980s, the pool of HLG-P32 acted as a perpetual spouter about 1 foot high. The vents were first seen in 1982. Switching back and forth between them, the eruptions generally recur every 4 to 5 minutes, last 40 to 60 seconds, and reach 1 to $1^1/_2$ feet high. The pool no longer erupts.

11. UNNG-HLG-P34 is another small pool with an ornamental geyserite rim. The play recurs every few minutes. It lasts vari-

ably from 5 seconds to 1 minute, splashing up to 2 feet high. A second, completely independent and cyanobacteria-lined vent occupies the same crater.

36. UNNG-HLG-P43 ("IVORY GEYSER"), named for the smooth, creamy geyserite within the crater, has become the premier geyser of the Lower Group. It was first seen during 1985 and has been continuously active, with little change, ever since. The play consists of both major and minor eruptions. A few minutes of quiet follow a major eruption. Then, a series of minor eruptions 1 to 3 feet high, lasting only a few seconds but each a bit stronger than the previous one, leads to the next major eruption. It reaches 7 feet high and may have a duration as long as 2 minutes. Major intervals depend on the number of minor eruptions that take place but are usually between 8 and 15 minutes long.

12. UNNG-HLG-P53 is nearly a perpetual spouter. "Ivory Geyser" (36) is the only Lower Group geyser that can reach a greater height. The pale blue pool sits within a 2-foot by 5-foot crater with a well-established runoff channel. Much of the crater and the channel is brilliantly colored by cyanobacteria, but the vent itself is nearly black because of manganese oxide minerals. Boiling above the vent is nearly constant, but it frequently increases in vigor so that the water is thrown 2 to 6 feet high. Such eruptions last as long as 2 minutes and may be followed by a few seconds of complete quiet, so that HLG-P53 comes close to matching the definition of a geyser.

13. UNNG-HLG-P54 is a perpetual spouter. It might have had some unobserved eruptions during 1986, when intermittent overflow was observed. The normal steady play is 1 foot high.

14. UNNG-HLG-P8 is a small but vigorous perpetual spouter that plays out of a small cone. It is surrounded by a washed area drained by significant runoff channels, but large eruptions have never been observed.

15. UNNG-HLG-P7 is as stable as a Yellowstone hot spring can be. Every observer during the past 20-plus years has reported exactly the same activity: perpetual spouting 1 foot high with no discharge. There is no indication that it has ever had periodic or more powerful activity.

Table 34. Geysers of the Lower and Middle Groups

Name	Map No.	Interval	Duration	Height (ft)
UNNG-HLG-P1	8	near steady	near steady	3
UNNG-HLG-P7	15	steady	steady	1
UNNG-HLG-P8	14	steady	steady	1
UNNG-HLG-P19	9	60 sec	5–20 sec	1
UNNG-HLG-P32	10	4–5 min	40–60 sec	1–2
UNNG-HLG-P34	11	minutes	5–60 sec	1–2
UNNG-HLG-P43 ("Ivory"), major	36	8–15 min *	1–2 min	1–7
UNNG-HLG-P53	12	frequent	sec–2 min	2–6
UNNG-HLG-P54	13	steady	steady	1
UNNG-HMG-P42	37	[1988]	3 min	1 1/2
UNNG-HMG-P56	38	[1988]	unknown	1

* When active.
[ ] Brackets enclose the year of most recent activity for extremely rare or dormant geysers. See text.

Middle Group

The Middle Group (Map DD, Table 34) was not known to contain any geyser until 1986, when two springs were active upstream along Witch Creek well away from the trail. The surroundings of the other hot springs indicate that none are geysers. This is the only group of Heart Lake springs that now has the trail passing directly among it. Several of the springs are small but pretty pools. There are also a few perpetual spouters.

37. UNNG-HMG-P42 lies at one end of a fracture within a shallow depression; vents at the other end of the crack do not

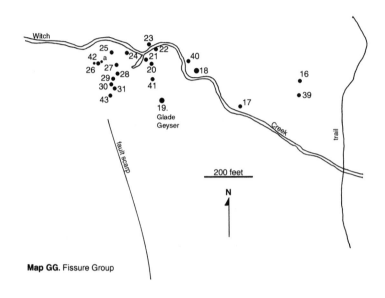

Map GG. Fissure Group

erupt. It was first seen as a geyser in 1986, when the play recurred with a high degree of regularity. Intervals were 6 to $6^{1}/_{2}$ minutes long, and all recorded durations were within plus or minus 9 seconds of 3 minutes. The play was $1^{1}/_{2}$ feet high. HMG- P42 was dormant by 1988.

38. UNNG-HMG-P56 is the northernmost member of the Middle Group, near HMG-P42 (37). It was first seen in eruption during 1987. The play was brief but frequent and was 1 foot high. Like HMG-P42 a few feet away, this geyser had returned to dormancy by the end of 1988. Both are now so completely dormant that their locations in a meadow trampled by wildlife are impossible to find.

Fissure Group

The Fissure Group (Map GG, Table 35) is the most extensive group in the Heart Lake Geyser Basin. The continuous bubbling, splashing, roaring, and steaming create a scene like that of an old steam works. Thus, the mountain behind the springs is known as Factory Hill. Geyser activity is most intense on and near the sinter-covered rise near the upper end of the group. Here is a long crack in the geyserite from which rise several geysers and numerous other hot springs jointly known as the Fissure Springs. A southward continuation of this fissure lines up with a sharp change in the slope of the hillside, and both may be evidence of recent fault activity. Witch Creek flows through the center of the Fissure Group, and much of its volume actually runs below ground in the fissure area. With a temperature greater than 85°F (30°C) in some of its upper reaches, Witch Creek is almost entirely hot spring runoff.

16. UNNG-HFG-P5 sits well apart from the main portion of the Fissure Group. It was not mapped by the 1973 USGS study but was active as a perpetual spouter 1 to 2 feet high in the late 1970s. It fell dormant around 1980. In its place is a nearby spring that began having eruptions in 1986. Apparently infrequent and yet to be seen in eruption, it has formed a large runoff channel.

39. UNNG-HFG-P3 is a pair of vents that developed along an old crack. Both are decorated with massive, convoluted geyserite rims and are colored black and orange-brown by mineral deposits. The play is perpetual but is seldom more than 1 foot high.

17. UNNG-HFG-P7 is a very interesting spring. The rectangular vent lies within a shallow basin several feet across. As with many springs in this area, the vent is colored black by mineral deposits (probably manganese oxide). As large steam bubbles rise into the bottom of the pool they create a rich blue, flamelike flashing that is perhaps the best seen anywhere in Yellowstone. The eruptive activity is usually frequent but erratic. It consists of vigorous bursting 1 to 8 feet high over durations of 2 to 20 seconds. Most intervals are less than 2 minutes long.

18. UNNG-HFG-P35 is the modern successor to a large pool or geyser. The crater is over 12 feet wide at the top and about 8 feet deep. Its sinter walls are deeply weathered, indicating a long period of inactivity. The modern geyser plays through a long, narrow crack at the bottom of the western crater wall. The play is nearly horizontal, reaching completely across the bottom of the crater, a span of 7 or 8 feet. Although some dormant periods are known, and there have also been times when the intervals were as long as several hours, most observers find the play recurring every 9 to 35 minutes. The typical duration is 30 seconds.

40. UNNG-HFG-P36 plays from a shallow pool within an eroded crater 10 feet wide and 6 feet deep. There are two vents in the pool. One acts as a vigorous perpetual spouter that jets at a low angle. The other vent is periodic, briefly bursting 1 to 4 feet high about every half minute.

19. GLADE GEYSER is Heart Lake's tallest and most spectacular geyser. Unfortunately, it has only brief eruptions at very long intervals when active, and dormancies are known. Glade is also somewhat controversial. Some people believe Glade is the same as the "Hissing Spring" described by Professor T. B. Comstock in 1873, but that description is difficult to rectify with Glade's location. Also, a single photograph dated 1957 shows Glade in eruption (except for the possibility that this is Hissing Spring, 1957 becomes the year of Glade's first known activity), but a special post-1959 earthquake survey of the Heart Lake Geyser Basin noted no spring whatsoever at Glade's site.

Glade erupts from a small cone, the only thermal feature within a large erosional alcove. Whatever its modern record has been, it seems clear that Glade has had a long history of eruptions. The oval vent at the top of the cone measures about 13 by 21 inches; it was only 8 by 9 inches in 1964, showing that the eruptions have caused substantial erosion. The play is a steady stream of water 30 to 60 feet high at an angle into the alcove. Glade's known activity has always been highly variable. It .might also be a long-term cyclic geyser.

Usually, on the rare occasions when people have spent extended time in the Fissure Group, the intervals have been found to exceed 24 hours; intervals as long as 60 hours are known. During the long hours prior to an eruption, the small pool intermittently boils and overflows. It is believed that these periodic episodes become stronger and longer shortly before the play and that it is one of these that finally triggers the eruption. A typical duration is just $1^1/_2$ to 2 minutes.

Glade is one of those geysers that seems to have several tricks to pull. In 1973 and 1974 there were always two eruptions in sequence, the second following the first at intervals of only 7 to 10 minutes *or* a few hours. At that time, most full-cycle intervals were longer than 40 hours. But in early 1984 Glade was having preliminary series of "minor" eruptions. Intervals of 2 to 3 hours were seen, and the play could last as long as 10 minutes and reach 30 feet high. The major eruptions, 45 to 60 feet tall, recurred as often as 18 hours and lasted more than 20 minutes, most of which was steam phase. There was then a span of 6 to 8 hours of quiet before the minor eruptions resumed. (A number of people have contended that this mode of activity could not possibly occur, but in fact it is the only time when I have personally seen Glade erupt.) Later in 1984 Glade was back to the long intervals and short durations of before. Since 1984 Glade has apparently continued to have intervals of 1 to 2 days. It had dormant spells during 1985, 1987, and 1993–1994.

41. UNNG-HFG-P138 is a small cone amid numerous hot springs between Glade Geyser (19) and Splurger Geyser (21). That it showed geyser activity in 1878 is implied by a notation about quiet intervals in that year's Geological Survey report, but nothing else is known. For modern observers it was usually dry, known to steam slightly only in cold weather. Then, in September 1993 it was seen in full eruption. One recorded interval was slightly more than 5 hours in length, and another exceeded 6 hours. The eruptions consisted of about 10 seconds of water jetting 15 feet high followed by another 35 to 40 seconds of strong steam phase.

A small geyserite cone in the Fissure Group on the Heart Lake Basin, which had never been known to erupt, this 15-foot geyser sprang to life during late summer 1993. (Photo by Clark Murray.)

The cone indicates a significant amount of prehistoric activity, so this geyser might be persistent. If so, it will be the second-largest geyser in the Fissure Group and among the four or five largest ever known in the Heart Lake Geyser Basin.

20. UNNG-HFG-P116 is located in a sandy-gravelly basin about 10 feet upslope from Splurger Geyser (21). The eruption is 1 to 2 feet high. At one time it seemed this geyser could be active only when Splurger was also active. At those times, eruptions typically recurred every 2 hours and lasted 13 to 25 minutes. More recently, however, any direct relationship with Splurger seems to have been lost. HFG-P116 presently has both intervals and durations hours to days long. It has had dormant periods, too, in which the crater has virtually disappeared because of erosion from the slope above.

21. SPLURGER GEYSER, also known as Triple Bulger Geyser, is one of the most impressive springs in the Fissure Group. The oval pool is colored aquamarine blue over each of the three vents. During an eruption the water is bulged up to 3 feet high over each vent, with occasional bursts of 5 to 6 feet. In addition to the main vents, there are four other spouting holes around the sides of the crater. Splurger has shown much variation over the years. In 1973 it was in eruption 40% of the time, with regular intervals of 42 minutes and durations of 24 minutes. Such action lasted until 1981. Splurger was then dormant from 1981 into 1986, when it was a perfectly quiet pool but still had a very high water discharge. Renewed activity in 1987 was as a perpetual spouter, but that was temporary. Splurger was again periodic in 1993, in eruption fully 80% of the time.

22. UNNG-HFG-P126 was probably once a more significant geyser than it is now. Its cone is massive, with the rim rising fully $2^1/_2$ feet above a geyserite mound. The present activity is far too small to have formed such a cone. There is a constant boiling of the water within the crater. Some splashes throw out a little water, and exceptional surges may reach 2 feet above the rim, but in most cases the activity is completely confined within the vent and the net discharge is zero. It is possible that this is the "Puffing Spring" described in passing by T. B. Comstock in 1873.

23. UNNG-HFG-P41 plays from a beautiful small crater right next to Witch Creek. The delicately scalloped sinter rim is lightly stained by iron oxides, giving it a pink and orange cast. The spring is a perpetual spouter about 2 feet high.

24. SHELL GEYSER is almost impossible to see clearly. The deep crater is carved into a nearly vertical cliff, 10 feet above Witch Creek. The back wall of the crater is fluted like a clam shell. The play of this geyser splashes against this wall so that most of the water falls back into the pool. Some more violently spraying bursts escape the crater and reach as high as 10 feet. Rarely, a nearly horizontal jetting arches outward as far as 15 feet; this may arise from a second vent near the back of the cavern The intervals between eruptions are usually 2 to 3 minutes long, and the duration is seldom more than 10 seconds. Shell sometimes regresses to perpetual spouting, but it has never been known to fall completely dormant.

25. HOODED SPRING is a perpetual spouter. It lies at the north end of the rift that gave the Fissure Group its name. Hooded Spring was named because of a sinter projection that extends partially out over the crater, deflecting the larger bursts of the eruption. This "hood" appears to be the remains of an old geyserite cone. The eruption is mostly 1 foot or less high, but relatively frequent surges spray as high as 3 or 4 feet. Just behind Hooded Spring, hidden back within the fissure, is another perpetual spouter; it plays 1 foot high.

42. SHELF SPRING is a long, oval pool on a sinter platform near the upper end of the Fissure Group. It used to be a beautiful, pale blue color that made it one of the prettiest features at Heart Lake. In June 1992 a debris flow dumped muddy sediment into the crater. Although the water has

long since cleared, the crater is now brownish, and the pool has lost its fine color. On the basis of heavily washed areas surrounding the entire crater, Shelf Spring apparently had some eruptions (or perhaps only heavy overflow) later in 1992, possibly because of plumbing system changes caused by the slide debris.

26. UNNG-HFG-P51 plays from a small cone between Shelf Spring (42) and the hillside. It behaves as a perpetual spouter, weakly splashing less than 1 foot high. Its general appearance is very similar to that of HFG-P52 (26a) on the opposite side of Shelf, but unlike that spring HFG-P51 has never been known to undergo true geyser eruptions.

26a. UNNG-HFG-P52 has a cone almost identical in appearance to that of HFG-P51 (26). No eruptions were ever witnessed until 1986, but continuing play has revealed a splash zone of beaded sinter and a runoff channel, neither of which is entirely the result of the modern activity. HFG-P52 currently plays at intervals of a few hours. The eruptions consist of vigorous splashing 1 to 4 feet high with heavy overflow for durations of 2 to 3 minutes. Most, if not all, of the "quiet" interval between the eruptions is involved in splashing to about 1 foot, so this spring should perhaps be called a variable perpetual spouter rather than a geyser, the eruptions being nothing more than occasional increases in the action.

27. UNNG-HFG-P91 is a small, double pool within jagged craters created by a steam explosion. Sometimes active as a perpetual spouter, as a geyser it shows both intervals and durations of 4 to 8 minutes. The 1- to 2-foot splashes would be higher were it not for an overhanging roof of sinter.

FISSURE SPRINGS (numbers 28 through 31 plus 43). The final five members of the Fissure Group are situated along the south-central portion of the rift that gave the group its name, within about 30 feet of each other. These, along with several other small geysers that are only irregularly and briefly active plus some nonerupting springs, constitute the Fissure Springs proper. These geysers are closely related to one another, and just a brief period of observation reveals their competitive activity. Any one of them may be much reduced in frequency and vigor because of a corresponding increase in the action elsewhere along the fissure.

28. UNNG-HFG-P70 is usually the most active geyser among the Fissure Springs. It is nearly, but not quite, a perpetual spouter, with pauses only a few seconds long. The vent, 8 feet long, is nothing more than a wide zone along the fracture. The fan-shaped eruption may be continuous for as long as 2 minutes, although a more typical duration is only 5 to 10 seconds. The jetting reaches several feet high, and exceptional surges to 12 feet have been seen. When HFG-P69 (29) has its stronger form of eruptions, this geyser will briefly be quiet.

29. UNNG-HFG-P69 spouts from the next opening along the fissure, south of HFG-P70 (28). Its eruptions generally recur every minute and last 5 to 10 seconds. The normal play is only a foot or two high, but at highly irregular times HFG-P69 has stronger eruptions. Then, the water can spray has high as 4 feet above the ground. It is only during these "major" eruptions that a cone adjacent to the fissure vent can also splash up to 1 foot.

30. UNNG-HFG-P68 lies in a very narrow opening in the rift. The vent is nowhere more than 2 inches wide, but it is more than 6 feet long. The activity of HFG-P68 is closely tied to that of HFG-P67 (31). When HFG-P67 is dormant, which is the usual case, HFG-P68 erupts frequently. The most powerful bursts are in concert with eruptions by HFG-P69 (29), which is adjacent to it along the rift. Some of the surges reach 3 feet above the ground. Both the intervals and durations are usually only seconds long, but this geyser sometimes declines so that the brief play is only 1 foot high at intervals as long as 5 minutes. Such weak play is the rule when HFG-P67 is active.

31. UNNG-HFG-P67 is rarely active; the only observed major eruptions took place during the early 1970s. Since then, it has been nearly dormant. During the active phases this geyser would overflow steadily between eruptions. The play began when the flow suddenly became very heavy. It quickly built into steady jetting that reached about 8 feet throughout the 15-second duration. Intervals were 11 to 17 minutes. Nearby geyser HFG-P68 (30) was essentially dormant when HFG-P67 was active. Now, with HFG-P68 active, P-67 surges upward and sometimes reaches overflow during the other geyser's quiet interval, but the only eruptions known since 1973 consisted of frequent but weak 1-foot splashing seen in 1978 and 1986.

43. UNNG-HFG-P57 ("FISSURE SPRINGS GEYSER") is the southernmost of the important geysers among the Fissure Springs. Its only known major eruptions took place in 1986. The action was regular, with intervals of about $3^1/_2$ minutes and durations of 27 to 36 seconds. The play was a strong jetting 10 to 12 feet high at a sharp angle. During the years before and since 1986, "Fissure Springs Geyser" has acted as a small perpetual spouter confined completely to its fissure vent.

Table 35. Geysers of the Fissure Group

Name	Map No.	Interval	Duration	Height (ft)
Glade Geyser	19	see text	1 1/2–20 min	30–60
Hooded Spring	25	steady	steady	1–4
Shelf Spring	42	rare	unknown	unknown
Shell Geyser	24	minutes	seconds	3–15
Splurger Geyser	21	minutes *	minutes	3–6
UNNG-HFG-P3	39	steady	steady	1
UNNG-HFG-P5	16	[1980]	steady	1
UNNG-HFG-P7	17	1–2 min	2–20 sec	1–8
UNNG-HFG-P35	18	9–35 min *	20–30 sec	2–6
UNNG-HFG-P36	40	12–30 sec	1 burst	1–3
UNNG-HFG-P41	23	steady	steady	2
UNNG-HFG-P51	26	near steady	near steady	1
UNNG-HFG-P52	26a	hours	2–3 min	1–4
UNNG-HFG-P57 ("Fissure Springs")	43	[1986]	30 sec	10–12

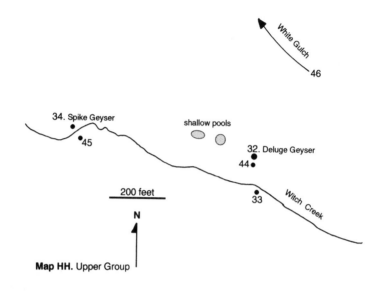

Map HH. Upper Group

Table 35 continued

UNNG-HFG-P67	31	[1973]	15 sec	8
UNNG-HFG-P68	30	sec–5 min	seconds	1–3
UNNG-HFG-P69	29	1 min	5–10 sec	4
UNNG-HFG-P70	28	seconds	sec–2 min	4–12
UNNG-HFG-P91	27	4–8 min	4–8 min	1–2
UNNG-HFG-P116	20	hrs–days *	hrs–days	1–2
UNNG-HFG-P126	22	rare	seconds	2
UNNG-HFG-P138	41	see text	50 sec	15

* When active.
[ ] Brackets enclose the year of most recent activity for extremely rare or dormant geysers. See text.

Upper Group

The Upper Group (Map HH, Table 36) is a short distance up Witch Creek from the Fissure Group. It covers a large area, but most of its activity is in the form of relatively cool and muddy acid springs. Alkaline springs with clear water and high temperatures are confined mostly to two small clusters immediately next to Witch Creek and several hundred feet apart from one another. At least five and possibly seven geysers are known. A portion of the Upper Group known as White Gulch extends far up the slope to the north. This is the area immediately below the Heart Lake trail at the scenic viewpoint one reaches when hiking into the area. Most geyser gazers leave the trail here, dropping down White Gulch to the geysers below.

32. DELUGE GEYSER is the largest deep, clear spring in the Upper Group. Named in 1878, it and Columbia Spring in the Rustic Group are the only deep, blue pools in the Heart Lake Geyser Basin. The crater has massive geyserite shoulders and internal formations and is surrounded by a wide sinter platform studded with smaller hot springs. It shows all signs of large eruptions, but the only party of observers to have seen bursting play was that of 1878. Without citing details, the group reported Deluge as 10 to 15 feet high and gave it its name. The only other known occasion when there were probably true eruptions was 1976, when the surroundings were found cleanly washed and grasses had been scalded around the edges of the platform. The modern activity consists of frequent boiling periods. The level of the quiet pool rises to a heavy overflow. Superheated water reaches the surface, resulting in a sizzling, spluttering eruption. The boiling commotion is seldom higher than 1 foot, and Deluge sometimes fails to do more than bubble during its overflow. The usual interval is 3 to 5 minutes and the duration 1 to 2 minutes.

44. UNNG-HUG-P16 erupts from a ragged vent at the edge of the runoff from Deluge Geyser (32). It appears to have formed quite recently and, in fact, was never mapped or reported prior to 1982. The play recurs every 5 to 7 minutes, when splashing 1 to 2 feet high lasts around 40 seconds. There is no relationship between the timing of this geyser and that of Deluge, despite their proximity.

33. UNNG-HUG-P11 plays from a crater just above Witch Creek directly opposite Deluge Geyser (32). The eruptions have excavated a small alcove in the slope above, implying considerable activity, but the only eruptions actually seen were in 1985. At that time the play was frequent, lasted about 1 minute, and reached 2 to 4 feet high. Since then, the crater has been filled with debris so that P11 acts as a frying pan spouter 1 foot high.

34. SPIKE GEYSER lies in the second cluster of alkaline springs, about 600 feet upstream from Deluge Geyser (32). In several ways Spike is one of the most intriguing geysers in Yellowstone. Starting with the earliest description in 1878, it has probably received more attention than most Heart Lake springs because of its strange cone. Although only 2 feet tall, the cone closely resembles the dead and dying cones of the Monument Geyser Basin (see Chapter 9). It stands near one end of a geyserite bridge that spans Witch Creek and is surrounded by an assortment of tiny vents that spout when Spike is active. Spike was in eruption during the early expeditions to Yellowstone but was dormant by at least 1909 and remained that way into the 1940s or possibly until after the 1959 earthquake. Either Spike itself or some of the minor vents surrounding it have been active during every known observation since then. The play is as curious as the cone. Very little water issues from the tiny vent at the top of the cone; what does emerge is squirted about 6 inches high. The tallest spout comes from a pencil-sized hole near the base of the cone. It briefly squirts, every second or so, a stream about 2 feet high. A small pool at the back side of the cone surges and boils steadily, throwing some water to about 1 foot. It has taken Spike a very long time to form its cone, yet the surrounding area is badly weathered. It looks as though Spike is a remnant of more vigorous prehistoric activity, and that long active periods may be separated by equally long dormancies.

45. UNNG-HUG-P27 ("YELLOW FUNNEL SPRING") is a small, ordinarily quiet pool that is very appropriately named. Its tem-

perature is often far below boiling, but on occasion it is hotter and bubbles quite vigorously. A single report of small splashing eruptions dating to 1984 might refer to another funnel-like vent a few feet from Yellow Funnel. That spring, HUG-P28, tends to have higher temperatures, and it was observed to be boiling vigorously in 1987 and 1991.

46. UNNG-HUG-P51. Scattered along White Gulch, the arm of the Upper Group that extends up the hillside northward toward the trail, are many hot springs. Most are small and muddy, and there are numerous mud pots and steam vents among them. Nonetheless, this unlikely setting has produced at least two geysers that were active at different times from one another during the 1980s. Both probably resulted from chance seasonal changes in normally noneruptive acid springs. Neither lasted for more than a few weeks.

Table 36. Geysers of the Upper Group

Name	Map No.	Interval	Duration	Height (ft)
Deluge Geyser	32	3–5 min	1–2 min	boil
Spike Geyser	34	steady	steady	1–2
UNNG-HUG-P11	33	steady	steady	1
UNNG-HUG-P16	44	2–7 min	40 sec	1–2
UNNG-HUG-P27 ("Yellow Funnel")	45	[1984]	unknown	1
UNNG-HUG-P28	45	unknown	unknown	boil
UNNG-HUG-P51	46	rare	sec–min	1–3

[ ] Brackets enclose the year of most recent activity for extremely rare or dormant geysers. See text.

Chapter 13

Other Yellowstone Geysers

Geysers are known to occur in several other areas of Yellowstone National Park. Although these areas are relatively inaccessible, this book would not be complete without mention of them. In all of these hot spring groups, geysers are small in number and are secondary to other types of hot springs, so they are not considered to be actual geyser basins. These areas are shown on Map II.

1. SEVEN MILE HOLE

Seven Mile Hole is one of the few parts of the Grand Canyon of the Yellowstone that can be reached by trail. About 7 miles downstream from the Lower Falls of the Yellowstone, it is famous for its fishing. The trail to the area follows the canyon rim from near Inspiration Point, then drops abruptly into the canyon; the elevation difference is about 1,200 feet in just the last $1^1/_2$ miles.

Hot springs occur in several small, scattered groups within Seven Mile Hole. One of the first to be reached is Halfway Spring, a small perpetual spouter that plays atop an impressively large geyserite cone. On occasion it may act as a geyser. Within another group of springs about halfway to the bottom of the canyon are two geysers. One, surprisingly, has an official name. When active, Safety-valve Geyser erupts every 10 to 20 minutes, has a duration of 2 to 3 minutes, and splashes about 3 feet high; more recently, it has behaved as a perpetual spouter. Nearby is a second geyser, but its height is

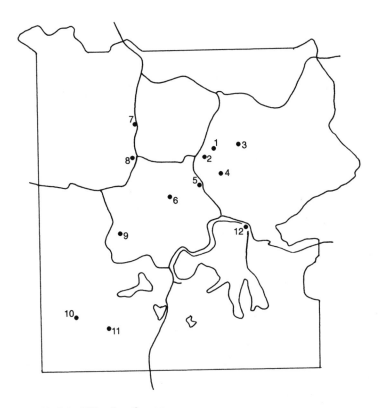

Map I I. Other Yellowstone Geysers

not more than 2 feet. At and near the canyon floor are several perpetual spouters that, again, may act as geysers at times.

2. THE GRAND CANYON OF THE YELLOWSTONE

The main part of the Grand Canyon is brilliantly colored from the Lower Falls about 2 miles downstream. The coloration is the result of hydrothermal rock alteration that has formed a mixture of numerous oxide minerals. The thermal area at the Grand Canyon has been active for a very long time. Some old geyserite deposits above the rim near Artist's Point are estimated to be between 300,000 and 600,000 years old. Today's hot springs are largely confined to the bottom of the canyon. They can be seen from the various viewpoints along the rim, but none is reached by trail. Several geysers are included.

On the east side of the river just downstream from the base of the Lower Falls (so close as to sometimes be within the spray) is a tiny hot spring group. Uncle Tom's Trail, which drops partway into the canyon, extended to the group before it was closed because of rock slides, so the springs received names in spite of their small sizes. Among them are Fairy and Watermelon Geysers and Tom Thumb Geyser, which is actually a perpetual spouter.

A short distance farther downstream and across the river is the site of another geyser. Directly below Red Rock Point, this Red Rock Geyser erupted 15 feet high during 1947. Smaller but frequent eruptions were recorded during 1991.

Visible in both directions along the river from Artist's Point are several other hot springs and geysers. None is named. The most important of these is a geyser that plays from a vent at the river's edge. It usually shows itself only with a bit of steam at a narrowing of the canyon upstream from the viewpoint. Eruptions are infrequent but over long durations jet water completely across the river. Downstream from the point are one additional geyser and at least six perpetual spouters.

3. JOSEPHS COAT HOT SPRINGS

Josephs Coat Hot Springs lies within the trail-less Mirror Plateau east of the Grand Canyon, and access requires both excellent wilderness skills and a special backcountry permit. The topographic maps show a Whistler Geyser at Josephs Coat, but it is a perpetual spouter that has probably never had periodic activity. Nearby, however, is Broadside Geyser. Its best-known activity was during 1978, when play up to 15 feet high recurred every 20 to 40 minutes for durations of 5 to 6 minutes.

4. BOG CREEK HOT SPRINGS

Along Bog Creek, southeast of Canyon Village and east of Hayden Valley, again not accessible by trail, are some small, unnamed thermal areas. In one of these there is a single geyser, named Enigma Geyser because of its unlikely location in an elevated, mostly acid group of hot springs. Observed on only three known occasions, it was active each time but with considerable changes in its performances. The intervals tended to be several minutes in length. Eruptions lasted only a few seconds, during which water was sprayed 6 to 10 feet high.

5. CRATER HILLS

The Crater Hills area is within Hayden Valley, about 1 mile west of the highway. Getting to the area involves some dangers, as this is prime bear country. In 1985 a Park ranger was mauled by a grizzly bear while casually walking in the area. There are numerous hot springs among the Crater Hills, only one of which is depositing geyserite. Crater Hills Geyser is in eruption more than it is quiet. The play reaches about 8 feet.

6. WESTERN HAYDEN VALLEY

Along Alum Creek in the far northwestern portion of Hayden Valley are several hot spring groups. One of these is known as Highland Springs. Located in the hills west of the valley proper, it contains some perpetual spouters and a single geyser, the well-named Miniature Geyser. Not far to the west are the Mary Mountain Hot Springs, which are really just an acid, westward extension of the Highland Springs. In Hayden Valley east of Highland Springs is Glen Africa Basin. Although not marked on any published map, it contains many perpetual spouters, some of which might act as geysers at times. Among the named features here are Pseudo Geyser, a cyclic spouter up to 15 feet high, Red Jacket Spring, which plays steadily to 8 feet; and Flutter–Wheel Spring, a drowned but vigorous fumarole within an echoing cavern. A single long interval–long duration geyser exists at the Alabaster Springs, about 2 miles north of Glen Africa Basin.

7. CLEARWATER SPRINGS

The Clearwater Springs are just north of Roaring Mountain, along the road between Norris and Mammoth. Geyser activity occurred here in 1918, but 1922, Yellowstone's fiftieth anniversary year, was when Semi–Centennial Geyser gained both notice and its name. Some of the eruptions reached 75 feet high. Minor intermittent bubbling has been seen during some recent seasons, but since Obsidian Creek flows directly through the crater, no eruptions can be expected.

8. UNNAMED AREA NEAR NORRIS GEYSER BASIN

Roughly 2 miles west of the Norris Museum is a thermal area that was almost never visited until the 1980s, when some very large mud explosions took place. Access is difficult, involving trekking across wet meadows, fording streams and marshes, and bushwhacking dense forest. The area contains a variety of springs, from mud pots to clear pools to geysers. The geysers have actually been known for years, primarily because of distant intermittent steam clouds visible on cold days. The largest now appears to be dead, or dormant and severely altered, because of landsliding. It erupted from a long crack in the ground, sending a fan-shaped spray of water as high as 30 feet. Some early reports probably referring to this spring imply eruptions much higher than that. Two other geysers play from murky pools, their highest splashes reaching perhaps 3 feet. Two or three other springs, including one of the deep, blue pools, might also be geysers, and there are several perpetual spouters. The mud explosions of the 1980s created impressive craters tens of feet deep and across where there had previously been no hot springs of any kind.

9. RABBIT CREEK

Although of ready access, the Rabbit Creek area was listed here in the previous editions of this book. Much has been learned during the past few years, so these hot springs have now been incorporated into Chapter 5, Midway Geyser Basin.

10. BOUNDARY CREEK

In the southwestern portion of Yellowstone are the hot springs along Boundary Creek. Because this is the closest thermal group in Yellowstone to the Island Park area outside the park where geothermal drilling was proposed, these hot springs were monitored closely during the 1980s. That they included two small geysers was a surprise. Eruptions were frequent then, but neither geyser was active in 1993.

11. FERRIS FORK OF THE BECHLER RIVER

Within a deep canyon along the Ferris Fork, extending from Three River Junction upstream about two miles, are several small hot spring groups. At least two geysers and one large perpetual spouter are known. The geysers, near the Junction, are small but frequent in their action. The spouter may act as a geyser at times, reaching up to 10 feet high.

12. SEDGE BAY, YELLOWSTONE LAKE

In early 1990, at a time when the water level of Yellowstone Lake was exceptionally low, a geyser was seen along the shoreline of Sedge Bay, southeast of Steamboat Point. The play recurred every $1^1/_2$ minutes, lasted 40 seconds, and splashed up to 3 feet high. The activity only persisted for a few weeks.

As of now, true geysers are not known to occur in any other thermal area of Yellowstone. However, the geysers of areas 3, 4, 8, 10, 11, and 12 were only discovered during the past two or three decades. Also, geysers and geyserlike action have historically been seen at Mud Volcano and Calcite Springs. It is possible that more geysers lie hidden in Yellowstone's backcountry.

Appendix:
Geyser Fields of the World

When this appendix appeared in the first edition of *The Geysers of Yellowstone* in 1979, it was the first presentation of information ever published about all of the known geyser fields of the world. Since then, much more has been learned. Geysers have been found in a few new areas; some other places have been proven to not include geysers after all. As with the rest of this book, this section has been completely rewritten.

The sources of information presented here are diverse. Geysers have been noted in the course of numerous geologic studies — geysers are rare enough to make their existence an important part of any geologic study — but few of these studies have been published for wide distribution. Nearly as often as not, these reports are written in some language other than English. Some are as much as 150 years old. Because of a misunderstanding among many early researchers, some warm artesian springs have been listed as geysers although they definitely are not. It has turned out, then, that the most valuable source of information about geysers in the modern world has been personal communications, mostly letters from geologists all around the world, plus personal journeys to many of the geyser fields around the Pacific Rim.

All of these studies have made one thing especially clear: Yellowstone National Park is far and away the greatest geyser field anywhere. The small area of the Upper Geyser Basin contains at least 20% of all of the geysers in the world and, taken alone, contains more geysers than any other field on earth. Even the Park's smaller, backcountry areas would rank

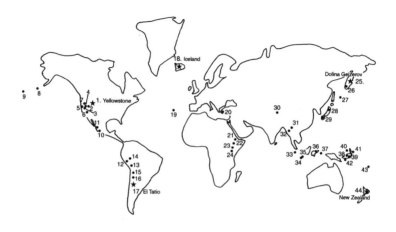

Map JJ. Geyser Fields of the World

among the handful of largest geyser fields. Yellowstone undoubtedly encompasses well over half of the world total.

These percentages are somewhat smaller than those cited in the earlier editions of this book, primarily because of recent findings on Russia's Kamchatka Peninsula, but one simple fact remains — geysers are extraordinarily rare features, restricted to generally small numbers in restricted geologic environments. It is possible that a few small geothermal areas with geysers remain to be discovered or publicized, but there are none of significant size yet to be found. Just why geysers are so common in Yellowstone is not known with certainty. It could be chance as much as anything. The existence of geysers is a complex matter, involving details such as water temperature, water supply, degree of self-sealing within the geothermal system, and, perhaps of utmost importance, the extent to which water has been both over-pressured beyond normal hydrostatic pressure and over-heated (or superheated) above the normal boiling point for a given depth and pressure. Yellowstone is a nearly perfect combination of factors that has scarcely been matched elsewhere. For example, Iceland contains more hot springs than does Yellowstone, yet the geysers there number only about twenty-five. Even that small number is enough to rank Iceland as one of the most important geyser fields on earth.

The fact that no place in the world can compare with Yellowstone must not be taken as a belittlement of other geysers. Icelanders and New Zealanders are justifiably proud of their geysers and have recently taken steps to assure their preservation. The Russians have created a national park around theirs, in large part because of the geysers, just as happened at Yellowstone. In fact, one is hard put to convince these people that Yellowstone really is better. Yet the combination of *all* other geyser fields of the world, listed here as forty-three in number, probably includes fewer than 500 geysers at most; 400 is a more realistic number of other geysers that exist at this time. These figures include a number of areas for which the best available information simply states "several geysers." All of the world's known geyser fields are shown on Map JJ and are summarized in Table 37.

Table 37. Summary of the Geyser Fields of the World

Name	Text Number	Number of Geysers†
Yellowstone National Park, Wyoming, U.S.A.	1	500
Dolina Geizerov, Kamchatka Peninsula, Russia	25	200
New Zealand	44	40 *
El Tatio, Antofagasta, Chile	17	38
Iceland	18	16 *
Kasiloli, New Britain Island, Papua–New Guinea	39	14
Deidei and Iamelele, Fergusson Island, Papua–New Guinea	42	12
Lihir and Ambitle Islands, Papua–New Guinea	41	9
Umnak Island, Alaska, U.S.A.	8	8
Carumas, Moquegua, Peru	12	8
Puchuldiza and Tuja, Tarapaca, Chile	16	8
Comanjilla, Guanajuato, Mexico	10	7
Chiang Mai, Thailand	31	5 *
Nakama Springs, Savusavu, Vanua Levu, Fiji	43	5
Tagajia, Xizang, People's Republic of China	30	4
Chaluo, Sichuan, People's Republic of China	30	4
Great Boiling Springs, Nevada, U.S.A.	4	3
Morgan Springs, California, U.S.A.	5	3

Table 37 continued

Long Valley, California, U.S.A.	6	3 *
Lake Bogoria, Kenya	24	3
Lampung–Semangko, Sumatra, Indonesia	33	3
Tapanuli, Sumatra, Indonesia	33	3
Ixtlan de los Hervores, Michoacan, Mexico	11	2
Pauzhetsk, Kamchatka Peninsula, Russia	26	2 *
Onikobe, Miyagi Prefecture, Honshu Island, Japan	28	2
Chapu, Xizang, People's Republic of China	30	2
Cisolok, Java, Indonesia	34	2
Garua Harbour, New Britain Island, Papua–New Guinea	38	2
Mickey Hot Springs, Oregon, U.S.A.	7	1
Calientes, Candarave, Tacna, Peru	13	1
Puentebello, Puno, Peru	14	1
Suriri, Tarapaca, Chile	15	1
Ayvacik, Turkey	20	1
Allallobeda, Danakil, Ethiopia	21	1
Abaya and Langano, Lakes District, Ethiopia	22	1
Logkippi, Kenya	23	1
Balazhang, Yunnan, People's Republic of China	30	1
Pai, Tavoy District, Myanmar (Burma)	32	1
Kerinci, Sumatra, Indonesia	33	1
Pasaman, Sumatra, Indonesia	33	1
Minahasa District, Celebes, Indonesia	36	1
Bacan Island, Maluku Group, Indonesia	37	1
Narage Island, Papua–New Guinea	40	1
Shiashkotan Island, Kuril Islands, Russia	27	many?
Kanaga Island, Alaska, U.S.A.	9	several
Beppu, Kyushu Island, Japan	29	several
Guhu, Xizang, People's Republic of China	30	unknown
Gunung Papandayan, Java, Indonesia	35	unknown
Beowawe, Nevada, U.S.A.	2	0 *
Steamboat Hot Springs, Nevada, U.S.A.	3	0 *
Volcan Furnas, Azores Islands, Portugal	19	0 *

† — Number of active geysers according to the best information currently available, sometimes many years old. As noted in Chapter 1 of this book, different authorities may derive different counts depending on their personal interpretation of the definition of "geyser."

* Areas in which significant geothermal development has affected the activity, reducing the number of active geysers. The three areas listed as 0 (zero) formerly contained significant numbers of geysers but now have none because of human geothermal developments or natural volcanogenic changes.

Each of the descriptions is followed by a numerical listing of references. The descriptive section is then followed by
an annotated bibliography of these references. It is hoped
that the entire work is accurate, but there are bound to be
some errors. However, this section is not designed as a
guidebook but only as a source of basic information. In that
capacity it gives an accurate idea as to the nature and distribution of geyser fields.

Finally, it must be noted that many of these geyser fields
are not what they once were. Mankind's ever-widening
search for energy has destroyed many of these geothermal
systems, and several of those that remain untapped are
being explored for potential development. As with the
expression "you can't have your cake and eat it, too," it is
impossible to exploit a geothermal system while also preserving its hot springs. The two are 100% incompatible. Even
Yellowstone has been threatened by developments outside
the Park boundaries. Geysers are disappearing from our
world. Were they a biological species, they would be on the
endangered species list.

1. YELLOWSTONE NATIONAL PARK, WYOMING, U.S.A. In terms
of the number of geysers, the power of the activity, and any
other category one would like to consider, Yellowstone is far
and away the world's largest and best geyser field. Its more
than 600 historically known geysers are scattered among
nine individual geyser basins, which range in size from the
Upper Basin with over 200 geysers to smaller areas with as
few as one geyser. With well over half of the world's geysers,
Yellowstone simply cannot be compared with anyplace else.

2. BEOWAWE, NEVADA, U.S.A. Beowawe is a small community,
little more than a whistle-stop on the railroad, halfway
between Battle Mountain and Elko in northern Nevada. The
geysers were found about 4 miles southwest of the town,
near the head of Whirlwind Valley. The gold rush pioneers
of the 1850s saw the steam clouds and took them to be perpetual dust devils; the area was not reported to contain gey-

"Teacup Geyser," one of the last geysers of significance on the valley floor at Beowawe, Nevada, had eruptions a few feet high until the early 1980s. One the large geyserite terrace above, where geothermal wells spouted constantly, there were once more than two dozen geysers.

sers until 1869 — with which it is interesting to note that geysers were confirmed at Beowawe before they were in Yellowstone. A graded public road leads to the hot springs, but the geysers themselves are on private land. Beowawe is now the site of a geothermal power plant, on-line as a producer of electricity since 1986. The Beowawe Geysers are dead as a result.

The Beowawe Geysers did not receive detailed study until 1934. At that time the small field contained at least a dozen spouters, enough to have made Beowawe one of the most significant geyser fields anywhere. Further studies during the 1950s revealed that as many as thirty of its springs were capable of geyser eruptions, although generally only a few were active at any given time. Indeed, with thirty of only fifty hot springs known as geysers, Beowawe probably held the highest proportion of spouting vents of any geyser area in the world. In fact, it generated enough attention that it was once proposed as a National Monument and later as a Nevada State Park.

The hot springs were distributed about two groups: a geyserite terrace on the hillside and a lower, sinter-covered shield on the valley floor. These two groups of springs are apparently separated by a major fault zone. Most of the activity was on the top of the Main Terrace. Among the geysers there was Beowawe Geyser, which erupted about 30 feet high. Others such as Spitfire, Teakettle, and Pin Cushion played frequently as high as 15 feet. The sinter shield in the valley below included just three geysers.

One of the earliest U.S. geothermal exploration programs was begun at Beowawe in the 1950s. Three deep steam wells were drilled on the Main Terrace. Testing of the wells for steam pressure and temperature immediately robbed most of the natural springs of water and heat. All of the geysers were destroyed, and most pools dried up before 1970, leaving only a few muddy springs and steam vents. Then, in the early 1970s, somebody used dynamite on two of the well caps. Both became steady spouters, erupting commingled steam and water to as high as 70 feet. Although one of these wells was later recapped, the Main Terrace only

"Teacup Geyser" was the last of the geysers at Beowawe, Nevada, to undergo strictly natural eruptions. It quit playing in the early 1980s shortly after a nearby geothermal power plant began producing electricity.

vaguely resembled what had been there before.

The springs on the valley floor were less affected by the drilling, and the clear alkaline springs remained into the 1980s. Three were geysers. One, a deep, blue pool, had true eruptions up to 10 feet high only infrequently, but it often acted as a boiling intermittent spring. Another geyser played from a small vent along a crack in the geyserite. The third geyser, when active, was the best of the lot. Its 2-foot-wide vent was centered in a shallow 10-foot-wide basin. The geyser erupted erratically, with intervals ranging from 2 to 4 hours, but the play typically lasted 10 minutes, sent some bursts over 10 feet high, and ended with a noisy steam phase. All descriptions of the Beowawe Geysers must be written in the past tense, however. New technology has allowed small geothermal systems of comparatively low temperature to be exploited. In 1986 the Whirlwind Valley power plant began producing electricity. The production wells are located on the Main Terrace, and the spent fluid is reinjected into the ground near the valley springs. For reasons geologists cannot thoroughly explain, there was a brief rejuvenation of many of the geysers shortly after the first production, but by 1987 all of the hot spring activity had quit. One of the most concentrated geyser fields anywhere is dead.

References: 3, 4, 5, 6, and 41.

3. STEAMBOAT HOT SPRINGS, NEVADA, U.S.A. Steamboat Springs is almost too accessible. The area lies astride U.S. Highway 395 just 9 miles south of downtown Reno, Nevada. It suffered severe damage from a lack of management while most of the local population was completely unaware of its rare importance. For a time during the early 1980s, it appeared that the situation was about to change. The Bureau of Land Management, in cooperation with Washoe County, had plans to establish a regional park. The area was cleaned, and interpretive signs were erected. But similar to Beowawe elsewhere in the state, geothermal developments quickly ended both the planned park and Steamboat as a geyser field.

The geyser activity at Steamboat Springs was continuously changing. Seldom did any spouter persist for more than a few months before an exchange of function caused its dormancy or death. On the other hand, there was always some degree of eruptive activity, and more than twenty-five of the springs had histories as geysers.

Most of the action was on the Main Terrace, west of the highway. Many different geysers had been active there. During the 1870s one of these was very regular and played as high as 75 feet. It became so well-known that the residents of Virginia City made trips to watch it play, and Dan DeQuille mentions the geyser in his famous book, *The Big Bonanza*.

Shortly after the Whirlwind Valley geothermal power plant began producing electricity near the Beowawe, Nevada, hot springs, several of the old geysers on the huge geyserite terrace were temporarily reactivated. The largest and most vigorous was "Geyser T-1." It and all the others stopped erupting in 1987.

"Geyser 40" at Steamboat Hot Springs played frequently and vigorously, reaching as much as 20 feet above its pool level and 10 feet above the ground, during the 1980s. It and all the other geysers at Steamboat stopped playing shortly after a geothermal power plant started operating in 1987.

Most other geyser activity on the Main Terrace has been of much smaller size, but in the 1980s Geyser #42w could reach over 20 feet high, and #40 played to 10 feet from a water level as far belowground.

The Lower Terrace, near the Steamboat resort east of the highway, contained fewer geysers. None ever matched the scale of those on the Main Terrace, but one was persistent, continuously active for more than 50 years.

The same technology that led to the destruction of Beowawe did the same to Steamboat Springs. The operators of the power plant, which began full commercial production in 1988, were supposed to monitor the natural springs and assure their preservation. That was not done. Although a few warm springs remain, no geyser has played on either the Main or Lower Terrace since early 1989 or before. Now, a second power plant is being built. Steamboat Hot Springs, where much of our modern understanding of how geothermal systems and geysers operate was developed, has joined the list of destroyed areas.

References: 1, 2, 3, 7, and 41.

4. GREAT BOILING SPRINGS, GERLACH, NEVADA, U.S.A. The Great Boiling Springs were first reported by John C. Fremont in 1845. He was impressed by periodic boiling and commented on the distance at which the noise could be heard. In more recent years, the hot spring area has been developed as a park, variously operated by the town of Gerlach or private interests; at other times it has served as a target range. That intermittent activity exists at Great Boiling Springs is certain, and some of the springs have almost unquestionably acted as geysers on occasion. Eruptions up to 5 feet high were reported in a 1984 travel magazine. The area also contains large mud pots that have been known to throw mud explosively as far as 100 feet. The future of Great Boiling Springs is uncertain. The area has been leased for geothermal exploration, and there is a high likelihood of a power plant being constructed during the 1990s.

A few miles north of Gerlach is Fly Ranch. Near the graded dirt road is the "Fly Ranch Geyser." It is actually a

drilled well that acts as a perpetual spouter, jetting a few feet high from several openings near the top of a travertine cone.
References: 3 and 41.

5. MORGAN SPRINGS, CALIFORNIA, U.S.A. Located just outside the south entrance to Lassen Volcanic National Park, the Morgan Springs used to be the site of a Forest Service campground. This small collection of very hot, flowing springs and pools included at least three geysers during the 1950s. The typical play was of long duration and was up to 3 feet high. There are no known reports of activity before those years. The Morgan Springs now lie within private property closed to normal access, and their current state is unknown.

A few miles away, and within the national park, is Terminal Geyser. Many reports state that it has always been a perpetual spouter, never known to have intermittent geyser eruptions. It is steady now, jetting constantly a few feet high from several openings. But in the 1870s it was reported to spout intermittently as high as 20 feet. Later, a 1925 publication about the geology of Lassen Park refers to Terminal as "Geyser." Two different 25-foot-wide pools were said to play "at times," and a photograph showing one of these with a person standing beside it implies that the height was least 8 feet.
References: 3, 8, and 41.

6. LONG VALLEY CALDERA, CALIFORNIA, U.S.A. The Long Valley Caldera is a huge volcanic explosion crater very much like that of Yellowstone, and it formed at about the same time. It is, therefore, logical that it should contain similar hot springs. It does, but the hot spring groups are small. The town of Mammoth Lakes and the Mammoth Mountain ski area are within the caldera.

Mentions of geysers are scattered throughout the literature; however, the reliability of the reports is sometimes questionable. Overall, there has been limited geyser activity. Starting in May 1980 and continuing for several years, the Long Valley area underwent a series of strong earthquake swarms. Some of the shocks had Richter magnitudes greater than 6. This action has been shown to be the result of intrusions of magma at a shallow depth, possibly presaging a new episode of volcanic eruptions in Long Valley. The intrusions altered the heat flow of the area, increasing the temperatures of several of the hot spring groups, and the earthquakes opened or enlarged existing plumbing conduits. The result was a few geysers.

The Casa Diablo Hot Springs are near the junction of U.S. Highway 395 and State Highway 203. Apparently, at least one geyser was active at Casa Diablo Hot Springs as early as the 1870s. It plus another also played in the 1930s, when the spray caused a hazardous ice buildup on the highway during the winters. One geyser was active during the early 1980s. Its activity was directly related to the status of a nearby steam well. If the well was turned on and producing, the geyser was all but dormant; when the well was off, the geyser sometimes played frequently. Its height was as much as 30 feet. There are now two geothermal power plants at Casa Diablo. As is the typical case, the energy production has destroyed the geyser and related springs, leaving only a few tepid, muddy pools at Casa Diablo.

At the swimming area at Hot Creek, which is operated by the U.S. Forest Service as a developed recreational area, several springs have histories as geysers, most notably following the 1980 earthquakes. One of these pools erupted up to 40 feet high. Play by the others was much smaller, seldom reaching over 3 feet, but it was frequent. This activity has gradually died down, and even the larger geyser seldom plays. It is likely that future earthquakes will rejuvenate the geysers.

Little Hot Creek is less well-known. A tiny area on an unimproved back road, all of its springs are small, the biggest pool being only about 2 feet across. Still, there are at least two geysers at Little Hot Creek. They play frequently and can reach as high as 2 feet.

Last is the Hot Bubbling Pool, across the stream from the fish hatchery. It is an intermittent spring if not a true geyser. The water level rises and falls as much as several feet, and vigorous bubbling accompanies the times of high water. Hot Bubbling Pool might have been a substantial geyser in prerecorded time. It now never fills its basin, but a very large runoff channel leads from the rim. Plans for a power plant at Hot Bubbling Pool are presently on hold because of environmental concerns, but if the plant is developed it could easily spell the demise of the more distant Hot Creek as well as Hot Bubbling Pool.

References: 3, 9, and 41.

7. MICKEY HOT SPRINGS, OREGON, U.S.A. Although Mickey Hot Springs, in southeastern Oregon, has been known as a site of geyserite deposits and hot springs for several decades, the fact that it possesses a single geyser was only discovered in 1986. Much of the time this spring behaves as a variable perpetual spouter 2 to 3 feet high, but during dry seasons, when there is no interference by near surface groundwater, it behaves as a true geyser. The best year for Mickey Geyser was 1991. It had intervals of 4 to 5 minutes, durations of about 1 minute, and heights up to 6 feet. The Bureau of Land Management has improved the area and installed some interpretive signs. Unfortunately, a permit for exploratory geothermal drilling has been issued for another group of springs a few miles away at Borax Lake. Although likely to exist for at least a few more years, Mickey Hot Springs is threatened.

Reference: 41.

8. UMNAK ISLAND, ALEUTIAN CHAIN, ALASKA, U.S.A. Umnak Island is one of the first and largest of the Aleutian Islands, quite close to the mainland of the Alaska Peninsula. Although the next island to the east, Unalaska, is quite well populated, Umnak is home to only a small community of Aleut people who live miles away from the hot springs. In the narrow midsection of the island — in Geyser Valley along Geyser Creek, which drains into Geyser Bight — are several groups of hot springs, three of which contain geysers. Although all are small, their activity is vigorous. Most recorded intervals have ranged between 3 and 10 minutes, with durations of about 3 minutes and heights of 1 to 10 feet. One of the geysers is capable of much larger eruptions, perhaps up to 20 feet high. The geysers were first studied in 1948. Subsequent visits during the 1970s and 1980s showed little overall change. Twelve springs have shown geyser activity, with about eight typically being active at any given time. In addition to the geysers, the area is notable for its assortment of large pools of great depth and beautiful coloration, matching some of the pools of Yellowstone.

References: 2, 10, 11, and 41.

9. KANAGA ISLAND, ALEUTIAN CHAIN, ALASKA, U.S.A. Kanaga Island is another of the Aleutian Chain but is much farther from the mainland, near Adak Island. The only ordinary access is to military personnel, and even that is rare. However, during a general survey of the geothermal resources of Alaska, it was discovered that Kanaga's hot springs include small geysers. No statistics were reported, except that no geyser evidently played more than about 2 feet high.

Reference: 41.

10. COMANJILLA, GUANAJUATO, MEXICO. Comanjilla is a fancy hot spring spa and hotel between the cities of Guanajuato and Leon, northeast of Guadalajara. All of the bathing pools are fed by the runoff from the hot springs and some shallow wells. The first description of these geysers was written in 1910. Since that report is the only known publication about the area, little activity was expected when I visited Comanjilla in 1981. However, the geothermal developments of the resort are low-grade, and the springs had not been substantially affected. Most of the geysers described in 1910 could still be identified. The largest, Geyser Humboldt, is usually dormant but plays up to 10 feet high when active. Another had frequent eruptions of 6 feet, and one hidden deep within a small cavern next to a swimming pool played very regularly every 2 hours. A total of seven geysers was seen, making this Mexico's largest existing geyser field.

References: 3, 12, and 41.

11. IXTLAN DE LOS HERVORES, MICHOACAN, MEXICO. The name roughly translates as "boiling pools," and Ixtlan certainly has its share of them. Located about midway between Guadalajara and Morelia, it is a large geothermal area. Because of its great number of mud pots, pools, and geysers, it has sometimes been promoted as "Mexico's Little Yellowstone." Unfortunately, it has also been the site of geothermal drilling. Both that and a nearly total lack of preservationist management have severely altered the natural springs.

The hot springs occur in several groups scattered along a 2-mile stretch of the valley. Geysers used to occur in all of the clusters. With descriptive names translating to Black, Coyote, White Rock, and Kitchen, for example, at least fourteen geysers were active in 1906 when they were visited by the International Geological Congress. Most were still active as recently as the 1950s, including Tritubulario (Three Vent) and Pozo Verde (Green Spring), each of which reached 10 to 15 feet high.

One of the geothermal wells at Ixtlan de los Hervores is spouting continuously, reaching perhaps 50 feet high. That area is fenced and is operated as something of a park. A few pesos are charged for admission, but the natural springs have been essentially destroyed.

A part of the easternmost area, behind the village of Salitre, has been relatively unchanged, although drilling also occurred there. At least two geysers were still active in 1981. One played at unknown intervals for as long as 10 minutes; it reached 3 feet high. The other was probably bigger but was not actually seen in eruption. However, the large geysers Tritubulario and Pozo Verde had both been dormant for a long enough time to have allowed large cacti to grow in their runoff channels.

References: 3, 13, 14, and 41.

12. CARUMAS, MOQUEGUA, PERU. The vicinity of Carumas, at about 12,000 feet elevation in the Andes Mountains of southern Peru, is filled with hot springs. All are of significantly high temperatures, and geysers are known to occur in three of the groups.

The best area is Sicoloque, where there are four geysers, one reaching over 12 feet high, one about 10 feet, and two around 4 feet. Indications are that these geysers have been active without significant change since before 1900. At Putina there are three geysers. One is about 12 feet high. Both of the others play to less than 3 feet. Sayasayani is the site of a single geyser 3 feet high. The waters of all of these areas and more are used for bathing and cooking, and evidence of Inca usage is found in numerous places.
References: 2, 3, and 41.

13. CALIENTES, CANDARAVE, TACNA, PERU. As in the Carumas area, (see #12), the hot water from the springs at Calientes has been used for medicinal bathing for hundreds of years. Incan ruins are abundant in the area. The elevation is nearly 14,000 feet above sea level. There are many boiling springs but only one certain geyser. In 1979 it erupted with extremely regular 55-minute intervals; the duration was 2 minutes, and the height was over 20 feet.
References: 2 and 41.

14. PUENTEBELLO, PUNO, PERU. The geysers of Puentebello occur within and immediately in front of a single limestone cavern. Generally, limestone is considered an improper material for the existence of geysers, as it does not have the inherent strength of siliceous sinter. Nevertheless, geysers exist at Puentebello. Within the cave, and therefore inaccessible because of the hot water and inhospitable atmosphere, are many geysers, all probably playing 3 to 6 feet high; these may be perpetual spouters. Just outside the cave is a truly periodic geyser with heavy discharge. It has a very short interval of only about 10 seconds, but during the quiet the water level drops and then refills the crater. The play consists of a few quick bursts 4 to 5 feet high.
Reference: 41.

15. SURIRI, PARINACOTA PROVINCE, TARAPACA REGION, CHILE. Nearly 15,000 feet up in the Andes of far northern Chile,

Suriri (also known as Polloquere) is often nearly impossible to reach. Although it lies within the Salar de Suriri Natural Monument, the access is by way of poor dirt roads that are completely closed during the November to March wet season. Very little observation has been conducted at Suriri. One small geyser was observed in 1944. As part of a geothermal survey of Chile, Suriri was surveyed in the 1960s, and a report was published in 1972. No geyser was actually described at that time. However, at least 230 hot springs are scattered about the valley, and several were said to act as "springs boiling up quite high." A more extended observation would probably reveal true geysers, possibly quite a few.
References: 12 and 32.

16. PUCHULDIZA, IQUIQUE PROVINCE, TARAPACA REGION, CHILE. Also located in northern Chile and high in the Andes Mountains, Puchuldiza is the least accessible of Chile's geyser fields. Overland travel through exceptionally rugged volcanic terrain (or a helicopter) is needed to reach the hot springs. Famous French volcanologists Katia and Maurice Krafft, who were killed by Japan's Mt. Unzen in 1991, cited their failure to reach Puchuldiza after a four-day effort as one of their greatest disappointments.

No details about the activity of the individual geysers at Puchuldiza have been published, but at least four were active in 1972. A short report published in 1993 referred to "a geyser 50 feet high at Volcanitos in northern Chile"; Puchuldiza has also been listed as Volcanitos de Aguas Puchuldisas, so this is probably the site of that geyser.

About 3 miles down the river draining the Puchuldiza field proper is a smaller thermal area known as Tuja. It also contains at least four geysers.
References: 16 and 41.

17. EL TATIO, EL LOA PROVINCE, ANTOFAGASTA REGION, CHILE. El Tatio is one of the world's premier geyser fields. Unlike Suriri and Puchuldiza farther north in Chile, El Tatio is readily accessible by vehicle and is frequently visited by tour groups. It is still quite far from cities, however, and this has helped "save" the geysers, at least for the time being. Although exploratory geothermal drilling has been done in the area, the geysers have recently (1993) been proposed for preservation within a national park. Access is by way of a rough road from the town of San Pedro de Atacama about 50 miles away. It is a long trip, and most tours to the geysers leave the town before dawn and return by afternoon, spending only a few hours among the hot springs. There are no commercial facilities. Under some circumstances it is possible to stay inside some old concrete cabins (there is a guard who should be given a generous tip), but any overnight stay still requires high-quality camping gear. Even though the bone-dry Atacama Desert is nearby, winter conditions are the rule at the altitude of 13,800 feet.

Of more than 300 hot springs at El Tatio, as many as 67 have been recorded as geysers. The record for a single observation is 38 geysers. None of the eruptions is of significantly large size, the tallest reaching perhaps 20 feet, but the action is vigorous. Several play from massive geyserite cones.

The El Tatio geothermal system also appears as hot springs across the crest of the Andes Mountains, near Laguna Colorada in Bolivia. Almost nothing is known about these springs. It is illegal as well as physically difficult to hike across the border from Chile. Access from the Bolivian side is possible through four-day jeep tours out of the town of Uyuni. A few geysers do exist.

This is about the sum total of what is known about El Tatio. Even with only 38 geysers, it ranks as either the third or fourth largest existing geyser field on earth, trailing only Yellowstone, Kamchatka, and perhaps New Zealand.

References: 2, 3, 16, 17, and 41.

18. ICELAND. Most discussions of the geysers of Iceland always seem to generalize, giving the impression that there is a single geyser basin. Reality is that although the large geysers of fame are confined to one small area, hot spring groups with geysers are scattered widely about the island. They total a large enough number of make Iceland probably the fifth largest geyser field in the world.

The names of the geysers are fascinating. Icelandic is a Viking tongue, largely unrelated to other modern languages, and many of these names are virtually unpronounceable by English-speaking people. The geyser basins bear such names as Torfastathir, Hruni, Reykir in Ölfus, and Borgarfjartharsysla. The geysers themselves also have some stupendous names such as Sturlüreykir, Svathi, Eyvindarhver, and Opherrishola. Each name has a specific meaning, and, like those of Yellowstone, they are often very descriptive. Most famous of all is Geysir. It is the namesake of all of the geysers in the world. Translated, the name means "gusher" or "spouter." The Icelandic people are proud of Geysir, and the name is copyrighted so it can never be applied to any other geyser.

Geysir is at Haukadalur. It rarely erupts now. Why this is so is uncertain; perhaps it is simply dormant because of an exchange of function with other springs in the area, or perhaps it was damaged after suffering through too many artificially induced eruptions (a practice that has now been banned). When active, the eruption may reach 200 feet high. Geysir is one of the world's truly major spouters, and it probably deserves its rank as the most famous geyser on earth. After all, it was first described way back in the year 1294 when it was seen by Saxo Grammaticus, an English monk.

Another important geyser at Haukadalur is Strokkur, whose name means "churn." Before 1900 it played in concert with Geysir, with some of its spouts also reaching 200 feet. After a long dormancy, Strokkur reactivated around 1970. Now, it gushes forth every 15 to 20 minutes, the brief bursts of most eruptions reaching 75 feet high. Three or four other, much smaller geysers occur at Haukadalur, which is maintained with a parklike atmosphere.

Another great concentration of geysers was at Reykir in Ölfus. Most of these can no longer be identified because of geothermal drilling for the space heating of greenhouses. Gone are Gryla, which played every 2 to 3 hours as high as 40 feet; Littli, which could reach 80 feet; and more than a dozen other geysers. A few geysers persist, however, and a trail system threads up the thermal valley to Svarth, Bath-stafuhver, and an unnamed geyser, each of which erupts a few feet high, and the manmade geysers known as Bogi I, Bogi II, and Gosi II, each of which is frequent and as high as 25 feet..

In far northern Iceland is Reykjadalur. Two geysers here have been active with little change for at least 200 years. Ysti-hver plays every 2 to 3 minutes, reaching 9 (rarely 20) feet high. Uxahver is less frequent and is 8 feet high. Odiphtong, a pool, has rare eruptions, and Sythstihver has been dormant since 1918.

Probably the most active basin in Iceland at present is at Hveravellir, almost exactly in the center of the island. It is within a barren desertlike region far from any town and so is seldom visited. It contains perhaps fifteen geysers, one of which is known to reach 15 feet high. In the 1800s Gamli Strokk played as high as 150 feet, but not a trace of its crater remains visible.

Additional geysers have been known in at least fifteen other areas in Iceland, but many of these have been altered or destroyed by geothermal developments.

Iceland is, to be sure, one of the foremost geyser fields in the world. Of course, the nation has virtually no other energy reserves, and geothermal energy is vital to the future of the country. Therefore, there has been virtually no attempt to preserve the geysers. Only the small area at Haukadalur has any real measure of protection, but even it has been proposed for development.

References: 1, 2, 3, 18, 19, and 41.

19. VOLCAN FURNAS, ISLA SAN MIGUEL, AZORES ISLANDS, POR-TUGAL. The name Furnas translates just as it sounds — "furnace." It is a volcano, probably only dormant rather than dead, within which are numerous hot springs. At the turn of the twentieth century there were several geysers, one erupting frequently to "several feet," but as of 1955 the activity had declined to a few intermittently boiling springs. If there are no geysers at Furnas now, there certainly may be again.

References: 2, 3, and 20.

20. AYVACIK, TURKEY. Boiling hot springs would not be expected near the northwest coast of Turkey, but several occur near the town of Ayvacik. This, in turn, is near the site of ancient Troy. Gayzer Suyu is the single geyser in the area, reported in 1968 to erupt frequently to about 6 feet. The only other known reference may not refer to Gayzer Suyu, but it's nice to think that it does, for it would then be the oldest reference to any geyser. This is the *The Iliad*, written by Homer around 700 B.C.
References: 2 and 21.

21. ALLALLOBEDA, DANAKIL DEPRESSION, ETHIOPIA. The Danakil Depression is a forbiddingly stark desert in east-central Ethiopia. It is a volcanic area within the northern part of the East African Rift system. Not far from Allallobeda is Hadar, where the remains of Lucy, First Family, and other early human ancestors were found during the 1970s. The hot springs are aligned along a fault zone. It may be that the name Allallobeda refers to a single spring here, a perpetual spouter as high as 20 feet. At least one other spring is a true geyser, but its eruption reaches only about 1 foot.
References: 22 and 41.

22. THE LAKES DISTRICT, ETHIOPIA. The highlands of southern Ethiopia, although still dry, are markedly different from the Danakil Depression. A series of large lakes occupies low areas in the Rift Valley. Hot springs are numerous; geysers are known in at least two places and very possibly exist in others as well. A very early report about these geysers referred to them under the name Ta'hou. The name is obsolete, for no modern reference to such a place can be found. Just which geysers comprised Ta'hou — these in Ethiopia or perhaps some in northern Kenya — is unknown.
Along the northwest shore of Lake Abaya is an extensive hot spring area. The geyserite platform is dotted with small cones and beaded deposits, both of which strongly imply geyser activity. During a long-term UN study in the mid-1960s no eruptions were seen, but when a member of that survey returned in 1979 he found one active geyser. Its

action was erratic but frequent and was up to 6 feet high.

In Lake Langano's North Bay is Geyser Island. Following an earthquake in 1906 one spring erupted powerfully, with some of the play reaching over 60 feet high. The play was extremely brief, perhaps a single burst, but it recurred every 30 seconds. Through the years the activity declined, and by 1966 the spring had regressed to intermittent overflow. An active geyser "at Lake Langano" in 1993 is probably this one.

References: 2, 3, 22, and 41.

23. LOGKIPPI, KENYA. Logkippi (also spelled Logipi, Lokipi, and so on) is a small lake a few miles south of the southern end of Lake Turkana (formerly Lake Rudolph) in northern Kenya. It would be a part of Lake Turkana except for some recent lava flows, which act as a dam. The Logkippi area includes several hot springs. Logkippi Geyser is reported to be nearly a perpetual spouter, reaching 8 to 10 feet above a raised sinter platform. A few of the other springs may also be geysers, given that one survey report cites the plural "spouting springs."

References: 2, 3, and 41.

24. LAKE BOGORIA, KENYA. Lake Bogoria (formerly Lake Hannington) in central Kenya is famed as one of the better flamingo nesting areas anywhere; at times, from a distance the lake looks pink because of the tremendous flocks of birds. Relatively little attention has been paid to the hot springs near the south end of the lake. Among these is at least one geyser. During the early 1970s Loburu Geyser erupted every 5 minutes, sending its water to a height of 5 feet or more. As of 1991, it was active as a highly variable perpetual spouter, sending a pulsating jet between 3 and 10 feet high. Several other springs in the immediate vicinity of Loburu were also spouting.

Farther north along the west shore of the lake is Maji ya Moto. It also includes hot springs, several of which are small geysers or perpetual spouters.

The East African Power & Light Company, a Kenyan government corporation, has done exploratory geothermal

drilling at Lake Bogoria. At one time plans were for a power plant to be operating before 1985; no construction has been done, however, and the hot springs remain in their natural state.
References: 2 and 41.

25. DOLINA GEIZEROV (GEYSER VALLEY), KRONOTSKY NATURE PRESERVE, KAMCHATKA PENINSULA, RUSSIA. The Kamchatka Peninsula is that extension of Siberia that points south into the north Pacific Ocean. Most Americans know about Kamchatka either from playing the game of Risk or because it is near where Korean Airlines Flight 007 was shot down a few years ago. One of the closest parts of the former Soviet Union to the United States, it was closed to outsiders until 1991. I am proud of having served as the leader of the first U.S. expedition allowed to spend time in Dolina Geizerov; that eight days during June–July 1991 revealed the valley to be the second largest geyser field in the world.

Kamchatka is an intensely volcanic place. Dolina Geizerov lies just outside the Uzon Caldera, a large Yellowstone-style volcanic explosion and collapse crater, and is low on the flank of Kikhpinych Volcano, which had some small, ashy eruptions in the 1890s. Several other active volcanoes are in the immediate vicinity. The Kronotsky Nature Preserve is the descendant of an area that was closed to hunting in the 1880s in order to preserve sables, but it is such a remote and rugged region that Dolina Geizerov wasn't discovered until 1941. World War II postponed explorations until the late 1940s, but within a few years the valley had been thoroughly mapped and its existence revealed to the outside world. The modern Kronotsky Nature Preserve is slightly larger than Yellowstone. With the development of limited tourism, trails and a camping area have been established, but there are no commercial facilities. As of 1994 access is achieved through expensive 120-mile helicopter flights from the city of Petropavlovsk-Kamchatskii, which are available only to organized adventure travel companies. This might change in the near future. The park is sorely strapped for funds, and the money of western tourists is the most

Geizer Velikan ("Giant Geyser") is probably the most famous geyser in the Valley of Geysers on Russia's Kamchatka Penninsula. The jet of water reaches over 100 feet high but lasts less than one minute.

Grot Yubileinyi ("Jubilee Grotto") rarely erupted prior to July 1991. Named after the fiftieth anniversary of the discovery of the Valley of Geysers on Russia's Kamchatka Peninsula, it seemed to celebrate the arrival of the first party of American geyser gazers (led by T. Scott Bryan, the author of this book). The eruptions lasted only a few seconds each but sent water jets more than 100 feet high and outward nearly 300 feet.

ready source of new income.

Published reports about Dolina Geizerov limited the discussion to about twenty-three geysers, and, since the same features were always discussed, the impression was that they were the only geysers present. In fact, there are at least 200 geysers. Most are relatively small, playing only a few feet high, but the intensity of the activity is extreme, with most geysers of any size having intervals of less than 1 hour. Fontan (Fountain), Malyi (Small), Bolshoi (Great), Troynoy (Three), and Pervenets (First Born) all reach 40 to 80 feet high, whereas Skalistyi (Rocky), Conus Khrustalnyi (Crystal Cone), Malenkii Prinz (Little Prince), and Shchell (Crack) play to lesser heights but with great frequency and regular-

Geizer Zhemchuzhnyi ("Pearl Geyser") is one of the taller cone-type geysers in the Valley of Geysers on Russia's Kamchatka Peninsula, reaching up to 40 feet high every 3 to 5 hours.

ity. Unknown prior to 1991 is Grot Yubileinyi (Jubilee Grotto). Named because of the fiftieth anniversary of the discovery of the valley, it can send its angled water jet as high as 100 feet and as far outward as 250 feet; only Yellowstone's Giant and Steamboat Geysers can play with more force. Velikan Geyser (Giant) is the largest of those that had received publicity. Although impressive in size at 90 to 120 feet high, the play lasts less than 1 minute, and the 5-hour interval is one of the longest in the valley. In addition to the geysers, Dolina Geizerov is studded with many small perpetual spouters, pools, mud pots, and steam vents.

As remote as it is, there has been some discussion of geothermal development near Dolina Geizerov. Russia is increasingly concerned about its environment, however, and the fact that Kronotsky Nature Preserve is listed by the United Nations as a World Heritage Site will probably assure its preservation.

References: 2, 3, 23, and 41.

26. PAUZHETSK, KAMCHATKA PENINSULA, RUSSIA. Near the southern tip of the Kamchatka Peninsula is the geothermal field of Pauzhetsk. The area is the site of Russia's only operating geothermal power plant, but at least two of its geysers are reported to remain. According to published literature none reaches more than a few feet high, but in 1991 geothermal geologist Slava Sviagintsev stated that some of the eruptions reach fully 30 feet high.

References: 2, 3, 24, and 41.

27. SHIASHKOTAN ISLAND, KURIL ISLANDS, RUSSIA. Similar to the Aleutians, the Kurils are the volcanic island chain between Japan and Kamchatka. It stands to reason that hot springs of the same sort should exist on these islands. Shiashkotan is a small island in the middle of the chain. Although it was called "the island of a thousand geysers" in a 1971 book, only a single geyser was actually described. It apparently erupted frequently and was several meters high. Two Russian volcanologists have recently stated that there are also geysers on another, unstated Kuril Island.

Reference: 41.

Geizer Malyi ("Small Geyser") was named not for the size of its eruption, which reaches over 70 feet high, but because its vent is smaller than that of nearby Geizer Bolshoi ("Great Geyser") (Photo by Genrich S. Steinberg, Russian Academy of Sciences.)

28. ONIKOBE SPRINGS, HONSHU ISLAND, JAPAN. Considering the number of volcanic zones in Japan, a number of which contain rhyolite rock, geysers are very few in number and presently exist in only one or two areas. There once was a large but infrequent geyser at the city of Atami, but it has been inactive since the 1950s. The geysers reported at Tsuchiya, Shikabe, Yunotani, and Tamatsukuri are probably all artificial, erupting from drilled wells.

The Onikobe Springs are in Miyagi Prefecture in northern Japan. A part of an extensive zone in which there are several resorts and sulfur mines, Onikobe includes two geysers among its hundred hot springs. One is strictly natural and plays about 5 feet high. The other is a natural spring that has been modified. The eruptions recur every 30 minutes, have durations of a few minutes, and reach heights as great as 45 feet. There are also several pools whose geyserite deposits show signs of large-scale geyser eruptions in the past. The geyser area has an entry fee.

References: 2, 3, and 41.

29. BEPPU, KYUSHU ISLAND, JAPAN.

The city of Beppu is a major hot spring resort. Boiling springs are common. Most act as perpetual spouters, but there is at least one geyser. Its name, Tatsumaki jigoku, translates into something like "The Water Spout from Hell." Its eruptions are frequent and several feet high. Another spring, commonly called "Dragon's Breath," sprays water out of a cavern to a distance of 10 or 12 feet into a pool.

References: 2, 3, and 41.

30. XIZANG (TIBET) AND VICINITY, PEOPLE'S REPUBLIC OF CHINA. "We marched for three successive days without coming to tents. Then we saw in the distance a great column of smoke rising into the sky. We wondered if it came from a chimney or a burning house, but when we got near we saw it was the steam rising from hot springs. We were soon gazing at a scene of great natural beauty. A number of springs bubbled out of the ground, and in the middle of the cloud of steam shot up a splendid little geyser fifteen feet high. After poetry, prose! We all naturally thought of a bath."

So wrote Heinrich Harrer in describing his *Seven Years in Tibet* (New York: E. P. Dutton, 1954). Unfortunately, there is no way of identifying his "nice" geyser. Xizang is known to have geysers in several places, but none of those recently studied seems to match Harrer's locality. Neither do they appear to match geyser fields described by Montgomerie in 1875. All told, Tibet may include as many as six separate geyser fields. There is also at least one within Sichuan (Szechwan) and still another in Yunnan. Very little is known about any of these areas, and the truth about Tibetan geysers is largely a mystery.

The Lahú Chu River is a remote place, its headwaters rising at an elevation of more than 17,000 feet. Geysers were first identified here by Montgomerie in a visit in 1872, and they were seen again in 1912. The better of two geyser basins along the river was Peting Chuja, where "about a dozen" geysers were described — the *smallest* reaching 20 feet high — among 100 other hot springs. A few miles farther up the river was Naisum Chuja. It reportedly included just two geysers, but both were said to spout 50 to 60 feet high. This number of geysers would make the Lahú Chu River one of the premier geyser fields in the world. No modern reference clearly describes hot springs at the given latitude and longitude. However, the early surveyors could well have been in error, and it is possible that Naisum Chuja is the same as the modern Bibiling. Bibiling, one of three thermal areas at

of which erupts at an angle from a vertical cliff to as high as 60 feet.

Tagajia is near the headwaters of the Lagetzanbo River at an altitude of almost 16,000 feet. There were four geysers in 1978. The two largest played to heights of 60 feet. The interval of one was about 3 hours. The other was cyclic, undergoing series of 10-minute eruptions separated by quiet of at least 36 hours; its eruption jetted at a 45-degree angle. According to former Yellowstone ranger Jeremy Schmidt, only one of these was active, as a perpetual spouter, in 1987.

Another geyser area is Chapu. Geysers such as Quzun

and Semi are reported to have increased the frequency of their eruptions by up to five times following an earthquake in 1959 (different from Yellowstone's earthquake in the same year).

With no details available, geysers are also reported at Guhu and Kue.

Little is known about the geysers in the other parts of China. Both are short distances outside Tibet. Chaluo, in Sichuan, is reported to include four geysers. The largest is cyclic in its activity. Major eruptions generally recur every 2 hours, last 15 to 20 minutes, and reach heights as great as 18 feet. Balazhang, in Yunnan, has a single geyser 3 feet high; it was not known to erupt prior to an earthquake in 1976.

Worth mentioning here is that one Chinese publication expressly states that a geyser eruption "must reach 3 meters (almost 10 feet) in height to be counted." That is a strange restriction not followed elsewhere in the world. Since boiling springs are described in many places other than those cited as containing geysers, one wonders how many geysers less than 10 feet high have been ignored by the Chinese. Nevertheless, in 1992 a respected geothermal expert visited Tibet with the express aim of seeing some of its geysers. His guides professed ignorance and led him only to lukewarm springs. No geyser of any size was seen. Thus, virtually all that is known about these areas is extracted from very old books and a few modern but cursory publications.

References: 2, 25, 26, 27, 28, 29 and 41.

31. CHIANG MAI PROVINCE, THAILAND. Thailand is certainly a well-explored place, yet the fact that there are geysers in northern Chiang Mai was only revealed by some geothermal studies dating to the 1970s. Geysers definitely exist in two localities and possibly in at least one other, each of which is separated from the others by more than 50 miles.

A few miles from Fang, near the border with Myanmar (Burma) and not far from Laos, are the hot springs of Ban Muang Chom. A small geothermal power plant has been operating there for several years, but somehow, as of 1991, the geysers had survived. One, next to the access road, had intervals of about 10 minutes, playing up to 6 feet high for a few minutes. A number of smaller geysers existed nearby.

Pa Pai is a tiny cluster of only seven hot springs along a geyserite terrace. Four are geysers. All have intervals of 15 to 45 seconds, durations of 5 to 10 seconds, and heights of up to 2 feet.

Somewhat more questionable is Pong Hom, where eruptions up to 20 feet high might rise from a perpetual spouter.
References: 3, 30, and 41.

32. PAI, MYANMAR (BURMA). The listing of a geyser at Pai in the Tavoy District of the Burmese panhandle seemed unlikely until the discovery of geysers in Thailand. The only written reference to the geyser was penned in 1864. It described the play as reaching 6 feet high.
References: 3 and 31.

33. SUMATRA, INDONESIA. Sumatra, the largest and northwesternmost of the Indonesian Archipelago, is intensely volcanic, and geysers have been reported in four localities. They are separated from one another by great enough distances to be considered as individual geyser fields. In only two, however, are true geysers positively known to exist. Taken from southeast to northwest, these fields include the following.

Lampung-Semangko. A caldera within this district at the far southeastern end of Sumatra used to contain geysers in a number of places, including one basin that reportedly contained a dozen or more geysers of substantial size. A few decades ago the entire region was disrupted by a series of powerful phreatic (steam-powered) eruptions, and most of the geysers were destroyed. Such activity is now restricted to two small hot spring groups. Near Waimuli there are two geysers, both playing only about 1 foot high. At Waipanas is a single geyser, which showed intervals of 10 seconds, durations of 5 seconds, and heights up to 12 feet during late 1971.

Kerinci. Kerinci is Sumatra's most active volcano, the centerpiece of a large national park established for the preservation of the Sumatran tiger and rhinoceros. The Geyser Gao Gadang is probably the largest in Indonesia — if it is a true geyser. The activity is dependent on atmospheric conditions, with eruptions only occurring when the air temperature is exceptionally high or the barometric pressure is very low. Then, it may erupt frequently (or perhaps steadily) to more than 70 feet high. Eruptions are rare at best and are only 3 feet high under other conditions.

Pasaman. Among the small cluster of Pasaman Hot Springs near the town of Panti is one possible geyser, playing 5 feet high.

Tapanuli. Within an area of a few square miles, geysers apparently occur within three hot spring groups, and a large perpetual spouter is found in another. Near the village of Sibanggor Jae is a single geyser, erupting 8 feet high. Tarutung also has a single geyser, which reaches perhaps 10 feet. The most extensive of these groups is at Silangkitang, where a geyser 8 feet high plays from a large pool, and several smaller geysers may exist. Finally, a muddy perpetual spouter at Sipirok jets a steady stream of acid water to about 60 feet.

References: 32 and 41.

34. CISOLOK, JAVA, INDONESIA. Cisolok is on the southwestern coast of Java. Most of the hot springs rise from the bed of the Cipanas River, and only those whose deposits have grown above the water level erupt. The deposits are unusual for a geyser area in that they are calcium carbonate (travertine) rather than siliceous sinter. Two geysers have been described. One reaches 12 to 17 feet high, and the other plays to just 1 foot. According to one writer these are only hot artesian springs, but they are listed as geysers by volcanologists with the Volcanological Survey of Indonesia.

References: 3 and 41.

35. GUNUNG PAPANDAYAN, JAVA, INDONESIA. Papandayan is one of Indonesia's most active volcanoes. Much of the surrounding countryside was devastated by a sideways explosion in 1772, and both the scenery and the hot springs are said to be magnificent. The springs definitely include boiling pools

and perpetual spouters. This area was not noted as a geyser locality by the Volcanological Survey of Indonesia in 1983, but a more recent travel guidebook cites "small geysers" as one of the region's lesser attractions.
Reference: 41.

36. MINAHASA DISTRICT, CELEBES (SULAWESI), INDONESIA.
Celebes is a large, very irregularly shaped island between the main Indonesian islands and the Philippines. The northeastern arm of the island contains the volcanic area of Minahasa, near the main city of Manado. Although hot springs are extremely common throughout the district, geysers are known to occur within just one group. Near the village of Toraget, a deep, clear pool erupts every 3 to 5 minutes. The play lasts only a few seconds and reaches 1 to 2 feet high. Other geysers have been recorded in this area, but most of their activity has been restricted to short periods of time following earthquakes.

In July 1994 a European Volcanological Society expedition found two geysers, each playing 7 to 10 feet high, within an extensive solfatara zone inside the crater of Mahawu Volcano.

Most reports about the hot springs at Airmaddidi (which means boiling water) imply that all of the springs are acidic and muddy. A small geyser or two might exist, but they will no doubt be destroyed because of a 300-megawatt geothermal power plant that was under construction in 1993.

Also in the Minahasa District is Nolok Volcano, which during the 1950s contained a boiling lake that periodically erupted as high as 150 feet. Such activity, seen in other areas of the world, is considered volcanic rather than geothermal.
References: 2, 3, and 41.

37. BACAN ISLAND, MALUKU GROUP, INDONESIA.
Bacan Island (also spelled Bactian, Batjan, and Bacjan) is one of the largest of the Maluku, or Molluca, Islands but is also one of the least developed. These islands are important historically under their old western name "Spice Islands." Bacan lies just off the southwest coast of the larger Halmahera Island.

The hot springs are of boiling temperatures, and several were apparently active as geysers during the 1800s. The largest was named Atoe Ri. No modern geothermal survey has been conducted on the island, and the present status of these springs is unknown.
References: 3 and 41.

38. GARUA HARBOUR, NEW BRITAIN ISLAND, PAPUA–NEW GUINEA.
New Britain is the large island immediately east of New Guinea. Garua Harbour, about midway along the north coast, is probably a caldera, and hot springs occur all around its shore.

Near the village of Pangalu north of the bay is a thermal area that includes two geysers. Both seem to come and go with time, sometimes being completely inactive and at others acting as perpetual spouters but also occasionally acting as periodic geysers. The larger of these can play as high as 25 feet; the other more typically reaches 6 feet.

Across the harbor is the town of Talasea. Scattered throughout the settlement are alkaline hot springs and extensive geyserite deposits. As of 1982 there were no geysers, but their past and future existence is likely.

Geysers have also been reported in the literature to occur on "Hannam Island, near Garua Harbour north of New Britain." Such a place does not exist; Hannam was the original name for what is now recognized as the Willaumez Peninsula, which is only partially separated from the mainland by Garua Harbour. This reference to geysers probably refers to Pangalu and/or Talasea.
References: 1, 2, 3, 33, and 41.

39. KASILOLI, NEW BRITAIN ISLAND, PAPUA–NEW GUINEA.
The Kasiloli thermal area is about 50 miles southeast of Garua Harbour at Talasea and 10 miles inland from Cape Hoskins. Although the active area is very small, measuring less than 1,000 feet in any dimension, it contains at least 14 geysers, ranking it among the largest geyser fields in the world. Tabe Geyser is cyclic in its action, the intervals ranging from 15

minutes to several hours in length. The duration is 3 minutes and the height in excess of 30 feet. The other geysers, none of which has been named, all play to between 1 and 4 feet. Access to Kasiloli is severely restricted by the natives of the region in order to preserve a population of unique megapode birds, which bury their eggs among the hot springs to be incubated by the geothermal heat.

References: 33 and 41.

40. NARAGE ISLAND, WITU GROUP, PAPUA–NEW GUINEA. Narage Island is a speck of dormant volcanism among the tiny Witu Island Group about 50 miles north of New Britain. Hot springs occur at a number of places around the island, and among them is one geyser. Early reports from the 1800s talk of eruptions as high as 30 feet, but now it is much weaker. In 1970 it exhibited intervals of 2 to 3 minutes, durations of 20 to 30 seconds, and a height of around 3 feet.

References: 2, 3, and 41.

41. LIHIR AND AMBITLE ISLANDS, NEAR NEW IRELAND ISLAND, PAPUA–NEW GUINEA. These islands lie off the east coast of New Ireland, forming the easternmost lands of the sprawling nation of Papua–New Guinea.

Lihir (or Lir) Island is small, measuring about 5 by $3^1/_2$ miles. There are several hot spring groups, and two *may* contain geysers. Near the coastline is a deep vent known as Roaring Spring. Its water level periodically rises and falls, accompanied by much noisy evolution of steam. A second area contains the Hot Air Blow Hole. This sounds like a steam vent, but the activity is described as periodic. Both of these springs are possible geysers. Copper deposits of low grade but huge volume have recently been identified on Lihir, and the island is apt to be devastated by mining.

Ambitle (or Anir, or Feni) Island is larger and contains more hot springs than does Lihir, and here geysers positively exist. At a low elevation, near a copra plantation, are numerous hot springs. Several show intermittent activity, and one is clearly a geyser, erupting irregularly but frequently to about $1^1/_2$ feet high. Inland 2 miles is another thermal area. It con-

tains several very hot, geyserite-lined pools. One of these is thought to be a large but infrequent geyser, playing as high as 30 feet. Elsewhere in this group may be as many as five other geysers plus a 10-foot perpetual spouter.
References: 1, 2, 3, 33, and 41.

42. FERGUSSON ISLAND, D'ENTRECASTEAUX ARCHIPELAGO, PAPUA–NEW GUINEA. Fergusson is the largest of the d'Entrecasteaux Islands, located near the southeastern tip of New Guinea. The thermal areas of interest, Deidei and Iamelele, are just a few miles apart.

At Deidei there are several geysers. No written report has specified the exact number, but one researcher recalled seeing about a dozen in 1956. Most of the eruptions were quite small, but one geyser frequently reached 15 feet, another played less often 5 to 10 feet high. In 1992 a special program about New Guinea was broadcast on public television. It showed vigorous geyser activity at an unidentified site, possibly Deidei.

Iamelele is a larger thermal area than Deidei, but geyser activity is much less intense. The several clusters of small hot springs all include sinter platforms, but only two contain large formations of geyserite. These are broad terraces dotted with small cones. Cones alone are indications of geyser activity, but small eruptions from just two or three of the springs were all that was seen in 1956.
References: 1, 3, 33, and 41.

43. NAKAMA SPRINGS, SAVUSAVU, VANUA LEVU, FIJI. Vanua Levu is the "second" island of Fiji, large but considerably less populated than Viti Levu. The town of Savusavu serves as a district capital but remains little more than a small South Seas settlement. Tourism is rapidly developing in the area, however, and several fancy resorts have recently opened within a few miles of the town.

The Nakama Springs are actually within the town, adjacent to the school grounds and near the Hot Springs Hotel. The thermal tract is tiny, measuring only about 100 by 60 feet, but at least five of its thirteen springs are geysers. The

Nakama Springs were first described in 1845. Additional reports were written in the 1860s and 1870s, all of which commented on the vigorous boiling and most of which either stated or implied intermittent activity. The first time distinct eruptions were recorded was during 1878. Two of the springs began to play and attracted considerable attention by jetting columns of water up to 60 feet high; both the intervals and durations were as short as 10 minutes. After just a few months, the springs reverted to small boiling, and no further eruptions were seen until the 1950s. Since then, only small geysers have been seen. The individual Nakama Springs tend to shift their locations, old vents filling in as new openings appear, and it is not known if any of the modern features play from the same craters as the geysers of 1878.

In 1993 I visited Nakama Springs and found five active as geysers. Most of the eruptions consisted of vigorous boiling that produced splashes as high as 2 feet. The intervals of three of these springs were only a few seconds, and their durations were as long as several minutes. One spring, largely hidden under some boulders that forced the water sideways, was more erratic, repeating every 2 to 12 or more minutes. Yet another evidently erupted about once a day. Natives who reside nearby use the springs for cooking vegetables such as cassava and taro, and there is some local discussion of improving the area for both continued native use and as an interpretive tourist attraction.

References: 3, 34, 35, and 41.

44. NEW ZEALAND. The thermal areas in the central part of New Zealand's North Island used to comprise the second largest geyser field in the world, trailing only Yellowstone. As many as 300 geysers or more have been known within the Rotorua-Taupo Volcanic Zone. Because of recent geothermal and hydroelectric developments, only about 40 geysers remain.

The best known of the geyser basins is at Whakare-warewa, just outside the city of Rotorua. The area is operated by the native Polynesians as part of the Maori Arts and

Pohutu Geyser, joined by the arching play of Prince of Wales Feathers Geyser, is now the largest of New Zealand's active geysers, with some play reaching over 100 feet high and at intervals as short as 15 minutes.

Crafts Institute. A number of these people live within the area, using the hot water for bathing, cooking, space heating, and so on. Although there is no geothermal development within "Whaka," extensive drilling in the city has had a serious impact on the geysers. About a dozen geysers were active in 1993. By far the largest are Pohutu ("Big Splash") and the adjacent Prince of Wales Feathers Geysers. For a brief time after Pohutu's eruption, this complex is quiet, but Prince of Wales Feathers soon begins jetting an angled, steady column. This gradually grows in strength, and about the time it reaches 30 feet high Pohutu joins in. At full force, Pohutu plays up to 100 feet high. Some intervals are as short as 15 minutes, and durations are as long as 10 minutes. Nearby Waikorohihi and Mahanga Geysers both show cyclic eruption patterns that, when active, can be frequent and up to 20 feet high. Kereru Geyser is very erratic, often splashing but rather uncommonly bursting up to 10 feet. In an area away from the tourist trails, a vigorous small geyser and several large perpetual spouters are an indication of renewed activity because of recovering water levels at depth. Near the Maori village several large pools have rare but powerfully bursting eruptions. In addition to the geysers, Whaka boasts several large mud pots; directly across the highway, the Arikikapakapa area has mud pots and pools as unique golf course hazards.

Currently, the largest concentration of active geysers in New Zealand is at the comparatively little-known Orakei Korako. Until 1961 Orakei Korako matched Yellowstone's Upper Geyser Basin. Well over 100 geysers and intermittent springs were known, 20 of which were of major proportions. Orakeikorako Geyser would sometimes erupt to 180 feet. When it was dormant, nearby Minguini would play, infrequently reaching a measured 295 feet high. Rameka played to 30 feet, Terata to 50, Porangi to 80, and Te Mimi-a-homai-te-rangi to 75, just to name a few. Most of these geysers are gone. In 1961 they were covered by the waters of Lake Ohakuri. Government geologists have called the destruction New Zealand's worst case of environmental vandalism. But above the lake level about 16 small geysers remain, and Orakei Korako is operated as a tourist attraction. The largest of the present geysers are Diamond, which reaches 8 to 25 feet; Cascade, which has strong bursts within a cavern; and Sapphire, which is frequent and as high as 10 feet.

The country around Lake Rotomahana was once the site of two of the largest geyserite formations in the world. The Pink and White Terraces were over 50 feet high and hundreds of feet broad. Playing from the crater atop the White Terrace was Te Terata, a geyser that sometimes put on spectacular displays. Not a trace of the terraces remains today. They were completely blown away by the explosive Mt. Tarawera–Rotomahana-Waimangu volcanic eruptions of 1886. But in the aftermath of those destructive blasts new and equally fascinating thermal features were formed. The star of them all — the star of all the world's known geysers — was the great Waimangu. Beginning in 1900 and lasting 4 years, Waimangu Geyser (whose name means Black Water) played like no other geyser has ever done. Eruptions were frequent and predictable. During some stretches of time it

New Zealand's Waimangu Geyser was the tallest geyser ever observed anywhere. Active between 1900 and 1904, some of its most powerful bursts reached 1,500 feet high.

was actually in eruption nearly half the time. All eruptions were several hundred feet high. Jets reaching 600 to 1,000 feet were common, and some even approached 1,500 feet high. Waimangu's death in 1904 came not because of changes to its plumbing system but because of groundwater changes caused by nearby landslides. The dominant features at Waimangu today are Frying Pan Lake, around whose shores are several small geysers, and Inferno Crater Lake, which varies its water level by more than 30 feet over regular cycles of about 38 days.

A few geysers also exist at Waiotapu, Waikite, Te Kopia, and Tokaanu, but these are all quite small and are largely secondary to other geothermal attractions such as mud pots and some of the largest pools in the world.

Once upon a time, Wairakei would have headed New Zealand's list. Its Geyser Valley was the site of at least 100 geysers, some of them large and spectacular. New Zealand's first geothermal power plant spelled their end and also destroyed the geysers at The Spa, a few miles away near Taupo.

The distance between Rotorua and Taupo is about 50 miles. Within this zone there are still enough geysers to rank New Zealand high on the list of world geyser fields. But so much has been destroyed. The tendency is for development to continue, for New Zealand is a nation with limited energy resources such as coal and oil. But some geologists and private citizens think there must be a better way, and the situation is improving. Recent legal action has resulted in limitations on geothermal production in Rotorua, and water levels and geyser activity are slowly recovering at Whakarewarewa. Waimangu-Rotomahana has been designated as a research area and preserve, and no new geothermal developments are planned near any of the other geyser basins. New Zealand stands to remain one of the major geyser fields on earth.

References: 1, 2, 3, 36, 37, 38, 39, 40, and 41.

OTHER POSSIBLE GEYSER FIELDS. The forty-four areas just described are those positively known to contain geysers at this time or in the recent past. In addition, a number of other localities around the world have been known or reported to contain geysers. Several of the following used to contain geysers, but for one reason or another they disappeared many years ago. For some, the answer as to whether geysers are present will have to wait for future explorations. These places are described briefly.

AMEDEE HOT SPRINGS, CALIFORNIA, U.S.A. The balance of evidence shows that the Amedee area would never have contained geysers, as the appropriate water chemistry and geyserite deposits are lacking. However, the town of Amedee (now long gone) once had a newspaper, *The Amedee Geyser*, and a historical reference contains the following report: "The greatest novelty of the area were the hot springs and geysers which erupted from the soil. Even the geyser was harnessed for a novel purpose — Amos Lane invented a clock which moved forward exactly 38 seconds with each spurt of the water, thereby keeping perfect time" (D. F. Myrick, *The Railroads of Nevada and Eastern California* [Berkeley: Howell-North Books, 1962], 353–354).

BRADY'S HOT SPRINGS, NEVADA. There probably was a geyser at Brady's in the 1840s (the earliest description was penned by a survivor of the Donner Party) and again in the 1920s, but there definitely has not been since then. All natural springs have now been destroyed by geothermal developments.

SALTON SEA, CALIFORNIA. Hot springs near what is now the southeast portion of the Salton Sea included a few small geysers, but they have been inundated by the lake's water since about 1950.

ARARO, MICHOACAN, MEXICO. In 1952 this scenic area near the eastern shore of Lake Cuitzeo north of Morelia was reported to contain several clear intermittent springs and one geyser or perpetual spouter among its sinter-lined pools and mud pots. A 1981 investigation was unable to find such springs.

QUETZALTENANGO DISTRICT, GUATEMALA. North of the bathing resorts of Aguas Georginas and Aguas Amargas are said to be "fumaroles and geysers for the traveller to see" (Reference #2). Also, southeast of the town of Zunil another thermal area was reported in *Geothermics* (vol. 2, no. 2 [1970]) to contain "geysers and fumaroles." One or the other of these may be the same locality seen by a member of the U.S. Geological Survey as including a large perpetual spouter, but that person denied that any true geyser exists anywhere in Guatemala.

VOLCAN PURACE NATIONAL PARK, COLOMBIA. The hot springs at Termales de San Juan are near this national park's visitor center and are traversed by an interpretive trail. The hot springs are described as being geysers with eruptions a few feet high. Unfortunately, the description also states that one can tell the temperature of the water by the color of its cyanobacteria. Since hot water cyanobacteria will not survive above 167°F (71°C), this implies that these pools cannot be geysers.

QUIGUATA, IQUIQUE PROVINCE, TARAPACA REGION, CHILE. A single reference published in 1967 lists Quiguata as containing geysers, in a table that includes Suriri, Puchuldiza, and El Tatio along with many other thermal areas of the Chilean Andes. Yet Quiguata is not mentioned in any other known report, and a geothermal geologist at the University of Chile professed no knowledge of such a place; not even the name was familiar to him. The latitude-longitude description places Quigata only 35 miles south of Puchuldiza, near the town and thermal resorts of Chuzmisa, from which mineral water is bottled and sold throughout northern Chile.

HELL'S GATE, KENYA. Hell's Gate, also known as Njorowa Gorge, is a long canyon traversed only by a trail south of Lake Naivasha. It certainly contains hot springs, which are listed as a major attraction in two published tourist guides and by the Kenya Ministry of Tourism and Wildlife. These sources talk of water jets several feet high. Geologists, however, report that these are probably (they apparently do not know for certain) fumaroles rather than either geysers or perpetual spouters.

YERIKE VOLCANO, CHAD. Hot springs definitely exist within the small caldera of Yerike Volcano, in the Tibesti Mountains of northern Chad. The temperatures are high enough to support fumaroles, and geysers have also been reported.

KERGUELEN ISLAND, SOUTH INDIAN OCEAN. Kerguelen, a large but virtually unknown island, is a part of French territory in the sub-Antarctic. Several groups of hot springs are known to occur in the southern part of the island, where seals warm themselves in the steam. A television documentary showed these springs to be hot, clear, deep pools, and the narrator mentioned "bubbling, splashing pools" (although none was shown in eruption).

FLORES ISLAND, INDONESIA. Geysers have been rumored to exist in a large thermal area at Magekabo, Ende District, in western Flores. Numbers cited in a personal communication to the author were "several" and heights "considerable." However, according to the director of a geothermal survey, the area is entirely acidic, containing steam vents and mud pots but no geysers or other spouting springs.

ALA RIVER, NEW BRITAIN ISLAND, PAPUA–NEW GUINEA. Deep in the heart of New Britain, along the Ala River, is a thermal area that definitely does include spouting springs. During a brief survey in 1978 these seemed to be perpetual spouters rather than true geysers. They also appeared to have temperatures below boiling so that their eruptions were caused at least partly by gasses other than steam. The time allotted for observation was very limited, though, so some of these springs could be geysers after all.

VUTUSUALA HOT SPRINGS, SAVO ISLAND, SOLOMON ISLANDS.

Savo Island is really nothing more than an active volcanic cone with a narrow, habitable coastal zone. Hot springs are numerous on the slopes of the mountain, and the Vutusuala Hot Springs are reported to contain "geysers, boiling mud, and hot springs" by two recent travel writers.

Finally, the following localities have been reported as containing geysers, but they definitely do not now and probably never have.

COSO HOT SPRINGS, CALIFORNIA. High-temperature springs with siliceous sinter deposits exist, but no geysers were ever observed. A large-scale geothermal power plant now operates at Coso Hot Springs.

AHUACHAPAN, EL SALVADOR. An acid area of mud pots and fumaroles, sometimes called "Hell's Half Acre," has been related to Yellowstone by several travel guides, but no geysers have ever existed. On occasion, the mud pots do have explosive eruptions, and several people were killed by such eruptions in 1990.

VOLCAN ALCEDO, ISLA ISABELA, GALAPAGOS ISLANDS, ECUADOR. Several references state that geysers occur within this caldera. According to naturalist Tui de Roy Moore, however, these are only fumaroles that occasionally become choked with surface water, resulting in steady jetting with a geyser-like appearance.

LARDARELLO, ITALY. This is the site of the world's first operating geothermal power plant. There were some very hot springs at Lardarello, but true geysers were never observed.

ZAMBIA AND ZIMBABWE, AFRICA. Several spots in each of these countries have been reported to contain geysers. Two — Chimanimani Geyser and Zongola Geyser in Zimbabwe — are steadily spouting artesian springs with near-boiling water. The other localities contain only a few lukewarm springs, and at the reported site of the Chilambwa Geyser, Zambia, there is no form of thermal activity whatsoever.

THE GEYSERS, CALIFORNIA. In spite of the name, The Geysers never included geysers. It was named because of steam clouds, which were mistaken for geysers during California's early history.

ARTIFICIAL "GEYSERS" IN THE WESTERN UNITED STATES. Highway maps often indicate geysers here and there around the American West. These are all drilled wells. They do erupt, sometimes spectacularly, but are totally artificial. Among these are the "Old Faithful of California" at Calistoga; Lakeview and Adel, Oregon; and Soda Springs, Idaho. The Crystal, Woodside, and Champagne Geysers near Green River, Utah, are even more different from true geysers. They are abandoned wildcat oil wells that act as "soda pop geysers." They play ice-cold water, Crystal to well over 100 feet, because of the evolution of dissolved carbon dioxide gas. The effect is similar to vigorously shaking a can of warm soda pop before popping it open. A "geyser" near Afton, Wyoming, erupts several feet high because of a periodic siphoning action along a stream that temporarily flows underground.

Annotated Bibliography
Geyser Fields of the World

1. Allen, E. T., and A. L. Day. 1935. *Hot Springs of Yellowstone National Park* Washington, D.C.: Carnegie Institute of Washington Publication Number 466. An early but intensive study containing descriptions of nearly all of Yellowstone's geyser areas and mention of some of the world's other geyser fields.

2. Van Padang, M. N., ed. 1951–165. *Catalogue of the active volcanoes of the world, including solfatara fields.* 21 vols. Naples, Italy: International Volcanological Association. A good source of all kinds of volcanic data, this is the only reference to several of the smaller geyser fields; information about geysers is often sketchy, though. Only 1,000 copies printed in English.

3. Waring, G. A. 1965. *Thermal springs of the United States and other countries of the world.* U.S. Geological Survey Professional Paper 492. Washington, D.C.: U.S. Government Printing Office. Not all-inclusive because of age, and not entirely reliable because of differences in the definition of a geyser, but still excellent as a comprehensive, general reference. Outstanding bibliography with 3,733 citations.

4. Nolan, T. B., and G. H. Anderson. 1934. Geyser area near Beowawe, Eureka County, Nevada. *American Journal of Science* 27:215–229. The earliest descriptive reference to Beowawe as it existed prior to any other study and long before geothermal drilling, with maps and photos.

5. Zoback, M. C. 1979. *A geologic and geophysical investigation of the Beowawe geothermal area, North-central Nevada.* Stanford: Stanford University Publications, Geological Sciences, vol. 16. A work that concentrates on the overall geology of the Beowawe system but does include information about the activity current as of the mid-1970s.

6. White, D. E. 1992. *The Beowawe Geysers, Nevada, before geothermal development.* Washington, D.C.: U.S. Geological Survey Bulletin 1998. A discussion of the general geologic framework of the Beowawe system along with a thorough summary of the geyser activity between 1945 and 1957. Large-scale map and color photos.

7. White, D. E. 1968. *Hydrology, activity, and heat flow of the Steamboat Springs thermal system, Washoe County, Nevada.* Washington, D.C.: U.S. Geological Survey Professional Paper 458-C. Includes a map showing and tables listing all of the important springs at Steamboat, including the geyser activity observed during detailed studies from 1946 to 1952.

8. Day, A. L., and E. T. Allen. 1925. *The volcanic activity and hot springs of Lassen Park.* Washington, D.C.: Carnegie Institute of Washington Publication 360. Notes that two different springs at Terminal Geyser had been known to spout up to 8 feet high.

9. Bezore, S. P., and R. W. Sherberne. 1985. *Monitoring geothermal wells and spring conditions in selected areas of California for earthquake precursors.* Sacramento: California Division of Mines and Geology Open File Report OFR 85-12 SAC. Mentions various activity changes among the Long Valley Caldera hot springs since the earthquakes of May 1980.

10. Byers, F. M., and W. W. Brannock. 1949. Volcanic activity on Umnak and Great Sitkin Islands, 1946-1948. *Transactions of the American Geophysical Union* 30:719–734. The first reference to geysers on Umnak Island, with details about the activity and small-scale maps of the individual hot spring groups.

11. Nye, C. J., and others. 1990. *Geology and geochemistry of the Geyser Bight geothermal area, Umnak Island, Aleutian Islands, Alaska.* Anchorage: Alaska Division of Geological and Geophysical Surveys, report to Department of Energy. Gives detailed descriptions of the hot spring activity in each of the Geyser Bight thermal groups, including geyser statistics.

12. Wittich, E. 1910. Geysers y mantiales termales de Comanjilla (Guanajuato). *Soc. Geologica Mexicana Bulletin* 6:183–188. A short descriptive work on the nature of geyser activity in 1906, with a map accurate enough to allow the individual springs to be identified today. (In Spanish)

13. Singletary, C. E. 1952. The hot springs, geysers, and solfatara of the northern part of Michoacan, Mexico. *Texas Journal of Science* 4:413–420. Includes very brief descriptions of the thermal areas at Ixtlan de los Hervores and Araro but gives no substantive details about the geyser activity beyond its basic existence. Photos.

14. Waitz, P. 1906. Los geysers d'Ixtlan. Text of a paper delivered at the 10th International Geological Congress, Mexico City. A field guide sort of report, this provides a lot of details about the individual geysers and other hot springs. Incorporates detailed map and photos. (In French)

15. Trujillo, P. 1972. *Estudio de las manifestaciones termales de Suriri.* 15 pp. An in-house report to the Geological Survey of Chile. Provides considerable detail about the early 1970s activity at Suriri, including a mention of the 1944 geyser. Detailed map. (In Spanish)

16. Lahsen, A. 1976. *La actividad geotermal y sus relaciones con la tectonica y el volcanism en el norte de Chile.* Primer Congreso Geologico Chileno, Santiago, August 2–7, 1976, pp. B105–127. Provides general information about numerous geothermal areas in Chile, especially Suriri, Puchuldiza, and El Tatio; includes Quiguata in a table only. (In Spanish)

17. Trujillo, P. 1969. *Estudio para el desarrollo geotermico en el norte de Chile — Manifestaciones termales de El Tatio.* 11 pp. An in-house report to the Geological Survey of Chile. Provides great detail about the geysers of El Tatio, with a large-scale map showing all springs. (In Spanish) Mr. J. Healy of New Zealand, who was involved in this study, appended to the map a numerical listing of those springs known as geysers.

18. Barth, T.F.W. 1950. *Volcanic geology, geysers, and hot springs of Iceland.* Washington, D.C.: Carnegie Institute of Washington Publication Number 587. The data in this volume are considerably out-of-date, as they were gathered mostly during the 1930s, but this is nonetheless the only work to cover all of Iceland's geyser basins. Many maps and photos.

19. Einarsson, T. 1967. *The Great Geysir and the hot spring area at Haukadalur, Iceland.* Reykjavik, Iceland: Geysir Committee. A small tourist guide to the area at Haukadalur, with photos and a map.

20. de Morais, J. C. 1953. *Boiling springs of Furnas, Azores.* Lisbon: Coimbra University, Museum of Mining and Geology Notes 35:48–75. Primarily about the geochemistry of the Furnas springs. The author briefly discusses the history and early existence of geysers. (In Portuguese, with English summary)

21. Erentoz, C., and Z. Ternek. 1968. *Thermal springs of Turkey, and a study of geothermal energy.* Ankara: Mineral Resources and Exploration Institute of Turkey Bulletin 70, foreign edition. Contains a brief mention of the geyser at Ayvacik.

22. United Nations Development Programme. 1973. *Geology, geochemistry, and hydrology of hot springs of the East African Rift System within Ethiopia.* UNESCO, Technical Publication DP/SF/UN/116. Provides tremendous detail about all of the many dozen geothermal areas within Ethiopia, numerous maps and tables, and photographs of Allallobeda.

23. Raik, A. 1963. *Nature investigations in the Far East.* Tartu: Academy of Sciences of the Estonian Soviet Socialist Republic, Tartu State University. Despite the general-sounding title, this work deals exclusively with the natural history of Dolina Geizerov, Uzon Caldera, and vicinity. One chapter is entirely about the geysers. (In Russian, with English chapter summaries)

24. Sugrobov, V. M. 1964. Effect of experimental exploitation of the Pauzhetsk deposit on surface manifestations and regime of the boiling springs. *Sibirskoye Otdeleniye* (Petropavlovsk-Kamchatskii, Kamchatka, Russia), Volcanological Station Bulletin 39:47–58. Gives brief mention of geysers at Pauzhetsk and implies the historical existence of numerous others.

25. Montgomerie, T. G. 1875. Narrative of an exploration of the Namcho, or Tengri Nur Lake, in great Tibet, made by a native explorer in 1871-2. *Royal Geographical Society* (of London) *Journal* 45:315–330. Includes mention of the localities and activity of geysers at Peting Chuja and Naisum Chuja on the Lahú Chu River.

26. Sapper, —. 1914. A narrative of a journey through Thibet. *Danckelmann's Mitteil.*, Ergänz 3, 44. A very short article in which the geysers of the Lahú Chu River are mentioned as to numbers and heights. (In German)

27. Liao, Z. 1979. *Setting of the geothermal fields of Tibet and a discussion of associated heat source problems.* Auckland: Geothermal Institute, University of Auckland, New Zealand. Report Number 79.17. Describes, mostly in passing, the geysers of Tagajia, Chapu, Guhu, and Namling.

28. Liao, Z., et al. 1979. Heat beneath Tibet. *Geographical Magazine* (London), May 1979, 560–566. A popularized and somewhat disorganized account in which the geysers of Tibet are described. Includes an excellent photo of a geyser at Tagajia.

29. Zhang, M. 1982. *The roof of the world.* New York: Harry N. Abrams, Inc., for Peking, People's Republic of China: Foreign Languages Press. A large coffee-table book. Chapter 4, "Geysers, Spouters, and Fumaroles," contains considerable detail about and numerous photos of the geysers, especially Tagajia.

30. Ramingwong, T., et al. 1979. *Geothermal resources of northern Thailand: A compilation.* Chiang Mai, Thailand: Department of Geological Sciences, Chiang Mai University. A short report in which a tabulation of hot spring areas includes mention of the geysers in the area. Mostly general, with no specific details provided.

31. Stevenson, J. F. 1864. Account of a visit to the hot springs of Pai in the Tavoy District. *Asiatic Society Bengal Journal* 34:383–386. Makes special note of the single geyser at Pai and also discusses general hot spring conditions and deposits.

32. Healy, J. 1972. *Geothermal reconaissance, Lampung District, South Sumatra.* Bandung, Java: Report to Volcanological Section, Geological Survey of Indonesia, 37-41. Locates and provides eruptive data for the existing geysers of the Semangko geyser field.

33. Reynolds, M. A.; Taylor, G. A.; Johnson, R. W.; and Heming, R. F., and I. E. Smith. 1950s, 1960s. A series of reports on the geothermal activity within the former territories of Papua and New Guinea. Canberra: Australian Bureau of Mineral Resources, unpublished reports 1954/63, 1956/9, 1956/25, and 1969/115. These miscellaneous papers cover the Fergusson Island areas, Talasea, Lihir and Ambitle Islands, and Kasiloli. Most of the reports are about 20 pages long plus detailed maps, tables, and some photographs. Although now about 40 years old, these are the only in-print studies of these areas.

34. Healy, J. 1960. *The hot springs and geothermal resources of Fiji.* Wellington: New Zealand Department of Scientific and Industrial Research Publication Number 136. Includes a description and historical accounting of the Nakama Springs at Savusavu, with detailed notes about the periodicity of the springs and a map.

35. Cox, M. A., 1980. *Preliminary geothermal investigations*

in the Savusavu area, Vanua Levu. Suva: Mineral Resources Department of Fiji, Geothermal Report Number 1. Primarily a discussion of water chemistry and temperatures, this includes brief descriptions of the Nakama Springs and a small-scale map useful for historical comparisons.

36. Grange, L. I. 1937. *Geology of the Rotorua-Taupo subdivision.* Wellington: Geological Survey of New Zealand Bulletin 37. The Rotorua-Taupo area contains all but one of New Zealand's geyser basins. The descriptions here are complete, although sometimes sketchy, and give good information about the geysers as they were prior to any significant geothermal developments. Many maps and photos.

37. Keam, R. F. 1955. *Volcanic wonderland.* Auckland, New Zealand: G. B. Scott. Contains brief descriptions of all of New Zealand's more important thermal areas, with frequent mention of and emphasis on geyser activity. Many photos.

38. Lloyd, E. F. 1972. *The geology and hot springs of Orakeikorako.* Wellington: New Zealand Geological Survey Bulletin 85. An outstanding book, this contains detailed descriptions of the geyser activity both historically and just before the inundation by Lake Ohakuri. Numerous photos, detailed maps, a table listing every hot spring in the area, and reams of other data.

39. Lloyd, E. F. 1975. *Geology of Whakarewarewa Hot Springs.* Wellington: New Zealand Department of Scientific and Industrial Research, Information Series Publication Number 111. Designed for visitors to the Whakarewarewa preserve, this colorful booklet includes descriptions of all of the geysers and other hot springs plus some information about the nearby Arikikapakapa mud pot area. Many color photos and a detailed, large-scale map.

40. Scott, B. J. 1992. *Waimangu — A volcanic encounter.* Rotorua, New Zealand: Waimangu Volcanic Valley. A small guidebook that provides basic information about most of

the individual thermal features in Waimangu Valley and around the shoreline of Lake Rotomahana.

41. Personal experiences of the author: personal visits, movies, television documentaries, slide shows, many small foreign-language publications, conversations, and so on. Most especially, written communications with geothermal geologists worldwide. It is these people above all who have provided much valuable data for this research. The documents and letters they have given me comprise a bibliographic list of more than 200 items about the geysers of the world. They cannot be thanked enough for their time and willingness to forward information to an initially unknown researcher.

Dr. Donald E. White, U.S. Geological Survey
Dr. Robert Christianson, U.S. Geological Survey
Dr. Thomas P. Miller, U.S. Geological Survey
Ms. Anna St. Johns, University of Oregon
Mr. Alberto Parodi I., Arequipa, Peru
Dr. Alfredo Lahsen A., University of Chile
Dr. Stefan Arnorsson, University of Iceland
Mr. Sebastian Bwire-Ojiambo, East African Power and Light Co., Nairobi, Kenya
Mr. Colin D. Kerr, Geological Survey of Zambia
Dr. L. A. Lister, University of Rhodesia (Zimbabwe)
Dr. Genrich Steinberg, Academy of Sciences of the U.S.S.R., Yuzhno, Sakhalin
Dr. Tatyana I. Ustinova, Burnaby, British Columbia (discoverer of Dolina Geizerov, Kamchatka)
Mr. Sergei A. Alekseev, Director, Kronotsky Nature Preserve, Kamchatka
Mr. Vitalii A. Nikolayenko, Chief Interpreter, Kronotsky Nature Preserve, Kamchatka
Mr. Slava Sviagintsev, Paratunka Geothermal Development, Kamchatka
Mr. Wishnu S. Kartokusumo, Volcanological Survey of Indonesia

Mr. R.J.S. Cooke, Senior Government Geologist, Papua–New Guinea

Dr. R. W. Johnson, Australian Bureau of Mineral Resources

Mr. Bradley J. Scott, New Zealand Institute of Geological and Nuclear Sciences

Dr. E. F. Lloyd, Geological Survey of New Zealand

Dr. R. F. Keam, University of Auckland, New Zealand

Mr. James Healy, Geological Survey of New Zealand

Glossary

Algae: colonial, single-celled plants; in Yellowstone, true algae are common in cold stream and lake water but are uncommon in any but the very coldest or acid geothermal water. Brightly colored forms of "blue-green algae" (properly called thermophilic cyanobacteria) live in thermal waters cooler than 167°F (75°C); these growths are commonly but incorrectly called algae.

Burst: applicable to fountain-type geysers, a burst may be a single throw of water or, in the case of those geysers having a series of short, closely spaced eruptions, may be one of the periods of spouting.

Complex: a cluster of springs or geysers that are so intimately associated that the activity of any one member will affect that of the others.

Concerted eruptions: simultaneous eruptions by two or more geysers within a *complex*, the eruption of one usually triggering the eruption of the other(s).

Cone-type geyser: a geyser whose eruption is jetted as a steady column of mixed water and steam from a small vent with little or no surface pool. The vent is often but not necessarily at the top of a built-up cone of geyserite.

Crater: may be synonymous with *vent;* more often, the crater is a broad, shallow depression within which is centered a comparatively small vent. A crater is also a wide, deep hole containing a pool.

Cyanobacteria: the modern and correct formal term for what has commonly been called blue-green algae or simply *algae.*

Cycle, or **Cycle interval:** for those geysers that tend to have short series of eruptions separated by comparatively long periods of noneruptive quiet, the time span from the start of one active phase of a geyser, through the following dormancy, to the start of the next active phase.

Cyclic: a geyser that has a series of eruptions at relatively short intervals separated from another, similar series by a relatively long span of quiet.

Dead: a former geyser that is no longer undergoing active cycles because of having permanently lost its supply of water. Must be used with extreme caution, as most seemingly dead features are only *dormant.*

Dormancy: a span of time during which a geyser temporarily ceases to erupt, usually because of *exchange of function.* Many geysers will be active for long periods of time and then go dormant. Note that dormant does not mean *dead.*

Duration: the period of time from the start of an eruption to the end of the same eruption.

Eruption: the spouting action of a geyser.

Exchange of function: the shift of energy and/or water from one geyser, other hot spring feature, or hot spring group to another, resulting in a decline of activity in the first and an increase in the latter.

Fountain-type geyser: a geyser whose eruption is a series of separate explosions or bursts of water, usually issuing from a pool with a large vent or crater.

Frequent: a general term for eruptions that are irregularly spaced in time yet occur often, usually separated by only a few minutes.

Fumarole: a steam vent; a fumarole is a hot spring in which the water supply is so limited that all water is completely and constantly converted to steam before reaching the surface.

Geyser: a hot spring in which eruptive activity is induced by the boiling of water at depth within a plumbing system, which forcibly ejects water out of the vent in an intermittent fashion.

Geyser basin: a portion of a geyser field within which groups of hot springs including geysers are found.

Geyser field: an expanse of land, large or small, that encompasses all of the geyser basins of a geographical region. Many of the world's geyser fields consist of a single geyser basin.

Geyserite: the variety of opal — technically, an amorphous hydrated silica — deposited by geysers and perpetual spouters, usually with a beaded surface; also, a general synonym for *siliceous sinter.*

Group: an assortment of hot springs and geysers that are considered as a unit on the basis of some geographical separation from other nearby thermal features.

Height: the distance from the ground to the top of a geyser's erupted water. The height listed in the tables and descriptions invariably expresses the range in maximum height per eruption and is not necessarily characteristic of the entire eruption.

Infrequent: a general term for eruptions that are very irregular, usually with intervals days to weeks long.

Intermittent spring: a hot spring that undergoes occasional quiet overflow without a bursting or jetting eruption.

Interval: the period of time from the start of one eruption (or eruptive sequence) to the start of the next. This is one of the most basic factors describing geyser activity and is also the most controversial. In some parts of the world it is taken to mean the period of time from the *end* of one eruption to the start of the next; in other words, the time of noneruptive quiet between eruptions. In those cases the term *period* is synonymous with the American *interval*. Americans do not seem to have a set term for the noneruptive quiet.

Irregular: the term for eruptions that show no evident pattern of distribution, with intervals ranging randomly from minutes to days in length.

Mud pot: an acid hot spring with a limited water supply; not enough water is present to carry away clay muds that are brought to or form at the surface so that they accumulate to form a thick, bubbly mud within the crater.

Period: in some international usage, the span of time from the start of one eruption to the start of the next; synonymous with the American *interval*.

Perpetual spouter: a spouting spring resembling a geyser but whose eruptive activity does not stop. Although included with geysers throughout this book, important mechanical differences mean that a perpetual spouter is not a true geyser.

Play: the eruptive activity of a geyser; a synonym for *eruption*.

Plumbing system: the subsurface network of tubes, cavities, and channels that makes up the water supply system of a hot spring; it is especially important for geysers in that it must contain a near-surface constriction, be pressure tight, and be accessible to relatively large volumes of water.

Preplay: any activity by a geyser, such as heavy overflow or splashing, preceding an eruption; it is useful in that preplay may be an indication that the time of eruption is near.

Rare: the general term for eruptions or active phases that almost never occur, many months to years sometimes passing between them.

Seldom: the general term for eruptions that are very widely spaced, several weeks to a few months often passing between them.

Siliceous sinter: the deposit of noncrystalline silica that is formed by most hot springs and geysers; used largely as a synonym for *geyserite*, which technically is only one form of siliceous sinter.

Sinter: a general term for any variety of hot spring deposit, regardless of chemical composition.

Sput: an informal term for a small geyser or perpetual spouter whose activity is relatively insignificant compared to that of surrounding features but whose action can have a deleterious effect on nearby geyser activity; also, a general term for the memgbers of a large group of small erupting features.

Thermophilic: literally "temperature-loving," used in reference to the life that lives within the hot springs and runoff channels, such as in *thermophilic cyanobacteria.*

Travertine: a hot spring deposit formed of calcium carbonate rather than silica; also called "calcareous sinter."

Uncommon: a synonym for *infrequent.*

Vent: the surface opening of the plumbing system of any hot spring; in geysers it is the point from which the eruption issues.

Suggested Reading

Allen, E. T., and A. L. Day. 1935. *Hot springs of Yellowstone National Park.* Washington, D.C.: Carnegie Institute of Washington Publication Number 466.

Bonney, O. H., and L. Bonney. 1970. *Battle drums and geysers — the life and journals of Lt. Gustavus Cheney Doane, soldier and explorer of the Yellowstone and Snake River regions.* Chicago: Swallow Press.

Brock, T. D. 1994. *Life at high temperatures.* Yellowstone National Park: Yellowstone Association.

Bryan, T. S. 1990. *Geysers: What they are and how they work.* Niwot, Colo.: Roberts Rinehart.

Haines, A. L. 1955. *Osborne Russell's journal of a trapper.* Lincoln: University of Nebraska Press.

————. 1977. *The Yellowstone story: a history of our first national park.* 2 vols. Yellowstone National Park, Wyoming: Yellowstone Library and Museum Association, with Colorado Associated University Press.

Kirk, R. 1972. *Exploring Yellowstone.* Seattle: University of Washington Press.

Langford, N. P. 1972. *The discovery of Yellowstone Park.* Lincoln: University of Nebraska Press.

Lystrup, H. T. 1969. *Hamilton's guide — Yellowstone National Park.* West Yellowstone, Mont.: Hamilton's Stores.

Macdonald, G. A. 1972. *Volcanoes.* Englewood Cliffs. N.J.: Prentice-Hall.

Marler, G. D. 1951. Exchange of function as a cause of geyser irregularity. *American Journal of Science* 249: 329–342.

————. 1964. *Effects of the Hebgen Lake earthquake of August 17, 1959 on the hot springs of the Firehole Geyser Basins, Yellowstone National Park.* Washington, D.C.: U.S. Geological Survey Professional Paper 435, 185–197.

————. 1968. *Studies of geysers and hot springs along the Firehole River, Yellowstone National Park, Wyoming.* Yellowstone National Park: Yellowstone Library and Museum Association.

————. 1973. *Inventory of thermal features of the Firehole River Geyser Basins, and other selected areas of Yellowstone National Park.* Washington, D.C.: National Technical Information Service Publication Number PB-221289; 648 pages.

Marler, G. D., and D. E. White. 1975. Seismic Geyser and its bearing on the origin and evolution of geysers and hot springs of Yellowstone National Park. *Geological Society of America Bulletin* 86: 749–759.

Paperiello, R. 1988. *The Heart Lake Geyser Basin — report and investigation.* Sacramento: Geyser Observation and Study Association (typescript manuscript).

The Geyser Observation and Study Association. 1989, 1990, 1992, 1993, 1994. GOSA Transactions. *Journal of The Geyser Observation and Study Association.* Sacramento, Calif.: GOSA.

White, D. E., R. O. Fournier, L.J.P. Muffler, and A. H. Truesdell. 1975. *Physical results of research drilling in thermal areas of Yellowstone National Park, Wyoming.* Washington, D.C.: U.S. Geological Survey Professional Paper 892.

White, D. E., R. A. Hutchinson, and T.E.C. Keith. 1988. *The geology and remarkable thermal activity of Norris Geyser Basin, Yellowstone National Park, Wyoming.* Washington, D.C.: U.S. Geological Survey Professional Paper 1,456.

Whittlesey, L. H. 1988. *Yellowstone place names.* Helena: Montana Historical Society Press.

————. 1989. *Wonderland nomenclature: A history of the place names of Yellowstone National Park.* Helena: Montana Historical Society Press; cooperatively reproduced by The Geyser Observation and Study Association, typescript manuscript; 2,242 pages.

Index of Geyser and Hot Spring Names

About the Author

T. Scott Bryan was a seasonal employee at Yellowstone National Park from 1970 through 1986, working in the maintenance division at Canyon for four summers and as a ranger-naturalist at Norris and Old Faithful after that. He held other National Park Service positions in Glacier National Park, Death Valley National Monument, Glen Canyon National Recreation Area, and the Los Angeles Field Office. Although no longer employed by Yellowstone, he returns to the Park for much of each summer season.

After serving in the U.S. Navy (during which time he was able to visit the geysers of Japan and New Zealand), he received his Bachelor of Science degree in geology at San Diego State University. His education continued at the University of Montana, where he received the Master of Science degree in 1974. He is now an instructor of geology, astronomy, and general physical sciences at Victor Valley College in Victorville, California. *The Geysers of Yellowstone* was his first book. He is also the author of *Geysers: What They Are and How They Work*, several articles on the natural history and geology of the American West, and scientific journal reports. Bryan and his wife Betty are the co-authors of *The Explorer's Guide to Death Valley National Park*.

Bryan is associated with The Geyser Observation and Study Association (GOSA), a nonprofit corporation devoted to furthering the study and understanding of geysers worldwide. In addition to his studies at Yellowstone, he aims to eventually visit every significant geyser occurrence on earth. So far, he has been to geyser fields in the contiguous United States, Mexico, Japan, Fiji, New Zealand, and, especially, the Kamchatka Peninsula of Russia, when he led the first-ever U.S. study group there in 1991.